ON
MEDIA
VIOLENCE

ON
MEDIA
VIOLENCE

W. JAMES POTTER

Sage Publications, Inc.
International Educational and Professional Publisher
Thousand Oaks ▪ London ▪ New Delhi

For information:

Sage Publications, Inc.
2455 Teller Road
Thousand Oaks, California 91320
E-mail: order@sagepub.com

Sage Publications Ltd.
6 Bonhill Street
London EC2A 4PU
United Kingdom

Sage Publications India Pvt. Ltd.
M-32 Market
Greater Kailash I
New Delhi 110 048 India

Printed in the United States of America

Library of Congress Cataloging-in-Publication Data

Potter, W. James.
    On media violence / by W. James Potter.
      p. cm.
    Includes bibliographical references (p.)and index.
    ISBN 0-7619-1638-5 (cloth: alk. paper)
    ISBN 0-7619-1639-3 (pbk.: alk. paper)
      1. Violence in mass media. 2. Mass media—Social aspects.
    3. Mass media—Influence. I. Title.
    P96 .V5 P68 1999
    303.6′02—dc21   99-6433

This book is printed on acid-free paper.

99 00 01 02 03 04 05 7 6 5 4 3 2 1

Acquiring Editor:	Margaret H. Seawell
Editorial Assistant:	Renée Piernot
Production Editor:	Astrid Virding
Editorial Assistant:	Patricia Zeman
Typesetter:	Lynn Miyata
Indexer:	Teri Greenberg
Cover Designer:	Candice Harman

Contents

Acknowledgments   vii

1. Overview and Introduction   1

PART I: Reviewing

2. Theories of Media Violence   11

3. Effects of Exposure to Media Violence   25

4. Violent Content on Television   43

PART II: Reconceptualizing

5. Violence   63

6. Schema and Context   85

7. Levels of Analysis   97

8. Development   109

9. Effects   121

10. Risk   139

11. The Industry's Perspective   153

PART III: Rethinking Methodology

12. Effects Methodologies and Methods   167

13. Content Analysis of Media Violence   195

PART IV: Lineation Theory

14. Axioms and Dictionary   211

15. Propositions   225

References   257

Author Index   287

Subject Index   296

About the Author   304

Acknowledgments

This book is a down payment on a debt I owe to many people who inspired and helped me in my scholarly career. First, I must thank the theoreticians—Albert Bandura, Leonard Berkowitz, George Gerbner, Rowell Huesmann, and especially Dolf Zillmann. While I have not always accepted all of their explanations, these scholars have given us the most important tools an area of scholarly study can have. I am also grateful to the hundreds of scholars who have directed their energies to doing the empirical work that extends our knowledge and reshapes our thinking about media violence. I have been fortunate to work with many graduate as well as undergraduate students on research teams where together we have explored the mysteries of how violence appears on television and how it affects us.

The most intense, mind-expanding, maddening, rewarding, frustrating, and exhilarating experience of my entire career was the four years I worked on the National Television Violence Study. This was the kind of project we all dream about—a think tank-like experience where you are submerged deeply in important research. I learned so much from my colleagues in Santa Barbara (Ed Donnerstein, Dale Kunkel, Dan Linz, and Barb Wilson) as well as my NTVS colleagues from other sites, such as the University of Texas at Austin (Ellen Wartella, Chuck Whitney, Dominick Larosa, and Wayne Danielson), University of Wisconsin (Joanne Cantor), and University of North Carolina (Frank Biocca and Jane Brown). Also crucial to the project and my learning were Don Roberts, who chaired the advisory board to the project, and the graduate research assistants at Santa Barbara (Mike Berry, Eva Blumenthal, Carrie Colvin, Tim Gray, and especially Stacy Smith). These are people who are very smart and care passionately about creating knowledge. This was continually obvious in the numerous meetings we held to plan the project, then to carry out its execution and the analyses of several million data points. In these meetings, everything was challenged from the wording of a phrase in a definition all the way to the very nature of social science. Most of the ideas in this book were forged in the crucible of that experience. Every time I lost an argument in one of these meetings, I would walk the beaches until I could figure out the flaw in my thinking or the "limitation" in the thinking of my colleague who won that argument. I spent a lot of time at the precipice of knowledge staring down into the abyss of mystery. I hope this book lays down a few planks of knowledge that will help us bridge some of the gap between what we understand now and what we need to understand in order to help viewers, policymakers, and programmers deal effectively with this problem that affects us all.

I am very thankful again for the professionals at Sage Publications. Margaret Seawell, acquisitions editor, Stephanie Hiebert, copyeditor, and Astrid Virding, production editor, are very demanding to work for but deliver high-quality service.

Finally, there is you, the reader. If the ideas in this book stimulate you to think differently or more deeply about media violence, then I thank you for your attention. If you want to argue with me, then let me know, and I'll thank you for your counter insights that will help me learn more. If you conduct research that falsifies or supports any of the propositions in Lineation Theory, then I thank you in advance for your contribution in helping us all walk the plank a few more steps into the mystery.

Overview and Introduction

Violence in American society is a public health problem. Although most people have never witnessed an act of serious violence in person, we are all constantly reminded of its presence by the media. The media constantly report news about individual violent crimes. The media also use violence as a staple in telling fictional stories to entertain us. Thus, the media amplify and reconfigure the violence in real life and continuously pump these messages into our culture.

The culture is responding with a range of negative effects. Each year about 25,000 people are murdered, and more than 2 million are injured in assaults (Steenland, 1993). On the highways, aggressive behavior such as tailgating, weaving through busy lanes, honking or screaming at other drivers, exchanging insults, and even engaging in gunfire is a factor in nearly 28,000 traffic deaths annually, and the problem is getting worse at a rate of 7% per year (Wald, 1997). Gun-related deaths increased more than 60% from 1968 to 1994, to about 40,000 annually, and this problem is now considered a public health epidemic by 87% of surgeons and 94% of internists across the United States (Ragan, 1998). Meanwhile, the number of pistols manufactured in the United States continues to increase—up 92% from 1985 to 1992 (Browning, 1994).

Teenagers are living in fear. A Harris poll of 2,000 U.S. teenagers found that most of them fear violence and crime and that this fear is affecting their everyday behavior (Applebome, 1995). About 46% of respondents said they have changed their daily behavior because of a fear of crime and violence; 12% said they carry a weapon to school for protection; 12% have altered their route to school; 20% said they have avoided particular parks or playgrounds; 20% said they have changed their circle of friends; and 33% have stayed away from school at times because of fear of violence. In addition, 25% said they did not feel safe in their own neighborhood, and 33% said they fear being a victim of a drive-by shooting. Nearly twice as many teenagers reported gangs in their school in 1995 compared to 1989, and this increase is seen in all types of neighborhoods; violent crime in schools increased 23.5% during the same period (Sniffen, 1998).

This problem has far-reaching economic implications. The U.S. Department of Justice estimates the total cost of crime and violence (such as child abuse and domestic violence, in addition to crimes such as murder, rape, and robbery) to be $500 billion per year, or about twice the annual budget of the Defense Department (Butterfield, 1996). The cost includes real expenses (such as legal fees, the cost of lost time from work, the cost of police work, and the cost of running the nation's prisons and parole systems) and intangibles (such as loss of affection from murdered family members). Violent crime is responsible for 14% of injury-related medical spending and up to 20% of mental health care expenditures.

The problem of violence in our culture has many apparent causes, including poverty, breakdown of the nuclear family, shift away from traditional morality to a situational pluralism, and the mass media. The media are especially interesting as a source of the problem. Because they are so visible, the media are an easy target for blame. In addition, they keep reminding us of the problem in their news stories. But there is also a more subtle and likely more powerful reason why the media should be regarded as a major cause of this public health problem: They manufacture a steady stream of fictional messages that convey to all of us in this culture what life is about. Media stories tell us how we should deal with conflict, how we should treat other people, what is risky, and what it means to be powerful. The media need to share the blame for this serious public health problem.

How do we address the problem? The path to remedies begins with a solid knowledge base. It is the task of social scientists to generate much of this knowledge. For the past five decades, social scientists and other scholars have been studying the topic of media violence. This topic has attracted researchers from many different disciplines, especially psychology, sociology, mental health science, cultural studies, law, and public policy. This research addresses questions such as these: How much media violence is there? What are the meanings conveyed in the way violence is portrayed? and What effect does violence have on viewers as individuals, as members of particular groups, and as members of society? Estimates of the number of studies conducted to answer these questions range as high as 3,000 (Donnerstein, Slaby, & Eron, 1994) and even 3,500 (Wartella, Olivarez, & Jennings, 1998).

After a great deal of research through decades, we are not yet able to offer confident answers to the important questions: What are all the risks of exposure to media violence? How can television programs provide us with useful warnings about the risk of the content in their narratives? Can exposure to some violence have positive effects, and if so, what are those positive outcomes and how can we increase their prevalence? What strategies can we use to protect children from negative effects of exposure to violence? Do risks of exposure continue even when someone has reached adulthood, and if so, what strategies can adults use to protect themselves from negative effects?

This book addresses these questions. It shows that we have partial answers for all of them, but that we need to complete additional tasks before we have answers strong enough to make a significant impact on people's everyday lives. In this book, I lay out my vision for what those additional tasks are and how they can best be accomplished. The book is organized into four parts, each addressing a different argument.

PART I: REVIEWING

First, I show that there is a rich literature of findings about media violence. The scholarly activity to this point has generated a great many findings about which scholars agree. We are certain that violent portrayals are pervasive in the media, especially the most dominant medium, television. We know that people use the cues in the portrayals of violence to construct meaning. Scholars strongly agree that exposure to media violence leads to negative effects both immediately during exposure and over the long term of continuous exposure. We also know that certain types of portrayals of violence, certain types of viewers, and certain environments increase the probability of negative effects.

The existing body of research has provided us with a great deal of knowledge about media violence. There has been some very insightful theorizing (Chapter 2). In addition, there have been some very useful lines of research in the areas of effects of exposure to media violence (Chapter 3) and content (Chapter 4).

PART II: RECONCEPTUALIZING

The second argument is that the research literature has some serious limitations—as do all research literatures. But with media violence, the limitations have grown to a point at which they are now suppressing the value of ongoing empirical research. Many of these limitations are conceptual. The ongoing research continues to reveal considerable disagreement on key issues. For example, there is fundamental disagreement about how violence should be defined in media portrayals. The thinking about what constitutes an effect from exposure to media violence is diverse. And the understanding about what factors lead to the various effects varies widely.

These conceptual limitations are excusable—even essential—when a line of research is new. When the questions greatly outweigh the findings, creativity of conceptualization and simplification of methods are highly valuable. In the early stages of researching an area, scholars must first explore the full range of conceptual alternatives open to them. They need to try all sorts of variables. They need to tinker with all kinds of definitions to characterize those variables.

Conceptually, we need to rethink many of our ideas, especially violence (Chapter 5), context (Chapter 6), levels of analysis (Chapter 7), human development (Chapter 8), effects (Chapter 9), risk (Chapter 10), and the media industries (Chapter 11).

In the literature on media violence, definitions for violence vary widely. There is no consensus. Some people define violence narrowly as physical harm, but others take a broader perspective, using definitions such as aggression, conflict, or antisocial behavior. Some scholars present formal definitions, but others treat violence as a primitive concept. These conditions make it very difficult to synthesize findings across studies.

Violence needs to be treated as a theoretical construct that is broad enough to include all the elements suggested by theoreticians, as well as all the risks found by researchers. In short, scholars need to recognize a broad template for the construct of violence. A broad template would serve as a salient agenda for what needs to be examined in the empirical research studies. Individual scholars may choose to ignore parts of the total construct when conducting their research, but by recognizing that there is a broad template—or map—scholars can position their findings more efficiently within an integrated pattern in the line of research. This issue is examined in Chapter 5.

We need to rethink the role of certain major contextual factors that have raised intriguing questions. Examples include the contextual factors of humor and realism. Many people feel that when an otherwise violent act appears humorous or as fantasy, it loses its status as violence. The challenge here is to find out why people turn off their perceptions of harm under such conditions. In addition, it is important to determine if these conditions turn off the harm itself, or only the perceptions of harm. This issue is addressed in Chapter 6.

We need to think more deeply about the multifaceted nature of media violence. Each of the facets can be examined at a different level: aggregate, cultural, and individual. We need to focus more on the unavoidable facts that people are individuals and that they differ in the way they construct meaning. Often their constructs are identical to those of others in society; thus, it is worthwhile to look at patterns in the aggregate. At other times, their constructions are contingent on their group conditioning, such as gender, age, religious orientation, or other cultural influences. And in other instances their constructions are purely idiosyncratic. Although cues for meaning exist in the context of the portrayals, often viewers do not perceive or process all those cues. Because people expose themselves to the media usually in a partially attentive, "automatic pilot" manner of processing, viewers take shortcuts to deriving meaning. This manner of processing leads to profound individual differences in interpretations. A great deal of understanding is to be mined in these differences; it is a serious shortcoming to wash them out with analytical techniques that treat variance within subjects as error. The challenge here is to design research strategies that examine both the differences and the commonalities. This issue is addressed in Chapter 7.

We need to take a broader view of human development and how it influences the effect of media violence on viewers (see Chapter 8). Many very good studies illustrate this perspective, but they are limited to children and to cognitive development. It is implicitly assumed that once children have cycled through the Piagetian stages of cognitive development, they have reached a plateau where they stay in a suspension of equilibrium with everyone else. We need to challenge this assumption and look at cognitive development as a lifelong process. In addition, we need to augment our view of development to include emotional and moral dimensions. Locating our research subjects on cognitive, emotional, and moral continua would give us a great deal more context for understanding how media violence exerts a variety of negative effects on different people. To construct more accurate assessments of risk, we need to consider development as both multidimensional and lifelong.

We need to broaden and deepen our conceptualization of effects. Too often the effect of media violence has been equated with imitation of violent portrayals. During the past decade or so, a few scholars have been generating convincing evidence that exposure to media violence also leads to the effects of fear and desensitization. In Chapter 9, I try to expand our thinking about the range of effects by arguing that at least a dozen different effects warrant our attention.

Perhaps the most useful task we can address is the conceptualization of risk. What does it mean to be in danger of a negative effect? This topic is addressed in Chapter 10. The most overlooked facet of media violence is the industry that produces and programs these harmful messages. Why does the industry depend so much on violence in its fictional narratives and news stories? What is it about violence that attracts viewers? These questions are addressed in Chapter 11.

PART III: RETHINKING METHODOLOGY

In addition to the conceptual tasks outlined in the previous section, we also need to address methodological tasks. This is the third argument. Our methods have much potential that we have yet to use fully in our research.

In early stages of a line of research, the research designs need to be fairly simple to reduce ambiguity in the empirical task. Although experiments with 2×2 designs oversimplify the phenomenon, these designs are of high value, because they give researchers the ability to identify more clearly the particular variables that lead to an effect. But now we need to be more rigorous in our decisions about sampling and measurement; more creative in our quantitative analyses, especially in the examination of relationships; and more critically analytical in our reviews of the literatures (Chapter 12).

When using the content analysis methodology, we need to realize that violence and its context are latent content that is best assessed using a normative point of view, not a criterion point of view set by experts. Once this shift to a normative coding scheme is accepted, there are implications for the testing of the reliability of the coding and the validity of the results (Chapter 13).

PART IV: LINEATION THEORY

The arguments presented in this book build to a suggested perspective for thinking about media violence. I call this perspective lineation because it uses the metaphor of a line in the making of distinctions and the drawing of connections. Lineation theory is a blend of explanations and speculations. The explanations highlight what we already know. The speculations provide direction for what we need to know.

This lineation perspective focuses attention on media violence while seeking to integrate thinking about the media industries, the content they produce, the effects of violent content on audience members and society, and the processes that lead to those effects. In constructing this perspective, I have attempted to weave together the findings of the empirical literature, key propositions in existing theories, and the arguments from the critical analyses. In short, this perspective rests on the foundation of ideas highlighted in the first 13 chapters.

The lineation perspective attempts to be inclusive; that is, it tries to avoid excluding any key ideas on media violence. The perspective also attempts to extend those key ideas in the current thinking into a new position by challenging some of the currently held assumptions and by suggesting revisions to the currently used practices. Thus, lineation is not a refutation of any of the previous research or thinking about media violence. Instead, it attempts to build on an integration of that thinking and then push on to a broader view of media violence and its effects.

Some readers may regard lineation more as a set of guidelines for future research than as a theory. In places, lineation does appear to be primarily a guide for thinking about the phenomenon rather than an explanation of the phenomenon. That is okay. In this book I am less interested in arguing that I have all the explanations right than I am in arguing for more useful and powerful research. Even if the results of that research falsify many of the speculations in the theory, I will regard that outcome as a very positive advancement.

NEED FOR A NEW PERSPECTIVE

In all lines of scientific scholarship, there comes a point at which research and thinking reach a critical mass. We are now at that point with research on media violence. The literature is large enough that we can see patterns emerge. It is becoming clear that certain types of studies will be much more valuable than others in moving our understanding forward. And it is very important that we become efficient with our small resources so that we can more quickly be successful at providing valid estimates of risk of exposure to different kinds of portrayals of violence. Policymakers need our help in programming the V-chip. And parents have waited long enough for guidance about how to control and enhance the exposure of their children—as well as themselves—to the media.

Thus, the purpose of this book is to lay out a vision for where the research should head and what the results should be to make a difference. We need to generate confident conclusions that can be used by policymakers and the general population as powerful tools in addressing this public health issue.

Although social science has great value in increasing our understanding of media violence, it has had its shortcomings. But the current shortcomings in the literature are not attributable to inherent limitations in social science methodologies of content analysis, experiment, and survey. Instead, the shortcomings reflect the difference between where social scientists want to be and what they have been able to accomplish in the relatively short time they have been working on explaining this phenomenon. These social science methodologies have not yet been used to their full potential in increasing our understanding of media violence.

This is not to say that qualitative methodologies are not also useful in the pursuit of this goal. The qualitative approach can be used to widen our perspective on the importance of considering individual differences and to keep us from focusing exclusively on aggregate patterns such that we miss the variety in the media violence content and the wide range of reactions viewers can have to this violence. However, I believe that the rich insights gained from qualitative approaches become even more useful when put to an empirical test using social science methodologies. These social science methodologies are essential tools for developing good answers to questions about the prevalence of kinds of media violence; about the microstructures in the effects process; and in understanding differential degrees of risk to exposures.

Social science can do a much better job of providing useful information to the public and to public policymakers. We need to go beyond our limitations by framing better questions about the nature of violence, about how it appears in context most often in the media, and about how variations of the media violence formula put people at risk for different, often conflicting, negative effects. To do this, we need to take a major step forward into a new generation of theorizing. Accomplishing this empirical work will require greater methodological sophistication. By "greater methodological sophistication," I do not simply mean more statistical tests. Instead, I mean that our use of methodological tools should be guided by more creativity in thinking about violence, effects, relationships, differences, groups, and processes.

The past research and theorizing have been extremely valuable as a start on this complex task. But repeating the past tests and methods will not do much to advance our understanding. We need to make many adjustments to go beyond our historical focus on "there are effects," shifting our attention much more to explaining the how and the why of those effects.

It is time to shift to a new perspective on media violence thinking and research. By "new perspective," I do not mean anything as grand as a Kuhnian shift in paradigm, one in which we need to alter our ontological or epistemological assumptions of the world. We do not need to do anything as radical as that. Furthermore, in calling for a new perspective, I do not mean that we should abandon the methodologies that have brought us this far. Instead, by calling for a shift in perspective, I am recommending that we ratchet up the rigor in our conceptualizations and increase the sophistication in our use of methodologies to realize more of the power in those procedures.

We need to recognize our accomplishments and use them as a foundation, thinking of them as Phase One research. But now we need to shift into a Phase Two perspective that builds on that foundation—rather than rejecting it—and shifts our focus to new questions, as well as to a deeper analysis of the older questions.

Phase One research has been concerned most with exploring possibilities; that is, it has sought to discover what *can* occur. Thus, it has asked questions such as these: Is there a disinhibition effect from exposure to media violence? Can viewers become desensitized to victims of violence? Can the viewing of violence that is portrayed as justified lead viewers to more risk of a negative effect?

Phase Two research is most concerned with determining *prevalence* and *strength;* that is, it seeks to document how widespread various effects are. So it asks questions such as the following: What percentage of children will exhibit a disinhibition effect after being exposed to media violence portrayed in a particular web of context? What degree of desensitization to victims is there in the general population of television viewers? Within the contextual web of violent portrayals, what is the strength of justification relative to other elements in the web? The focus here is on assessing how much of the processes and effects operates in the aggregate and how much is traceable to differences in interpretations among individuals.

The studies in the existing literature on media violence exhibit a Phase One perspective. There are exceptions, of course, but our literature has been predominantly Phase One. This is not a shortcoming of the field. Phase One research has been a necessary, unavoidable stage in this—and any other—line of research. We need to begin by exploring possibilities, by developing and redeveloping constructs, by trying out different definitions, and by inventorying the possible processes and effects. The research on media violence has been very successful in addressing Phase One issues. We have made a solid beginning.

We have accomplished enough by this point to warrant moving into a Phase Two perspective on media violence research. Such a shift is not only warranted, but also necessary to avoid squandering our precious few resources. It is time for this line of research to move forward substantially. In short, I recommend that we ask more of our research so that we can give more to policymakers and the public.

PART I

Reviewing

2

Theories of Media Violence

A wide range of theories provides explanations about aggression and the media's role in creating or shaping it. In this chapter, I review the contributions made by the theoreticians by organizing those major theories into four groups. The first three of these categories (biological theories, ecological theories, and cognitive theories) focus their explanations primarily in one domain. The fourth category (interactionist theories) draws ideas from across domains.

BIOLOGICAL THEORIES

Biological theories focus primarily on human physiological characteristics to explain the genesis and shaping of aggression. From this biological point of view, aggression has been explained in terms of instincts and hormones.

Instinct

Animal ethologists view aggression as an instinct. For example, Lorenz (1963) says that the instinct of aggression in animals serves three primary functions: (a) to balance the distribution of animals of the same species against the available supporting environment, (b) to drive intraspecies combat that results in the selection of the "fittest" animals for reproduction, and (c) to drive intraspecies combat associated with mating selections for organisms that are adapted for extraspecies fighting, as well as intraspecies challenges. This instinct generates energy. This aggressive energy must periodically be discharged by an appropriate releasing stimulus. The media often present such stimuli.

In his later thinking, Freud (1933) proposed that humans are ruled by two instincts. One of these is the *eros,* or life instinct, which includes the libido that causes people to create and prolong life. The other is *thanatos,* or the death instinct, which urges people toward disintegration and the destruction of self and others. Freud said that humans need to aggress to relieve hostility and to push the death wish away from themselves. Some critics have rejected Freud's contention that aggression is instinctive, preferring instead to think of it as a reactive force (Horney, 1939). More generally, other scholars (e.g., Parke & Slaby, 1983) have criticized this explanation of aggression for relying too much on instinctual factors and not enough on learning.

Hormones

Hormones have also been regarded as responsible for aggressive behavior. The relationship between hormones and behavior is seen as bidirectional; that is, a high level of testosterone in a person's body can lead to aggressive behavior, and aggressive behavior can trigger higher levels of testosterone. However, the relationship is not linear, nor is it direct; there are many intervening variables.

When hormones are used as an explanation for aggression, sex and age differences become especially prominent. Boys are found to be more aggressive than girls in much of the research. In addition, younger males are generally more aggressive than older males. These differences in aggression are strongly correlated with differences in testosterone levels.

ECOLOGICAL THEORIES

Ecological theories focus primarily on influences from the environment that act on a person over the long term. The primary ecological influences are family, religion, education, and the media. All the messages from these institutions create an environment that can teach people about violence and aggression.

Goldenstein (1994) points out that there are physical and social ecologies. Theories of physical ecology explain aggression primarily in terms of housing structures, population density, ease of access to neighborhoods and buildings, zoning, lighting, traffic patterns, and so on. Theories of social ecology focus on explanatory variables of social disorganization, social inequality, income inequality, unemployment, differential economic opportunity, ethnic mix, family structure, population mobility, and the like.

The media, especially television, provide people with a great deal of information about social ecologies. Moreover, the television set is a part of a person's physical ecology. The locations and numbers of television sets can be responsible for violent behavior. For example, Goldenstein (1994) says that much of the violence in people's living rooms "appears to occur in front of and, in a sense, in response to television viewing, i.e., conflict over one's view of the screen being blocked or which channel to watch, or arguments initiated by differing reactions to program content" (p. 17).

Confluence

Dishion, Patterson, and Griesler (1994) have developed a confluence theory to bring together two environmental influences: family and peers. For families in which discipline is harsh, erratic, and lax, the incidence of juvenile delinquency is high. Coercive families develop a pattern of negative reinforcement in which parents punish children for "bad" behavior, thus coercing them to be "good." When children comply, they are ignored rather than rewarded. In this situation, children usually adapt to the attempted conditioning by being aversive when they are coerced by parents. When parents recant on their coercion, children stop being aversive and there is peace. Children learn that responding with aversive behavior (whining, yelling, etc.) works as a tool to stop coercion. Over time, the parents erratically give up on coercing their children. The adaptive behavior of these children spills over into school, where they are likely to be problem students in terms of inattentiveness and noncompliance when being forced to learn something.

Peer influence is also an important factor. Ecological factors such as neighborhoods, schools, communities, and classrooms all determine the people with whom children come in contact. Children seek acceptance into social networks, and they look for similar children with whom to form friendships. Thus, aversive children are likely to bond with other aversive children, and the bonds of friendship among these like children are strengthened through further aggressive behavior. Some of this bonding can be with characters on TV through parasocial interaction.

Socialization

Socialization is the gradual, long-term process that teaches children about society's rules, attitudes, values, and norms. Institutions transmit their meaning to each new generation through this process.

Socialization can be regarded as an ecological theory, because it uses environmental factors to explain why certain people are shaped by their experiences to be aggressive. Parents are generally regarded as the primary agents of socialization, but all other ecological factors (such as family, school, neighborhood, church, and media messages) also exert their influences (Bronfenbrenner, 1979; Parke & Slaby, 1983).

Lippmann (1922) highlighted the importance of media in this socialization process by pointing out that newspapers—the dominant form of mass media of his time—present the public with information about events that people cannot experience in real life. Thus, the media are powerful agents of socialization because they give the public a great deal of information that cannot be confirmed by sources other than the media.

Berger and Luckmann (1966) extended Lippmann's ideas by theorizing that socialization consists of three main processes: internalization, externalization, and objectivation. Internalization is the process by which people learn about their social world and thereby become a product of it. People learn to observe the rules and lessons of society.

Externalization is the process of typifying behavior either on a small scale or on a large scale. On a small scale, people express attitudes and behaviors as they interact with one another in a social world. Particular attitudes and behaviors become common in certain situations; that is, people develop habits. On a large scale, we can see that certain behavioral patterns are continually exhibited by a wide range of people.

Objectivation is the process by which the externalized products of human activity attain the character of objectivity; that is, they become accepted as legitimate. When these patterns are used by others, this typified pattern can become an institution. Once an institution becomes established, it controls human conduct with its previously defined patterns of conduct. As people conform to these patterns, the institution gains credibility and acceptance. Over time, institutions are regarded as having a reality of their own. In this case, they are said to have been "objectified."

Berger and Luckmann argued that the most important vehicle of reality maintenance is conversation—not so much the explicit words as the implicit meanings. The content does not define the world as much as the assumptions behind the conversation define the background of a world that is silently taken for granted. That which is never talked about becomes forgotten. That which is talked about becomes clearer as reality. Thus, conversations can alter behavior when they are supported by significant others with whom an individual has established a strongly affective identification.

Berger and Luckmann drew an interesting contrast between primitive and complex societies. They observed that primitive societies show a high proportion of institutionalized activity, because most problems are held in common by all members of that society. In contrast, complex societies have very few problems held in common by all people, and therefore there is almost no common stock of knowledge. The United States is a highly complex society, so we should ordinarily expect very little sharing of a common stock of knowledge. However, we have very highly developed mass media, especially television, that can serve as an institution to convey a common experience to all members of our complex society and thus bring us all together. The media give us all the same ability to witness the same conversations and to participate vicariously in many actions with surrogate significant others.

Cultivation

Cultivation refers to the long-term formation of perceptions and beliefs about the world as a result of exposure to the media. The term was introduced by George Gerbner in 1969 with the publication of "Towards 'Cultural Indicators': The Analysis of Mass Mediated Message Systems." In this article, Gerbner argued for the importance of moving beyond examining short-term effects of the media to looking at how the media exert subtle but cumulative effects over a long period of time. He posited that "changes in the mass production and rapid distribution of messages across previous barriers of time, space, and social grouping bring about systematic variations in public message content whose full significance rests in the cultivation of collective consciousness about elements of existence" (p. 138). Rather than use the phrase *long-term effects,* Gerbner used the term *cultivation,* because he was interested in the more diffuse effects on perceptions that are shaped over a long period of exposure to media messages.

Cultivation theory is composed of essentially two constructs (cultivation indicators and television exposure) linked together in one primary proposition that states the following: Heavier viewers of television are more likely to believe that the real world is like the television world than are lighter viewers. Gerbner uses the term *cultural indicators* to refer to the elements in the messages that reflect our culture. He draws an analogy with economic and social indicators, which are continually gathered in an effort to monitor the economy and society. Major cultivation indicators are the beliefs that people hold about crime, violence, and victimization (Bryant, Carveth, & Brown, 1981; Carveth & Alexander, 1985; Doob & Macdonald, 1979; Gerbner et al., 1977; Hawkins & Pingree, 1980, 1981a; Morgan, 1983, 1986; Potter, 1991a, 1991b; Rouner, 1984; Signorielli, 1990; Weaver & Wakshlag, 1986; Wober, 1978; Zillmann & Wakshlag, 1985).

Cultivation is classified here as an ecological theory, because it uses only television messages as its explanation for how people come to think about aggression. Furthermore, exposure is conceptualized purely in terms of time. A primary assumption is that television is a world in which a small set of messages is consistently presented over and over again across the television landscape. Gerbner, Gross, Jackson-Beeck, Jeffries-Fox, and Signorielli (1978) said that the world presented on television is uniform across programs and over years, and that some types of portrayals are repeated so often that viewers come to believe that the real world operates in the same way as the world that is so constantly portrayed on television. Gerbner et al. argued, "Although some of these lessons may be enhanced by a preference for watching crime or police shows, they cannot and need not be specifically related to specific elements of those or other shows. They can and should be seen as generalized responses to the central dynamics of the world of television drama" (p. 205).

The central proposition of cultivation theory predicts a positive linear relationship between the amount of exposure to television and cultivation indicators. Although the prediction is expressed in very general terms, a practice has developed in which the relationship is qualified with the use of "third variables" such as gender, age, educational level, and other demographic characteristics that are thought to indicate a person's social position in the environment. Thus, controlling for these variables is believed to remove the socializing influences of all major institutions—leaving a clearer assessment of the influence of the media.

By 1980, Gerbner, Gross, Morgan, and Signorielli had refined cultivation theory with the addition of the concepts of resonance and mainstreaming. Mainstreaming was defined as follows: "Those groups who in general are *least* likely to hold a television related attitude are *most* likely to be influenced toward the 'mainstream' television view; and those who are most likely to hold a view *more* extreme than the television view may be 'coaxed back' to the 'mainstream' position" (p. 18). For example, Gerbner, Gross, Morgan, and Signorielli (1982) found evidence of a mainstreaming effect on the general topic of political orientation. Among lighter viewers, there was a relatively wide difference in attitudes toward blacks, personal conduct, communism, free speech, federal spending, and taxes. The differences in those attitudes were smaller among medium viewers and smallest among the heaviest viewers.

Gerbner, Gross, Morgan, and Signorielli (1980) introduced the concept of resonance by explaining that the cultivation relationship can vary across subgroups; that is, cultivation is stronger (it resonates) in some groups more than in others. As evidence, they presented a pattern of data showing that in suburban neighborhoods there is a cultivation effect (heavier viewers are more likely to score high on the Perceptions of Danger Index) among low-income people ($r = .10$), but that the effect is even stronger among high-income people ($r = .20$).

COGNITIVE THEORIES

Cognitive theories are concerned with human thinking. The two families of cognitive theories—cognitive abilities and construct accessibility—acknowledge that the human mind interacts with outside stimuli, but their explanations focus attention on the workings of the mind.

Cognitive Abilities

The theories of cognitive abilities focus on how a person's developmental level leads to the cognitive processing of certain types of messages and how that processing can lead to effects (Flavell, 1977). According to the Swiss psychologist Jean Piaget, children progress through four stages of cognitive development. At lower levels of development, children are prevented from processing certain messages or understanding certain concepts. When it comes to processing information from the media, children younger than 5 are likely to have difficulty in distinguishing fantasy from reality-based programming, in inferring motives of characters, and in connecting a consequence with an action presented earlier in a narrative. Thus, violent television content has a different effect on younger children than it does on older children, because children in the two age groups differ substantially in their cognitive abilities.

Construct Accessibility

In his classic work on perceptual readiness, Bruner (1957) theorized that not all constructs stored in a person's memory have an equal probability of being used to interpret events. When people are confronted with an event, they usually have several relevant constructs in their memory to help them interpret it. Which one of these will people choose? Bruner says that people will choose the construct that is the most accessible.

Several factors influence which constructs are most accessible at any given time. First, a temporal dimension says that the most recently used constructs are the most accessible. Second, an association dimension says that constructs are linked together in the mind and that particular portrayals can activate these associations. Thus, a visual of a gun could activate the aggression construct. Third, emotions and motivations are important. These states bring certain constructs to the fore of memory. In an angry person, for example, aggressive constructs are more accessible than peaceful constructs.

Sanbonmatsu and Fazio (1991) say that "the media are instrumental in developing the constructs that are available in memory, and in determining which of those constructs are chronically accessible" (p. 57). These theoreticians explain that when people see a portrayal of a bad cop on television, that perception of police officers becomes the most accessible one in their memory. Later, when the same people see a police officer in real life, they tend to think the officer is bad.

INTERACTIONIST THEORIES

Interactionist theories consider both intraindividual qualities and the relevant characteristics of the person's environment. The key intraindividual characteristics are a person's traits and states, especially frustration. Environmental factors include the people and the qualities of the immediate environment, as well as society at large. These theories view aggression or violence as a person-environment event.

Drive

Generally, drive theories posit that individuals are motivated by internal needs that are influenced by stimuli external to them. The most important drive theory related to violence is the frustration-aggression hypothesis, which was formulated by Dollard, Doob, Miller, Mowrer, and Sears (1939). Their thinking was innovative, because it represented a break with the theorizing up to that point, which stated that aggression was instinctual. They were strongly influenced by biological theories and psychoanalytical thinking and built on the ideas in those traditions by translating Freudian theory into testable behaviorist terms.

Their main proposition was that when people become frustrated, they respond aggressively. Thus, frustration is seen as the antecedent of aggression. Frustration is a necessary condition for aggression, but it is not a sufficient condition; frustration can occur without aggression.

Excitation Transfer

This theory places the focus on a person's physiological state as an explanation for aggressive behavior. Zillmann (1982) says that arousal is "a unitary force that energizes or intensifies behavior" (p. 53). He argues that the media can be used to reduce or increase arousal states. In the reduction condition, the media absorb viewers' attention and thus distract them from fixating on an unpleasant arousal state. This distraction cuts the rehearsal process, in which people keep thinking about the unpleasant arousing experience. This thinking initiates the decay of physiological arousal and eventually brings on relief.

The media can also increase arousal when they present exciting portrayals. Media entertainment (especially portrayals of violence, but also of erotica and humor) can stimulate excitatory reactions physiologically. Once aroused, people remain in this excitatory state beyond the length of the stimulus material.

Zillmann (1971) theorized that not only is arousal a key element in explaining aggressive effects from the media, but arousal that is generated with one activity or message can be transferred to another activity. In an experiment, he found that arousal can be transferred from one type of stimulus to another type of effect and that the strongest arousal leads to the strongest effects. For example, he showed participants an erotic film, an aggressive film, or a neutral film. The film that led to the most subsequent aggression among the participants was not the aggressive film, but rather the erotic film, because the erotic film was more arousing than the aggressive one.

Zillmann (1991b) also explains that arousal is viewed as an energizer of thoughts and behaviors. However, the energy needs direction, because arousal by itself is not guided. So the residual arousal from a viewing experience can lead to either prosocial or antisocial reactions, depending on the prevailing social circumstances and the dispositions of the individual.

Catharsis

As an explanation for aggression, catharsis was first suggested by Aristotle, who argued that drama provides audiences with a way to purge their feelings of fear, grief, pity, anger, and other negative emotions. This explanation was taken up by drive theorists, who said that when a drive, such as aggression, is increased to a certain point, a person must find a way to reduce it. Thus, catharsis requires a component that is internal to the person (drive or emotion), as well as a component that is external (the media message).

This theory has a troubled past as an explanation of aggressive effects. When a series of empirical tests was published in support of the theory (Feshbach, 1955, 1961, 1972), those tests were criticized (Comstock, Chaffee, Katzman, McCombs, & Roberts, 1978; Liebert, Sobol, & Davidson, 1972; Wells, 1973). Berkowitz (1962) argued that the reduction of aggression that Feshbach found was due not to catharsis, but to inhibition induced by the experiment.

Catharsis, however, still exists as a theory. Reviews still continue to acknowledge its place as an explanation of aggressive effects (Comstock et al., 1978; Gunter, 1994; Signorielli, 1991).

Social Learning

The primary contribution of social learning theory is its greater emphasis on environmental cues as elicitors of aggression rather than an exclusive focus on characteristics internal to the individual, such as drives. The central proposition is that aggressive behavior is learned and maintained through environmental experiences either directly or vicariously.

Social learning theory explains that viewers, especially children, learn social and cognitive skills by watching the behavior of others in social situations and then imitating that behavior (Bandura, 1977). There are four subprocesses: (a) attentional processes—that is, how well the observer attends to the model; (b) retention of the observed behavior through symbolic coding and mental rehearsal of the model's actions; (c) motor reproduction, or the behavioral enactment of the previously acquired behavior that depends on the physical capacity of the observer; and finally (d) the reinforcement and motivation that determine whether the actions observed will be translated into behavior by the observer.

The theory says that the same dynamic takes place when viewers observe behavior in the media, especially aggressive behavior. Individuals who act aggressively might feel a sense of self-satisfaction and pride, or they might experience self-criticism; therefore, there is a process of self-reinforcement.

Initially, social learning theory had a strong behaviorist flavor in its explanation that behaviors were learned through experience with rewards and punishments. Behaviors that are rewarded are learned; then over time the learned behaviors that are rewarded are reinforced. In contrast, behaviors that are punished are avoided, and these behaviors are eventually extinguished.

Over time, Bandura (1986) moved away from a behavioral orientation and more toward a cognitive one. He called this evolution in thinking social cognitive theory (which I will discuss a little later in this chapter). This theory builds on social learning theory by emphasizing the cognitions in the processes of influence. It focuses on the rules and strategies that are observed and learned in social situations.

In this reformulation, Bandura (1986) emphasized a person's internal self-regulating processes. Social cognitive theory focuses on how the child interprets the meaning of events. Children evaluate the models by watching the reactions of other people to the models, by watching the self-evaluative standards used by the models themselves, or by using their own intuition.

Priming Effects

Berkowitz (1965) initially developed what he called cue theory, which stated that when angry people are exposed to television violence, those portrayals signal them to behave aggressively. The elements in the portrayal (guns, particular kinds of characters, etc.) serve as cues. When these cues are later encountered in real life, viewers are reminded of the violence, and this reminder increases the likelihood that they will behave aggressively.

With cue theory, Berkowitz (1974) explained that frustration may create a readiness for aggression, but aggression-eliciting cues are what are necessary for aggression to occur. Thus, two conditions must be met—one internal to the person (the drive of frustration or anger) and one in the environment (suitable cues). Classical conditioning is the mechanism that assigns cues their aggressive-inducing potential.

Berkowitz (1984) has elaborated cue theory and now refers to it as cognitive-neoassociation theory. He extended his thinking to account for the instances of aggression that he did not think were accounted for in other theories. Specifically, he felt that the explanations available at the time focused only on how aggression arises when a person is wronged. Berkowitz, however, observed that aggression can result even when people are not stimulated by actions aimed at them personally. For example, an environment with high temperatures can make people feel angry or frustrated even though the heat is not created for them individually. As explained by the cognitive-neoassociation theory, the effects process begins with an aversive event that stimulates a chain reaction leading to anger, which is an emotion people feel when they become inclined to assault someone verbally or physically.

With anger, there are usually two built-in emotional networks: fight and flight (Berkowitz, 1994). With the fight network, anger leads to aggression. With the flight network, anger leads to escape and avoidance, which is a fear response. Berkowitz argues that any aversive event usually activates both networks, although one is usually dominant, given a person's learning, genetics, and particular situation.

How does an aversive event lead to the emotion of anger? Berkowitz says that each person builds associative networks that link up physiological reactions, feelings, motor responses, and thoughts or memories. Thus, certain types of physiological patterns are linked with angry feelings, hostile thoughts, and aggressive motor responses. These connections differ in strength but are often weak. When an associative network exists, the activation of any one of its components activates the other parts in proportion to their degrees of association. If people think back on a previous episode when they were very angry, they are likely to feel anger, experience hostile thoughts, and perhaps even express some aggressive behaviors in the present.

Another key idea in Berkowitz's theory is *spreading activation.* This concept means that when a person becomes aware of a cognition, an activation process is triggered in which awareness radiates from the particular cognition—called a node—along associative paths to other mental nodes. Thus, the associated information is also activated or primed. For example, when people watch a violent episode on television, their awareness of that perceived act spreads (or primes awareness) to information associated with that type of portrayal. This process happens automatically, with little, if any, conscious thought. Thus, watching a violent episode on television automatically calls up memories and feelings of other aggressive events and perceptions. A single exposure to violence in the media can quickly bring up an entire mind-set about how to behave aggressively.

Key to the triggering of networks is the aversive event and how a person attributes it. "Aggression is in the mind of the beholder, and a movie will not activate aggression-associated thoughts unless the viewer regards what is seen as aggression" (Berkowitz, 1994, p. 41). When people believe that an event was deliberately directed at them and that the event wrongly kept them from satisfying their desires, they are very unhappy—usually angry. When people attribute the event to mishap, however, even though they may still feel unhappy (usually frustrated), this negative feeling is not as strong as when they attribute the event as deliberately directed at them.

In addition to attribution, other factors influence the strength of the emotion. Environmental characteristics (temperature) and personal characteristics (depression or sadness) have been found to be influences. Furthermore, the ability to self-regulate behavior is important. Sometimes people are able to activate higher-order cognitive processes that can restrain or alter the more primitive emotional reactions. These cognitions become increasingly influential as aroused people think about their feelings and actions.

Cues are still important. Viewers who see a target in real life that resembles the target in a media portrayal are more likely to aggress when angry. In addition, viewers who identify with the aggressor in the media will be more likely to aggress in real life when presented with a similar situation to that of the media aggressor. And when the media portray violence as having a successful outcome, viewers are more likely to be cued to try aggression as a strategy in real life.

Social Cognition

The main proposition of this theory is that aggressive behavior is determined by how the individual interprets environmental events (Eron, 1994). According to this theory, there are some very important explanatory constructs, such as environmental cues, attitudes, response biases, perceptual sets, and schemas. Borrowing from Bandura (1977), Eron argues that another important explanatory construct is self-efficacy—that is, how competent a person feels in responding in certain ways, such as aggressively or nonaggressively. He says that social behavior is controlled by learned programs for that behavior. These programs, or scripts, have been learned throughout life and are used as guides for people to figure out what to do in social situations. When people are faced with a certain social situation, they use the cues in that situation to select a script as a guide. They then evaluate the usefulness of that script in guiding their interpretations.

Guerre, Nucci, and Huesmann (1994) add moral cognition as an important explanatory construct. They define moral cognition as "moral judgments or moral reasoning, characterized by justification of actions according to underlying conceptions of justice" (p. 19). They found that delinquents use lower stages (à la Kohlberg's conception) of moral reasoning than nondelinquents.

Huesmann (1986) argued that there is a cumulative learning process during childhood in which aggressive scripts are learned through observation of media portrayals. Then later in life, when certain cues are present in media portrayals, aggressive behavior is triggered. Although early childhood television habits are correlated with adult criminality, certain intervening variables (especially intellectual achievement, social popularity, identification with TV characters, and belief in the reality of TV violence) shape the effect.

Sometimes referred to as script theory, this explanation was developed by Huesmann (1988), who used some of the ideas from social cognition to illuminate how people are affected by media violence. He said that young children construct cognitive maps, or scripts, through observational and enactive learning. The media influence the construction of these scripts. During the primary learning process, children observe the behavior of others and encode this information into scripts that can be stored in memory. Then during the secondary learning process, children use the scripts as guides for their own behavior. If a script is useful (their behavior is successful), it is reinforced. But if a script presents problems, children will alter the elements or structure of the script. This enactive learning does not require actual behavior on the part of the child; enactive learning can happen through mental rehearsal, in which additional encoding can take place and the child can connect similar subscripts into a more general script.

While children are first constructing these scripts, they use them in a controlled manner; that is, they think about what they are learning, and they slowly work through the construction to keep control of the process. After the scripts are well learned, they become automatic; that is, the scripts operate very rapidly, and the person has little awareness of the mental operations involved. The older a script becomes and the more it is used (rehearsed and enacted), the more resistant to modification it becomes.

RECOMMENDATIONS

We need a synthesis across complementary theories. Generally speaking, the development of theories about the effects of media violence on individuals has been relatively cooperative, with the existing theories being rather complementary to one another. The differences in explanations across the theories are attributable to differences in perspectives of the various theoreticians. For example, the theories of social learning, priming effects, and social cognition seem to have many more similarities among them than differences. They all regard the environment as offering stimuli that set off a process that is primarily cognitive and leads to a behavioral effect, while also allowing for attitudinal and cognitive effects. The cognitive process is guided by scripts, schemas, or associative networks—all of which are learned by experiencing of social situations over time. These learned tools then help the individual interpret the meaning of a given stimulus. The three theories differ in how they elaborate the process, but none of those elaborations predicts a process that is substantially different from the processes envisioned in the other two theories. Researchers cannot use the theories to operationalize a critical test in which the explanation of one of these theories could be supported, thus falsifying the explanations of the other two theories.

Theories are also complementary in another sense. For example, an ecological theory, such as cultivation, focuses on the environment as a cause of the effect. But nothing in cultivation would rule out the addition of cognitive elements to explain the process of that effect. Instead, cultivation simply has a different perspective that favors an ecological view.

We need more conflicting theories. When two or more theories offer conflicting explanations, scholars' attention focuses on critical tests to determine which explanation is most useful. There are a few examples of theoreticians setting up a critical test between their creations and another theory. In the development of cue theory, Berkowitz ran a critical test against Feshbach's catharsis theory and found that his participants increased their aggression (as he predicted) instead of decreasing their aggression (as catharsis theory would predict). Zillmann ran a critical test of his excitation transfer theory against cue theory and found that aggression was enhanced by both violent and sexual content, so arousal appeared to be a better explanation for aggressive behavior than cues were. The overall development of theory could benefit by more critical tests.

We need a broader explanation of media violence that includes the component of content creation, as well as content patterns and effects. Currently there is an imbalance in theorizing: The effects component is rich in theory and research, the content pattern component exhibits a good deal of research but little theory, and the content creation component has relatively little theory or research.

Within the content creation component, we need theories to explain why violence is used so often in all sorts of television narratives and why these narratives are programmed across the entire spectrum of the television and film landscapes. Within the content pattern component, we need to develop theories that explain the narrative patterns of violence and move beyond the research focus on the prevalence of individual characteristics. Within the effects component, we need additional theories or broader theories that will explain a greater range of effects, both positive and negative. Perhaps most important, however, we need a more general framework for thinking about the interdependencies among all three of these components.

3

Effects of Exposure to Media Violence

Does exposure to violence in the media lead to effects? With each passing year, the answer is a stronger yes. The general finding from a great deal of research is that exposure to violent portrayals in the media increases the probability of an effect. The most often tested effect is referred to as *learning to behave aggressively.* This effect is also referred to as direct imitation of violence, instigation or triggering of aggressive impulses, and disinhibition of socialization against aggressive behavior. Two other negative effects—desensitization and fear—are also becoming prevalent in the literature.

Exposure to certain violent portrayals can lead to positive or prosocial effects. Intervention studies, especially with children, have shown that when a media-literate person talks through the action and asks questions of the viewer during the exposure, the viewer will be able to develop a counterreading of the violence; that is, the viewer may learn that violent actions are wrong even though those actions are shown as successful in the media portrayal.

The effects have been documented to occur immediately or over the long term. Immediate effects happen during exposure or shortly after the exposure (within about an hour). They might last only several minutes, or they might last weeks. Long-term effects do not occur after one or several exposures; they begin to show up only after an accumulation of exposures over weeks or years. Once a long-term effect eventually occurs, it usually lasts a very long period of time.

This chapter focuses on the issues of both immediate effects and long-term effects of exposure to media violence. Most of the studies have examined immediate effects rather than longer-term effects. In addition, a few studies (e.g., Bryant, Carveth, & Brown, 1981; Van der Voort, 1986) do both, by measuring effects immediately after the treatment exposure and sometime later, such as a week or more, to see if the effects have changed.

TABLE 3.1 Summary of Major Findings About Effects of Exposure to Media Violence

Immediate Effects

1. Exposure to violent portrayals in the media can lead to subsequent viewer aggression through disinhibition.

2. The immediate disinhibition effect is influenced by viewer demographics, viewer traits, viewer states, characteristics in the portrayals, and situational cues.

3. Exposure to violence in the media can lead to fear effects.

4. An immediate fear effect is influenced by a set of key factors about viewers and the portrayals.

5. Exposure to violence in the media can lead to desensitization.

6. An immediate desensitization effect is influenced by a set of key factors about viewers and the portrayals.

Long-Term Effects

7. Long-term exposure to media violence is related to aggression in a person's life.

8. Media violence is related to subsequent violence in society.

9. People exposed to many violent portrayals over a long time will come to exaggerate their chances of being victimized.

10. People exposed to many violent portrayals over a long time will come to be more accepting of violence.

From the large body of effects research, I have assembled 10 major findings. These are the findings that consistently appear in quantitative meta-analyses and narrative reviews of this literature. Because these findings are so widespread in the literature and because they are so rarely disputed by scholars, they can be regarded as empirically established laws (see Table 3.1).

IMMEDIATE EFFECTS OF VIOLENT CONTENT

The first six laws illuminate the major findings of research into the immediate effects of exposure to media violence. Immediate effects occur during exposure or within several hours afterward.

1. *Exposure to violent portrayals in the media can lead to subsequent viewer aggression through disinhibition.* This conclusion is found in most of the early reviews (Baker & Ball, 1969; Chaffee, 1972; Comstock, Chaffee, Katzman,

McCombs, & Roberts, 1978; Goranson, 1970; Hapkiewicz, 1979; Liebert, 1972; Liebert, Neale, & Davidson, 1973; Liebert & Poulos, 1975; Liebert & Schwartzberg, 1977; Maccoby, 1964; Roberts & Schramm, 1971; Shirley, 1973; Stein & Friedrich, 1972; Tannenbaum & Zillmann, 1975). For example, Stein and Friedrich closely analyzed 49 studies of the effects of antisocial and prosocial television content on people 3 to 18 years of age in the United States. They concluded that the correlational studies showed generally significant relationships (r = .10 to .32) and that the experiments generally showed an increase in aggression resulting from exposure to television violence across all age groups.

This conclusion gained major visibility in the 1972 Surgeon General's Report which stated that there was an influence, but this conclusion was softened by the industry members on the panel. Ten years later, the conclusion was put forth again in a major report issued by the National Institute of Mental Health (1982): "Most of the researchers look at the totality of evidence and conclude, as did the Surgeon General's Advisory Committee, that the convergence of findings supports the conclusion of a causal relationship between televised violence and later aggressive behavior" (p. 37).

Some of the early reviewers disagreed with this conclusion (Howitt & Cumberbatch, 1975; Jones, 1971; Kaplan & Singer, 1976; Kniveton, 1976; Lesser, 1977; Singer, 1971). For example, Lesser organized criticisms of these findings into five categories: (a) lack of distinction between filmed and TV violence, (b) restriction to an immediate effect, (c) inadequate exploration in the observational learning experiments of the developmental function of imitation in children's play, (d) questionable definitions and operationalizations of aggression, and (e) the artificial nature of laboratory experiments that limits the ecological validity of the findings.

In the two decades since this early disagreement, a great deal more empirical research has helped overcome these shortcomings, so most (but not all) of these critics have been convinced of the general finding that exposure to media violence can lead to an immediate disinhibition effect. All narrative reviews since 1980 have concluded that viewing of violence is consistently related to subsequent aggressiveness. This finding holds in surveys, laboratory experiments, and naturalistic experiments (Comstock, 1985; Comstock & Strasburger, 1990; Friedrich-Cofer & Huston, 1986; Geen, 1994; Heath, Bresolin, & Rinaldi, 1989; National Institute of Mental Health, 1982; Roberts & Maccoby, 1985; Rule & Ferguson, 1986). For example, Roberts and Maccoby concluded that "the overwhelming proportion of results point to a causal relationship between exposure to mass communication portrayals of violence and an increased probability that viewers will behave violently at some subsequent time" (p. 576). Also, Friedrich-Cofer and Huston concluded that "the weight of the evidence from different methods of investigation supports the hypothesis that television violence affects aggression" (p. 368).

Meta-analytical studies that have reexamined the data quantitatively across sets of studies have also consistently concluded that viewing of aggression is likely to lead to antisocial behavior (Andison, 1977; Carlson, Marcus-Newhall, & Miller, 1990; Hearold, 1986; Paik & Comstock, 1994; Wood, Wong, & Chachere, 1991). For example, Paik and Comstock conducted a meta-analysis of 217 studies of the effects of television violence on antisocial behavior and reported finding a positive and significant correlation. They concluded that "regardless of age—whether nursery school, elementary school, college, or adult—results remain positive at a high significance level" (p. 537). Andison looked at 67 studies involving 30,000 participants (including 31 laboratory experiments) and found a relationship between viewing and subsequent aggression, with more than half of the studies showing a correlation (r) between .31 and .70. Hearold looked at 230 studies involving 100,000 participants to determine the effect of viewing violence on a wide range of antisocial behaviors in addition to aggression (including rule breaking, materialism, and perceiving oneself as powerless in society). Hearold concluded that for all ages and all measures, the majority of studies reported an association between exposure to violence and antisocial behavior.

There is still some criticism of this conclusion (Freedman, 1984; McGuire, 1986; Stipp & Milavsky, 1988). Stipp and Milavsky argued that there were two major problems with the research. First, they felt that the findings of laboratory experiments cannot be generalized to real-world applications, especially when the studies use mild forms of aggression and then predict that serious antisocial activity will be triggered in society. Second, they were skeptical of the use of survey data, especially when attitudinal measures are used to reflect behavior and when researchers use survey data to make causal claims about the effects of exposure to media violence. They called for more naturalistic studies that take into account the new media environment, in which VCR use has shifted much of the viewing into movie content that is very different from what the television broadcast networks typically program.

On balance, it is prudent to conclude that media portrayals of violence can lead to the immediate effect of aggressive behavior, that this can happen in response to as little as a single exposure, and that this effect can last up to several weeks. Furthermore, the effect is causal, with exposure leading to aggression. However, this causal link is part of a reciprocal process; that is, people with aggressive tendencies seek out violent portrayals in the media.

2. *The immediate disinhibition effect is influenced by viewer demographics, viewer traits, viewer states, characteristics in the portrayals, and situational cues.* Each human is a complex being who brings to each exposure situation a unique set of motivations, traits, predispositions, exposure history, and personality factors. These characteristics work together incrementally to increase or decrease the probability of the person's being affected.

2.1. *Viewer Demographics.* The key characteristics of the viewer that have been found to be related to a disinhibition effect are age and gender, but social class and ethnic background have also been found to play a part.

- *Demographics of Age and Gender.* Boys and younger children are more affected (Comstock et al., 1978; Stein & Friedrich, 1972). Part of the reason is that boys pay more attention to violence (Alvarez, Huston, Wright, & Kerkman, 1988). Moreover, younger children have more trouble following story plots (Collins, 1973, 1983), so they are more likely to be drawn into high-action episodes without considering motives or consequences. Age by itself is not as good an explanation as is ability for cognitive processing.

- *Socioeconomic Status.* Lower-class youth watch more television and therefore more violence (Chaffee & McLeod, 1972; Huesmann, Lagerspetz, & Eron, 1984; Stein & Friedrich, 1972).

- *Ethnicity.* Children from minority and immigrant groups are vulnerable because they are heavy viewers of television (Berry & Mitchell-Kernan, 1982; Greenberg, 1988).

2.2. *Viewer Traits.* The key characteristics of viewer traits are socialization against aggression, intelligence, cognitive processing, and personality type.

- *Socialization Against Aggression.* Family life is an important contributing factor. Children in households with strong norms against violence are not likely to experience enough disinhibition to exhibit aggressive behavior. The disinhibition effect is stronger in children living in households in which parents have sociopathic beliefs (Heath et al., 1989); in households in which children are abused by parents, watch more violence, and identify more with violent heroes (Heath et al., 1989); and in families that have high-stress environments (Borduin, Mann, Cone, & Henggeler, 1995; Tangney, 1988; Tangney & Feshbach, 1988).

Peer and adult role models have a strong effect in this socialization process. Male peers have the most immediate influence in shaping children's aggressive behaviors in the short term; adult males have the most lasting effect 6 months later (Hicks, 1965).

- *Intelligence.* Sprafkin, Gadow, and Grayson (1987) ran an experiment on 46 learning-disabled children (6-10 years old) in which the children were exposed to either six aggressive cartoons or six control cartoons. There was no main effect of condition on subsequent aggression, but there was an interaction with IQ: The low-IQ group became significantly more physically aggressive following the control cartoons than they did following aggressive cartoons.

• *Cognitive Processing.* Viewers' reactions depend on their individual interpretations of the aggression. Rule and Ferguson (1986) said that viewers first must form a representation or cognitive structure consisting of general social knowledge about the positive value that can be attached to aggression. The process of developing such a structure requires that viewers attend to the material (depending on the salience and complexity of the program). Then viewers make attributions and form moral evaluations in the comprehension stage. Then they store their comprehension in memory.

Cognitive processing is related to age. Developmental psychologists have shown that children's minds mature cognitively and that in some early stages they are unable to process certain types of television content well. At age 3, children begin watching television using an exploratory approach in which they actively search for meaning in content. But until age 5, they are especially attracted to and influenced by vivid production features, such as rapid movement of characters, rapid changes of scenes, and unexpected sights and sounds. Children seek out and pay attention to cartoon violence, not because of the violence, but because of the vivid production features. By ages 6 to 11, children have developed the ability to lengthen their attention spans and make sense of continuous plots. In addition, children who have learning disabilities are more susceptible to a disinhibition effect (Sprafkin, Liebert, & Abelman, 1992).

• *Personality Type.* The more aggressive the person is, the more influence viewing of violence will have on that person's subsequent aggressive behavior (Comstock et al., 1978; Stein & Friedrich, 1972). And children who are emotionally disturbed are more susceptible to a disinhibition effect (Sprafkin et al., 1992). Lagerspetz and Engblom (1979) classified each of their participants into one of four personality types: aggressive, constructive, submissive, and anxious. In the play period following viewing, personality accounted for more differences than the type of film seen: The submissives and constructives showed an increase in aggressive play after seeing the violent film.

2.3. *Viewer States.* The degrees of physiological arousal, anger, and frustration have all been found to increase the probability of a negative effect (Carlson et al., 1990; Geen, 1975; Geen & Berkowitz, 1967; Liebert & Schwartzberg, 1977; Schuck, Schuck, Hallam, Mancini, & Wells, 1971; Tannenbaum, 1972; Thomas, 1982; Worchel, Hardy, & Hurley, 1976; Zillmann, Bryant, Comisky, & Medoff, 1981; Zillmann & Sapolsky, 1977).

• *Aroused State.* Portrayals (even if they are not violent) that leave viewers in an aroused state are more likely to lead to aggressive behavior (Berkowitz & Geen, 1966; Donnerstein & Berkowitz, 1981; Tannenbaum, 1972; Zillmann, 1971).

• *Emotional Reaction.* Viewers who are upset by the media exposure (negative hedonic value stimuli) are more likely to aggress (Rule & Ferguson, 1986; Zillmann et al., 1981). Such aggression is especially likely when people are left in a state of unresolved excitement (Comstock, 1985). In addition, Ekman et al. (1972) found that when boys who were watching violence on television exhibited happy facial expressions while viewing, they were more likely to be aggressive during subsequent play. In his meta-analysis of 1,043 effects of television on social behavior, Hearold (1986) concluded that frustration and provocation contributed to the sizes of effects. However, the sizes of the effects are still positive and strong even when viewers are not frustrated, so frustration is not a necessary condition, but rather a contributory condition. Furthermore, aggression by angered people is higher after they watch a film in which the violence is portrayed as seeking revenge rather than in a professional's role as a fighter (Geen & Stonner, 1973).

• *Degree of Identity.* It has been well established that the more a person, especially a child, identifies with a character, the more likely the person will be influenced by that character's behavior (Anderson, 1983; Cantor, 1994; Dorr, 1981; Hicks, 1965; Huesmann, Lagerspetz, & Eron, 1984; Leyens & Picus, 1973; McLeod, Atkin, & Chaffee, 1972; Paik & Comstock, 1994; Perry & Perry, 1976; Tannenbaum & Gaer, 1965; Turner & Berkowitz, 1972).

Identity seems to be a multifaceted construct composed of similarity, attractiveness, and hero status. If the perpetrator of violence is perceived as *similar* to the viewer, the likelihood of learning to behave aggressively increases (Lieberman Research, 1975; Rosekrans & Hartup, 1967). When violence is performed by an *attractive* character, the probability of aggression increases (Comstock et al., 1978; Hearold, 1986). Attractiveness of a villain is also an important consideration (Heath et al., 1989). Liss, Reinhardt, and Fredriksen (1983) conducted two experiments on children in kindergarten through fourth grade and found that "the superheroes are compelling, attractive, and evidently above reproach, making their actions highly visible and favorable for generalized imitation" (p. 184).

2.4. *Characteristics in the Portrayals.* Reviews of the literature are clear on the point that people interpret the meaning of violent portrayals and use contextual information to construct that meaning (Comstock et al., 1978; Comstock & Strasburger, 1990; Gunter, 1985; Hearold, 1986; Heath et al., 1989; Liebert & Schwartzberg, 1977).

In the media effects literature, there appear to be five notable contextual variables: rewards and punishments, consequences, justification, realism, and production techniques. Two other contextual factors—presence of weapons and eroticism—are also often thought to contribute to the disinhibition effect; however, the research on these two factors is mixed.

- *Rewards and Punishments.* Rewards and punishments to perpetrators of violence provide important information to viewers about which actions are acceptable (Comstock et al., 1978; Comstock & Strasburger, 1990). However, there is reason to believe that the effect does not work with children younger than 10, who usually have difficulty linking violence presented early in a program with its punishment rendered later (Collins, 1973).

In repeated experiments, viewers who watch a model rewarded for performing violently in the media are more likely to experience a disinhibition effect and behave in a similar manner (Bandura, 1965; Bandura, Ross, & Ross, 1961, 1963a, 1963b; Liebert & Baron, 1973; Rosekrans & Hartup, 1967; Walters & Parke, 1964). But when violence is punished in the media portrayal, the aggressiveness of viewers is likely to be inhibited (Comstock et al., 1978). In addition, when nonaggressive characters are rewarded, viewers' levels of aggression can be reduced (Lando & Donnerstein, 1978).

The absence of punishment also leads to disinhibition. That is, the perpetrators need not be rewarded in order for the disinhibition effect to occur (Bandura, 1965). Furthermore, the reward or punishment need not be consistent to have an effect on viewers. Rosekrans and Hartup (1967) ran an experiment on 64 children of ages 36 to 71 months. They found that participants who were exposed to inconsistently reinforced models (not media portrayals, but rather real people) showed more imitative aggression than did participants exposed to a consistently punished model. However, they did not act as aggressively as participants who were exposed to a consistently rewarded model.

- *Consequences.* The way in which the consequences of violence are portrayed influences the disinhibition effect (Berkowitz & Rawlings, 1963; Comstock et al., 1978; Comstock & Strasburger, 1990; Goranson, 1969; Gunter, 1985; Heath et al., 1989; Liebert & Schwartzberg, 1977). For example, Goranson showed people a film of a prize fight in which either there were no consequences or the loser of the fight received a bad beating and later died. The participants who did not see the negative consequences were more likely to behave aggressively after the viewing.

A key element in the consequences is whether the victim shows pain, because pain cues inhibit subsequent aggression (Baron, 1971a, 1971b, 1979; Sanders & Baron, 1975). Moreover, Swart and Berkowitz (1976) showed that viewers could generalize pain cues to characters other than the victims.

- *Justification.* Reviews of the effects research conclude that justification of violent acts leads to higher aggression (Bryan & Schwartz, 1971; Comstock, 1985; Comstock et al., 1978; Comstock & Strasburger, 1990; Gunter, 1985; Hearold, 1986; Meyer, 1972; Paik & Comstock, 1994; Rule & Ferguson, 1986). For example, Bryan and Schwartz observed that "aggressive behavior in the service of morally commendable ends appears condoned.

Apparently, the assumption is made that moral goals temper immoral actions. . . . Thus, both the imitation and interpersonal attraction of the transgressing model may be determined more by outcome than by moral principles" (p. 58).

Several experiments offer support for these arguments. First, Berkowitz and Rawlings (1963) found that justification of filmed aggression lowers viewers' inhibitions to aggress in real life. In this study, the experimenters showed their participants a 7-minute prizefight scene. In the justified condition, participants were told that the target (a man who took a bad beating in the fight) was a scoundrel. In the nonjustified condition, participants were told that the target was not really bad. Similar designs and results were found in other studies (Berkowitz & Powers, 1979; Geen, 1975, 1981; Meyer, 1972).

Justification is keyed to motives. Brown and Tedeschi (1976) found that offensive violence was regarded as more violent even when the actions themselves were not as violent. For example, a verbal threat that is made offensively is perceived as more violent than a punch that is delivered defensively.

The one motive that has been found to lead to the strongest disinhibition is vengeance (Berkowitz & Alioto, 1973; Geen & Stonner, 1973, 1974; Hoyt, 1970). For example, Berkowitz and Alioto introduced a film of a sporting event (boxing and football) by saying that the participants were acting either as professionals wanting to win or as motivated by vengeance and wanting to hurt the other. They found that the vengeance film led to more shocks and longer duration of shocks in a subsequent test of participants. When violence was portrayed as vengeance, disinhibition was stronger than when violence was portrayed as self-defense (Hoyt, 1970) or as a means of achieving altruistic goals (Geen & Stonner, 1974).

Young children have difficulty understanding motives (Collins, 1973; Collins, Berndt, & Hess, 1974). For example, Collins (1973) ran an experiment on children aged 8 to 15 to see if a time lag from portrayal of motivation to portrayal of aggression changed participants' behaviors or interpretations. Participants were shown either a 30-minute film in which federal agents confronted some criminals or a control film of a travelogue. In the treatment film, the criminals hit and shot the federal agents, displaying negative motivation (desire to escape justice) and negative consequences (a criminal fell to his death while trying to escape). Some participants saw the sequence uninterrupted; others saw the motivation, followed by a 4-minute interruption of commercials, then the aggression. Both 18 days before the experiment and then again right after the viewing, participants were asked their responses to a wide range of hypothetical interpersonal conflict situations. There was a difference by age. Third graders displayed more aggressive choices on the postviewing measure when they had experienced the separation condition; sixth and 10th graders did not exhibit this effect. The author concluded that among younger children, temporal separation of story elements obscures the message that aggression was negatively motivated and punished.

Justification is also keyed to appropriateness of the violent action. People assess aggressive acts as appropriate especially when those acts are retaliation for previous aggression (Brown & Tedeschi, 1976; Kane, Joseph, & Tedeschi, 1976). For example, Tedeschi and colleagues conducted experiments in which participants took turns administering electric shocks to each other as a form of feedback in learning tasks. The researchers found that when participants administered a degree of shock similar to what they had received, such retaliation was not regarded as violent. However, acts of retaliation that were stronger (in terms of number of shocks) than an initial act of aggression were regarded as much more violent. The researchers reported that participants' judgments of violence were attributable much more to the appropriateness of the retaliation than to the actual number of shocks administered. Therefore, the judgment of violence does not rest solely with the type of act performed but is also keyed to the context of surrounding events.

• *Realism.* When viewers believe that the aggression is portrayed in a realistic manner, they are more likely to try it in real life (Atkin, 1983; Berkowitz & Alioto, 1973; Berkowitz & Geen, 1966, 1967; Donnerstein & Berkowitz, 1981; Eron, 1982; Feshbach, 1976; Geen, 1975; Huesmann, Lagerspetz, & Eron, 1984; Jo & Berkowitz, 1994; Thomas & Tell, 1974).

• *Production Techniques.* Certain production techniques can capture and hold attention, potentially leading to differences in the way the action is perceived. Attention is increased when graphic and explicit acts are used to increase the dramatic nature of the narrative (Huston-Stein, Fox, Greer, Watkins, & Whitaker, 1981), to increase positive dispositions toward the characters using violence (Comisky & Bryant, 1982), and to increase levels of arousal, which is more likely to result in aggressive behavior (Berkowitz & Geen, 1966; Bjorkqvist & Lagerspetz, 1985; Donnerstein & Berkowitz, 1981; Zillmann, 1971). At age 3, children begin watching television using an exploratory approach in which they actively search for meaning in content. But until age 5, they are especially attracted to and influenced by vivid production features such as rapid movement of characters, rapid changes of scenes, and intensity of unexpected sights and sounds. Children seek out and pay attention to cartoon violence not because of the violence but because of the vivid production features. In addition, Huston-Stein et al. (1981) found that preschool children exhibited greater visual attention to the TV screen when high action was being shown. But they found no differences in terms of attention to violence itself; the attention was stimulated by action. Participants who saw high action with high violence exhibited higher aggression and lower imagination in playtime following the viewing.

Another production technique that influences how viewers interpret violence is suspense. Comisky and Bryant (1982) conducted an experiment on 150 undergraduates to see what factors contribute to dramatic suspense. They varied the degree of uncertainty about the outcome and the audience disposition toward the hero-protagonist. Both of these treatment factors were found to be significant. Ratings of suspense were at a maximum when the hero's chances of success or survival were a long shot (1 chance in 100). Suspense was minimal when success or failure was absolutely certain. Furthermore, suspense increased with increasingly positive dispositions toward the protagonist.

- *Presence of Weapons.* The results here are mixed. The presence of weapons has been found to elicit more aggressive behavior in some laboratory experiments (Berkowitz & LePage, 1967; Caprara, Renzi, Amolini, D'Imperio, & Travaglia, 1984; Page & O'Neal, 1977); in field experiments (Turner, Layton, & Simons, 1975); and in studies conducted in countries such as Sweden (Frodi, 1975), Belgium (Leyens, Cisneros, & Hossay, 1976), and Italy (Caprara, Renzi, et al., 1984).

In contrast, no weapons effect was found in other laboratory studies (Cahoon & Edmonds, 1984, 1985; Halderman & Jackson, 1979; Page & Scheidt, 1971). Some studies even found an opposite effect, in which the presence of weapons lowered aggression (Buss, Booker, & Buss, 1972; Ellis, Wienir, & Miller, 1971; Turner et al., 1975).

The differences in results appear to be traceable to the type of dependent measure. For example, studies that used real behavior as the dependent variable showed a weapons effect (Berkowitz & LePage, 1967; Caprara, Renzi, et al., 1984; Frodi, 1975; Leyens & Parke, 1975; Page & O'Neal, 1977). But when the dependent variable is self-report, there is less support for the weapons effect. For example, Cahoon and Edmonds (1984, 1985) did not find such an effect on self-report measures of behavioral control. They said that the "weapons effect is a weak variable requiring further research to delineate the conditions of its occurrence" (1985, p. 57). Participants who see weapons and are given a chance to physically harm (shock) someone will show a weapons effect. But when participants are asked to report their own hostility in hypothetical situations, they do not show a weapons effect.

The weapons effect also seems to be sensitive to the type of participants. Page and Scheidt (1971) ran three experiments on college students and were able to find the weapons effect in only one experiment, in which the participants were slightly sophisticated and were aware of the purpose of guns. This conclusion is reflected in a meta-analysis of experiments on situational aggression cues by Carlson et al. (1990), who reasoned that the weapons effect is limited to participants who are low in sophistication and evaluation apprehension.

- *Eroticism.* Two meta-analyses concluded that violence portrayed in an erotic context exerts an especially strong negative effect (Allen, D'Alessio, & Brezgel, 1995; Paik & Comstock, 1994). When aggression is linked with erotica, it leads to increased aggression subsequently in real life (Donnerstein,

1980a), especially toward females (Donnerstein & Barrett, 1978; Donnerstein & Berkowitz, 1981; Donnerstein & Hallam, 1978). In addition, erotic films without aggression can lead to aggression in real life (Donnerstein & Barrett, 1978). Although both aggressive and erotic films lead to greater aggression among experimental participants, the effect of the erotic films might be a bit stronger (Donnerstein & Hallam, 1978; Peterson & Pfost, 1989).

No sex effect was found by Smeaton and Byrne (1987). In an experiment, they showed their participants either a nonviolent erotic film (clips from *Body Heat* and *Crimes of Passion*), nonerotic violence (*Friday the 13th, Halloween,* and *Pieces*), or neutral control material. Participants viewed the 30-minute films with a female confederate and then filled out a questionnaire. Contrary to their expectations, the researchers found no effects of the film on sexual aggression measures. However, an effect was traceable to the participants' feeling of their masculinity.

Why these conflicting findings? The effect seems to be influenced by the emotional state of the viewer. To illustrate, Zillmann et al. (1981) conducted an experiment and found that most aggression (retaliation against someone who provoked them) occurred with participants who were exposed to erotica that was arousing and displeasing. Exposure to nonarousing and pleasing erotica or to nonerotica failed to reduce aggression. In addition, Zillmann and Sapolsky (1977) found that provoked subjects were more annoyed and engaged in more retaliatory behavior after being exposed to erotica. With unprovoked participants, exposure to the erotic film had no effect.

The effect also seems to be keyed to the type of erotic portrayal. Donnerstein, Donnerstein, and Evans (1975) argued that erotic stimuli have two components (arousal and attentional shift) that interact with anger arousal either to inhibit or to facilitate aggressive behavior. Mild erotica can have an inhibiting effect on subsequent aggression. Zillmann et al. (1981) varied the excitatory potential (high, low), the hedonic valence (negative, positive), and the type of content (erotic, nonerotic) of visual stimuli (photographs shown on a VCR to control exposure time). Retaliatory aggression was highest with high-excitatory, negative-hedonic stimuli.

2.5. Situational Cues. When viewers are exposed to violence, they experience negative arousal, which brings up certain cognitive schemas. Viewers are then primed for aggressive action. Once primed, the presence of weapons or cue value of perpetrators (such as their names) can lead to action (Carlson et al., 1990; Comstock, 1985; Jo & Berkowitz, 1994).

3. Exposure to violence in the media can lead to fear effects. The best available review is by Cantor (1994), who defines fear effect as an immediate physiological effect of arousal, along with an emotional reaction of anxiety and distress.

4. *An immediate fear effect is influenced by a set of key factors about viewers and the portrayals.*

4.1. *Viewer Factors.*

• *Identification With the Target.* The degree of identification with the target is associated with a fear effect (Comisky & Bryant, 1982; Feshbach & Roe, 1968; Tannenbaum & Gaer, 1965; Zillmann, 1982, 1991b; Zillmann & Cantor, 1977). For example, characters who are attractive (Zillmann, 1982, 1991a), who are heroic (Comisky & Bryant, 1982; Zillmann & Cantor, 1977), or who are perceived as similar to the viewer (Feshbach & Roe, 1968; Tannenbaum & Gaer, 1965) evoke viewer empathy. When a character with whom viewers empathize is then the target of violence, viewers experience an increased feeling of fear.

The identification with characters can lead to an enjoyment effect. For example, Tannenbaum and Gaer (1965) found that participants who identified more with the hero felt more stress and benefited more from a happy ending in which their stress was reduced. However, a sad or indeterminate ending increased participants' stress.

• *Prior Real-Life Experience.* Prior experience with fearful events in real life leads viewers, especially children, to identify more strongly with the characters and events and thereby to involve them more emotionally (Hare & Blevings, 1975; Himmelweit, Oppenheim, & Vince, 1958; Sapolsky & Zillmann, 1978).

• *Belief That the Depicted Violent Action Could Happen to the Viewer.* When viewers think there is a good chance that the violence they see could happen to them in real life, they are more likely to experience an immediate fear effect (Cantor & Hoffner, 1990).

• *Motivations for Exposure.* People expose themselves to media violence for many different reasons. Certain reasons for exposure can reduce a fear effect (Dysinger & Ruckmick, 1933; Zillmann, 1978, 1982). If people's motivation to view violence is entertainment, they can employ a discounting procedure to lessen the effects of fear (Cantor, 1994).

• *Level of Arousal.* Higher levels of arousal lead to higher feelings of fear (Cantor, Ziemke, & Sparks, 1984; Cantor, Zillmann, & Bryant, 1975; Hoffner & Cantor, 1991; Nomikos, Opton, Averill, & Lazarus, 1968; Zillmann, 1978).

• *Ability to Use Coping Strategies.* When people are able to remind themselves that the violence in the media cannot hurt them, they are less likely to experience a fear effect (Cantor & Wilson, 1984; Koriat et al., 1972; Lazarus & Alfert, 1964; Speisman, Lazarus, Mordkoff, & Davidson, 1964).

 • *Developmental Differences.* Children at lower levels of cognitive development are unable to follow plot lines well, so they are more influenced by individual violent episodes, which seem to appear randomly and without motivation (Cantor & Sparks, 1984; Cantor & Wilson, 1984; Cantor, Wilson, & Hoffner, 1986).

 • *Ability to Perceive the Reality of the Portrayals.* Children are less able than older viewers to understand the fantasy nature of certain violent portrayals (Dorr, 1980).

   4.2. *Portrayal Factors.*

 • *Type of Stimulus.* Cantor (1994) says that the fright effect is triggered by three categories of stimuli that usually are found in combination with many portrayals of violence in the media. First is the category of dangers and injuries, stimuli that depict events that threaten great harm. Included in this category are natural disasters, attacks by vicious animals, large-scale accidents, and violent encounters at levels ranging from interpersonal to intergalactic. Second is the category of distortions of natural forms. This category includes familiar organisms that are shown as deformed or unnatural through mutilation, accidents of birth, or conditioning. And third is the category of experience of endangerment and fear by others. This type of stimulus evokes empathy for particular characters, and the viewer then feels the fear that the characters in the narrative are portraying.

 • *Unjustified Violence.* When violence is portrayed as unjustified, viewers become more fearful (Bryant et al., 1981).

 • *Graphicness.* Higher levels of explicitness and graphicness increase viewer fear (Ogles & Hoffner, 1987).

 • *Rewards.* When violence goes unpunished, viewers become more fearful (Bryant et al., 1981).

 • *Realism.* Live-action violence provokes more intense fear than cartoon violence does (Cantor, 1994; Cantor & Hoffner, 1990; Cantor & Sparks, 1984; Geen, 1975; Geen & Rakosky, 1973; Groebel & Krebs, 1983; Gunter & Furnham, 1984; Lazarus, Opton, Nomikos, & Rankin, 1965; Osborn & Endsley, 1971; Sparks, 1986; Surbeck, 1975; von Feilitzen, 1975). For example, Lazarus et al. found that showing gory accidents to adults aroused them physiologically less when the participants were told that the accidents were fake. This effect has also been found with children (Cantor & Hoffner, 1990; Cantor & Sparks, 1984; Sparks, 1986). In addition, fear is enhanced when elements in a portrayal resemble characteristics in a person's own life (Cantor, 1994).

5. *Exposure to violence in the media can lead to desensitization.* In the short term, viewers of repeated violence can show a lack of arousal and emotional response through habituation to the stimuli (Averill, Malmstrom, Koriat, & Lazarus, 1972; Davidson & Hiebert, 1971; Pillard, Atkinson, & Fisher, 1967; Wilson & Cantor, 1987).

6. *An immediate desensitization effect is influenced by a set of key factors about viewers and the portrayals.* Children and adults can become desensitized to violence upon multiple exposures through temporary habituation. But the habituation appears to be relatively short-term (Mullin & Linz, 1995).

6.1. *Viewer Factors.* People who are exposed to larger amounts of television violence are usually found to be more susceptible to immediate desensitization (Cline, Croft, & Courrier, 1973; Thomas, 1982; Thomas, Horton, Lippincott, & Drabman, 1977).

6.2. *Portrayal Factors.* There appear to be two contextual variables that increase the likelihood of a desensitization effect: graphicness and humor.

• *Graphicness.* Graphicness of violence can lead to immediate desensitization (Cline et al., 1973; Lazarus & Alfert, 1964; Lazarus, Speisman, Mordkoff, & Davidson, 1962; Speisman et al., 1964). In experiments in which participants are exposed to graphic violence, initially they have strong physiological responses, but these responses steadily decline during the exposure (Lazarus & Alfert, 1964; Lazarus et al., 1962; Speisman et al., 1964). This effect has also been shown with children, especially among the heaviest viewers of TV violence (Cline et al., 1973).

• *Humor.* Humor contributes to the desensitization effect (Gunter, 1985; Sander, 1995).

LONG-TERM EFFECTS OF VIOLENT CONTENT

Long-term effects of exposure to media violence are more difficult to measure than are immediate effects. The primary reason is that long-term effects occur so gradually that by the time an effect is clearly indicated, it is very difficult to trace that effect back to media exposures. It is not possible to argue that any single exposure triggers the effect. Instead, we must argue that the long-term pattern of exposure leads to the effect. A good analogy is the way in which an orthodontist straightens teeth. Orthodontists do not produce an immediate effect by yanking teeth into line in one appointment. Instead, they apply braces that exert very little pressure, but that weak pressure is constant. A person who begins wearing braces might experience sore gums initially, but even then there is no observable change to the alignment of the teeth. This change in alignment cannot be observed even after a week or a month. Only after many months is the change observable.

It is exceedingly difficult for social scientists to make a strong case that the media are responsible for long-term effects. The public, policymakers, and especially critics of social science research want to be persuaded that there is a causal connection. But with a matter of this complexity that requires the long-term evolution of often conflicting influences in the naturalistic environment of viewers' everyday lives, the case for causation cannot be made in any manner stronger than a tentative probabilistic one. Even then, a critic could point to a "third variable" as a potential alternative explanation.

7. *Long-term exposure to media violence is related to aggression in a person's life.* Evidence suggests that this effect is causative and cumulative (Eron, 1982). This effect is also reciprocal: Exposure to violence leads to increased aggression, and people with higher levels of aggression usually seek out higher levels of exposure to aggression.

Huesmann, Eron, Guerra, and Crawshaw (1994) conclude from their longitudinal research that viewing violence as a child has a causal effect on patterns of higher aggressive behavior in adults. This finding has appeared in studies in the United States, Australia, Finland, Israel, Poland, the Netherlands, and South Africa. While recognizing that exposure to violence on TV is not the only cause of aggression in viewers, Huesmann et al. conclude that the research suggests that the effect of viewing television violence on aggression "is relatively independent of other likely influences and of a magnitude great enough to account for socially important differences" (p. 331).

The long-term disinhibition effect is influenced by "a variety of environmental, cultural, familial, and cognitive" factors (Huesmann & Miller, 1994, p. 165). A major influence on this effect is the degree to which viewers identify with characters who behave violently (Eron, 1982; Huesmann, Lagerspetz, & Eron, 1984). For example, Eron found that the learning effect is enhanced when children identify closely with aggressive TV characters. He argued that aggression is a learned behavior, that the continued viewing of television violence is a very likely cause of aggressive behavior, and that this is a long-lasting effect on children.

Once children reach adolescence, their behavioral dispositions and inhibitory controls have become crystallized to the extent that their aggressive habits are very difficult to change (Eron, Huesmann, Lefkowitz, & Walder, 1972). Both IQ (Chaffee & McLeod, 1972) and achievement (Huesmann, Lagerspetz, & Eron, 1984) have been found to be related to this effect. Huesmann et al. concluded that low IQ makes the learning of aggressive responses more likely at an early age, and this aggressive behavior makes continued intellectual development more difficult into adulthood.

Evidence also suggests that the effect is contingent on the type of family life. In Japan, for example, Kashiwagi and Munakata (1985) found no correlation between exposure to TV violence and aggressiveness of viewers in real life for children in general. But an effect was observed among young children living in families in which the parents did not get along well.

8. *Media violence is related to subsequent violence in society.* When television is introduced into a country, the violence and crime rates in that country, especially crimes of theft, increase (Campbell & Keogh, 1962; Centerwall, 1989; Furu, 1962, 1971; Halloran, Brown, & Chaney, 1970; Hennigan et al., 1982; Schramm, Lyle, & Parker, 1961; Williams, 1986b). Within a country, the amount of exposure to violence that a demographic group typically experiences in the media is related to the crime rate in neighborhoods where those demographic groups are concentrated (Messner, 1986). Finally, some evidence suggests that when a high-profile violent act is depicted in the news or in fictional programming, the incidents of criminal aggression increase subsequent to that coverage (Phillips & Hensley, 1984).

All these findings are subject to the criticism that the researchers have only demonstrated co-occurrence of media violence and real-life aggression. Researchers are asked to identify possible "third variables" that might be alternative explanations for the apparent relationship, and then to show that the relationship exists even after the effects of these third variables are controlled. Although researchers have been testing control variables, critics are still concerned that one or more important variables that have yet to be controlled may account for a possible alternative explanation of the effect.

9. *People exposed to many violent portrayals over a long time will come to exaggerate their chances of being victimized.* This generalized fear effect has a great deal of empirical support in the survey literature (see Signorielli & Morgan, 1990). But this relationship is generally weak in magnitude, and it is sensitive to third variables in the form of controls and contingencies (Hawkins & Pingree, 1982; Potter, 1996). The magnitude of the correlation coefficients (r) is usually low, typically in the range of .10 to .30, which means that exposure is able to explain only less than 10% of the variation in the responses of cultivation indicators.

Care must be taken to interpret the strength of the relationship in the context of the control variables. For example, Potter and Chang (1990) found that when the predictive power of the set of control variables is compared to the predictive power of the exposure measures, the control variables show a much greater relationship on all cultivation measures used. Although researchers report that they have found a cultivation relationship, a stronger finding is usually that the control variables are an even better predictor and should not be ignored. This finding provides further support for the conclusion that cultivation tests that do not use control variables result in coefficients that are spuriously large.

The magnitude of the cultivation effect is relatively weak even by social science standards. Cultivation theorists have defended their findings by saying that even though the effect is small, it is persistent (e.g., see Gerbner, Gross, Morgan, & Signorielli, 1981).

This cultivation effect is also remarkably robust. In the relatively large literature on cultivation, almost all the coefficients fall within a consistently narrow band. Not only is this effect remarkable in its consistency, but this consistency becomes truly startling when one realizes the wide variety of measures (of both television exposure and cultivation indicators) that are used in the computations of these coefficients.

10. *People exposed to many violent portrayals over a long time will come to be more accepting of violence.* This effect is the gradual desensitizing of viewers to the plight of victims, as well as to violence in general. After repeated exposure to media violence over a long period of time, viewers lose a sense of sympathy with the victims of violence. Viewers also learn that violence is a "normal" part of society, that violence can be used successfully, and that violence is frequently rewarded.

The probability of this long-term effect is increased when people are continually exposed to graphic portrayals of violence. For example, Linz, Donnerstein, and Penrod (1988a) exposed male participants to five slasher movies during a 2-week period. After each film, the male participants exhibited decreasing perceptions that the films were violent or that they were degrading to women.

CONCLUSION

After more than five decades of research on the effects of exposure to media violence, we can be certain that there are both immediate and long-term effects. The strongest supported immediate effect is the following: Exposure to violent portrayals in the media increases subsequent viewer aggression. We also know that there are other positive and negative immediate effects, such as fear and desensitization. As for long-term effects, we can conclude that exposure to violence in the media is linked with long-term negative effects of trait aggression, fearful worldview, and desensitization to violence. The effects process is highly complex and is influenced by many factors about the viewers, situational cues, and contextual characteristics of the violent portrayals.

4

Violent Content on Television

Social scientists have published more than 60 separate analyses of violent content on television around the world (see Tables 4.1 and 4.2). These content analyses began almost as early as television broadcasting itself, and they continue today. They have been especially numerous since 1980. Although most of these studies have been conducted by independent scholars—usually university professors—some have been conducted by citizen action groups (Center for Media and Public Affairs, 1994; Lichter & Lichter, 1983; "NCTV Says," 1983); some have been funded by industry groups (Cole, 1995, 1996; *National Television Violence Study,* 1997, 1998) or private foundations (Kunkel et al., 1998); and some have been conducted by the television industry itself (Columbia Broadcasting System, 1980).

Within this activity, three content analysis projects stand out as major because of their groundbreaking nature, their size, and their influence. First is the series of content analyses of physical violence by George Gerbner and his colleagues at the University of Pennsylvania. This study is noteworthy because the same methods were used each year for 22 years beginning in 1967. Second, Bradley Greenberg and his colleagues conducted a 3-year analysis of television programming in the mid-1970s. This study is important, because it broadened the examination of physical violence to include verbal aggression and other forms of antisocial activity. Third is the *National Television Violence Study* (NTVS), which was funded for 3 years by the National Cable Television Association. Although it narrowed the focus again to physical violence, it analyzed narratives at three levels: macro level (the entire program), midlevel (the scene), and micro level (the violent act). It also had the best sample of any content analysis of television. Its composite week of more than 3,000 hours of programming for each of 3 years is a representative sample of all television programming across 23 channels in all parts of the day.

TABLE 4.1 Content Analyses of Television Violence

In the United States	
Year	*Author(s)*
1954	Head
1954	Smythe
1961	Schramm, Lyle, & Parker
1963	Lyle & Wilcox
1972	Clark & Blankenburg
1972	Gerbner
1973	Dominick
1976	Gerbner & Gross
1976	Poulos, Harvey, & Liebert
1976	Slaby, Quarfoth, & McConnachie
1977	CBS, Office of Social Research
1977	Franzblau, Sprafkin, & Rubinstein
1977	Gerbner, Gross, Eleey, Jackson-Beeck, Jeffries-Fox, & Signorielli
1978	Gerbner, Gross, Jackson-Beeck, Jeffries-Fox, & Signorielli
1979	Harvey, Sprafkin, & Rubinstein
1980	Columbia Broadcasting System
1980	Gerbner, Gross, Morgan, & Signorielli
1980	Gerbner, Gross, Signorielli, & Morgan
1980	Greenberg, Edison, Korzenny, Fernandez-Collado, & Atkin
1982	Gerbner, Gross, Morgan, & Signorielli
1982	Kaplan & Baxter
1983	Estep & Macdonald
1983	Lichter & Lichter
1983	"NCTV Says"
1985	Baxter, Riemer, Landini, Leslie, & Singletary
1986	Brown & Campbell
1986	Gerbner, Gross, Morgan, & Signorielli
1986	Sherman & Dominick
1987	Potter & Ware
1992	Lichter & Amundson
1993	Sommers-Flanagan, Sommers-Flanagan, & Davis

TABLE 4.1 Continued

In the United States

Year	Author(s)
1994	Center for Media and Public Affairs
1994	Oliver
1995	Cole
1995	Potter, Vaughan, Warren, Howley, Land, & Hagemeyer
1996	Cole
1997	*National Television Violence Study*
1997	Potter, Warren, Vaughan, Howley, Land, & Hagemeyer
1998	Cole
1998	Kunkel, Farinola, Cope, Donnerstein, Biely, & Zwarun
1998	*National Television Violence Study*
1999	*National Television Violence Study*

In Countries Other Than the United States

Year	Author(s)	Country
1972	British Broadcasting Corporation	United Kingdom
1972	Halloran & Croll	United Kingdom
1972	Shinar, Parnes, & Caspi	Israel
1981a	Iwao, de Sola Pool, & Hagiwara	Japan
1981b	Iwao, de Sola Pool, & Hagiwara	Japan
1982	Forum for Children's Television	Japan
1982	Williams, Zabrack, & Joy	Canada and the United States
1985	McCann & Sheehan	Australia
1987	Cumberbatch, Lee, Hardy, & Jones	United Kingdom
1987	Gunter	United Kingdom
1988	Cumberbatch, Jones, & Lee	United Kingdom
1988	Forum for Children's Television	Japan
1990	Goonasekera & Lock	Asia
1990	Hagiwara	Japan
1993	Broadcasting Standards Council	United Kingdom
1993	Mikami	Japan
1993	Mustonen & Pulkkinen	Finland
1994	Kapoor, Kang, Kim, & Kim	Korea
1995	Gunter & Harrison	United Kingdom

TABLE 4.2 Summary of Content Findings

The Presence of Violence in the Television World

1. Prevalence of violence is widespread.

2. Prevalence of violence varies across types of programs.

3. Rates of violence are high.

4. Rates of violence fluctuate across different types of programs.

5. Rates are higher for verbal violence than for physical violence.

6. As for duration, violence appears in only a small percentage of time in television programming.

7. Rates are shifting from major to minor types of violence.

8. Violent crime is much more frequent on TV than in real life.

Profiles of Characters Involved With Violence

9. Most perpetrators are males.

10. Most perpetrators are white.

11. Most perpetrators are middle-aged.

12. Victims and perpetrators are similar demographically.

13. A high proportion of the violence is committed by "good" characters.

The Context of Violent Portrayals

14. Most of the violence is intentional, and usually the motives are not prosocial.

15. Consequences for the victims are rarely shown.

16. The perpetrators often are not punished.

17. Much of the violence is justified.

18. Weapons are often found in violent acts.

19. The presentation style is rarely graphic and explicit.

20. Much of the violence is portrayed in a humorous context.

21. Violence is often shown in a fantasy context or in an unrealistic pattern.

Patterns in Countries Other Than the United States

22. The United States leads the world in the prevalence of violence on television.

23. Character portrayals generally conform to U.S. patterns.

24. Context generally conforms to U.S. patterns.

The content analysis literature on media violence has focused almost exclusively on the medium of television. One exception is the work of Clark and Blankenburg (1972), who compared violence across several mass media: movies, television, novels, popular magazine fiction, comic books, and newspapers. But despite this narrow focus on one medium, the literature still exhibits a wide diversity of methodological features (see Chapter 12). This variety is one of the most positive characteristics of the content analysis literature. When we see some findings emerge consistently across many different studies, we can be confident that those findings are fairly robust.

The following sections list 24 findings in four categories: (a) the presence of violence in the television world, (b) profiles of characters involved with violence, (c) the context of violent portrayals, and (d) patterns in countries other than the United States.

THE PRESENCE OF VIOLENCE IN THE TELEVISION WORLD

Consumerism more consistently glamorized than violence

1. *Prevalence of violence is widespread.* Regardless of the definition, the units of analysis, the sample, or the types of coders, content analyses consistently find that violence is prevalent across the entire television landscape. Such has been found to be the case across a wide range of studies by academics (e.g., see Gerbner, Gross, Morgan, & Signorielli, 1980; Greenberg, Edison, Korzenny, Fernandez-Collado, & Atkin, 1980; *National Television Violence Study,* 1997, 1998; Potter et al., 1995; Potter & Ware, 1987; Schramm, Lyle, & Parker, 1961; Smythe, 1954; Williams, Zabrack, & Joy, 1982), citizen activists (Lichter & Lichter, 1983; "NCTV Says," 1983), and members of the television industry itself (Columbia Broadcasting System, 1980).

For example, Gerbner and Signorielli (1990), looking back over the 22 years of their content analyses, reported that 80% of all analyzed shows (three networks during prime time and Saturday morning) contained violence. The NTVS found violence in 60% of the 9,000 programs it analyzed across 23 channels and 3 years (Smith et al., 1999). The Center for Media and Public Affairs (1994) found that 68% of all series contained at least one violent scene.

2. *Prevalence of violence varies across types of programs.* Although violence is found across the entire television landscape, certain types of shows exhibit a higher prevalence than others (Smith et al., 1999; Wilson et al., 1997, 1998). The NTVS found that premium cable channels show the highest prevalence of violence, with 85% of its programs containing some physical violence, followed by basic cable channels (59%), independent channels (55%), commercial broadcast networks (44%), and public broadcast stations (18%). As for genres, 90% of all movies contained some violence, followed by drama series

(72%), children's series (66%), music videos (31%), reality-based programs (30%), and comedy series (27%).

- *Nonfiction.* Lyle and Wilcox (1963) analyzed Los Angeles television news and found that 17.5% of the items were stories about crime, major accidents, and disasters. This figure compared to only 13.2% of stories devoted to these categories in four local newspapers. Several years later, Clark and Blankenburg (1972) found the same results in an analysis of national television news and four large newspapers, with 44.6% of the stories on television displaying violence, whereas only 25.0% of the stories in newspapers dealt with violence. More recently, the NTVS found that 38% of its 384 analyzed nonfiction programs contained visual violence, and another 18% contained talk about violence (Whitney et al., 1997).

- *Music Videos.* There is also a high prevalence of violence in music videos. For example, Baxter, Riemer, Landini, Leslie, and Singletary (1985) analyzed 62 MTV videos and found that 53% contained violence. Sherman and Dominick (1986) analyzed 166 concept (nonperformance) videos and found that more than 56% of all videos contained some violence. Brown and Campbell (1986) analyzed 112 videos on MTV and Black Entertainment Television and found that half of all characters engaged in some form of antisocial behavior. Sommers-Flanagan, Sommers-Flanagan, and Davis (1993) broke their 40 MTV videos down into 313 segments and found that only 6% of all segments showed explicit aggression, but another 25% of segments contained implicit aggression.

- *Children's Programming.* Schramm et al. (1961) found that more than half of the programs children were most likely to watch displayed violence that played an important part in the narratives. Gerbner says that children's Saturday morning programs are by far the most violent genre (Gerbner & Signorielli, 1990). From 1967 to 1985, 94% of all children's (weekend daytime) programming contained violence. In addition, 81.7% of all leading characters were involved in violence (Signorielli, 1990).

3. *Rates of violence are high.* The number of violent acts per hour remains high across the television landscape in general, although the rate fluctuates from study to study and from year to year. Reported rates of physical aggression range from a low of 5 acts per hour (Center for Media and Public Affairs, 1994) upward to 8.1 (Potter & Ware, 1987), 8.7 (Potter et al., 1995), 9.0 (Williams et al., 1982), 10.0 (Lichter & Amundson, 1992), and 14.6 (Greenberg et al., 1980). Some of this variation is due to differences in methods across studies.

When the definitions of violence, sampling, and units of analysis are repeated each year, there are still fluctuations, as demonstrated by Gerbner and Signorielli (1990), who reported regular cycles of rates from 6.7 to 9.5 acts per hour over the 22 years of their analyses.

4. *Rates of violence fluctuate across different types of programs.* Such fluctuation is especially apparent when verbal violence is also documented. For example, Potter and Ware (1987) report higher rates of aggression (physical and verbal) in some program types, such as action adventure programs (44.3 acts per hour), compared with situation comedies (25.0), episodic series (15.9), and continuing series (14.8).

• *Nonfiction.* Rates of violence are high in nonfiction programming (Oliver, 1994; Potter et al., 1997), but usually not as high as in fictional programming (Lichter & Amundson, 1992; Potter et al., 1995; Smith et al., 1999; Wilson et al., 1997, 1998). For example, Potter et al. (1997) found the rate of antisocial activity on reality-based programs to be 32.5 acts per hour, and within the set of reality-based programming, national news shows had the highest rate, 44.5 acts per hour. Using the same definition, Potter et al. (1995) found the rate to be 38.2 for fictional programming.

• *Music Videos.* Sherman and Dominick (1986) analyzed 166 concept (nonperformance) videos and found an average of 2.9 acts per violent video.

• *Children's Programming.* Studies that compare violence across genres have consistently found Saturday morning cartoons to be the highest on physical violence. From the earliest days of television, the programming designated for children has exhibited very high rates of physical violence (Gerbner & Signorielli, 1990; Greenberg et al., 1980; Poulos, Harvey, & Liebert, 1976; Schramm et al., 1961; Smythe, 1954). Smythe found that children's drama had more than three times the rate of violence than general-audience drama (22.4 vs. 6.0 acts per hour), but that the highest rate (36.6) was in children's comedy drama. Gerbner and Signorielli said that children's Saturday morning programs are by far the most violent genre. From 1967 to 1985, children's programming exhibited a rate of 20.1 violent acts per hour, which is three times the average found on prime-time television (Gerbner & Signorielli, 1990). Greenberg et al. found that the rate of physical violence on Saturday morning cartoons (25.9 acts per hour) was 40% higher than for the next genre—action-adventure programs (18.3 acts per hour).

• *Situation Comedies.* Although situation comedies have low rates of physical violence, they consistently have the highest rates of verbal violence (Greenberg et al., 1980; Potter et al., 1997; Williams et al., 1982). For example, Greenberg found a rate of 33.2 acts of verbal violence per hour in the mid-1970s, and the same rate was found 20 years later (Potter & Vaughan, 1997).

5. *Rates are higher for verbal violence than for physical violence.* Studies that look at both physical and verbal forms of violence have consistently found verbal forms to occur more frequently. Williams et al. (1982) found a ratio of

1.1 acts of verbal aggression to every act of physical aggression in their analysis of American and Canadian prime-time television in 1980. Potter and Ware (1987) reported a ratio of 1.4:1 in prime-time television in 1985. Greenberg et al. (1980) reported a ratio of about 1.8:1. Potter and Vaughan (1997) found a ratio of 2.4:1. Of course, definitions and samples differ across these studies, but even so, the findings are so robust that they continue to emerge: Verbal aggression is at least as prevalent as physical aggression on television.

6. *As for duration, violence appears in only a small percentage of time in television programming.* Less than 5% of programming time is violent. For example, Gerbner, Gross, Signorielli, Morgan, and Jackson-Beeck (1979b) examined 10 years of data and found a range of 2.2 to 3.7 min/hr (an average of 2.4). Thus, only 4% of the time was there violence on the screen in the United States. The NTVS found a difference in duration depending on the type of program. With reality-based shows (public affairs, talk, documentaries, but not breaking news), 3.3% of program time contained visual violence, and another 2.4% exhibited talk about violence (Whitney et al., 1997). In fictional programs, the duration was much higher (12.9%), largely because the coding of fictional violence included the time for threats that built up to the violent act (Wilson et al., 1997).

7. *Rates are shifting from major to minor types of violence.* To see this trend, we need to consider both physical and verbal forms of violence. For example, Potter and Vaughan (1997) replicated the study of Greenberg et al. (1980) to see if rates of different types of violence changed from the mid-1970s to the mid-1990s. They found that overall rates of physical violence stayed the same (12.7 vs. 12.3 acts per hour), but rates of verbal violence had climbed (from 22.8 to 27.0). This change is even more clear with two genres in particular. With situation comedies, the rate of physical violence stayed the same (7.2 acts per hour), but the rate of verbal violence went up from 33.5 to 41.9 acts per hour. With action-adventure programs, physical violence stayed about the same (18.2 vs. 21.5), but verbal violence went up (from 22.0 to 28.6).

8. *Violent crime is much more frequent on TV than in real life.* In his analysis of prime-time drama and comedy, Dominick (1973) reported that 60% of all programs portrayed at least one crime, with murder and assault ranked as the two most frequent crimes. In real life, burglary and larceny are the two most prevalent crimes.

Oliver (1994) reported that in reality-based police shows, 87% of criminal suspects were associated with violent crimes, but only 13% of all crimes in the real world are violent; therefore these TV shows greatly overrepresent violent crime. On television, 49.7% of all crimes were murders, compared to less than

0.2% in the United States. The TV world also displays inflated percentages of robbery (19.5% on TV vs. 5.0% in real life) and aggravated assault (14.8% vs. 7.0%).

PROFILES OF CHARACTERS INVOLVED WITH VIOLENCE

9. *Most perpetrators are males.* It is much more rare to see a female committing an act of violence compared to a male (Dominick, 1973; Gerbner, Gross, Morgan, & Signorielli, 1980; Greenberg et al., 1980; *National Television Violence Study,* 1997, 1998; Potter et al., 1995; Potter & Ware, 1987; Poulos et al., 1976; Williams et al., 1982). The percentage of perpetrators who are males ranges from about 71% to 85%. For example, Poulos et al. analyzed the content of children's Saturday morning television programs and found that 71% of all characters (376 human and 142 animal characters) were male. They said, "Inasmuch as males tended to be portrayed as more aggressive but less sympathetic or understanding than females, the image of males as both more potent and more callous than females is being perpetuated" (p. 1055).

10. *Most perpetrators are white.* It is much more rare to see an ethnic minority committing an act of violence compared to a white character (Dominick, 1973; Gerbner, Gross, Signorielli, & Morgan, 1980; Greenberg et al., 1980; *National Television Violence Study,* 1997, 1998; Potter et al., 1995; Potter & Ware, 1987; Poulos et al., 1976; Sherman & Dominick, 1986; Williams et al., 1982). The proportion of aggressors who are white is typically about 75% to 90%.

11. *Most perpetrators are middle-aged.* In most content analysis studies, middle-aged characters, defined as between the ages of 20 and 50, commit about 75% to 95% of all violent acts (Dominick, 1973; Gerbner, Gross, Signorielli, & Morgan, 1980; Greenberg et al., 1980; *National Television Violence Study,* 1997, 1998; Potter et al., 1995; Potter & Ware, 1987; Sherman & Dominick, 1986; Williams et al., 1982).

12. *Victims and perpetrators are similar demographically.* Victims are likely to be white, middle-aged males (Greenberg et al., 1980; *National Television Violence Study,* 1997, 1998; Potter et al., 1995; Potter & Ware, 1987; Sherman & Dominick, 1986; Williams et al., 1982). However, the analyses of Gerbner, Gross, Signorielli, and Morgan (1980) show that women are more likely to be victims than perpetrators (Signorielli, 1990).

13. *A high proportion of the violence is committed by "good" characters.*
The Center for Media and Public Affairs (1994) reports that "violence on
television is typically not a tool of evil . . . most violence in network shows is
committed by positive characters" (p. 12). This conclusion is based on the
center's finding that much of the violence (42%) is committed primarily by
"positive" characters, whereas negative or criminal characters account for
20% of the violence and neutral characters for 17%. "Good" characters are
sometimes operationalized as heroes, and when they are, heroes are found to
commit as many antisocial acts as villains do (Potter & Ware, 1987).

In the realm of crime, Dominick (1973) found that almost one third of all
law enforcers committed violence on entertainment television. On reality-based
crime shows, such as *Cops* and *America's Most Wanted,* Oliver (1994) reported
that although 51% of police officers used aggressive behaviors, only 19% of
criminal suspects did.

However, this pattern was not found in the NTVS project (Wilson et al.,
1997, 1998). In those analyses, 45% of perpetrators were bad characters and
24% were good characters. Why the discrepancy? Two explanations are possible. First, perhaps the difference can be traced to the type of violence. For
example, Potter and Ware (1987) reported that in general, 26% of antisocial acts
are committed by heroes, 28% by villains, and 46% by secondary characters.
But when we look at only serious violence, the pattern changes: Negative
characters commit 37%, positive characters 25%. Another explanation is that
the NTVS greatly expanded the number of channels examined beyond the major
broadcast networks. Perhaps the good characters are the largest proportion of
perpetrators on the major networks, and the bad characters take over on the
other channels.

THE CONTEXT OF VIOLENT PORTRAYALS

14. *Most of the violence is intentional, and usually the motives are not prosocial.* Rarely is violence portrayed as an accident (Dominick, 1973; Larsen, Gray,
& Fortis, 1968; *National Television Violence Study,* 1997, 1998; Potter et al.,
1995, 1997; Smith et al., 1999; Williams et al., 1982; Wilson et al., 1997, 1998).

As for motives in fictional shows, Williams et al. (1982) reported that in
97% of violent acts on television, the perpetrators intended harm. Potter et al.
(1995) found that 58% of the acts were malicious and 33% were inconsiderate.
In addition, in half the acts, the motive was to hurt the victim either physically
or emotionally. Dominick (1973) reported that the most popular motives for
crime are greed (32%) and avoidance of detection (31%). The *National Television Violence Study* (1997, 1998) found that most of the violent interactions
were intentionally motivated, by personal gain (30%), protection of life (26%),
or anger (24%) (Smith et al., 1999; Wilson et al., 1997, 1998). In nonfiction,

Potter et al. (1997) found that 60% of motives for violence consisted of maliciousness.

Another way to examine motives is to make a distinction between motives that are internal (desires of characters) and those that are external (forced by one's role or by others). Estep and Macdonald (1983) reported that 24% of motives for antisocial acts on the top-rated television shows were internal. Using a broader sample of all prime-time programming several years later, Potter and Ware (1987) found that 39% were internally motivated; that is, violent acts were not forced by external conditions such as threats, poverty, and so on.

15. *Consequences for the victims are rarely shown.* In most portrayals of violence, the victim is not shown in pain or suffering (Center for Media and Public Affairs, 1994; Dominick, 1973; *National Television Violence Study,* 1997, 1998; Potter et al., 1995; Sherman & Dominick, 1986; Williams et al., 1982). In fictional programming, Williams et al. (1982) reported that more than 81% of violent acts depicted no impairment to the victims. In 76% of violent scenes, no physical outcome of the violence was shown, and 90% of the scenes showed no emotional impact on characters (Center for Media and Public Affairs, 1994). The *National Television Violence Study* reported that in 47% of all violent interactions absolutely no harm was shown, and in 58% of violent scenes, the target showed no pain. In addition, in only 16% of all programs with violence was there a portrayal of long-term negative consequences such as psychological, financial, or emotional harm (Smith et al., 1999; Wilson et al., 1997, 1998). The same pattern was found in music videos. Sherman and Dominick (1986) reported that in almost 80% of all violence in performance music videos, no outcome of the violence was shown.

In nonfictional programming, Potter et al. (1997) found that 53.4% of the violent acts had no consequences for the victim, and 17.2% had only minor consequences. News programs were more likely to show major harmful consequences than were other types of nonfictional programming. The *National Television Violence Study* reported that 87% of acts of visual violence in reality-based programs showed no long-term negative consequences (Whitney et al., 1997).

16. *The perpetrators often are not punished.* Rarely are negative consequences to the perpetrators shown (Dominick, 1973; Potter et al., 1995, 1997; Potter & Ware, 1987; Smith et al., 1999; Wilson et al., 1997, 1998). For example, Potter and Ware found that only 12% of violent acts were portrayed as being punished. The *National Television Violence Study* reported that 19% of violent interactions in fictional programming were shown as punished, and another 8% were shown with both reward and punishment immediately after

the action. When looking at the entire show, the rates of punishment were higher, because another 40% of perpetrators were punished at the end of the show (Smith et al., 1999; Wilson et al., 1997, 1998). Still, about 37% of the perpetrators remain unpunished anywhere in the program for committing a violent act.

As for nonfiction, Potter et al. (1997) reported that 77.4% of the violent acts are not punished in any way. Dominick (1973) found that although most criminals are usually tracked down and caught, only 5% are shown during a trial or even have their trial mentioned during the drama. Furthermore, almost one third of all law enforcers commit violence on entertainment television, and they are never punished. In reality-based programming, 67% of acts show no punishment (Wartella, Whitney, et al., 1998; Whitney et al., 1997).

Much of the violence on television is portrayed as successful, except for violence perpetrated by criminals (Estep & Macdonald, 1983; Oliver, 1994; Williams et al., 1982). For example, Williams et al. found that the most common reaction to aggression by victims was to allow the violence to occur without striking back (29.1%) or to withdraw from the encounter (15.8%).

"There is a definite tendency for television programs to project content in which socially approved goals are most frequently achieved by methods that are not socially approved," observed Larsen et al. (1968, p. 100). The exception to this pattern of the successful use of violence is with criminals. In reality-based crime shows, violent crime is usually portrayed as unsuccessful. For example, Oliver (1994) reported that about 78% of crimes on these shows are cleared (perpetrators are arrested), and in the remaining 22% the suspect eludes arrest. This pattern of frequently arresting perpetrators is not matched by real-world statistics, which show that only 18% of crimes are cleared by an arrest. The same unrealistic pattern is found in fictional crime drama. Estep and Macdonald (1983) analyzed crime dramas in the 1980-1981 season and found that 72% of the murder suspects and 60% of the robbery suspects were portrayed as arrested, and a large percentage of crimes were resolved with the criminal suspect's death (14% of murder suspects, 19% of robbery suspects). These findings are consistent with those of Dominick (1973), who reported that 88% of crimes in prime-time fiction were portrayed as solved.

This high level of success and low level of punishment tells viewers that violence is not bad. Larsen et al. (1968) concluded that "a state of anomie is consistently being portrayed on television dramatic programming" (p. 111).

17. *Much of the violence is justified.* The amount of justification changes depending on the perspective from which it is judged. Potter and Ware (1987) found that 93% of violent instances were justified from the perspective of the perpetrator—not by society. That is, if the perpetrator was portrayed as regarding the violent act as warranted, the coder recorded it as justified. But if the perpetrator displayed a negative feeling, such as remorse, the act was coded as unjustified from the character's point of view.

The results would be different if the judgment of justification were made from the point of view of society. The NTVS defined justification primarily in terms of motives: Violence used to protect oneself or one's family or to retaliate against an attack was regarded as justified. With this perspective on justification, the NTVS found that 32% of all violent interactions were judged to be justified by the coders (Wilson et al., 1998).

18. *Weapons are often found in violent acts.* The NTVS said that in fictional programming, guns are used in one fourth of all violent interactions, and that other kinds of weapons are used in another one third of all violent interactions. The most prevalent form of violence, however, was natural means—the use of nothing more than the perpetrator's body (Smith et al., 1999; Wilson et al., 1997, 1998).

In reality-based programming, guns were used in 44% of visually depicted violent interactions (Wartella, Whitney, et al., 1998; Whitney et al., 1997). In music videos, 35% of the violent acts were committed with a weapon (Sherman & Dominick, 1986).

19. *The presentation style is rarely graphic and explicit.* The NTVS (Wilson et al., 1997, 1998) found that within fictional programming, rarely (10% of the time) is violence shown graphically—that is, shown closer than in a distant shot. Less than 3% of all violent scenes feature a close-up of the violence. In addition, only 15% of violent scenes showed any blood or gore.

In reality-based programming, violence is graphic in only 7% of acts, and intense in only 10% of acts (Wilson et al., 1997, 1998). In contrast, in 38% of instances in which people talked about violence, the descriptions were graphic (Wartella, Whitney, et al., 1998; Whitney et al., 1997).

20. *Much of the violence is portrayed in a humorous context.* Humor is a common context for violence (*National Television Violence Study,* 1997, 1998; Potter et al., 1995; Signorielli, 1990; Smythe, 1954; Williams et al., 1982). For example, Smythe found that about one fourth of all acts and threats of violence were committed in a humorous context, and that the humorous context was more common in programs for children than in those for a general audience. In Gerbner's analyses from 1967 to 1985, children's (weekend daytime) programming was found to have the highest rates of violence, but 73% of that programming presented violence in at least a partly comic context, compared to only 20% of prime-time programming using a comic context to present violence (Signorielli, 1990). More recently, the NTVS found that 39% of violent interactions occur in a humorous context in fictional programming, but only 3% of acts in reality-based programs are coupled with humor (Wartella, Whitney, et al., 1998; Whitney et al., 1997). Potter and Warren (1998) found that when presented in a humorous context, the violence also appeared with other contextual factors that tended to trivialize it.

21. *Violence is often shown in a fantasy context or in an unrealistic pattern.* The *National Television Violence Study* reported that about half of the violent acts were shown in a fantasy context, such as with anthropomorphized animals and puppets (Smith et al., 1999; Wilson et al., 1997, 1998). But the concept of realism is more complex than simply determining whether or not there are puppets.

Potter et al. (1995) explored this issue by examining violent content from the perspectives of replicated and contextual reality. As for replicated reality, they found that most of the aggression was at the less serious end of the spectrum, with serious assaults and deaths relatively rare compared to less serious assaults and verbal violence. As for the serious violence of a criminal nature, males are represented as perpetrators more than females, which is realistic. But African Americans are underrepresented, as are younger perpetrators. As for contextual reality, there were some differences between true fantasy shows (cartoons, science fiction, etc.) and shows with realistic settings. Fantasy violence is more likely to be humorous, less likely to be punished, and more likely to have a perpetrator with a malicious intent.

Rates of violent crime are much higher than rates of nonviolent crime, a pattern that is opposite to that of crime in the real world (Dominick, 1973; Oliver, 1994). In addition, Oliver found that on reality-based police shows, demographics deviate from the real world significantly. Among television police officers, only 9% are African American, but in the real world 17% of all police officers are African American. Among criminal suspects, the demographics are very similar to real-world criminal suspects. In addition, white characters were more likely to be portrayed as police officers than as criminal suspects, whereas African American and Latino characters were more likely to be portrayed as criminal suspects than as police officers.

Contextual reality was assessed in terms of how closely television portrayals follow the pattern of how violence unfolds in real life. Potter et al. (1995) point out a substantial difference in the patterns in the area of consequences of violence. In real life, violence carries serious physical, emotional, and psychological consequences. But in the television world, the portrayal of violence largely neglects the harmful consequences for the victims (Center for Media and Public Affairs, 1994; Dominick, 1973; *National Television Violence Study,* 1997, 1998; Potter et al., 1995; Sherman & Dominick, 1986; Williams et al., 1982). Television presents to viewers a very unrealistic picture of the nature of violence.

PATTERNS IN COUNTRIES OTHER THAN THE UNITED STATES

22. *The United States leads the world in the prevalence of violence on television.* Violence is less prevalent on TV in countries other than the United States (Cumberbatch, Lee, Hardy, & Jones, 1987; Gunter, 1987; Iwao, de Sola Pool,

& Hagiwara, 1981a; Kapoor, Kang, Kim, & Kim, 1994; Mustonen & Pulkkinen, 1993). In Great Britain, for example, Cumberbatch et al. used Gerbner's definition of violence and found that only about 30% of all programs contained any violence and that the overall rate was 1.7 acts per hour. The Broadcasting Standards Council (1993) reported higher figures, saying that 52% of programs contained violence, with an average of 4.0 scenes per hour. The highest rate was found on national news (7.5 scenes per hour); the rate for children's programming was 2.6.

In Korea, only one third of prime-time programs were found to contain violence. In addition, less than 8% of all leading characters were involved in violence (Kapoor et al., 1994).

In Finland, Mustonen and Pulkkinen (1993) examined a complete week of broadcasting, including news and sports and found that there were 3.5 aggressive acts per hour across all programs, 5.6 in fictional programming. The physical forms of violence made up the majority, 2.7 acts per hour. Mustonen and Pulkkinen found cartoons to have the highest hourly rate, as well as the highest ratings of brutality across all genres. They attributed much of the aggression to importation from other countries. Among programs produced in Finland, the rate of violence was 1.5 acts per hour, whereas imported programs had a much higher rate: 5.6 acts per hour for programs imported from Europe, 12.1 for programs imported from North America.

An eight-country comparison in Asia with Western television found that Asian television in general contains fewer incidents of violence but that suffering is glorified and blood is frequently shown (Goonasekera & Lock, 1990; Hagiwara, 1990). However, the two cultures were the same in the pattern of heroes and villains being equally likely to commit violence. Heroes, however, are shown suffering much more in Asian television.

Duration appears to be shorter in other countries. For example, in Finland, Mustonen and Pulkkinen (1993) found that about 2.4% of overall programming (3.9% of fictional programming) was violent. In Japan, Iwao et al. (1981a) found that on average 2.3 min/hr of programming time, or about 4% of all programming time, was violent.

Exceptions. There are several exceptions to the overall finding that violence is lower on television in countries other than the United States. In Australia, for example, McCann and Sheehan (1985) found patterns similar to those in the United States. Using Gerbner's definition of violence, they analyzed the content of 59 hours (80 programs) and found that 79% of cartoons, 73% of all fictional programming, and only 4% of nonfiction programming contained violence. On average there were 5.4 violent episodes per hour; the rate for cartoons was 10.2 (the highest rate), for fiction 7.2, and for nonfiction 0.4.

Williams et al. (1982) found 18.5 acts of aggression per hour in North American television. Much of their sample came from U.S. programming, and this programming was higher in conflict and aggression than Canadian programming. Furthermore, the duration of the aggressive scenes from U.S. television was substantially greater.

In Japan, Iwao et al. (1981a) used Gerbner's definition and found the presence of violence to be about the same in Japan as in the United States. They found violence in 81% of programs, compared to Gerbner's 80% in the United States; in Japan, 2.3 min/hr were violent, compared with 2.4 in the United States; and the proportion of characters committing violence was 46.3% in Japan, compared with 46.0% in the United States. Cartoons were found to have the highest rate of violent scenes per hour (14.3)—even higher than samurai dramas (8.7). Iwao et al. also found that highly violent shows were generally less popular among viewers, so over time the rate of violence dropped (Iwao, de Sola Pool, & Hagiwara, 1981b).

Studies that have looked at both fictional and nonfictional programming in countries other than the United States find much more violence in fictional programming (Broadcasting Standards Council, 1995; Mustonen & Pulkkinen, 1993). These findings match the findings from the United States (Lichter & Amundson, 1992; Potter et al., 1995, 1997).

23. *Character portrayals generally conform to U.S. patterns.* As with U.S. television, a very high percentage of aggressors in foreign-television violence are males (70% to 95%), and seldom are they younger than 20 or older than 50 (Cumberbatch et al., 1987; Kapoor et al., 1994; Mustonen & Pulkkinen, 1993; Williams et al., 1982).

In Finland, "aggressors were two times more likely to be 'baddies' than 'goodies' " (Mustonen & Pulkkinen, 1993, p. 181). The same is true in Japan (Iwao et al., 1981a) and Korea (Kapoor et al., 1994). But in Australia, the pattern of good characters as aggressors is more prevalent; McCann and Sheehan (1985) found that heroes were the aggressors in 42% of episodes, and villains were the aggressors in 54%. In addition, heroes were the victims in 66% of acts, and villains were the victims in 29%.

In Israel, most of the characters involved in violence were male and middle-aged (20-39 years old). In addition, whereas perpetrators were much more likely to be bad characters, victims were equally likely to be bad or good (Shinar, Parnes, & Caspi, 1972).

24. *Context generally conforms to U.S. patterns.* As for motives, Mustonen and Pulkkinen (1993) found that spontaneous acts of aggression were much more frequent (57%) than planned aggression (27%) and that the percentage of first-strike acts (76%) was much higher than that of retaliatory acts (12%). They said that "TV narration emphasized the act of aggression much more than its consequences. Aggressive acts were used as a climax point of a story. They were usually stressed with detailed visual cues, ravishing music, or other sound effects, while a noticeable proportion (36%) of the consequences were presented only as hints or not shown at all" (p. 181).

In Great Britain, the Broadcasting Standards Council (1993) reported that 17% of violent scenes were comic, 59% showed harmful consequences within the scene, and 40% showed some form of weapon being used to inflict harm.

In Japan, violence was shown with a high use of guns, unrealism, and justification (Forum for Children's Television, 1988). In addition, the rate of verbal violence was higher than that of physical violence (Forum for Children's Television, 1982). But on Japanese television, victims are usually shown suffering. "The protracted agony that characters suffer shocks U.S. viewers of Japanese TV and leaves them convinced that Japanese TV is much more violent than their own" (Iwao et al., 1981b, p. 31).

In Israel, the weapon was usually natural means, and harmful consequences for the victims are seldom portrayed (Shinar et al., 1972).

CONCLUSION

The examination of violence on television has been an active area of research, generating more than 60 published content analyses, most of which have been conducted in the past 20 years. The findings indicate that television shown in all parts of the world contains a great deal of violence and that this violence usually is portrayed in an antisocial manner; that is, the portrayals contain many elements that would lead viewers to experience negative effects.

PART II

Reconceptualizing

5

Violence

What is violence? This question appears deceptively simple. In our everyday lives, we treat violence as a primitive concept; that is, we know it when we see it. But when we have to write a definition, it is difficult to translate our understanding into words. Instead of using a formal definition, we usually define violence ostensively: We point to examples. This ostensive method of defining violence is useful in everyday life.

As scholars, however, we have the responsibility of providing a formal definition that explicates our conceptualization of violence. Such a definition clarifies the perimeter of the conceptualization such that we know which actions are included and which are excluded. Because many elements need to be considered when we are delineating a definition of violence, the task is not simple. For illustration of some of what is involved in this task, consider the eight questions in Table 5.1. Answering these questions in the simplest manner (by yes or no) yields 256 different combinations for the answers to the whole group of questions. When we realize that some of these questions have more than two possible answers and that there are more than these eight questions, we can begin to appreciate how much variety is possible in definitions of violence.

How we define television violence makes a big difference for two reasons. One reason is that the broadness of the definition is directly related to counts of violence on television. For example, if you answered no to all eight questions in Table 5.1, then your definition would yield about one act of violence on TV per hour. But if you answered yes to all eight questions, your definition would yield about 40 acts of violence per hour on average. The amount of violence you see on the screen is determined by what you regard in your mind as violence. You can dramatically reduce the amount of violence you perceive on television by simply making your definition more restrictive. Another reason why the broadness of the definition is important is that it sets the parameters

① counts w/ vary w/ definition

② research parameters

63

TABLE 5.1 Key Elements in Definitions of Violence

---

1. Does the act have to be directed toward a person? Gang members swing baseball bats at a car and totally destroy it. Is this violence?

2. Does the act have to be committed by a person? A mud slide levels a town and kills 20 people. Do acts of nature count as violence? (Remember that nature does not write the scripts or produce the programming.)

3. Does the act have to be intentional? A bank robber drives a fast car in a getaway chase. As he speeds around a corner, he hits a pedestrian (or destroys a mailbox). Do accidents count as violence?

4. Does the act result in harm? Tom shoots a gun at Jerry, but the bullet misses. Is this violence? What if Tom and Jerry are cartoon characters and Tom drops an anvil on Jerry, who is momentarily flattened like a pancake. A second later, Jerry pops back to his original shape and appears fine. Is this violence?

5. What about violence we don't see? If a bad guy fires a gun at a character off-screen and we hear a scream and a body fall, but we don't see it, is this violence?

6. Does the act have to be physical (such as assaults), or can it be verbal (such as insults)? What if Tom viciously insults Jerry, who is shown through the rest of the program experiencing deep psychological and emotional pain as a result? What if Tom embarrasses Jerry, who then runs from the room, trips, and breaks his arm?

7. What about fantasy? If 100 fighting men transform themselves into a single giant creature the size of a 10-story building, which then stomps out their enemies, does this count as violence?

8. What about humorous portrayals? When the Three Stooges hit each other with hammers, is this violence?

---

for effects research. Activity that is not included in the definition likely will not be tested in experiments to determine effects.

In this chapter, I work toward a broad definition of television violence by first analyzing how theoreticians and empirical researchers have defined it. Next, I analyze use of the term by television content researchers to illuminate the overlaps and uniquenesses in definitions. I then examine how the public defines violence. The chapter concludes with recommendations about how I think violence should be defined.

OVERVIEW OF SCHOLARLY DEFINITIONS

Several terms (such as *aggression, conflict, crime,* and *antisocial behavior*) are sometimes used by researchers as synonyms for *violence* and sometimes refer to concepts related to or overlapping with violence. In this chapter, these terms will be regarded as a set for several reasons. First, when we survey the literature we can see that they do constitute a set of behaviors in which one character intends to or accidentally causes harm to another. Thus, the behaviors in this set are distinguished from positive or prosocial behaviors and neutral behaviors. Furthermore, it is assumed (a) that these behaviors warrant monitoring on a medium as pervasive as television because these acts have the potential for influencing the behavior or attitudes of viewers and (b) that this influence is antisocial. There is a legitimate debate among scholars concerning the degree of harmful influence across the different types of acts and therefore about whether certain acts should be considered as warranting the label "violent." We will examine this argument in detail in the recommendations section.

Definitions by Theoreticians

Let's begin with the focal concept of aggression. In the analysis of these conceptualizations, note that the key differences in the definitions are in the characteristics of harm, intentionality, and whether the act can be verbal or if it needs to be physical. For example, Dollard, Doob, Miller, Mowrer, and Sears (1939), in the early classic book *Frustration and Aggression,* defined aggression as "an act whose goal-response is an injury to an organism (or an organism surrogate)" (p. 11). Clearly, intention to injure is paramount in this definition. Therefore, accidents do not count. Bandura (1973) moves beyond the simplicity of this definition by defining aggression as "behavior that results in personal injury and in destruction of property. The injury may be psychological (in the form of devaluation or degradation) as well as physical" (p. 5). He adds, "Aversive effects cannot serve as the sole defining characteristic of aggression. Individuals who hurt others while performing a socially sanctioned function (e.g., dentists repairing teeth or surgeons cutting into flesh) would not be considered as acting in an aggressive manner" (p. 5). In addition, "a person who attempted to hurt another individual by firing a gun at him or by striking him with a lethal object, but who happened to miss the unsuspecting victim, would be judged as behaving violently" (p. 5). Thus, Bandura focuses his definition on both intentionality and harm.

Like Bandura, Mees (1990) takes a social norms approach to defining aggression by focusing on intention and harm. Mees elaborates the conception of intention by arguing that there are three modes: (a) thoughtlessness (the aggressor should have taken possible dangers into consideration but did not), (b) inconsideration (the aggressor knows that the action will cause distress or harm but accepts this and places his or her own interests above those of others), and (c) maliciousness (wickedness is accepted and intended by the aggressor). These three modes can be distinguished by two dimensions: active versus passive responsibility, and direct versus indirect responsibility. The first dimension refers to the degree of involvement in the aggressive act, the second to the degree of moral culpability. Passive responsibility, for example, applies both to people who guarantee the aggressive act is done by making it possible and to

*Mees
on
harm*

onlookers who do nothing to stop the act. Furthermore, Mees elaborates on the idea of harm by saying that there are three possible types: (a) harm from distress (interference with one's freedom from physical or mental harm), (b) legal harm (violation of an accepted standard of social interaction), and (c) harm from moral guilt (disregard of the moral aspects of people's fundamental attitudes).

Berkowitz

Berkowitz (1993) broadens the definition further, by defining aggression as "any form of behavior that is intended to injure someone physically or psychologically" (p. 3). This definition includes physical and symbolic harm and characterizes violence as an extreme form of aggression. Berkowitz proposes four dimensions for categorizing aggression: (a) instrumental versus emotional (acts done for purposes of coercion, establishment of power, or management of an impression are instrumental; those intended primarily to inflict harm are emotional), (b) physical versus verbal, (c) indirect versus direct (how direct the attack is on the aggressor's primary target), and (4) controlled versus impulsive (premeditation). Berkowitz (1994) defines emotional aggression as "behavior aimed at the verbal or physical injury of a target, that is instigated by some circumstance that aroused negative feelings" (p. 36).

The inclusion of verbal forms in addition to physical forms is reinforced by Velicer, Govia, Cherico, and Corriveau (1985), who based their conceptualization on the Buss-Durkee Hostility Inventory and constructed seven dimensions of aggression:

*Velicer
7 dimensions*

1. Assault (physical violence against others)

2. Indirect aggression (malicious gossip, slamming doors, temper tantrums)

3. Irritability (grouchiness, rudeness, quick temper)

4. Negativism (oppositional behavior, usually against authority figures)

5. Resentment (jealousy and hatred of others, especially related to mistreatment)

6. Suspicion (projection of hostility onto others, distrustfulness)

7. Verbal aggression (arguing, shouting, including threats and curses)

Muncer, Gorman, and Campbell (1986) took a receiver perspective. They asked television viewers (prison inmates and college students) to group violent acts together into kinds. In analyzing those groupings, they found that three dimensions were used to make the categorizations: (a) physical versus verbal aggression, (b) violence between strangers versus violence between acquaintances, and (c) provoked versus unprovoked violence (intentionality).

Gunter (1985) suggests a multifaceted definition that takes into consideration both the behavior of the perpetrator of violence and the consequences from the victim's point of view. From the perpetrator's point of view, he says that "violence is often defined in terms of the intensity or seriousness of the harm doer's behaviour" (p. 2). The key idea from the perpetrator's point of view is whether the behavior is considered excessive or unrestrained. Also important are the elements of justification and motive. Instrumental violence (designed to achieve a goal) is different from expressive violence (occurring spontaneously from anger or rage). Another dimension of motive is whether the violence is intentional. If we exclude the intention to cause harm, we can include accidents and natural disasters in the definition of violence.

Huesmann and Miller (1994) define aggressive behaviors as "behaviors by one individual that are intended to injure or irritate another individual" (p. 155). They exclude accidents, which are violent but lack intention. They also exclude assertive behaviors, such as are exhibited by salespeople.

Perhaps the broadest definition of aggression by a theoretician was suggested by Eron (1987), who defined aggression as "an act that injures or irritates another person" (p. 435). Note that this definition removes the intentionality requirement of Huesmann and Miller's definition. It excludes self-hurt but does include accidents, as well as aggression that is socially acceptable. It also includes injury to property and theft.

Definitions in Content Analysis Literature

Researchers who design content analyses have come up with a variety of definitions (see Table 5.2). The most consistently used definition of violence is that developed by Gerbner. Gerbner and his colleagues have used this definition for more than 25 years, making it possible for comparisons across a long span of time. This definition has become a standard for examining violence on television and has been used in content analyses by other researchers in the United States (Sherman & Dominick, 1986; Slaby, Quarfoth, & McConnachie, 1976), as well as in other countries (Cumberbatch, Lee, Hardy, & Jones, 1987; Halloran & Croll, 1972; Iwao, de Sola Pool, & Hagiwara, 1981a; Kapoor, Kang, Kim, & Kim, 1994; McCann & Sheehan, 1985; Mikami, 1993).

Several teams of researchers have expanded the definition of Gerbner and his colleagues. For example, the *National Television Violence Study* (NTVS) codes behavioral acts, an approach very similar to the conception of Gerbner, but it also codes credible threats and harmful consequences. Actions apparently leading to a violent act are coded even though the behavioral act never materialized. In addition, if a violent act took place off-screen and only the harmful consequences were shown, it too is coded. Thus, this coding is an expansion of Gerbner's conception of violence.

A three-category system was also developed by Williams, Zabrack, and Joy (1982), who began with Gerbner's definition of violence as a core. They then expanded their perspective by adding the broader concept of aggression, which they defined as "behavior that inflicts harm, either physically or psychologically, including explicit or implicit threats and nonverbal behaviors" (p. 366). Thus, aggression includes violence. Broader still is their concept of conflict, which includes both aggression and therefore violence. So their three categories

TABLE 5.2 Definitions of Violence and Related Concepts

Definitions of Violence

Gerbner, Gross, Jackson-Beeck, Jeffries-Fox, and Signorielli: "The overt expression of physical
   force, with or without weapon, against self or other, compelling action against one's will on
   pain of being hurt or killed, or actually hurting or killing" (1978, p. 179).
       These authors also require that violence be plausible and credible, which rules out idle
   threats, verbal abuse, or comic gestures with no credible violent consequences. The violence
   may be intentional or accidental. In addition, violent accidents, catastrophes, and acts of nature
   are included.
       "Any act that fits the definition, regardless of conventional notions about types of violence
   that may have 'serious' effects, is coded. This includes violence that occurs in realistic, serious,
   fantasy, or humorous contexts. 'Accidental' violence and 'acts of nature' are recorded because
   they are always purposeful in fiction, claim victims, and demonstrate power" (Signorielli,
   1990, p. 89).

Center for Media and Public Affairs: "Any deliberate act of physical force or use of a weapon in
   an attempt to achieve a goal, further a cause, stop the action of another, act out an angry im-
   pulse, defend oneself from attack, secure some material reward or merely to intimidate others"
   (1994, p. 3).
       This definition excludes unintentional acts, sports, acts of nature, animal attacks unless used
   as a weapon by a human aggressor, verbal or emotional abuse, and acts that happen off-screen.

American Broadcasting Corporation (ABC): "A specific, manifest behavior of violence involving
   actual or potential harm to life or destruction of objects. Acts are classified into four major categories: Threats, Assaults, Violence of Nature and Human Accidents" (Wurtzel & Lometti,
   1984, p. 92).

National Coalition of Television Violence (NCTV): "Hostile and intentional acts of one person
   against another through physical force" ("NCTV Says," 1983).

Gunter and Harrison: "Any overt depiction of a credible threat of physical force or the actual use
   of physical force, with or without a weapon which is intended to harm or intimidate an animate
   being or a group of animate beings. The violence may be carried out or merely attempted, and
   may or may not cause injury. Violence also includes any depiction of physically harmful consequences against an animate being (or group of animate beings) that occur as a result of unseen
   violent means" (1995, p. 45).

National Television Violence Study (NTVS): "An overt depiction of a credible threat of physical
   force or the actual use of such force intended to physically harm an animate being or group of
   beings. Violence also includes certain depictions of physically harmful consequences against
   an animate being or group that occur as a result of unseen violent means" (1997, p. I-48).

Definitions of Aggression

Williams, Zabrack, and Joy: This conceptualization is built on a hierarchy of conflict, aggression,
   and violence. Conflict had three manifestations: "as argument, as nonaggressive conflict, or as
   aggressive conflict. Aggressive conflict is designated as aggression or violence according to the
   following definitions: Aggression is behavior that inflicts harm, either physically or psychologically, including explicit or implicit threats and nonverbal behaviors. Violence is physically aggressive behaviors that do, or potentially could, cause injury or death" (1982, p. 366).

Mustonen and Pulkkinen: "Any action causing or attempting to cause physical or psychological
   harm to oneself, another person, animal, or inanimate object, intentionally or accidentally. Psychological harm was understood as assaulting another's self verbally or non-verbally, e.g., by
   threatening, forcing, submitting, or mocking. Verbal reports of aggression and aggression without clear visual cues were not coded" (1993, pp. 177-178).
       Mustonen and Pulkkinen say they based their definition of aggression on Williams et al.,
   1982, instead of on Gerbner's definition of violence so that they could move beyond an emphasis on physical aggression and include psychological harm.

TABLE 5.2 Continued

Definitions of Aggression (continued)

Potter, Vaughan, Warren, Howley, Land, and Hagemeyer: "Any action that serves to diminish in some physical, social, or emotional manner" (1995, p. 497).
   This definition "includes a wide range of portrayals, as suggested by Berkowitz's conception. We include verbal forms of aggression, not just physical forms. We include psychological and emotional harm to the victim, not just physical harm. We include indirect as well as direct attacks. (If A shoots at B but misses and instead hits C, then this counts as aggression against C.) And we include impulsive or non-premeditated acts of aggression" (p. 497). The receiver of the aggression can be another person, the perpetrator him- or herself, or a nonhuman entity such as an animal, an inanimate object, or society in general.

Oliver: Oliver (1994) developed a coding scheme for four types of aggressive behaviors: verbal aggression, threat of physical aggression, unarmed physical aggression, and armed physical aggression. Basing her definitions on Greenberg, she defines verbal aggression as noxious symbolic messages containing criticism, insults, cursing, or a negative affective reaction. Threats of physical aggression are overt verbal and nonverbal warnings of intentions to cause physical harm to a person. Unarmed physical aggression is the attacking of one human being by another that involves contact with any body part but that does not involve weapons or other objects. When weapons or objects are used in an assault, it is regarded as armed physical aggression.
   Only aggressive behaviors performed on-screen were coded.

Potter and Ware: "Any attempt by one character to harm another character" (1987, p. 672).
   This definition includes physical acts (destruction of property, larceny, burglary, robbery, armed robbery, assaults both with and without a weapon, rape, and killing) and symbolic acts (deceit, insults, and threats).

Sommers-Flanagan, Sommers-Flanagan, and Davis: These researchers code characters on explicit aggression, implicit aggression, and aggression with sexuality. Explicit aggression is defined as "instances of actual acts intended to inflict pain or injury" or in which "someone establishes dominance over another by using forceful means" (1993, p. 747). Implicit aggression is defined as "instances that do not directly portray violence but suggest aggression, portray themes of aggression, or depict the threat of inflicting pain or injury" and includes the leading up to or the aftermath of an aggressive act without actually seeing the act. And aggression with sexuality is an act of aggression that has sexual overtones or that is primarily sexual (1993, p. 747).

Definitions of Antisocial Behavior

Greenberg, Edison, Korzenny, Fernandez-Collado, and Atkin: "That which is psychologically or physically injurious to another person or persons whether intended or not, and whether successful or not" (1980, p. 102).
   These authors started with Gerbner's definition but expanded their focus because they wanted "to examine a fuller range of negative social behaviors available from television. A variety of noxious behaviors other than violence is available on television" (p. 102). They delineated four major components: physical aggression, verbal aggression, theft, and deceit. They chose these negative behaviors because they were "considered as modelable by social learning theorists and child psychologists" (p. 102).
   Within the physical aggression category, they began with Gerbner's definition but expanded it beyond attacks (with and without weapons) and included physical control or restraint of others, physical invasion of privacy, and elaborated fighting, such as fist fights among multiple people in which individual acts are indistinguishable. They added verbal aggression (verbal hostility, verbal rejection, and verbal threats) along with deceit and theft because these behaviors were also considered disruptive of society, and they provided models of behavior for viewers.

are nested rather than mutually exclusive, as are the three categories of the NTVS.

The broadest scope is displayed in the work of Greenberg (1980), who, like other researchers, begins with Gerbner's definition. But Greenberg expands the scope by arguing that television presents a wider variety of noxious behaviors that can be modeled by viewers, and therefore the frequency of their presence should be documented. He enumerated four major components: physical aggression, verbal aggression, theft, and deceit. This broader perspective has influenced other scholars (Brown & Campbell, 1986; Kaplan & Baxter, 1982; Oliver, 1994; Potter, Vaughan, Warren, Howley, Land, & Hagemeyer, 1995; Potter & Ware, 1987). For example, Oliver coded four types of aggressive behaviors: verbal aggression, threat of physical aggression, unarmed physical aggression, and armed physical aggression. A similarly broad definition was used by Mustonen and Pulkkinen (1993), who also included verbal aggression, such as threatening, forcing, or mocking.

On the other end of the definitional spectrum is a very conservative definition developed by the Center for Media and Public Affairs (1994). The many adjectives and conditions in this definition limit its scope, excluding unintentional acts, sports, acts of nature, animal attacks (unless used as a weapon by a human aggressor), verbal or emotional abuse, and acts that happen off-screen.

The most unusual definition in the set is the one used in the UCLA Television Monitoring Project, which was funded for 3 years by the broadcast television networks (Cole, 1995, 1996). This project sought to avoid using "an elaborate and exact" or a "precise" definition of violence on the grounds that "no matter how well the definitions were drawn, there would be those who felt that some important aspect of the problem should or should not have been included" (Cole, 1995, p. 22). Cole elaborates, "We put our focus not on establishing a correct, narrow definition of violence, but rather on distinguishing between violence that raises issues of concern and that which does not. Our broad definition includes sports violence, cartoon violence, slapstick violence— anything that involves physical harm of any sort, intentional or unintentional, self-inflicted or inflicted by someone or something else. We even included verbal threats of physical violence, although these were of secondary importance" (1995, p. 22). If a coder saw something in a program that fit this definition, it was not to be coded as violence unless the coder felt that it "raised a concern." Coders were given 14 criteria to use when considering the issue of concern, but they could ignore any of them in making their personal judgments about whether the actions within a show warranted concern. These criteria are as follows: time of show, presence of an advisory for viewers, whether the violence was integral to the story, graphicness, length of violence, number of scenes in a show, glorification of violence, who commits the act, realism, consequences, the manner in which violence is used to attract viewers, the alternatives to violence presented, weapons, and intentionality. In essence, the only programs that were identified as violent were those that somehow raised a concern. All other programs were categorized as nonviolent.

The most salient characteristic of the definitions in Table 5.2 is that they can be divided into three groupings according to their focal term: *violence, aggression,* or *antisocial behavior.* This three-part grouping generally reflects the broadness in what is coded. The definitions of violence usually specify the most narrow set of behaviors. The use of the term *aggression* usually opens up the scope to include verbal acts. The use of the term *antisocial* opens the scope even more.

[handwritten note in margin: focal terms]

The broadness of the definition is related to the number of acts that will be found in the content analyzed. Focusing on violence, Gerbner found an average of about 8 acts per hour over 22 years (Signorielli, 1990). The National Coalition of Television Violence reported a slightly higher figure (9.7 acts of violence per hour) on prime-time television ("NCTV Says," 1983), and the Center for Media and Public Affairs (1994) reports a lower figure (5 acts per hour).

When the term *aggression* is used, studies find higher rates. In their content analysis of North American television, Williams et al. (1982) found an overall rate of 18.5 acts of aggression per hour, of which 9 were physical aggression. Potter and Ware (1987) found a total of 19.4 violent acts per hour, of which 8.1 were physical violence. In Finland, Mustonen and Pulkkinen (1993) found an average of 3.5 violent acts per hour across all programs. Had they limited their definition to physical violence, the rate would have been 2.7 acts per hour.

Finally, there is the concept of antisocial behavior. Greenberg, Edison, Korzenny, Fernandez-Collado, and Atkin (1980) reported that an average prime-time hour of television contains 38 acts of antisocial behavior, consisting of 22 acts of verbal aggression, 12 acts of physical aggression, and 4 acts of deceit. Potter and Vaughan (1997) found 42.1 antisocial acts per hour— 12.3 physical aggression, 27.0 verbal aggression, 2.2 deceit, and 0.6 theft.

Analysis of Definitions

In this section we will use the three primary dimensions (intentionality, harm, and verbal vs. physical) of the definitions of theoreticians that were analyzed earlier and add to that list the concerns of nonhuman targets, off-screen acts, fantasy, and humor to set up a matrix for comparing the definitions used in the content analysis literature (see Table 5.3).

Note that the consistent distinction between violence and aggression is that whereas the studies that focus on violence limit themselves to physical acts, the studies that use the term *aggression* or *antisocial* also include verbal acts. This important distinction will be addressed in more detail later.

There are no consistent patterns across terms (*violence, aggression, antisocial*). It is also interesting that most of the definitions allow for unintentional

TABLE 5.3 Comparing Definitions of Violence or Aggression

Study	Acts of Nature	Accidents	No Harm	Nonphysical	Off-Screen	Nonhuman Target	Fantasy	Humor
			Are These Elements Included in the Counting?					
Gerbner and colleagues (multiple works)	Yes	Yes	Yes	No	No	Yes	Some	Some
Gunter and Harrison, 1995	No	Some	Yes	No	No	Yes	?	?
Center for Media and Public Affairs, 1994	No	No	Yes	No	No	No	?	?
National Television Violence Study, 1997, 1998	Some	Some	Yes	No	Yes	Yes	Yes	Yes
"NCTV Says," 1983	No	No	?	No	?	No	?	?
ABC[a] (in Wurtzel & Lometti, 1984)	Yes	Yes	Yes	No	?	Yes	?	?
Mustonen and Pulkkinen, 1993	Yes	Yes	Yes	Yes	?	Yes	?	?
Williams et al., 1982	?	?	No	Yes	?	?	?	?
Potter et al., 1995	Yes	Yes	Yes	Yes	Yes	Yes	Yes	Yes
Oliver, 1994	No	Yes	Yes	Yes	No	Yes	?	?
Sommers-Flanagan et al., 1993	No	No	Yes	Yes	Yes	No	?	?
Potter and Ware, 1987	Yes	Yes	Yes	Yes	No	Yes	Yes	Yes
Greenberg et al., 1980	No	Yes	Yes	Yes	No	Yes	?	?

a. The definition used by ABC is included in this analysis for purposes of comparison. No results of content analyses have been published by ABC; instead, this commercial broadcast network uses this definition for internal monitoring of prospective programs and episodes by its Broadcast Standards and Practices Department.

acts to be coded. Accidents and acts of nature count as acts of violence. In addition, almost all these definitions would count acts that did not result in harm.

For the remaining four characteristics—off-screen acts, nonhuman target, fantasy, and humor—the pattern is mixed, but still there is no consistent difference across terms. Especially with fantasy and humor, none of the definitions specifically deals with these characteristics. But with some studies, the researchers have separate variables for these characteristics, so it can be inferred that acts with these characteristics are not excluded from the coding.

In summary, there was only one consistent difference between the terms of *aggression* and *violence*—in both the definitions and the analysis across key elements. Violence is limited to physical acts; aggression also includes verbal forms. Furthermore, the large number of definitions makes it appear that conceptualization varies widely. However, the thinking converges considerably across many of the key elements in the definitions. Thus, we are led to the following question: What is the best type of conceptualization? This issue will be addressed later in this chapter, but first we need to examine how the public defines violence.

THE PUBLIC'S DEFINITION OF VIOLENCE

How is the term *violence* used in everyday language about the media? Before we begin this examination, we must realize that "the terms 'violence' or 'aggression' receive almost indiscriminate use, not simply by journalists with reference to TV portrayals, but also by ordinary people in everyday life" (Gunter, 1985, p. 2).

The public seems to be most concerned about being shocked or offended. Therefore, the most important element in their conceptualization of violence is graphicness. I conducted a study (Potter & Berry, 1999) to determine which characteristics in portrayals of violence are most associated with participants' ratings of the violence in those portrayals. The results showed that ratings of graphicness are by far the most important predictor of ratings of violence consistently across all stimulus tapes. This finding does not vary by gender, weekly amount of TV viewing, experience as a victim of violence, religiosity, or political conservatism. I concluded that when people watch shows with high rates of sanitized violence, they are not shocked and therefore are not concerned with the violence.

The public's definition of violence, however, is more complicated than simply equating violence with graphicness. Other elements are part of the public's formulation of the idea of violence. For example, the public does not think of cartoons as violent (Howitt & Cumberbatch, 1975), even though content analyses continually find cartoons to have the highest rates of violence of any type of television program (Gerbner, Gross, Jackson-Beeck, Jeffries-Fox,

& Signorielli, 1978, Greenberg et al., 1980; *National Television Violence Study,* 1997). The humor and fantasy of cartoons discount the violence.

In general, viewers do not pay much attention to violence compared to other program features (British Broadcasting Corporation, 1972), or when they do pay attention, violence is not an important factor that takes away from or adds to their enjoyment of programs (Diener & De Four, 1978; Diener & Woody, 1981). But when a violent portrayal is unusually graphic or when it strongly cuts across the grain of a person's learned schema for media violence, it interrupts viewers' flow of enjoyment, and viewers experience high attention along with a negative affect.

Researchers have found that several characteristics in the portrayals get the attention of viewers among the public when they see something that could be considered violent in the media. One of these studies (Forgas, Brown, & Menyhart, 1980) reported these characteristics as the following: (a) probability of occurrence (the likelihood of the act happening in everyday life), (b) justifiability (the degree to which sympathy lies with the aggressor or the victim), (c) provocation (the degree to which the aggressor performed a premeditated first strike or was responding with an emotional reaction), and (d) control (the degree to which the act was officially sanctioned or evoking punishment). These authors conclude that "perceived severity is not the most important attribute of aggressive incidents" (p. 225) and that people are more sophisticated in their judgments, taking contextual characteristics into consideration when judging the degree to which a particular act is aggressive.

The work of Gunter (1985) delivers a similar conclusion. He found viewers' ratings of seriousness to be related to four major factors: realism of the setting, physical form of the violence, degree of harm to victims, and physical setting of the violence. First, Gunter found that viewers' ratings of the seriousness of violent acts were higher as the fictional settings were closer to everyday reality in terms of time and location. In contrast, violent acts "depicted in clearly fantastic settings such as cartoons or science-fiction were perceived as essentially non-violent, non-frightening and non-disturbing" (p. 245). Gunter found ratings of seriousness to be related to portrayals that featured shootings and stabbings (Gunter & Furnham, 1984) and acts that took place in contemporary compared to noncontemporary or fantasy settings (Gunter & Furnham, 1983). Greenberg and Gordon (1972) found that weapon-induced violence was regarded as more violent. Second, violent acts that portray stabbings and shootings are rated more serious than portrayals of either more minor forms (such as fist fights) or more major forms (such as cannon fire). Third, the degree of harm to victims was found to be related strongly and consistently to ratings of seriousness. Interestingly, the most serious acts were the nonfatal harm followed closely by killings. And fourth, with the physical setting of the violence, indoor violence was rated as more serious than outdoor violence.

DIFFERENCES IN CONCEPTIONS OF VIOLENCE

Profound differences exist between how social scientists conceptualize violence and how the public sees it. From a scientific point of view, cartoons that feature characters such as Road Runner or Bugs Bunny are very violent; in fact, cartoons are consistently rated the most violent of all programs on television. The characters in these shows are continuously being stabbed, shot, hit with heavy objects, blown up, rocketed into the sky, and flattened into the ground. Social scientists who make strong statements about the harmfulness of viewing cartoons (such as those involving Bugs Bunny, Road Runner, or Ren and Stimpy) or live-action programs (such as *The Three Stooges* or *America's Funniest Home Videos*) put themselves in danger of being regarded as fuzzy-thinking academics. Most viewers would not regard any of these programs as violent. Critics (such as Morrison, 1993) look at this situation and conclude that social scientists must use poor definitions of violence.

It is not that scientific content analyses use "poor" definitions. Instead, the definitions used by scientists and the public are based on different concerns. The public is concerned primarily with being shocked by severe harm to victims. Social scientists are concerned primarily with harm to viewers.

Viewers' judgments of the degree of violence are not based on the actual number of violent acts in the program. In addition, children have been found to rate the frequency of violence in particular programs as lower than the frequency found in content analysis (Van der Voort, 1986). Instead, the public focuses on context. In the public's judgment, the degree of violence is associated with graphicness, realism, harm, and degree of justification. If a great number of shootings, stabbings, hittings, and the like take place in a fantasy, humorous context in which the perpetrators are justified and the victims show no real harm—such as in children's cartoons—viewers likely will not "see" violence.

In contrast, social scientists count the number of acts that meet their definition to determine whether the show is violent or not. Social scientists then examine context to judge harm to viewers. Using this method, social scientists continually find cartoons to be the most violent of all television genres.

Cartoons do present very high rates of shootings, stabbings, bombings, and the like. These are violent actions. Even Morrison recognizes this when he says that the cartoon *Tom and Jerry* contains so much violence that if you took away the violence you would be left with nothing. But the public discounts these actions when they appear in a fantasy or humorous context, such as a cartoon. The public reasons that when Tom and Jerry are stabbed or blown up, they are not really hurt, so when there is no harm there is no violence.

In contrast, scientists are less concerned with the harm to characters than they are with the potential harm to viewers. A social scientist who watches a cartoon such as *Tom and Jerry* sees many violent actions that are in a sanitized (low reality, high humor, no harm) contextual pattern and knows that this context increases the likelihood that viewers will become desensitized. Social scientists also see the high justification as a contributing agent to a disinhibition effect.

Tom and Jerry would be considered very violent by content analysts and not violent at all by the public. The difference in definitions is traceable to the focus of concern. The public wants formulaic action—that is, safe, sanitized violence (no graphicness, low harm) that does not threaten them (not shocking, low reality), and in which the good guys are strong and prevail (high revenge, high justification). When members of the public see this formula in action, they see no violence and no need to complain. When social scientists see this pattern, they see no reason to discount the actions. On the contrary, they see a high potential of viewer harm, and there are strong reasons to complain.

The differences in definitions lead to an apparent problem of ecological validity. The definitions used by social scientists appear too abstract and out of touch with real people. We could close the definitional gap by simply accepting the public's definition of violence. But given what we know about effects, that would be unethical. We would then become part of this public health problem rather than using our knowledge to effect a solution. The definitional gap, of course, needs to be closed. But it is the public that needs to move its conception. The problem is not with our definition. Instead, the problem is with our failure to educate the public better. The public has much to learn from us.

As social scientists, we have much more to learn from the public. We need to be more sensitive to how individuals interpret violence. Several critics of social science have been bothered by researchers' focus on their scientific definitions instead of on how viewers interpret violence. For example, Buckingham (1993) observes that "much of the research takes 'violence' as a homogeneous category, and tends to ignore crucial distinctions between different types of violence" (p. 12). He continues, "While there have been attempts to classify types of television violence . . . these have typically been based, not on the judgments of viewers who are actually exposed to the programmes, but on the supposedly objective judgments of researchers" (p. 12).

Van der Voort (1986) also saw this lack of attention to viewer interpretations as a problem. He found that the judgments of 9- to 12-year-olds about the amount of violence contained in a program differ little from those of adults. However, their estimates do differ from those found in content analyses. Van der Voort said, "Programs that are extremely violent according to 'objective' content analysis can be seen by children as hardly containing any violence. This, for example is the case with violent cartoons of the *Tom and Jerry* type" (p. 329). He argued that content analysts might find only one act of violence in a program, but for children this one act might be enough for them to regard the entire program as very violent. He suggested that "a 'subjective' determination of the violence-content of a program based on children's mean violence ratings is preferable to an 'objective' content-analytical assessment" (p. 330). However, Van der Voort's language reveals an assumption that content analysis is objective in some sense and free of individual interpretations. Clearly, this is not the case.

Even if coders could be fully trained to follow all coding rules systematically, they would still have to make many difficult interpretations. And even if they encountered a program that did not require any difficult interpretations, the coding rules themselves are really indicators of a person or persons' subjective interpretations codified into a coding manual. As seen earlier in this chapter, a scholar must make many judgments in constructing a definition of violence, and each of these judgments is subjective. The results of scientific content analyses are never objective—they can't be. However, good content analyses are systematic counts using a consistently applied definition of violence. For the results of content analyses to be useful to the public, the definition of violence must be understood and accepted.

Unless scholars consider the received view, their definitions will not resonate with those of the viewing public. Scholars cannot have a definition that will tag certain programs as violent if the public does not also regard the same shows as violent.

Should the definition of violence be based on what viewers believe or on what scholars believe? The beliefs of both viewers and scholars are important bases for definitions of violence. But these two bases serve different purposes. We need to use viewer interpretations as a basis for violence in order to find out what most upsets them and leads them to criticize television content. We also need to use scholars' knowledge of effects as a basis for violence in order to focus on portrayals of risk. Neither definitional basis is superior in general. Thus, usefulness as a basis for a definition of violence depends on where we want to extend our understanding.

Of course, there will be some discrepancies between the received view and the scholarly view. Scholars have access to much more information on this topic than do viewers. For example, scholars know what elements in portrayals are most likely to lead to harm. Most viewers are not aware of this information, or they are operating on false assumptions. Such is the case with graphicness. Viewers regard portrayals that have low levels of graphicness as not being very violent. However, scholars know that a steady diet of this sanitized violence desensitizes viewers. I am not arguing that harm to viewers should be the primary criterion for defining violence. Instead, I am saying that when violence occurs, it is a mistake for viewers to discount that violence merely because it is not graphic or because little harm to the victims is shown.

On this definitional issue, both sides need more education. Social scientists need to attend more to receiver definitions of violence and focus on how the salient and interruptive characteristics of violence contribute to or reduce the risk for a negative effect. The public needs to attend more to the case being made by social scientists who document types of violent portrayals.

IMPLICATIONS FOR RESEARCH

The way violence is defined has implications for research—both content analyses and effects studies. With content analysis, broader definitions will yield larger counts of violence. Therefore, broader definitions are more useful because they can account for the entire spectrum of violent acts. If some researchers want to eliminate certain actions, they can. But if we do not measure broadly, we cannot add later.

A broad definition of violence would also allow researchers to get a better picture of how patterns of violence change over time. If our definition of violence were limited to only the most serious and criminal physical forms, we would miss this shift, and we would have information to conclude only that the amount of violence has dropped. But if we have a wider definition that includes the less serious forms of physical behaviors, then we can see that there has been a shift from serious to less serious forms. For example, the rate of murder shown on television has decreased since the early days of TV (Gerbner, Gross, Morgan, & Signorielli, 1980). And if we had an even broader definition of violence (including verbal forms), we would have an even broader perspective to see that the overall rate of violence has actually increased. Although the rate of physical violence has not changed over time, the rate of verbal violence has been increasing. When Potter and Vaughan (1997) replicated the study of Greenberg et al. (1980) to see if rates of different types of violence had changed from the mid-1970s to the mid-1990s, they found that overall rates of physical violence stayed the same (12.7 vs. 12.3 acts per hour) but rates of verbal violence had climbed (from 22.8 to 27.0 acts per hour). This change is even more clear within two genres. With situation comedies, physical violence stayed the same (7.2 acts per hour), but verbal violence went up from 33.5 to 41.9 acts per hour. With action-adventure programs, physical violence was about the same (18.2 vs. 21.5 acts per hour), but verbal violence was up (from 22.0 to 28.6 acts per hour).

Another advantage of using a broad definition that catalogs types of violence is that it provides effects researchers with some guidance. For example, if serious acts of violence (such as killings) are disappearing and lesser forms of violence (such as insults) are increasing, then stimulus materials in experiments should feature insults. Although the effects literature ostensibly appears to be limited to physical violence, a close examination reveals some examples of verbal violence being tested. Verbal violence can be found as part of the media treatment variable (Geen, 1975; Thomas & Drabman, 1975; Thomas & Tell, 1974). In these studies, arguments with insults and intimidation led up to a fist fight. And sometimes, verbal violence is featured in the media treatment. In one study, viewers were shown a brief film depicting a businessman and his secretary in a hostile verbal interaction (Carver, Ganellen, Fromming, & Chambers, 1983). In another study, Berkowitz (1970) had women listen to a tape recording of either a hostile comedy routine by Don Rickles or a nonaggressive routine by George Carlin.

Sometimes verbal violence appears as a treatment variable (used to anger participants) in addition to the media exposure treatment. Although most of these studies used electric shocks to produce anger in their participants, some had an experimenter insult the participants to make them angry (Baron, 1977; Berkowitz, 1974; Berkowitz & Rawlings, 1963; Donnerstein & Berkowitz, 1981; Goranson, 1969; Leyens & Picus, 1973; Mussen & Rutherford, 1961; Turner & Berkowitz, 1972).

Finally, verbal violence is sometimes included as a dependent variable. Hapkiewicz and Stone (1974) evaluated experimental participants based on a variety of measures of aggression, one of which was verbal aggression. Berkowitz and Alioto (1973) had their participants evaluate another participant in the study; this retaliation was not physical (such as administering electric shocks) but symbolic (ratings on a form).

To date, the reporting of results from these studies does not make it possible to draw conclusions about the relative contributions of different kinds of violence on viewers' disinhibitions. It is time for experimental researchers to bring the type of violence more prominently into their designs so that they can assess the relative influence of different kinds of violence. Perhaps the less serious forms of violence pose the greatest risk to viewers. Perhaps because the inhibitions that prevent viewers from imitating insults and lies are much lower than the inhibitions that prevent them from imitating assaults, a small reduction in a person's inhibition would be more likely to show up as a behavioral effect with the less serious forms of violence. This important issue needs to be addressed by experimenters before we can make an accurate assessment of viewer risk.

RECOMMENDATIONS

We need a broader definition of violence. When we use a broader scope in looking at the range of behaviors on television, we gain a fuller understanding of their relative frequencies. Furthermore, it is important to monitor these patterns over time because the television landscape has shown a shift away from the most serious forms of violence, such as murders. With a narrow definition of violence limited to only the most serious and criminal physical forms, we would miss this shift.

Should we limit our concern to only physical acts, or should we also examine the prevalence and effects of verbal forms of violence? Implicit in this question is a concern about risk of harm. Harm can be regarded from two perspectives: harm to the portrayed victim and harm to the television viewer. From the perspective of the portrayed victim, a physical assault is usually more serious than an insult, but this need not always be the case. Portrayed victims might easily recover from the scrapes and bruises of a physical assault, but they might be shown as never recovering (psychologically or emotionally) from a harsh insult. Even more important, we must consider this issue from the perspective of the television viewer. Viewing "less serious" acts of violence, such as verbal insults, might have a disinhibiting effect on viewers. Furthermore, the disinhibiting effect of viewing verbal violence might be more likely to result in behavior than the effect of viewing physical violence because the sanctions are weaker.

I prescribe the following definition: Violence is a violation of a character's physical or emotional well-being. It includes two key elements—intentionality and harm—at least one of which must be present. In addition, I suggest we move beyond binary coding—that is, limiting the coding to recording the presence or absence of violence. I recommend that all acts of violence be coded on eight continua:

1. Level of act (from serious to minor)

2. Type of act (physical forms and verbal forms)

3. Intentionality (from premeditation to accident)

4. Degree of harm to the victims

5. Type of harm (physical, emotional, psychological)

6. Level of openness (covert to overt)

7. Level of reality (from fantasy to full reality)

8. Level of humor (from farce to serious)

Recording violence on all these dimensions would result in a more complete picture of the nature of violence on television. Effects researchers could then use this richer information to design their stimulus materials more precisely instead of regarding violence as a monolithic concept. There are many different kinds of violence, and these different kinds are likely to influence viewers in different ways.

Once we agree on a broad definition, we need to address the following question: What do we use as a label for this conceptualization? I propose that we use the term *violence*. I make five arguments to support this suggestion. First, the general public thinks in terms of violence rather than aggression, hostility, or antisocial behaviors when it refers to this category of actions on television. Furthermore, the common dictionary definitions do not limit violence to interpersonal physical acts. For example, one dictionary defines violence as covering violation of property; "exertion of physical force so as to injure or abuse (as in effecting illegal entry into a house)"; acts of nature; "intense, turbulent, or furious and often destructive action or force (the violence of the storm)" (*Webster's Ninth New Collegiate,* 1983, p. 1316). In addition, there is reason to believe that the concept of violence is not limited to physical forms in the general public, as evidenced by a dictionary definition of violence that includes "rough or immoderate vehemence, as of feeling or language" (*Webster's New Universal,* 1989, p. 1594).

A second argument is that scholars frequently use several terms as synonyms for violence. Furthermore, even scholars who make a distinction between violence and aggression and think of violence as excluding verbal forms often use definitions that would also allow for the inclusion of verbal forms. For example, Signorielli (1990) says that "violence is a complex social scenario and its purpose is usually to dominate, control, and terrorize—in short, to make people do things they do not want to do. Symbolic violence, such as that seen on television, demonstrates the same lessons but in an entertaining and painless way. Television tends to confirm and cultivate the traditional distribution of power in the symbolic and real worlds—domination by white males. It tells us who can get away with what against whom, where the safe or dangerous places are, and what one's chances of encountering or falling victim to violence may be. We would postulate that the lessons of violence, and especially victimization, are fear, intimidation, and a sense of vulnerability" (p. 88). When reading the preceding sentences in this paragraph, is it not possible to see a case being made for attention to verbal violence? What element in this perspective would force us to exclude verbal forms?

A third argument is that a broad definition includes an examination of a wider range of negative effects. Cantor (1994) argues that a definition of violence should include natural disasters and attacks by vicious animals; distortions of natural forms, such as monsters, mummies, ghosts, vampires, and the like, all of which are associated with threats of violence even if they don't actually commit a violent act; and acts in which characters are put in danger or exhibit fear of harm, even when they do not end up being harmed. She observes that these elements are often not included in definitions of violence in content analyses. However, these elements are instrumental in causing fear, especially in children.

Monitoring a wider range of negative effects puts us as researchers in a better position to document differential effects across viewer groups. For example, Lagerspetz and Bjorkqvist (1994) found that males are much more likely than females to exhibit direct aggression, but the opposite is true with indirect aggression. Therefore, both genders aggress frequently; they just use different means of expression. There are cultural and biological reasons why males are more likely to aggress physically and overtly. With indirect aggression, "the aggressor can stay unidentified and thereby avoid both counterattack from the aggressor and disapproval from the rest of the community" (p. 133). Indirect aggression can be physical (e.g., secretly setting fire to another person's belongings), but it is usually verbal (e.g., spreading nasty gossip). So if violence is conceptualized purely as overtly physical activity, the concern about boys' behavior will be given high priority, and concern about girls' behavior will be ignored.

A fourth argument is that viewers often regard verbal acts as more violent than physical acts. For example, Brown and Tedeschi (1976) found that offensive violence was regarded as more violent even when the actions themselves were not as violent. For example, a verbal threat that is made offensively is perceived as more violent than a punch that is delivered defensively.

Finally, a fifth argument is that the activity that is currently separated by some researchers into three or more categories (such as violence, aggression, and antisocial behavior) is composed of acts that are frequently interlaced in narratives. Patterson, Reid, and Dishion (1992) have shown that behaviors such as lying, stealing, and fighting tend to come in a package and are highly intercorrelated. Although these behaviors are topographically dissimilar, they are functionally equivalent (Patterson, 1974). Because viewers have become used to seeing these acts occur together, the acts have become associated with one another. Over time, viewers may become conditioned to level out the distinctions; that is, viewers may become less likely to see important distinctions across these individual acts and instead perceive them all as one mass of violent activity.

More than two decades ago, Stein and Friedrich (1972) observed, "Virtually all of the research on television content and behavior limits the definition of violence to physical injury or damage. The verbal abuse, aggressive humor, and control over other people by threat or imperative that are so prevalent on television are not included in most investigations" (p. 290). Since that time, researchers have been expanding their perspective on harmful content. Let's hope this trend toward more complete inventories of television content continues.

We need to understand more about how the public defines violence. The way the public defines violence is not simple and straightforward. The definition appears to take into consideration the factors of graphicness, realism, humor, harm to victims, motivation of perpetrators, justification, and appropriateness.

There are also some paradoxes in the public's definition. One of these puzzles is that programs are not judged by the number of violent acts. Thus, programs with 2 or 20 acts could both be judged violent if those acts were graphic with a high degree of harm to the victims, were in a realistic, non-humorous context, were unjustified, and exhibited a stronger response than the situation called for. In addition, it appears that many of these characteristics can be absent if one or more of the remaining characteristics that are present are very strong.

Another paradox is how fantasy and humor can wipe out perceptions of violence. When either of these characteristics is present (especially humor), most viewers regard the violence as absent, even if all other factors are present. This "Road Runner paradox" allows viewers to experience some of the highest rates of graphically violent acts while feeling that they are watching no violence. For example, in a British sample, respondents did not rate cartoons as particularly violent (Howitt & Cumberbatch, 1974). Social scientists know that humor as a context for violence can lead to disinhibition and desensitization effects. But the prevailing opinion in the public is that humor not only protects viewers from a negative effect, it in essence erases the violence. People look at all the cartoon mayhem that is pushed into the realm of absurdity through fantasy and humor and let down their guard, thinking it is a harmless diversion.

6

Schema and Context

Research clearly shows that viewers are affected by many factors that appear in narratives of media violence. The important questions now are the following: Do viewers see these factors in portrayals of violence, and if so, how do they interpret them? *How* do these factors influence individuals?

In this chapter, I first show how schema theory can be a very useful perspective in understanding what people perceive in narratives and how people construct meaning from the information they perceive. The key information in the narratives is referred to as contextual factors. When social scientists have a better understanding of the prevalent patterns of contextual factors of violent narratives, we can design better studies of effects. This is the argument I make in the second part of this chapter.

SCHEMA THEORY

Schema theory explains that we use templates (called schemas) to guide our perceptions. Schemas tell us what to look for in our experiences. Schemas also help us interpret the meaning of those experiences. Interpretive schemas have been defined as "people's cognitive structures that represent knowledge about a concept or type of stimulus, including its attributes and the relationship among the attributes" (Fiske & Taylor, 1991, p. 139).

With television viewing, people use a certain type of schema often referred to as a story schema, or script. Scripts are learned sets of related actions that define typical situations one finds on television (Biocca, 1991). These scripts are learned early in life as children hear the same types of stories over and over again (Kintsch & van Dijk, 1978). These story schemas are well developed in children as early as age 7 (Meadowcroft & Reeves, 1989).

Scripts are composed of patterns of contextual information. When viewers see certain contextual elements in a television narrative, they access their mental scripts cued by those elements. The scripts contain additional infor-

85

mation (beyond the cues) that sets up viewers' expectations and helps them interpret the continuing action. Some of this contextual information is about the plot: What motivates the violence, and is the violence justified? Some of the information deals with the characters who are perpetrators, as well as those who are victims, of the violence: Are they heroic and attractive? And some of the information deals with the outcome of the violence: Is the victim harmed, and is the perpetrator punished or experiencing remorse?

Schema theory focuses attention on how individuals make interpretations. Schemas differ across individuals, because individuals are different in terms of their experiences, perceptual abilities, cognitive styles, and emotional reactions. These differences explain why individuals vary widely in their perceptions of violence. Not all people judge the same violent incident in the same way. Some may perceive certain acts as violent; others will not. Gunter (1985) found that light viewers of television and females were likely to rate all kinds of violence, except cartoons, as less suitable for children. In contrast, heavier viewers exhibited the same pattern as all viewers in general in rating the violence of shows, but their ratings were more extreme. Viewers with an external locus of control tended to rate crime drama as more violent, more realistic, and more upsetting than other viewers did. In addition, more physically aggressive viewers tended to perceive physical unarmed violence as less violent than did more verbally aggressive viewers (Gunter & Furnham, 1984). Older viewers tended to perceive violence as more harmful than younger viewers did (Gunter, 1983).

Differences in perceptions of violence are also related to personality types. Highly emotional people were found to perceive violent acts as more serious than less emotional people do (Gunter & Furnham, 1983). In addition, people who cared less for others were more likely to perceive less harm in the violence than were people who showed more caring (Gunter, 1983).

Although individuals differ profoundly in the composition of their schemas, similar elements may be found in the schemas of all people—or at least large groups of people. All television viewers may have become socialized to certain expectations about violent narratives. This commonality is what makes the schema such a useful hypothetical construct. Researchers can use schemas as a device for looking at patterns in the aggregate as well as for idiosyncratic differences across all individuals.

This search for similarities and differences is conducted on the elements of contextual factors. Specifically, researchers look for the ability of people to perceive certain contextual factors in violent narratives. If all viewers perceive the same factors and construct the same meaning from them, the phenomenon is aggregate; that is, we have all learned to look for the same things and to arrive at the same interpretations. But if viewers differ significantly in terms of what they perceive in the narratives, the phenomenon is strongly individual.

THE IMPORTANCE OF CONTEXT

Content analysts rarely reported the context surrounding violent acts until the mid-1980s. One example is Dominick (1973), who looked at the contextual variables of motive and resolution of criminal acts portrayed on prime-time television. By the 1980s, the measuring of context was becoming a feature in many reports on television violence. For example, Williams, Zabrack, and Joy (1982) examined the contextual factors of intentionality, consequences of the act, and humor of the presentation. Sherman and Dominick (1986) looked at the outcome of violent acts and the use of weapons. Potter and Ware (1987) *examples* examined reward, justification, motivation, and hero status of the character.

By the mid-1990s, content analyses were typically looking at dozens of contextual variables. In Finland, for example, Mustonen and Pulkkinen (1993) coded 43 variables for each aggressive act. They organized the variables into four groups: (a) program context (such as temporal settings, realism, and *variables* atmosphere), (b) justification for aggression (motivational base, intentionality, *for* legality), (c) seriousness of aggression (severity of acts and their conse- *aggressive* quences), and (d) dramatization of portrayal (camera range, amount of suffer- *act* ing, realism of portrayals of the consequences). Potter, Vaughan, Warren, Howley, Land, and Hagemeyer (1995) looked at 42 variables, and the *National Television Violence Study* (1997) examined 23.

Because these contextual characteristics are used by viewers to construct their meaning of violent portrayals, it is important to conduct a series of effects studies to examine how the information contained in these cues is processed by viewers. These essential efforts must begin with good conceptualizations of the various contextual factors. This chapter examines seven of these factors: re- *factors* wards and punishments, harmful consequences, motives, justification, realism, identification, and humor. Although this examination is limited to these seven factors for purposes of illustration, the recommendations at the end of this chapter apply to the development of measures for all contextual factors.

My argument with each of these contextual factors is that it is most useful to develop as broad a conceptualization as possible. In that way we can operationalize a full range of content measures to document what forms of these characteristics are most prevalent. In addition, a broad conceptualization can guide a wider variety of operationalizations of treatments in effects studies so that we can examine which forms of the contextual characteristics have the most effect on viewers.

Rewards and Punishments

We know from effects research that when characters are rewarded in media portrayals—as well as in real life—people who watch those portrayals are more likely to learn to behave in a similar manner. The absence of punishment also shows this modeling effect (Bandura, 1965). Therefore, we know that reward and punishment constitute an important contextual element and a key part of a person's schema about violence.

What should be regarded as a reward? Does it have to be something physical, such as money? Or can it be something nonphysical, such as praise from others or a desired reputation? Does it need to be the presence of something, or can it be the absence of harm? For example, if a criminal robs a liquor store and barely gets away after a chase by police, can he be regarded as in a state of reward even if he did not get any money? Is relief from being caught rewarding?

What should be regarded as punishment? Being caught and put in jail would be regarded as punishment for a criminal. However, what if the criminal got away with a crime but was condemned by her friends? Can punishment be internal to the person, such as feelings of remorse?

My argument for the conceptualization of rewards and punishments—as with all other contextual variables—has three parts. First, I argue that reward and punishment should be conceptualized broadly. A broad conceptualization would include all forms of rewards and punishments.

Second, there should be clearly conceptualized components. For reward and punishment, I suggest a two-dimensional matrix as a heuristic to think about the different components. One dimension is the list of physical, tangible, overt elements in a portrayal. Such elements would include property gained (or lost), as well as verbalizations and gestures from other characters. The other dimension is the list of elements internal to the perpetrator of the action. Such elements would include emotional reactions (happiness, remorse) and psychological states (stress of being chased, relief from getting away, satisfaction from executing revenge, etc.).

A third part of my argument is that there should be a concern with ordinality or intensity. Not all rewards are equally good. When we document the presence of rewards and punishments in content analyses, we need to account for the different types. Then in experiments we need to test the effects of the most prevalent types found in television portrayals.

It is important to understand if rewards and punishments are categorical or if there is some overlap. Perhaps a minor form of punishment could be more rewarding than a weak form of traditional reward. To illustrate, consider two scenarios. In the first scenario, a criminal easily robs a store and gets $10. In the second scenario, a criminal gets no money in a robbery and is chased by police; in the chase, the criminal loses all his money, tears his clothes, and breaks his arm, but he gets away. The first criminal may feel punished, whereas the second criminal feels rewarded.

Harmful Consequences

Harmful consequences—like rewards and punishments—do not form a simple continuum. This factor is more complex, because it has many different facets. One scholar who has speculated on this topic is Mees (1990), who argues that three types of harm can be distinguished: (a) harm from distress (interference with one's freedom from physical or mental harm), (b) legal harm (violation of an accepted standard of social interaction), and (c) harm from moral guilt (disregard for the moral aspects of people's fundamental attitudes).

Most of the effects research focuses on harm from distress to the victim. These studies show that when violence is portrayed with no consequences (i.e., lacking pain, suffering, sorrow, or remorse), viewers are not likely to feel inhibited in performing aggressively, and their levels of aggressive behavior usually increase. This conclusion was argued by Comstock, Chaffee, Katzman, McCombs, and Roberts (1978) in their extensive review of the effects literature. Stein and Friedrich (1972), however, concluded that this effect did not exist in their review of the literature. But more recent reviewers are convinced that this is an important contextual factor (Comstock, 1985; *National Television Violence Study,* 1998).

As with rewards, harmful consequences should be conceptualized with attention to ordinality or intensity. In the public's mind, this ordinality does not follow medical harm. For example, Greenberg and Gordon (1972) found that violent acts that portray stabbings and shootings are rated more serious than portrayals of either more minor forms (such as fist fights) or more major forms (such as cannon fire). The most serious of acts were nonfatal harm, followed closely by killings. This counterintuitive finding was also reported in subsequent studies (Gunter, 1985; Potter & Berry, 1999).

Motives

What are the different types of motives for violence on television? Taking a social norms approach as a foundation, Mees (1990) argued that viewers assess characters' motives in terms of moral culpability. He then conceptualized three modes of intention that underlie conceptions of motivation for aggressive acts: (a) thoughtlessness (the aggressor should have taken possible dangers into consideration but did not), (b) inconsideration (the aggressor knows that the action will cause distress or harm but accepts this fact and places his or her own interests above those of others), and (c) maliciousness (the aggressor accepts and intends wickedness). These three modes can be distinguished by two dimensions of responsibility: active versus passive, and direct versus indirect. The first of these dimensions refers to the degree of involvement in the aggressive act, the second to the degree of moral culpability. Passive responsibility, for example, would apply both to people who guarantee the act is done by making the aggressive act possible and to onlookers who do nothing to stop the act.

Perhaps the most important distinction among motives is between those that are offensive (first strike) and those that are defensive (retaliation). In their content analysis of Finnish television, Mustonen and Pulkkinen (1993) catego-

offensive rized motivations for aggression as defensive or offensive. Among the offensive
aggression motives, there were five values: instrumental, masochistic, reactive-
expressive, sadistic, and altruistic.

④ Justification

The motives and values of the perpetrators of violence, as well as the targets,
are important elements in affecting viewers' judgments about the justification
of violence (Ball-Rokeach, 1972). How do viewers make this judgment? As
illustrated in the previous section, viewers are influenced by the apparent
motives of the perpetrators when they assess the meaning of the violence.
Retaliatory motives, such as revenge, appear to be the strongest in leading to
disinhibition. The causal path may go from motives to justification to disinhibition. That is, when a motive legitimates the violence, that violence is regarded
as justified, and viewers are more likely to exhibit a disinhibition effect.

A viewer's interpretation of justification may be linked to a context of
reward. Ball-Rokeach (1972) argued that when violence is presented as legitimate, characters' behaviors "are rewarded by others with praise, acceptance,
status, and the like. They can also see themselves as moral, responsible, and
good people because their behavior is so regarded by themselves and others"
(pp. 101-102).

deviant vs. normative violence Ball-Rokeach also made an important distinction between deviant and normative violence. The deviant violence is "socially disapproved" and caused by
"some personal or social system deficit while normative or socially approved
violence is caused by normal processes of conflict, change and control" (Ball-
Rokeach, 1980, p. 45). Thus, viewers of televised violence must constantly
make judgments about the meaning of the portrayals and decide which are
legitimate, and therefore good uses of violence, and which are bad. Ball-
Rokeach (1972) predicted that "there are probably only a very few situations in
which an act of violence is clearly legitimate in the eyes of all concerned"
(p. 102). These situations would be portrayals in which characters protect the
lives of others or in which characters are acting in socially sanctioned roles.
Thus, police officers who use violence to capture violent criminals who have
related to motive hurt innocent citizens are generally regarded by everyone as behaving legiti-
mately. Thus, justification is related to motive.

Rule and Ferguson (1986) argued, "Overall the studies seem to show that
there are degrees of justification, depending upon one's moral philosophy. For
example, from an 'eye for an eye' philosophy, vengeance may be perceived as
more justified than prosocial aggression; consequently, the degree of perceived
justification will affect the extent to which aggression is inhibited" (p. 36).
Gunter (1985) reinforced this position by arguing that the legal or moral context
of the portrayed behavior is an important mediator of public perceptions of
violence. Defensive or altruistic aggression may be interpreted as milder than
offensive, intentional, or sadistic aggression.

Realism

When analyzing how viewers judge the realism of a portrayal, we need to focus on two issues. First, we need to examine cues. Second, we need to consider how viewers use those cues to interpret reality.

Cuing

What elements in media narratives cue viewers about reality? One answer is that viewers look for cues in the portrayal that mimic real life, such as a victim with the same name or traits as someone in real life whom the viewer dislikes (Berkowitz & Geen, 1966, 1967; Donnerstein & Berkowitz, 1981; Geen & Berkowitz, 1967). Furthermore, Gunter (1985) has shown that viewers' discriminations between portrayals become more refined when the portrayals are perceived as more true to life and when viewers feel a greater familiarity with their own settings.

Another answer deals with how the characters are presented. Violence performed by human-type characters leads to more intense responses than violence performed by cartoon characters or puppets (Gunter & Furnham, 1984; Osborn & Endsley, 1971; Surbeck, 1975). For example, Osborn and Endsley found that participants responded more emotionally to the violence when human characters were involved. The human violence was also rated as the most scary, and participants recalled more details after being exposed to this type of violence than to nonhuman violence. Cantor (1994) says that children are especially sensitive to the similarity of depicted characters to real people, so when human characters perform violence, children are much more likely to experience a fear effect.

Setting is also a cue. Gunter and Furnham (1984) reported that violence in contemporary settings is rated as more serious than that in more remote settings. Violence in contemporary British and American crime dramas was considered more serious than violence in westerns, science fiction films, and cartoons, regardless of the type of violent act depicted or the consequences to victims. The authors noted that as the settings in which violence occurred more closely approximated those found in everyday life, such portrayals were rated as more realistic. The realistic portrayals were also rated as more violent, more frightening, more personally disturbing, more likely to disturb people in general, less humorous, and less suitable for children.

Genre is important to viewers in interpreting reality. Downs (1990) asked children to judge the reality of specific televised events shown on videotape. He concluded that the children were making their judgments of reality on the basis of format, that is, on whether or not the show was a cartoon. Gunter and Furnham (1984) ran an experiment in which they had British viewers rate five types of programs. Viewers rated the crime dramas as more realistic and more frightening and disturbing than the more fantasy fare of westerns, science fiction, and cartoons. Cartoons were rated as least violent and most suitable for children. The genre of news, of course, rates highest in realism. Thus, news was consistently rated as a more upsetting genre than other types of programs (Aisbett & Wright, 1989).

Interpretation

Interpreting the overall reality of a program or a narrative is a multidimensional task. For example, Hawkins (1977) measured children's reactions to the reality of television programming and found two dimensions: magic window and social expectations. Children are able to make separate judgments about whether the actions in the narrative actually happened (magic window) and whether the narrative contained lessons they could use in their own lives (social expectations). Other researchers have found three dimensions (for a review, see Potter, 1988a).

Judging reality usually begins with an assessment of whether a portrayal actually happened. But viewers rarely stop at this judgment. There is more to judging reality. Viewers—especially in evaluating fictional content—make assessments about whether something *could* happen as portrayed. Anything that could never happen is fantasy. So the judgment must move beyond the actualities of occurrence and consider the possibilities that different characters could be people encountered in real life and that particular situations could actually occur.

Judgments about reality are related to viewers' cognitive developmental differences. As children age, they are better able to distinguish reality from fantasy, and this increase in understanding is especially prominent from ages 3 to 5 (Taylor & Howell, 1973). Wright, Huston, Reitz, and Piemyat (1994) found that by age 5, children can distinguish the factuality of programming—that is, they can tell the difference between fictional programs and news or documentary—and that they improve with age. The learning comes not in believing that TV is fiction; 5-year-olds know this. The learning comes in figuring out what is nonfiction. This process is referred to as developing an adult discount. But this adult discount relates only to the dimension of the magic window (Hawkins, 1977). Among older children, Hawkins found no discounting on the dimension of social expectations.

Van der Voort (1986) challenged the notion that the adult discount is fully developed at age 12. He found that although children's perceptions of reality decreased from ages 9 to 12 for fantasy programs, there was no change in their perceptions of the reality of so-called reality-based programs. It appears that children base their perceptions of reality not on the accuracy of portrayals or information, but on the probability that something could occur in their lives. By age 12, they have not developed an understanding that in many ways news is a construction by journalists just as fictional programming is a creation of writers.

Identification

What cues about characters lead viewers to identify with those characters? One answer is that viewers are likely to identify with characters who are portrayed as heroes. For example, Liss, Reinhardt, and Fredriksen (1983) conducted two experiments on children from kindergarten through fourth grade to determine the impact of heroes in cartoons. They found that "the superheroes are compelling, attractive, and evidently above reproach, making their actions highly visible and favorable for generalized imitation" (p. 184).

Research has found that other characteristics are also related to identification, such as attractiveness of appearance (Hoffner & Cantor, 1985) and perceived similarity to oneself (Lieberman Research, 1975; McLeod, Atkin, & Chaffee, 1972; Perry & Perry, 1976; Tannenbaum & Gaer, 1965). Given these personal judgments about attractiveness and similarity, it is no wonder that viewers vary widely in their identification with characters. It is unlikely that any character on a television series has no viewers identifying with him or her.

Humor

There are many different forms of humor. People watching a particular show are likely to vary widely in terms of their reaction to humor. Some people might miss some forms of humor—such as satire or irony—altogether.

A laugh track is an obvious cue to viewers that a show is humorous. But laughter is neither a necessary nor a sufficient condition for a humorous context, because a producer can indicate a humorous context without using laughter at all. For example, a Three Stooges or Laurel and Hardy film contains many scenes of violence in a humorous context, but no characters laugh, and no laugh track cues the audience. Still, because of their farcical nature, the audience recognizes that these portrayals are meant to be humorous.

The presence of laughter does not automatically signal a humorous context. Laughter by itself is not a sufficient condition. In order for laughter to signal humor, it must be clear that those laughing find the situation funny. If instead laughter is triggered only to cover a person's embarrassment or if it is used in a false or ironic manner, then neither the motive nor the effect is humorous.

Conceptualizing humor is a complex task, because the judgment about humor changes depending on one's perspective. One perspective is to judge the humor in the eyes of the perpetrator of the violence. Perpetrators might find their actions funny, but no one else does. For example, the sadistic perpetrator, such as the Joker on *Batman,* finds his actions very funny, but the victims and the audience find no humor in the violence. Second, humor can be judged from the perspective of the victim, who might find the action funny while no one else does. For example, a character falls down some stairs and onlookers are shocked and concerned, but the victim jumps up laughing, saying he was playing a joke. As long as the character is not portrayed as using laughter to cover his embarrassment, the cues tell the viewer that the character feels the violence is genuinely humorous. Third, in the shared perspective, all characters regard the violence as funny. This perspective is exhibited when several characters take turns hurling insults at each other as if it were a game. Although the insults grow harsher, both players are having fun. And fourth, a violent scene may be humorous to the audience only. For example, the violence is treated very seriously by the characters in the portrayal, but the way it is executed is farcical or exaggerated, and the audience is meant to laugh at the silliness. This is the case with Laurel and Hardy and the Three Stooges.

Conceptualizing humor is a complex task for yet another reason. Viewers can use humor either to enhance or to detract from the influence of violence. For example, Freud (1960) theorized that hostile humor can often serve as a form of disguised attack against a target, thus providing the person making the joke with an opportunity to release emotional tension and/or purge hostile impulses. In his review of the experimental literature, Baron (1977) found support for the enhancing quality of hostile humor.

When humor is linked to violence, it has been found to lower inhibitions toward committing acts of aggression by subjects in controlled experiments (Baron, 1978; Berkowitz, 1970). Zillmann (1979) argued that humor can increase a viewer's arousal, which leads to a greater probability of behaving aggressively in real life.

Viewers can use humor to detract from the influence of violence. In an essay speculating about humor, Berger (1988) said that the thing humor does particularly well is "to help break set—that is, change one's assumptions about something, gain a new perspective, escape from a previously held pattern of beliefs and expectations" (p. 246). He also pointed out that humor has social and cultural value and helps people, collectively, deal with anxieties and stress. He said, "Comedy emphasizes survival; tragedy leads, almost inexorably, to death and destruction" (p. 247).

In reviewing the experimental literature on the relationship of humor and aggression, Baron (1977) said that exposure to nonhostile humor reduces subsequent aggression by previously angered persons. The explanations for this are (a) humor induces emotions incompatible with aggression, and (b) humor shifts attention away from prior annoyance. In an experiment, Baron (1978) found that exposure to exploitive sexual humor (but not nonexploitive sexual humor) significantly reduced the strength of participants' later attacks against a victim.

When humor is used to interrupt violence, it has been found to reduce the effect of violence, whereas violence without associated humor was more likely to lead to higher rates of aggressive behavior (Lieberman Research, 1975). However, Mueller and Donnerstein (1977) say that this effect may be limited to females.

Although viewers can use humor in several ways, humor is presented to trivialize violence on television (Potter & Warren, 1996). As evidence for this conclusion, Potter and Warren found that when humor was linked to violence, it was typically at the lower end of the violence spectrum. More than 88% of the total linkages found were in the lesser violence categories of verbal hostility and intimidation, and only about 2% were in the serious assault or property damage categories. About 94% of the linkages showed no major consequences of harm; in 88% of the linkages, the violence was not punished; and in 97% of the linkages, the perpetrator showed no remorse for committing the violence.

The trivialization of violence is troubling, because the more trivial forms of violence are more likely to be imitated. Bandura (1994) finds that easily imitated acts are more likely to be adopted than those beyond a person's mental and physical capabilities. This finding suggests that physical violence is only one form of aggressive or antisocial behavior that should be examined. A person who may not be capable of physical violence for moral and/or physical reasons may find verbal violence (e.g., insulting someone or verbally threatening them) a more acceptable alternative. These easily imitable forms of violence (harsh language, intimidation, and minor assaults) are already within the viewers' mental and physical capabilities. Social cognitive theory would predict that any inhibitions to imitating these acts would be reduced by their portrayed context of humor, lack of punishments, and lack of harmful consequences to the victims.

It is important for content analysts to document not just the presence of humor with violence, but the different kinds of humor. This information should then be translated into experiments in which the type of humor is varied. Not all humor is the same. Humor varies in tone (hostile to self-effacing), intensity, and type (slapstick, irony, etc.). Experimenters need to take more of a receiver orientation and ask their participants for their reactions to the humor. If researchers were to measure these personal reactions, they likely would find a great deal of variation even within experimental treatments. Should the influence of these differences in personal reactions to humor be covaried in the analysis? Doing so would make for a more controlled experiment and keep a sharper focus on patterns in the aggregate. But I argue that it is much more interesting to treat the personal reactions to humor as an independent variable so that the influence of this variable can be tested both as a main effect and in interaction with the other independent variables in the design.

RECOMMENDATIONS

This chapter does not conclude with broad and elaborate definitions of each contextual variable. That work needs to be conducted with much more speculation and research. Instead, I give some general guidelines to be used in developing more useful definitions of context.

We need to develop broader conceptualizations of all contextual factors. A broad conceptualization leads researchers to operationalizations of a fuller range of content measures for documenting what forms of these characteristics are most prevalent. In addition, a broad conceptualization can guide a wider variety of operationalizations of treatments in effects studies so that we can examine which forms of the contextual characteristics have the most effect on viewers.

We need to develop more elaborate conceptualizations of contextual factors. Each contextual factor is likely to be multifaceted. Theoreticians need to speculate more on the components of each and on whether these components show ordinality. For example, it is not likely that all viewers will regard all rewards as equal. Not all forms of violence are equally harmful, and not all forms of justification are the same. We need to test for possible differences in ordinality by posing the question, Is the ordinality (such as strength or serious- ness) of the contextual factor related to the probability of an effect? Without ordinality, contextual factors can be treated only as categorical. Ordinality requires greater precision in measurement and greater insight into determining the relative influence of facets of a contextual factor in the complex process of influence.

We need to examine how viewers' schemas incorporate context. Schemas guide viewers to pay attention to certain cues and ignore others. We have a good idea about which contextual factors get viewers' attention. More examination of how cues work in combination is needed. We need to know which cues are dominant and how certain cues can cancel out the perception of other cues.

Schemas also guide viewers in the use of this cuing information in making judgments about the meaning in narratives. We need to examine how viewers' schemas are constructed so that we can understand the associative networks among the cues and how those networks lead to effects. Effects are based on the meanings that viewers hold for narratives and interactions. The construction of that meaning is guided by schemas. The key to understanding the effects of media violence is to understand viewers' schemas.

7

Levels of Analysis

Quantitative and qualitative scholars differ not just in terms of their methods, but also in terms of how they view phenomena. With media violence, social scientists focus on patterns in the aggregate and make claims that all humans are the same—that is, that all our brains are wired in the same way. Thus, when presented with a particular stimulus, we will all behave in the same way.

Qualitative scholars claim that meaning making is an individual enterprise and that although we all learn how to make meaning of symbols through interactions with others, ultimately the meaning is ours to make. Whereas each television program presents a vast array of particular symbols carefully crafted to achieve a certain effect on the desired audience, each viewer interacts with those symbols in a way specific to his or her experience of meaning. Therefore television viewing is a very active process of meaning making (Fiske & Hartley, 1978). Different individuals have learned different connotations for each symbol. Because viewers weigh the symbols differently, individual interpretations differ widely.

These differences in perspective about the phenomenon being examined trigger criticism. Social scientists are skeptical about the ability of qualitative researchers to provide generalized findings about how humans process violent content and are affected by it. In contrast, qualitative scholars criticize social scientists for not treating humans as unique individuals. For example, Buckingham (1993) complains that the primary limitation of what he calls mainstream (i.e., social science) research on television violence is that it does not take into account how viewers construct meaning from it. He observes that "much of the research takes 'violence' as a homogeneous category" (p. 12) and that "attempts to classify types of television violence . . . have typically been based, not on the judgments of viewers who are actually exposed to the programmes, but on the supposedly objective judgments of researchers" (p. 12).

This controversy is over not methods, but perspective. Each side has a different vision about what the phenomenon is. The phenomenon of media violence, however, is multifaceted. Given this multilayered perspective on the phenomenon, the question is not, At which level does this phenomenon exist? We know the answer to this question; the phenomenon exists at all these levels. Instead, the question is, How can we conduct the best research at each level? The examination of each facet requires a different perspective and a different set of methods, as can be seen in both studies of content and studies of effects.

CONTENT STUDIES

Television shows are complex narratives. In analyzing them, researchers need to recognize that the meaning of the violence can be conveyed in different narrative strata. For example, within television shows are brief incidents of violence, each typically lasting several seconds and each telling its own mini-story about a character interaction. There are also scenes, each lasting perhaps a minute or two. And at the most macro level is a narrative that spans the entire length of the program and provides a more complete context for interpreting violent scenes and violent interactions.

At each level, an interweaving of elements forms a web of context. If the contextual web is identical across all narrative strata, viewers are presented with a consistent series of information that can be used efficiently to construct interpretations of the meaning of the violence in that program.

But the contextual web across strata likely is not consistent. To illustrate, an hour-long action-adventure episode might portray criminals committing six acts of violence during the first 50 minutes of the program. For each of these violent acts, the criminals are not caught or punished, so they continue to cause havoc, thus making it possible for the program-length narrative to continue. The consequences to the victims are largely ignored, because the goal is to keep the plot moving forward in an exciting manner. Then, in the last few minutes, the criminals engage in a shoot-out with police. The criminals are wounded and finally stopped from committing any more violent acts. In the final scene, we see all the victims gathered for a trial and testifying about their suffering. In such a narrative, a content analysis focused on the micro level would count seven acts of violence, of which only one was accompanied by the portrayal of punishment to the perpetrators and none depicted harm to the victims. Thus, researchers who make their analysis only at a micro level would conclude that the program, with its preponderance of no punishment and no pain, was teaching an antisocial lesson. However, if researchers used only a macro-level analysis of the entire narrative, they would conclude the opposite: that people who commit violence are always punished and that violence does result in harm to the victims.

The preceding example is hypothetical. However, empirical evidence supports the notion that stories are different across narrative strata. Using the *National Television Violence Study* (NTVS) database, Potter and Smith (in press) found the portrayal of harm to vary across the micro and macro units in about one third of the programs that contained violence. Furthermore, the dissonance across levels of analysis varies across genres and is highest in children's programs. This finding is especially troubling, because children have more difficulty making sense of narratives when contextual cues are in conflict.

Content analyses of television violence typically use one of three levels. At the macro level, the entire show is the unit. If violence occurs anywhere in the show, the entire program is categorized as violent. The problem with this approach is that a 2-hour movie that contains one act of violence would be put in the same category as a half-hour cartoon with 20 acts of violence.

The micro level focuses on the individual act of violence. Each time a violent act (such as a slap) is committed, it is recorded as another unit. The problem with this approach is that in some instances, such as fights, the counting of each individual act as a unit might be seen as inflating the frequency of violence. For example, if characters X and Y each throw 20 punches at each other during a 1-minute fight, the micro-level approach would require the coder to record each of the 40 punches as individual acts (units) of violence. But if the fight were used as the unit, one act of violence would be recorded.

There are several midlevel units of analysis, such as scenes and sequences. A scene usually is defined as a unity of characters, place, and action. The recording of violence at the scene level results in a smaller number of violent acts than the recording of violence at the micro level. The problem with conducting a sequence-level analysis is in the degree of difficulty in writing rules that specify the beginning and ending points of a sequence in such a manner that coders can attain an acceptable level of reliability.

Some studies have used multiple units of analysis. For example, Williams, Zabrack, and Joy (1982) coded at two levels. The global level was the program; coders rated the tone of the program and general characteristics of the characters. The second level was the segment, which was defined by a change in setting, time, or both. Several studies coded at the program and act levels (Gerbner, Gross, Morgan, & Signorielli, 1980; McCann & Sheehan, 1985). Gunter and Harrison (1995) coded at both the act and the sequence levels.

The NTVS used three units: program, sequence, and what they call PAT, which is a violent interaction (A) between a perpetrator (P) and a target (T). Each time one of these elements changed, a new PAT was coded throughout the continuing violent sequence. But as long as the PAT elements remained the same, even though there were multiple instances of the same act, such as repeated punches, only one unit was coded.

EFFECTS STUDIES

Media effects, in the simplest sense, can be examined at three major facets or levels: macro, cultural, and individual. The macro level focuses attention on patterns in the aggregate of all humans. It addresses the question, How are we all alike? The cultural level is most concerned with patterns in homogeneous groupings of people as delineated by shared cultural experience. It addresses the question, What are the shared meanings of the people in this particular culture? The individual level looks for the uniquenesses within individuals. It addresses the question, How is it possible that meaning is not shared?

Social scientists have typically focused on the aggregate level, especially in early effects studies. Thus, the so-called bullet, or hypodermic needle, approach assumed that all people were influenced in the same way by a powerful medium. This was a useful starting place for studying media effects. Very early experiments followed a kind of one-step direct-effect model, in which researchers tested different types of messages and tried to link them with different kinds of effects. The limits of this model were reached fairly quickly, and researchers shifted into an intervening variable model in which they began testing all sorts of characteristics of viewers as the intermediate step between media messages and effects. The goal was to identify the intervening variables that reduced as well as increased the probability that viewers would experience an effect. The intervening-variable model has been dominant in the past three or more decades. During that time, a great deal of research has been conducted to locate the factors that contribute to the effects process.

The focus of all this research was to provide explanations that accounted for the most variance—that is, to develop explanations that would apply to large aggregates. With this motivation and its strong empirical testing of hypotheses, social science research has moved our understanding about the effects of exposure to media violence from a point of intuitive speculations to a relatively high level of information within a period of several decades. We are now confident that exposure to media violence can lead viewers to immediate as well as long-term negative effects (reviewed in Chapter 3). We know a great deal about how individual characteristics of viewers are associated with various negative effects. We have also developed a long list of individual contextual factors that influence the effects process.

Paralleling the efforts of social scientists is the tradition of qualitative researchers, who are operating from a different perspective. They have focused on individuals and how individuals receive the messages. Qualitative researchers reject the mechanized view of humans in which brains are thought to be hardwired to process stimuli in a preordained manner. Instead, qualitative researchers argue strongly that humans are active meaning makers and that constructions of meaning differ widely across individuals. "Violence is not a simple fact about a television programme, which acts as an irresistible cause of enactments of violence by viewers. It is part of a complex structure of meanings, which are interpreted, mediated and acted on in very different ways" (Hodge & Tripp, 1986, p. 9). Hodge and Tripp said that "children watching television are not 'zombies.' Children are learning important and complex structures of meaning, and developing capacities for thinking and judgement that are a necessary part of the process of socialization. What they learn from television does not enter and remain in their heads as a self-contained and erroneous body of knowledge" (p. 10). Television interacts with the children both positively and negatively, "leading to new kinds of learning, new kinds of discrimination, as well as to opportunities being missed by television producers" (p. 8).

Some qualitative scholars are more interested in midlevels of the phenomenon, in some cases dealing with people in groups. For example, social scientists have conducted contingent analyses in which they recognize that people cluster into meaningful groups.

Over time, the two types of researchers have converged somewhat. Qualitative scholarship does not focus only on the use of symbols by individuals; many scholars are interested in the cultural aspects of people in groups and how they receive the messages. In one example, David Morley (1980) argues in *The Nationwide Audience* that a person's social class is a strong determinant of how he or she constructs meaning from television narratives.

Social scientists have recognized that there are few robust patterns in the aggregate and that there are many more interesting ones in demographic groups, so they run contingent analyses. For example, social scientists realize that individuals vary widely in their perceptions of violence (Gunter, 1985). Not all people judge the same violent incident in the same way. Some people may perceive certain acts as violent, whereas others do not. These differences are attributable to factors such as amount of television viewing, age, locus of control, personality, and trait aggressiveness (Gunter, 1983; Gunter & Furnham, 1984). Another example is in the work of criminologists, who conduct many contingent analyses and identify stronger findings within particular groups than in the aggregate of all people. Chiricos, Eschholz, and Gertz (1997) found no general cultivation effect in the aggregate; that is, exposure to any news medium was not related to fear of crime. But when the general population was disaggregated, they found that television news consumption was related to fear for middle-aged white females.

PROBLEMS WITH SOCIAL SCIENCE PRACTICES

As is evident in the preceding examples, social scientists are often aware of the multilevel nature of media violence. However, this awareness is not consistent. In some cases, social scientists appear confused about this issue of levels. This confusion limits the value of social science. Four examples of these limitations are discussed in the text that follows.

The first limitation is the use of poor grouping measures as the intervening variables. The practice of using grouping variables is a valuable step away from dealing with all people as uniform in their reactions to violence. Grouping variables can account for important differences. However, we must be careful in choosing what to treat as a useful grouping variable. When we choose a poor grouping variable, we are likely to find a great deal of variance within groups; with our statistical procedures we ignore this variation, thus making it appear that we are not interested in individual differences and falsely treat everyone within a group as the same. In addition, we are likely to find a very small difference (if any at all) across groups. If we run our test on enough participants, the power of the test increases to a point at which even very small differences become statistically significant; in short, we "get results." But when we report these results, we often confuse statistical significance with substantive significance. So when we make a big deal of an across-group difference (e.g., a one-third standard deviation), it appears that we focus on the trivial group difference while ignoring the massive individual differences within groups. This apparent focus is what triggers criticism from qualitative researchers. It is not that social scientists are unaware of individual differences or that individuals interpret violent messages differently. Instead, it is that social scientists often act as if they are mesmerized by their traditional methods and measures and don't examine how they can update those methods and measures as the cutting edge of knowledge moves.

An example of a poor grouping variable is sex. In the early years of effects research, sex was a useful grouping variable. It was worth examining if there were large differences between girls and boys. That research has failed to show much about any enduring physiological differences in reactions to violence across the sexes. And over time, the differences in cultural conditioning between boys and girls have eroded. Today, social scientists must consciously ask themselves an important pair of questions: Do you believe that all females are the same in their reactions to violence? Do you believe that all females are different in their reaction compared to all males? Unless we can answer yes to both of these questions, we must reject sex as an important grouping variable and spend our research resources on testing more promising variables. The variable of sex holds a useful place in the history of the examination of the effects of violence (see Donnerstein & Barrett, 1978; Donnerstein & Berkowitz, 1981; Mueller & Donnerstein, 1977; Schuck, Schuck, Hallam, Mancini, & Wells, 1971). But now we need a better explanatory grouping variable, such as masculinity, which places the focus more on psychology than on biology (Smeaton & Byrne, 1987).

 A second limitation is that social scientists too often choose to work with "surrogate" variables. By *surrogate variables,* I mean the readily available measures that attempt to represent—but are not actual measures of—the active influences on an effect. Surrogate variables include age of participants (Liebert & Baron, 1972), socioeconomic status (Hapkiewicz & Stone, 1974), and social class (Kniveton & Stephenson, 1975). Let's consider age as an example. With children, age in years is used as a surrogate for cognitive developmental level. But not all children of the same age are at the same level of cognitive development, so age is only a rough estimation of cognitive level. Sometimes age is used to represent experience with television or degree of socialization.

More active (nonsurrogate) variables include agents such as natural aggression (Dubanoski & Kong, 1977; Friedrich & Stein, 1973; Josephson, 1987; Wilkins, Scharff, & Schlottmann, 1974), trait anxiety (Berkowitz & Geen,

1967), trait irritability (Caprara, Renzi, Amolini, D'Imperio, & Travaglia, 1984), personal hostility (Gunter & Furnham, 1984), and learning disabilities (Sprafkin, Gadow, & Grayson, 1987).

It is understandable why social scientists often use surrogate measures. Such measures are easier to obtain. It is much easier to ask children their ages than to administer a good test of cognitive development or to conduct an in-depth inventory of their experience. Surrogate variables have their value in early stages of research programs, in which a priority is to sort quickly through large numbers of variables to identify the most promising ones. But once the line of research has identified the strongest avenues of explanation, it becomes essential to begin orienting toward measuring the essence of the influence. The task shifts its focus away from sorting through alternative variables toward finding the strongest explanatory variables. The stronger explanatory variables are usually people's interpretations rather than their demographics. For example, Chiricos, Hogan, and Gertz (1997) found that the cultivation effect of fear of crime was not related to the actual demographics (ethnic makeup) of one's neighborhood; instead, fear was related to a person's *perception* of the ethnic balance.

A third limitation is a preference for lower-level measurement. For example, a measure of sex is nominal, with only two categories. But measuring masculinity on a gender scale might offer a 20-point distribution. Thus, a masculinity scale highlights the variance and offers more options in analyses. One option is to use the response distribution to categorize participants into groups. For example, on a 20-point masculinity scale, researchers could divide participants into high masculinity, gender balance, and high femininity by selecting cutoff points of the scale (such as 20 to 15 as high masculinity, 14 to 8 as balanced gender, and 7 or below as high femininity). This practice is questionable because doing so would treat the difference of someone scoring 20 and someone else scoring 9 the same as the difference between someone scoring 15 and someone else scoring 14. The other choice is to preserve the variance in the response distribution, thereby acknowledging the differences among individuals. When we go to the trouble of using higher-level measures in constructing a distribution, it seems foolish to revert to past, more primitive practices of converting the distribution into a categorical variable.

A fourth limitation is a mismatch between method and level of phenomenon. Social scientists get themselves into trouble when they make macro-level assumptions while examining a cultural or individual phenomenon. For example, an experimenter might assume that all participants in a given treatment condition interpret the stimulus in the same way. This assumption helps the experiment focus attention on differences across treatments. When experimenters find within-treatment differences, they assume the differences are attributable to an error and use them as a benchmark against which to compare the size of their between-group differences in their analyses of variance. But what is really being tested in these experiments is how participants construct meaning from the stimuli and how they act on those constructions. In experiments that have no (or very little) within-treatment variation, the phenomenon being tested is truly a macro-level phenomenon. More than likely—as anyone who reads this literature finds obvious—the phenomenon is an individual or a cultural phenomenon, as indicated by how the variance is distributed. Thus, it seems strange that quantitative researchers would assume a macro-level phenomenon when as empiricists, they could easily look at all their data and determine the level in which the patterns reside. When they do this, they are likely to find evidence at all three levels, thus making the reporting of their results much more insightful.

The same assumption underlies much of survey research. Rarely do survey researchers ask respondents for their interpretations of various violent portrayals, and surveys focus on aggregate patterns rather than on individual differences. With cultivation research, for example, not only is there no acknowledgment of individual interpretations, but the theory is based on the assumption that television messages are the same throughout the television landscape and that all viewers interpret the messages in the same way.

A mismatch of level of phenomenon with research design is also indicated when experimenters tell their participants how to interpret certain key elements in the context of the violent portrayals. In some studies, for example, participants are told that the action was either real or fictional (Berkowitz & Alioto, 1973; Geen, 1975; Thomas & Tell, 1974). To illustrate, Berkowitz and Alioto (1973) showed a World War II documentary depicting U.S. Marines capturing a Japanese-held island. By taped introduction, about half of the 51 male undergraduate participants were told that the movie was a documentary, and the other half were told that the film was a Hollywood enactment. The researchers found that participants who were told that the film was realistic exhibited more of a disinhibition effect; the interpretation of reality made a difference, but that interpretation was given to the participants.

In some studies, participants are told certain things about the perpetrators or victims of the violence. Berkowitz and Geen (1967) told their participants that the protagonist in a filmed fight was a bad person or a good person, hence deserving the beating or not. In other experiments, participants were told by researchers how to interpret motivation for a particular violent act (Berkowitz & Powers, 1979; Berkowitz & Rawlings, 1963; Geen, 1981; Geen & Stonner, 1973, 1974; Hoyt, 1970) or specifically whether the violence was justified (Geen, 1981; Meyer, 1972).

Some researchers have found themselves using an interpretive scheme to explain their results. For example, several researchers have concluded that people are influenced by the "appropriateness" of aggressive acts, especially those that are in retaliation for previous aggression (Brown & Tedeschi, 1976; Kane, Joseph, & Tedeschi, 1976). For example, Tedeschi and colleagues conducted experiments in which participants took turns administering electric shocks to each other as a form of feedback in learning tasks. The researchers found that when participants administered a degree of shock similar to what they had received on earlier trials, such retaliation was not regarded as violent. However, acts of retaliation that were stronger (in terms of number of shocks) than an initial act of aggression were regarded as much more violent. The researchers reported that participants' judgments of violence were attributable much more to the appropriateness of the retaliation than to the actual number of shocks administered. Therefore, the judgment of violence does not rest solely with the type of act performed, but is also keyed to the participants' interpretations of surrounding events.

AN ILLUSTRATION OF MULTILEVEL ANALYSIS: IDENTIFICATION

What follows is an analysis of how social scientists have dealt with the variable of identification in research on media violence. It serves as an example of how a variable can be examined at all three levels.

Some early experiments on media effects were designed to see if identification by viewers with a character in a violent portrayal affected their subsequent behavior (Leyens & Picus, 1973; Perry & Perry, 1976; Turner & Berkowitz, 1972). These researchers were looking for patterns in the aggregate, and they ignored the possibility of individual interpretations. For example, Turner and Berkowitz (1972) told one group of participants to watch a film and to imagine themselves being the victor who delivers a brutal beating to his opponent in a prizefight. These participants were asked to push a button each time the hero hit his victim. The experimenters found the participants in this treatment condition to be more aggressive than participants who were given no instructions. Note how the participants were treated like machines; that is, they were told what to do and when to do it.

What this study really demonstrates is that people can be programmed to identify with a particular character and that this programming can lead to increases in aggressive behavior. These results document an aggregate behavior. Although this is an interesting finding, it is far more important to treat identification with violent characters at an individual level and frame the question as follows: What leads individual viewers to identify with a violent character?

Over time, the social science research has been shifting its perspective more toward this question. For example, Liss, Reinhardt, and Fredriksen (1983) conducted two experiments on children from kindergarten through fourth grade to determine the impact of heroes in cartoons. They found that "the superheroes are compelling, attractive, and evidently above reproach, making their actions highly visible and favorable for generalized imitation" (p. 184). They also reported that all children were able to distinguish between protagonists and antagonists. Although the findings still focused on the aggregate, there was more awareness of the received view; that is, the judgments of characters came from the children rather than from the experimenters.

Research has found that other characteristics, such as attractiveness of appearance (Hoffner & Cantor, 1985) and perceived similarity to oneself (Lieberman Research, 1975; McLeod, Atkin, & Chaffee, 1972; Perry & Perry, 1976; Tannenbaum & Gaer, 1965), are also related to identification. Given these personal judgments about attractiveness and similarity, it is no wonder that viewers vary widely in their identification with characters. It is unlikely that any character on a television series has no viewers identifying with him or her.

Not only are differences in identification traceable to elements about the characters, but elements about the viewers could also account for these differences. With children, cognitive developmental differences subdivide the group. As children develop cognitively, they are better able to distinguish reality from fantasy, and this increase in understanding is especially prominent from ages 3 to 5 (Taylor & Howell, 1973). Wright, Huston, Reitz, and Piemyat (1994) found that by age 5, many children can distinguish the factuality of programming— that is, they can tell the difference between fictional programs and news or documentary.

Social science research is enlarging its focus. This is a positive step in the direction of making quantitative methods more useful. However, it is important that designers of experiments position their treatments and measures more cleanly at particular levels of the phenomenon.

RECOMMENDATIONS

Researchers need to be clear about the level of phenomenon they are interested in examining. It is best not to make an assumption that a study is tapping into only one level. Instead, empiricists should conduct their analyses to determine how the variance is apportioned across levels. In this way it will become more clear at what level the phenomenon is strongest.

We need to get away from the assumption that all viewers are subjected to the same effect of violence when they see the same message. This simply is not the case. Viewers make a wide range of interpretations, and if we, as researchers, are to understand the effects process more fully, we need to focus on the interpretive process, as well as the influence process, as illustrated in the individual-interpretations model.

Identification, for example, appears to be an individual-differences phenomenon. But it is possible that after years of conditioning, we all have come to share the same ideas about what makes an attractive or heroic character.

More research is needed at a truly individual level. Most of the experimental research has been conducted at the group level, in which researchers focus on a particular category of people, such as children or heavy viewers of TV violence. Of course, data are gathered from the units (individual people) within the group, but the characteristics and differences across individuals are ignored (or treated as error variation) as the analysis focuses on patterns in the aggregate of the group.

We need to use grouping variables sparingly. The most promising route toward understanding individual interpretations is not to group individuals by demographic, psychological, or other characteristics. Not all males are alike in their interpretations, nor are all heavy viewers of television. Grouping individuals introduces error variance because people are grouped together not because they agree on interpretations, but because they share an easily observable characteristic. This categorization creates within-group variation that is then regarded as error. The strategy of running multivariate analyses on a large number of these grouping variables with the intention of increasing predictive power actually expands the total error as within-group error is increased with each additional variable entered. A better strategy is to focus on using a person's individual interpretations of contextual information to predict that individual's summary judgment of violence in a portrayal.

8

Development

Researchers studying media effects have treated children as a special group because children have been regarded as highly susceptible to negative effects from exposure to violence. Although there are many reasons for such heightened susceptibility, researchers have generally focused on the single reason of cognitive development, especially as conceptualized by Jean Piaget. The results of this research support the notion that children's minds mature as they age and that children's levels of mental maturity are related to how they process information from media narratives. Children of different ages are thus at different levels of risk of a harmful effect.

The research on developmental differences and how they relate to media effects displays two troubling limitations. One limitation can be traced to an assumption that once people have reached the teenage years, their minds are fully developed, so from a cognitive point of view there is no reason to treat a 15-year-old differently from a 55-year-old. Researchers who test the effects of media violence recognize that viewers may differ in terms of experience, media preferences, socioeconomic status, and many other characteristics—but not in terms of their mental capacity to process media messages after they reach early adolescence.

A second limitation is the practice of equating a person's development with his or her cognitive stage. Although cognitive development is very important, strong arguments can also be made for the importance of considering emotional and moral development in building an explanation of the effect of media violence on individual viewers. In this chapter I briefly review the thinking in all three realms: cognitive, emotional, and moral.

THE COGNITIVE REALM

Children have been treated as a special group with the expectation that they are especially susceptible to television violence. This susceptibility is attributed primarily to children's lower stage of cognitive development. It is believed that at young ages, people have a low ceiling of ability; that is, additional practice and experience will not help until the mind matures to a point at which it is able to handle higher-level skills. It is assumed that early childhood is a series of stair steps to higher levels of cognitive ability, but that once people reach the age of about 12, their capacity stays on a plateau the rest of their lives.

The seminal theoretician in this area is the Swiss psychologist Jean Piaget, who argued that a child's mind matures from birth to about 12 years of age, during which time it goes through several identifiable stages (Smith & Cowie, 1988). Until age 2, children are in the sensorimotor stage; then they advance to the preoperational stage from 2 to 7 years of age. Then children progress to the concrete operational stage, and by age 12 they move into the formal operational stage, where they are regarded as having matured cognitively into adulthood.

In each of these stages, children's minds mature to a level at which they can accomplish a new set of cognitive tasks. For example, in the concrete operational stage (7-12 years of age) children gain the ability to organize objects into series. If you try to teach this skill to a child of age 3, you will fail—no matter how organized and clear your lessons are.

Cognitive Development and Media

When children interact with the media, we can see these cognitive stages in operation. Sometimes children's lower cognitive abilities make them more susceptible to media effects, but at other times lower development can act as protection. For example, Collins (1973, 1983) found that young children are less able to understand relationships between motives and aggression and therefore may be more prone to imitate inappropriate behaviors. However, very young children seem to be protected because they do not understand the significance of violence, so they do not imitate it.

Children begin paying attention to the TV screen as early as 6 months of age (Hollenbeck & Slaby, 1979), and by the age of 3, many children have developed regular patterns of viewing of about 1 to 2 hours per day (Huston et al., 1983). By ages 2 to 11, Nielsen data indicate that children are viewing between 28 and 30 hours per week, and this exposure amount is fairly stable through these years.

At age 3, children begin watching television using an exploratory approach, in which they actively look for meaning in content. But until age 5, they are especially attracted to and influenced by vivid production features such as rapid movement of characters, rapid changes of scenes, and intense or unexpected sights and sounds. Therefore, a large part of the reason that children seek out and pay attention to cartoon violence is not the violence, but all the sound, color, and motion.

In an exploratory mode, children monitor the TV set not for unfolding stories, but for individual actions that are very high profile. They look for action over dialogue or conversation. They look for motion, color, music, sound effects, and unusual voices. They have great difficulty following the elements in a plot and understanding character development, as well as motivations for actions (Wartella, 1981).

By about age 4, children shift out of the exploratory mode and into a search mode. Thus, they begin developing an agenda of what to look for. Their attention does not simply bounce haphazardly from one high-profile action to another. By ages 6 to 11, children have developed the ability to lengthen their attention spans and make sense of continuous plots. A continuous story line holds their attention better than do disconnected segments in a magazine-type format. Children at this age still use formal features (interesting visual and audio cues, such as animation, children's voices, special effects) to decide what is important to attend to. For example, they interpret a laugh track as signaling that a program is a comedy.

By ages 10 to 12, children have developed an understanding of motives of characters and how those motives influence action. With this understanding comes a greater ability to distinguish among characters along more dimensions. Children of this age are not limited to understanding characters on only their physical traits, but can also infer personality characteristics. During this time, children increase the amount of their TV viewing, and much of this additional viewing is of violent programs. "Children between the ages of nine and twelve enjoy program violence more and are less inclined to regard violent actions on television as 'terrible' " (Van der Voort, 1986, p. 330) than are younger children. However, Van der Voort points out that although older children enjoy viewing violent programs, their preference for these programs is not for the violence itself; they are viewing most likely because the programs are more adult fare.

As children grow older, they are able to understand better the violence in fictional programs. As they age, they are less likely to see the violence in programs, and their general level of arousal diminishes. In addition, as children age, they "gradually watch the programs shown with less emotion, absorption and fear, and with more detachment" (Van der Voort, 1986, p. 332). Children's tendency to identify with television characters, however, was not found to decrease with age, as "television characters—even those in cartoons—appeared to maintain their attraction" (p. 332).

Not all children at a given age process narratives in the same way (Van der Voort, 1986). Factors such as preference for violence, perception of reality, and degree of identification with characters vary substantially at a given age. Van der Voort observed that one set of children who were absorbed in watching violent videos found the violence realistic, which led to a stronger emotional reaction, which in turn led to a belief that the violence was terrible, which did *not* lead to aggressive behavior in real life. In contrast, other children, who were also absorbed in viewing violence and believed it to be realistic, were found to have an uncritical attitude toward program violence, which led to their being more jaded and less emotionally involved, which in turn led to more aggressive behavior in real life.

Differential Cognitive Development

Stage theories of childhood cognitive development have come under criticism for being too discrete (e.g., see Gardner, 1983). Critics say that even Piaget could not consistently demonstrate that all children of a given age operate at the same developmental stage. There are differential rates of cognitive development. Information-processing theories, which look at the second-by-second processing of messages, argue that children of exactly the same age can process the same messages in very different ways. In addition, the symbol systems approach to development argues that children attach different meaning to the symbols in a message because of their differing experiences from life and contact with the media.

Research on the effects of media violence clearly indicates that factors in children's environments influence their rates of development and hence their understanding of these messages. For example, children of low socioeconomic status enjoy the violence in programs more, approve of violent behavior more, and identify with television characters more than do children of higher socioeconomic status (Van der Voort, 1986). Family life is also an important contributing factor. For example, children who are abused by parents watch more violence and identify with violent heroes more (Heath, Bresolin, & Rinaldi, 1989). Children in families that have high-stress environments receive less support and are more vulnerable to the effects of media violence (Borduin, Mann, Cone, & Henggeler, 1995; Tangney, 1988; Tangney & Feshbach, 1988). In contrast, children in households with strong norms against violence are not affected as much behaviorally (Heath, Bresolin, & Rinaldi, 1989).

Elaborating on the idea of environment, Hodge and Tripp (1986) used semiotic analysis to construct an explanation for how children are socialized by their environment into certain ways of thinking. They argue that children from working-class families are taught to see the world in simpler terms; thus, working-class children are cognitively deprived compared to children who are socialized to think in more complex terms about the world. When it comes to television exposure, working-class children "tend to represent issues in terms of black and white, not in shifting shades of gray" (p. 98). Television exposure, despite its enormous variety of messages and its ability to stimulate, cannot by itself lead children to expand their cognitive abilities.

Adult Cognitive Development

Developmental researchers who are influenced by Piaget focus all their attention on the cognitive development of children up to age 12. It is assumed that a person's mind is fully mature at that point. This idea has been defused throughout much of media effects research and shows up in other forms. For example, Eron, Huesmann, Lefkowitz, and Walder (1972) argued that once children reach adolescence, their behavioral dispositions and inhibitory controls have become crystallized to the extent that their aggressive habits are very difficult to change.

A growing literature is documenting how adults continue to experience cognitive changes throughout their lives. For example, Sternberg and Berg (1987) showed that throughout adulthood, people's intelligence changes not so much in the level of IQ, but in terms of a shift in type from fluid to crystalline. Fluid intelligence is the ability to be creative and see patterns in complex sets of facts. Crystalline intelligence is the ability to memorize facts. Sternberg and Berg said that "crystallized ability is best measured by tests requiring knowledge of the cultural milieu in which one lives, for example, vocabulary and general information, whereas fluid ability is best measured by tests requiring mental manipulation of abstract symbols, for example, figural analogies and number series completions" (p. 4). They pointed out that research has shown that "whereas crystallized ability seems to increase throughout the life span, although at a decreasing rate in later years, fluid ability seems first to increase and later to decrease" (p. 4).

[margin note: adults. experience continuing changes]

Evidence also suggests that a person's mind continues to mature throughout adolescence and adulthood in terms of cognitive style, which is a person's approach to organizing and processing information (Hashway & Duke, 1992). Cognitive styles mature by changing along the subdimensions of field dependency, tolerance for ambiguity, conceptual differentiation, and reflection versus impulsivity. Although no research yet has examined the relationship of these cognitive developmental factors on either the interpretation or effects of exposure to media violence, the speculations that follow illustrate the potential usefulness of these variables.

Field Dependency *vs Field Independent*

Perhaps the most important dimension in cognitive styles is the degree to which a person is field dependent. People vary by degrees according to their abilities to distinguish between signal and noise in any message. Noise is the chaos of symbols and images; signal is the information that emerges from that chaos. People who are highly field dependent become stuck in the field of chaos—seeing all the individual details but missing the big picture, which is the signal. Field-independent people are able to sort quickly through the field to identify the elements of importance and ignore the distracting elements (Witkin & Goodenough, 1977).

[margin note: field dependent vs independent]

For example, when watching a story of violence in a television news show, field-independent people are able to identify the key information—the who, what, when, where, and why—of the story. They quickly sort through what is said, the graphics, and the visuals to try to make sense out of the essence of the event being covered. Field-dependent people "see" the key elements along with all the other peripheral elements in the news story, but they are less able to distinguish between what is of central importance and what is background.

When watching a fictional narrative of violence, field-independent people quickly identify the salient information from the context and construct their meaning for the portrayal. In contrast, field-dependent people are confused by all the contextual elements, so they are likely to select an element haphazardly to construct their meaning.

Tolerance for Ambiguity   High tolerance = more critical viewers

Every day we encounter people and situations that are unfamiliar. To prepare ourselves for such situations, we have developed sets of expectations (schemas) for people and events. What do we do when our expectations are not met and we are surprised? People who have a low tolerance for ambiguity tend to ignore these discrepant messages. In contrast, people who have developed a high tolerance for ambiguity are more willing to follow observations into unfamiliar territory that goes beyond their preconceptions.

During exposure to media violence, people with a low tolerance for ambiguity are likely to encounter the messages on the surface and latch onto easily accessible schemas. If the surface meaning fits their schema, the message is left unexamined and reinforces the existing schema. If the message does not meet the easily accessible schema, it is ignored. In contrast, people with a high tolerance for ambiguity do not have a barrier to analysis. They are more willing to break any message down into components and make comparisons and evaluations in a quest to understand the nature of the message; that is, they are more critical viewers.

Conceptual Differentiation

People who classify objects into a large number of mutually exclusive categories exhibit a high degree of conceptual differentiation (Gardner, 1968). In contrast, people who use a small number of categories have a low degree of conceptual differentiation.

Related to the number of categories is category width (Bruner, Goodnow, & Austin, 1956). People who have few categories to classify something usually have broad categories, so as to contain all types of messages. If a person has only one category for all media violence, then this category is likely to contain a wide variety of portrayals. In contrast, someone who has many categories will have narrower ones. For example, we could divide violence into fantasy and realism. Within the realistic category are the subcategories of breaking news, docudrama, and serious drama. Within the subcategory of breaking news are the sub-subcategories of hard news and feature news. As we break a concept down into more and more levels, the width of the resulting categories narrows, and the examples within each category become more homogeneous.

As people see a new portrayal, they must categorize it. Levelers tend to focus on similarities across portrayals, thus categorizing new portrayals with previous types. In their goal to build cohesive cognitive schemas, they often fail to recognize small differences and gradual changes over time. In contrast, sharpeners focus on differences across portrayals. They try to maintain a high degree of separation between new portrayals and older ones (Pritchard, 1975). *sharpeners*

What do people focus on when they make their conceptual differentiations in the sorting process? There are two broad types of sorting strategies: descriptive and inferential. The descriptive strategy relies on easily observable physical characteristics on which everyone would agree. For example, if you were shown pictures of a dozen people and asked to sort them into groups, you might choose the criteria of gender, ethnicity, or age. These characteristics are usually observable in pictures, and all sorters are likely to observe the same thing. An inferential strategy requires making a judgment on abstract characteristics. For example, you might judge some of the people in the pictures to be sad and others to be happy and categorize them according to this inferential criterion. We cannot "see" sadness, or any other emotion, motive, thought, or personality characteristic directly; instead we infer these characteristics when we see particular cues. But the cues are only indicators; they are not the characteristic itself.

Reflection Versus Impulsivity — *deciding about messages*

This dimension separates people in terms of how quickly they make decisions about messages and how accurate those decisions are (Kagan, Rosman, Day, Albert, & Phillips, 1964). People who take a long time and make lots of errors are regarded as slow or inaccurate, those who are quick and make few errors are fast or accurate, those who take a long time and make few errors are reflective, and those who are quick and make many errors are impulsive.

In sum, cognitive development offers an important perspective on the effects of media violence. However, it is very limiting to accept the assumption that people stop developing cognitively once they reach the teen years. Adults and adolescents range along continua that are cognitive in nature and that address skills that can be developed. For example, adults can develop their cognitive abilities by becoming more field independent by learning to focus more on signal and less on noise, by developing a higher tolerance for ambiguity and being willing to scan more messages and to do so with more depth, by developing knowledge structures with more categories of varying widths as well as being comfortable with inferential and descriptive sorting strategies, and by moving away from making impulsive sorting decisions.

Cognitive development explains many of the differences in media effects across individuals. Children's minds mature, thus making it possible for them to understand important characteristics about the media. But the minds of adults also continue to mature and change. When researchers take a broader view of cognitive development, they can locate their research subjects along these continua and use this additional information to explain the variance in effects of media violence.

EMOTIONAL DEVELOPMENT

Media messages can arouse emotions in people of all ages. Emotions do not need to be learned in the sense that we learn to recognize words in order to be able to read. Instead, emotions are hardwired into our brains (Goleman, 1995). Regardless of the culture in which we are raised, we all can recognize in ourselves and others the basic emotions of anger, sadness, fear, enjoyment, love, surprise, disgust, and shame.

Awareness and control of emotions can be developed both throughout childhood and in adulthood. Salovey and Mayer (1990) point out that people develop emotionally in five areas: ability in reading emotions (empathy), emotional self-awareness, harnessing emotions productively, managing emotions, and handling relationships. It is not difficult to see how each of these would be related to media effects. People who are more highly developed along these lines will have a stronger and more appropriate emotional reaction to violence in the media while exercising greater control over their personal behaviors in real life.

We attain higher levels of emotional development by gaining experience with emotions and by paying close attention to our feelings as we interact with the media. With greater experience with emotions, we are able to make finer discriminations. For example, we are all familiar with anger because that is one of the basic emotions. But it takes experience with this emotion to be able to tell the difference between hatred, outrage, fury, wrath, animosity, hostility, resentment, indignation, acrimony, annoyance, irritability, and exasperation. In addition, fear has a range of subemotions: phobia, terror, panic, fright, dread, consternation, apprehension, anxiety, nervousness, wariness, qualm, edginess, and concern.

Emotional development is closely linked to cognitive development (Goleman, 1995). For example, very young children cannot follow the interconnected elements in a continuing plot; instead, they focus on individual elements. Therefore they cannot understand suspense, and without such an understanding they cannot become emotionally aroused as the suspense builds. So a child's ability to have an emotional reaction to media messages is low not because of a lack of ability to feel emotions, but because of a lack of ability to understand what is going on in certain narratives.

Emotions and cognitions are also closely linked throughout adulthood. Goleman (1995) explains, "We have two brains, two minds—and two different kinds of intelligence: rational and emotional. How we do in life is determined by both—it is not just IQ, but emotional intelligence that matters. Indeed, intellect cannot work at its best without emotional intelligence" (p. 28). Goleman broadens the conception of intelligence, then shows how a person's emotional development interacts with a broad range of cognitive abilities. He cites physiological data to show that emotions are part of the brain and are triggered by the capacity of the body.

Viewer-Message Interaction

Whether a message evokes an emotional response rests with the combination of the message itself and the way the viewer or reader interprets it. The sequencing of elements in a message fosters a mood that affects emotional responsiveness. A message element is assigned meaning only in the context given by the perceived pattern and themes of the entire message. Viewers and readers develop interpretive schemas to use in giving meaning to individual parts of a communication. The schemas can function as an aid and basis for recalling the substance of the story; particularly salient items are remembered. Schemas constitute a basis for perceiving similarity in communication experiences that differ in details.

Understanding of emotions is based on verbal and nonverbal cues from characters, situational cues, and proper coordinated interpretation of both sets of cues. With adults, if cues are not coordinated, situational cues are given precedence. Children give precedence to verbal and nonverbal cues.

What kinds of cues can trigger emotions in us? We can begin to answer this question by understanding how media narratives can evoke emotions. Four findings need to be emphasized.

First, people are more likely to have stronger emotional reactions when exposed to realistic narratives in realistic settings. Realistic elements draw viewers more strongly into the narrative by reminding them of their real lives and actual experiences. Thus, the narrative will resonate more with the personal experience of the viewers, and the viewers' remembrances and imaginations will be engaged to a higher degree. On the other hand, desensitization is enhanced when people believe the action viewed is fantasy and when they believe that everything will work out all right in the end (Cantor, 1994).

Second, people have a stronger emotional reaction to narratives that feature characters with whom they can identify. The influence of this variable on leading to aggressive behavior has been well established with children (Anderson, 1983; Dorr, 1981; Hicks, 1965; Huesmann, Lagerspetz, & Eron, 1984; Leyens & Picus, 1973; McLeod, Atkin, & Chaffee, 1972; Perry & Perry, 1976; Tannenbaum & Gaer, 1965; Turner & Berkowitz, 1972), as well as with young adults (Leyens & Picus, 1973).

Why do people identify with television characters involved in violence? This important question has been examined in children but not adults. With children, one characteristic that has been found to increase identification is the hero status of the character. Liss, Reinhardt, and Fredriksen (1983) conducted two experiments on children from kindergarten through fourth grade to determine the impact of heroes in cartoons. They found that all children are able to distinguish between protagonists and antagonists and that "the superheroes are compelling, attractive, and evidently above reproach, making their actions highly visible and favorable for generalized imitation" (p. 184).

Third, narratives that follow a conventional pattern are easy for viewers to follow and can evoke some standard emotions. But to evoke really strong emotions, the narrative has to surprise the viewer by changing the formula or bending the rules to take the viewer over the edge.

Fourth, massive exposure to arousing stimuli, especially sex and violence, can substantially diminish emotional reactions to such stimuli. This phenomenon is called excitatory inhibition. Spontaneous recovery from reduced responsiveness does occur after the massive exposure is discontinued.

In sum, emotional development is tied to cognitive development. The emotional reactions of children who cannot read or follow visual narratives are limited to reactions of microelements in messages. As people develop their emotional abilities, they are better able to "read" emotions in media portrayals and are better able to make finer discriminations among emotions. In contrast, people who are relatively undeveloped emotionally may not be able to experience as many emotions vicariously through characters, might experience inappropriate emotions, might be desensitized to many emotions by constant exposure to superficial treatments of news stories and formulaic fictional plots, and might be unable to control their behaviors when they are aroused or angered by media violence. Thus, differences in emotional development could well explain much of the variance in the effects of exposure to media violence.

MORAL DEVELOPMENT

Like Piaget, Lawrence Kohlberg studied the development of children. Whereas Piaget was concerned with cognitive development, Kohlberg focused on moral development. He envisioned three levels of moral development: preconventional, conventional, and postconventional. The centerpiece is *conventional*, which stands for fair, honest, concerned, and well regarded—characteristics of the typically good person (Kohlberg, 1966, 1981).

The preconventional stage begins at about age 2 and runs to about 7 or 8. During this period, the child is dependent on authority. Inner controls are weak. Young children depend on their parents and other adults to tell them what is right and to interpret the world for them. The child's conscience is external; that is, the child must be told by others what is right.

During the conventional stage, children develop a conscience for themselves as they internalize what is right and wrong. They distinguish between truth and lies. Their behavior is still motivated by the threat of punishment.

The postconventional stage begins in middle adolescence, when some people are able to transcend conventional notions of right and wrong as they focus on fundamental principles. This process requires the ability to think abstractly and therefore recognize the ideals behind society's laws. This level is characterized by a sense that being socially conscious is more important than adhering to legal principles.

Kohlberg's stages are not fixed stages that everyone follows in sequence. People can move around among the stages, given particular problems and moods. However, these stages are hierarchically ordered such that the more evolved person is one who operates most consistently at the highest stages of moral development.

Gilligan (1993) has extended the ideas of Kohlberg by arguing that moral development shows a gender difference. Men base their moral judgments on rights and rules; women tend to think in terms of care and cooperation. So in a conflict situation, women are likely to try to preserve relationships. Men will search for a moral rule and try to apply it.

Advances in moral development do not necessarily come with age. For example, Van der Voort (1986) found no evidence that children judge violent behavior more critically in a moral sense as they age. He found no reduction in the approval of the "good guys'" behavior. And as children aged, they were even more likely to approve of the violent actions of the bad guys. So although children acquire additional cognitive abilities with age, they do not necessarily acquire additional moral insights.

People of any given age show a range of moral development. In addition, older children are not automatically more highly developed morally than are younger children. A person's position along the moral development continuum likely would be a valuable piece of information in any explanation of the various effects of exposure to media violence.

RECOMMENDATIONS

We need to expand the idea of cognitive development beyond childhood into adolescence and adulthood. Theoreticians need to provide us with guidance about how our minds continue to develop beyond Piaget's last stage of formal operations. Researchers need to build measures of cognitive development into their designs that measure the effects of exposure to violence on participants older than 12.

We need to broaden our concept of development to areas other than cognitive abilities. A person's development cognitively, emotionally, and morally is all interrelated. This full spectrum of development is likely to be a major explanatory factor of why certain people are more affected by media violence than are others. Our reactions to portrayals of violence require cognitive processing; if adults vary in the degree to which they perceive and process contextual cues, there will be important differences in how violence affects them. Our reactions to portrayals have an important emotional component; if people vary in the degree of their awareness of these emotions and their ability to control these emotions, there will be important differences in how violence affects them. In our reactions to portrayals of violence, we must make moral judgments about the action; if people vary in their abilities to work through problems of morality, there will be important differences in how violence affects them.

9

Effects

In December 1997, a 14-year-old boy interrupted a prayer meeting before school by pulling out a gun and killing three classmates in West Paducah, Kentucky. The boy told investigators that he had seen this done in a movie (The Basketball Diaries), *which featured a teenage boy dreaming about breaking down a classroom door and methodically gunning down five classmates while students cheered. The 14-year-old said, "It was like I was in a dream, and I woke up." (Bridis, 1997, p. A8)*

In March 1998, two boys (ages 13 and 11) lay in ambush with a cache of stolen weapons (nine high-powered rifles and handguns) as their classmates filed out of school in Jonesboro, Arkansas, during a fire drill. The young snipers killed four students and one teacher, as well as wounding 10 others (Mills & Kemper, 1998). Two months later, police in St. Charles, Missouri, uncovered a plan by three sixth-grade boys to pull a false fire alarm on the last day of school, then kill their fellow classmates as they filed out of the building. Police said the boys planned to copy the Jonesboro massacre. ("Sixth-Graders Were Planning," 1998)

In May 1998, a 15-year-old boy in Springfield, Oregon, was expelled from his school for carrying a firearm. The next day, he opened fire in the cafeteria, killing one of his classmates and wounding 25 others. (Murphy & McDermott, 1998)

In February 1996, Flaviano Hernandez was killed in front of his 4-year-old son when he was chased down and stopped at a Los Angeles intersection by a motorist who was infuriated that Hernandez had hit his car and not stopped.

People would have no difficulty identifying these acts as violent and then generalizing that our society is a violent one. Public opinion would be very negative about these occurrences. <u>Many people might blame the media for causing these horrible acts.</u> A recent poll found that 70% say they believe

blame the media

that violence on television causes people to behave violently occasionally; this figure is an increase from the 58% who reported holding such a belief in 1989 (Lowry, 1997). A *U.S. News & World Report* poll found that 92% of Americans think that television contributes to violence in this country, and 65% think that entertainment programs on television have a negative influence on American life ("Culture & Ideas," 1994). Even college professors think that the influence of television is mostly negative. According to a poll of 500 college-level teachers and communication scholars, 66% believed that exposure to television increases aggressive behavior (Bybee, Robinson, & Turow, 1982).

Even though most people believe that media violence is harming others and society in general, they do not feel they personally are being affected. There is an obvious explanation for this opinion pattern. People are aware of the high-profile violent events reported in the media. People know that others are committing violent acts, but they also know that they personally have never committed any atrocities. The problem with this reasoning is that people equate effects with atrocities. Media violence has many different effects. A person can be profoundly influenced by exposure to media violence without ever having committed a violent crime.

Media researchers themselves are not sure how many effects there are:

- Liebert and Schwartzberg (1977) see two primary effects: direct imitation and disinhibition.

- Hearold (1986) sees three primary effects: learning, incitement of violent acts, and catharsis.

- The *National Television Violence Study* (1997, 1998) perceives three primary effects: learning, desensitization, and fear.

- Comstock, Chaffee, Katzman, McCombs, and Roberts (1978) see four major effects: imitation, disinhibition, desensitization, and catharsis.

- Condry (1989) observes four primary effects: cultivation, imitation, disinhibition, and arousal versus desensitization. He says he considers arousal and desensitization together because they are part of the same process or mechanism, and aggression is positively related to both.

- Signorielli (1991) sees five primary effects: catharsis, observational learning, disinhibition, arousal, and cultivation.

- Gunter (1994) lists seven primary effects: catharsis, arousal, disinhibition, imitation, desensitization, cultivation, and fear.

The purpose of this chapter is to expand thinking about the range of possible effects of exposure to media violence. I present a list of 19 possible effects. This list is not meant to be definitive. Future research might find more effects, might cross some of the effects off this list, or might present a convincing case for combining two or more effects into one. This list is presented here to guide research by expanding our outlook on effects and by making us more sensitive to possible subtle differences across the variety of those effects. As the list will show, I am sometimes using several terms to label what is probably one effect; in other instances, I use one term to label what is likely many different effects.

[handwritten: list will change]

EXPANDING THINKING ABOUT EFFECTS
OF MEDIA VIOLENCE

To organize thinking about the range of possible effects on individuals, I begin with a matrix. One dimension of the matrix is the timing of the effect—either immediate or long-term. Recall from Chapter 3 that immediate effects happen during exposure or within a very short period of time afterward. They can last a long time, or they can dissipate within minutes. Long-term effects require an accumulation of exposure before they begin to emerge.

[handwritten: Dimensions (1) timing]

The second dimension of the effects matrix is the type of effect: physiological, emotional, cognitive, attitudinal, or behavioral. Physiological effects influence a person's automatic bodily processes, such as heart rate, blood pressure, pupil dilation, galvanic skin response, sweating, and so on. Emotional effects have a physiological basis, but the individual is aware of the physiological change and labels it either in a positive manner (e.g., love) or a negative manner (e.g., fear, hatred, anger). Cognitive effects are intellectual ones in which the mind acquires new information or the mind is active in generating the effect, such as generalization. Attitudinal effects are the creation, alteration, or reinforcement of a person's opinion. Behavioral effects activate people to perform an action.

[handwritten: (2) type]

Table 9.1 shows this 10-cell matrix. A total of 14 effects fit into one of these cells. Other effects cannot be put neatly into a cell. Some effects span several cells vertically or horizontally; these are the combination effects, which will be illuminated at the end of this chapter. First I will work through the 10 blocks on the grid with effects that lend themselves more easily to clean classification.

Physiological Effects

Media can influence our automatic bodily systems. These systems usually are beyond our conscious control; an example is contraction of the pupil of the eye when we look at a bright object. A suspenseful mystery elevates the blood pressure and heart rate. A horror film triggers rapid breathing and sweaty palms. A patriotic song might raise goose bumps on the skin. Erotic pictures can cause vaginal lubrication, penile tumescence, and increased heart rate (Malamuth & Check, 1980). A farce might make us laugh and unable to stop even when laughing becomes painful. Or music can calm and relax us by reducing our heartbeat and bringing our rate of breathing down to a regular, slow pace.

[handwritten: sweaty palms, goose bumps]

TABLE 9.1 Overview of Media Effects

Type of Effect	Timing of the Effect	
	Immediate	Long-Term
1 Physiological	1 Temporary fight or flight	2 Physiological habituation
2 Emotional	3 Temporary fear	4 Emotional habituation
3 Cognitive	5 Learning specific acts and lessons	6 Generalizing patterns 7 Learning social norms
4 Attitudinal	8 Creation or change of attitudes	9 Reinforcement of attitudes or beliefs
5 Behavioral	10 Imitation or copying 12 Disinhibition 11 Activation, triggering, or instigation 13 Attraction	14 Generalizing to novel behaviors

+ COMBINATION EFFECTS (P 132) – Catharsis, narcotizing,
excitation transfer, long-term triggering, cultivation

1. *Temporary Fight or Flight*. Exposure to violence can temporarily arouse people physiologically. During exposure, a person's heart rate and blood pressure increase. These physiological changes are the body's way of preparing to respond to the violence as if it were a real threat to the viewer. This type of arousal dissipates usually within an hour after exposure.

Tannenbaum and Zillmann (1975) found that participants who are exposed to violent material become physiologically aroused. When they label this arousal anger, they are more likely to aggress against others. But this effect is short-lived (Doob & Climie, 1972).

2. *Physiological Habituation*. This effect is the building up of physiological or emotional tolerance over the long term. With repeated fight-or-flight responses, the human body gradually builds up a resistance to exposure to media violence. For example, the first time people see a horror film, their bodies respond with a fight-or-flight reaction by substantially increasing heart rate and blood pressure. As they continue to view horror films over the years, the bodily reactions to these stimuli become less substantial; heart rate and blood pressure

still increase, but not as much. These viewers are building up a physiological tolerance to this type of message. In the extreme case, with massive exposure to this type of message, all physiological reactions to horror might even be extinguished.

Cline, Croft, and Courrier (1973) found evidence of this effect when they observed that children who were heavy TV viewers (watching 25 or more hr/week) were much less responsive to television violence in terms of physiological measures of arousal than were very light viewers (less than 4 hr/week). *example*

Zillmann (1982) explained habituation when he said that over time, "the depiction of both aggressive and sexual behavior became increasingly explicit and 'graphic.' It appears that stronger and stronger stimuli were called upon to provide the audience with excitement and, more important here, that the use of more and more powerful material became necessary to get the job done. At the heart of this impression is the suspicion that audiences have become callous, mainly because their arousal reactions have become habituated. In other words, initially strong excitatory reactions have become weak or have vanished entirely with repeated exposure to stimuli of a certain kind; and correspondingly, initially strong affective reactions have been blunted" (p. 61).

This habituation effect can begin with a single exposure to media violence. For example, Geen (1981) told participants in one study that the aggressive acts they saw were either justified or not justified. He found that participants who saw the violence characterized as justified were more aggressive, but only if they had been aroused beforehand by a tape low in violence; participants who had been aroused by a violent tape previously were not as aroused by the second viewing and therefore were less aggressive.

This habituation effect generalizes to real-world violence. Thomas, Horton, Lippincott, and Drabman (1977) found that participants who had seen violence on television were later less aroused by real-life scenes of aggression.

(2) Emotional Effects

The media can make us feel things. They can trigger strong emotions, such as fear, rage, and lust. They can also evoke weaker emotions, such as sadness, peevishness, and wariness. Emotional reactions are related to physiological changes. In fact, some psychological theoreticians posit that emotions are nothing more than physiological arousal (Schachter & Singer, 1962; Zillmann, 1991a, 1991b). If we feel a very high level of arousal and don't like it, we might label the feeling hate. But if we like the feeling, we might label it love. In Table *love+ hate* 9.1, emotions are treated primarily as feelings triggered by exposure to media violence.

3. *Temporary Fear.* One of the earliest recorded effects of media violence is that violence in films can produce intense fright reactions (Blumer, 1933; *fright*

Cantril, 1940; Dysinger & Ruckmick, 1933; Himmelweit, Oppenheim, & Vince, 1958; Sapolsky & Zillmann, 1978; Schramm, Lyle, & Parker, 1961; von Feilitzen, 1975; Wertham, 1954). Research on the immediate emotional reaction of fear, especially in children, has continued over the decades (Cantor, 1994; Cantor & Hoffner, 1990; Cantor & Reilly, 1982; Cantor & Sparks, 1984; Cantor, Wilson, & Hoffner, 1986; Osborn & Endsley, 1971; Sparks, 1986; Sparks & Cantor, 1986; Wilson, 1985; Wilson & Cantor, 1985).

The results of this line of research are fairly consistent. Fright as an immediate emotional response is typically of relatively short duration, but it may endure on occasion for several hours or days, or even longer. Its components are anxiety, distress, and increased physiological arousal, which are frequently engendered in viewers as a result of exposure to specific types of media productions (Cantor, 1994).

4. *Emotional Habituation.* Some portrayals are presented so often that we can no longer treat them with wonder or awe. Our tolerance has been increased so that the things that used to horrify or even upset us no longer do. This building of tolerance is especially important with the issue of violence. Viewing TV violence leads to lowered sensitivity to aggression and violence. And when people are exposed to violence continuously for a long period of time, this lowering of sensitivity is reinforced. For example, Van der Voort (1986) found this effect with children in the Netherlands: Heavy viewers of television became habituated to violence, and this habituation had a desensitization effect. The manifestation of this habituation was that heavy viewers became less quickly frightened by violent programs. Van der Voort also found a reduction in empathy among heavy viewers, who become jaded to the violence.

As children age, they are not as emotionally affected by certain portrayals that caused fear when they were younger. This inuring to violent portrayals is not attributable to accumulated exposure. There is something else. Cantor (1994) explains, "As children mature cognitively, some things become less likely to disturb them, whereas other things become potentially more upsetting" (p. 230). Younger children (ages 3-8) are frightened primarily by animals, the dark, supernatural beings, and anything that looks strange or moves suddenly. They focus on perceptually salient characteristics of portrayals, such as size, appearance, loud music, and the like. They are likely to be frightened by something that looks scary but is really harmless. Older children (ages 9-12) fear acts of physical destruction, as well as acts of personal injury to themselves and their relatives. They are affected strongly by the anticipation of bad events even more than the occurrence. Adolescents exhibit fear of personal injury and social fears, as well as fears of political, economic, and global issues. They are sensitive to psychological harm and physical harm.

As children age, their cognitive development shifts their strongest fear reactions from one type of portrayal to another; that is, they are more responsive to realistic and less responsive to fantastic dangers depicted in the media. This change is attributable to a shift from <u>perceptual processing</u> (something that looks scary) to <u>conceptual processing</u>. The repetitive exposure to media violence likely works in conjunction with the changes in cognitive ability to lead to a habituation effect for certain types of media violence.

But even after people have completed their childhood cognitive development, they can be gradually habituated to emotional responses to media violence. Thomas, Horton, Lippincott, and Drabman (1977) argued that "repeated observation of violent acts in dramatic television programs can result in the <u>blunting of viewers' emotional sensitivity to similar aggressive actions</u>" (p. 457).

Exposure to media violence may also have a <u>counterhabituation effect</u>. Cantor (1994) argues that "studies of long term effects do not provide evidence of a diminution of emotional responses with repeated exposure to stressful films," and "heavy viewing of frightening media is not associated with a lowering of reactivity to such fare" (p. 226). She <u>speculates that long-term exposure to violence may actually increase fear</u>. Clearly, more research is needed on this long-term effect.

Cognitive Effects

5. *Learning Specific Acts and Lessons.* If <u>learning is defined as the acquisition of facts so that they can be recalled later</u>, then exposure to media messages can certainly lead to an immediate learning effect. As we watch a movie, for example, we might learn how to defend ourselves with our fists or how to give someone we dislike a severely witty tongue-lashing.

Almost all of this learning from media violence is incidental; that is, we are viewing fictional programming for the purpose of being entertained, not for the purpose of becoming informed. And the producers of fictional programming are not trying to teach us anything about violence; they simply want to arouse and entertain us. Yet <u>learning takes place incidentally to the entertainment</u>. We encode into memory the particular details, as well as the implied lessons of certain portrayals.

<u>For incidental learning to occur, the learner must be passive</u>, not active. And this passiveness makes incidental learning a dangerous thing in the eyes of many television critics. <u>When viewers are passive, their defenses are down.</u> They are not aware that any learning is taking place, and hence they are not actively evaluating and processing the information.

6. _Generalizing Patterns._ A person watches a local news program and hears a story about a house that was vandalized in an area near his apartment. Then he hears on the radio that a local bank was robbed. Next he reads the newspaper and sees that there was an assault in his town the previous night. He has learned three facts—one from each message. But later that night he might generalize from these three facts and draw a conclusion that crime has become a real problem in his town. This specific conclusion was not given to him by the media, but the media provided him with some facts that set up his jump to this conclusion.

The mass media have been found to provide consistent messages that lead viewers to construct generalizations about the amount of crime and violence in society (Gerbner, Gross, Jackson-Beeck, Jeffries-Fox, & Signorielli, 1978; Hawkins & Pingree, 1982; Potter, 1994).

Sometimes such generalization results in a conclusion that does not reflect the real world. In such instances, one of three conditions exists: (a) The person has acquired false information from the media; (b) the person has been exposed to an imbalance of information (extreme depth in one narrow area and no breadth), and the result is a distorted picture; or (c) the person has accumulated a great number of facts and has not properly sorted or organized them.

7. _Learning Social Norms._ The learning of social norms is a special case of generalizing patterns. People can generalize patterns from individual exposures to the media even when those patterns are not social norms. For example, through repeated exposure to media violence, a person overestimates the rate of crime and the percentage of crimes that are cleared by an arrest. Although these are generalizations, they are not social norms. Social norms are generalized patterns from social information, rather than factual information. Social norms deal more with the rules of behavior in social situations than with society's factual parameters, such as the numbers of lawyers, crimes, trials, and executions.

As people gradually construct their generalizations about social norms from viewing individual media portrayals of violence, they look at how that violence is portrayed. For example, viewers have been found to generalize to a social norm that violence is acceptable in certain situations when they frequently see it justified in those situations (Collins, 1973; Hoffner & Cantor, 1985; Kaplan & Singer, 1976; Leifer & Roberts, 1972; Linne, 1976; Siegel, 1958; Thomas & Drabman, 1978).

Furthermore, the sheer repetition of violent portrayals is enough to lead people to generalize that violence is a typical way of dealing with problems in society. For this reason, the amount of exposure to TV violence is related to a willingness to use violence, suggest violence as a solution to conflict, and perceive violence as effective (Liebert, Neale, & Davidson, 1973; Tan, 1981). An empirical test of this relationship was conducted by Thomas and Drabman (1978). In an experiment on third and fifth graders, participants heard descriptions of nine conflict situations and were asked to predict how the average child would react in such a situation and what behavior would be most morally correct. Children who had been shown an aggressive film first were significantly more likely to choose aggressive responses as normative. As for moral correctness, younger participants and boys were more likely to allow for aggression. This effect was also found for college-age participants who viewed violent films during a 5-day period (Zillmann & Weaver, 1997). Consumption of gratuitous violence consistently fostered greater acceptance of violence as a way to resolve conflict resolution.

Generalizing to social norms can be a problem for younger children. Researchers have found that until about age 8, most children are unable to comprehend motives for aggression when the portrayal of the motive is separated from the portrayal of the aggression itself. When there is such a separation, younger children focus more on the aggressive act itself as their basis for evaluating the aggressor. Older children are able to link the motive to the act and take this into consideration when evaluating the aggressor (Collins, 1973; Collins, Berndt, & Hess, 1974). Therefore, the generalizations made by younger children often differ from those of older children.

These social norms learned from media messages are often applied in real-world situations. For example, Siegel (1958) found that children used the media portrayals to make attributions about real people. Children who had heard a radio play about a taxi driver who used aggression to solve his problems were more likely to believe that real-life taxi drivers are aggressive.

Attitudinal Effects

We have known for a long time that the major effect of the media is the reinforcing of already existing attitudes, opinions, and beliefs (Berelson & Steiner, 1964; Klapper, 1960), but the media can also create and change beliefs (McGuire, 1973). This effect works in the long term and in the short term (Adler et al., 1980; Atkin, 1982; Gerbner, Gross, Morgan, & Signorielli, 1994; Tan, 1981).

8. *Immediate Creation or Change of Attitudes.* A person's attitude can be created or changed with as little as a single exposure to the media. For example, researchers have shown that when people are exposed to a violent television show, they show an immediate drop in sympathetic attitude (Drabman & Thomas, 1974; Molitor & Hirsch, 1994; Thomas & Drabman, 1975). Among children and adults, even watching a single violent film can make them temporarily less aware of and less concerned about aggressive acts in others (Drabman & Thomas, 1974).

9. *Long-Term Reinforcement of Attitudes or Beliefs.* Because the media provide so many messages of violence and because those messages are usually

presented with the same cluster of contextual factors, viewers' existing attitudes about violence are reinforced over time. This is a clear conclusion of many research studies (Cline et al., 1973; Drabman & Thomas, 1974; Greenberg, 1975; Kaplan & Singer, 1976; Thomas & Drabman, 1975; Thomas et al., 1977).

⑤ Behavioral Effects

Most of the experimental effects research has focused on behavioral outcomes. Researchers expose participants to violent portrayals and then watch what the participants do in response.

10. *Imitation or Copying.* This effect may be the one that is most responsible for the public's negative opinion about the effect of media violence. Periodically, a copycat crime appears in the news. In addition, criminals sometimes use the defense that they saw a violent act on television and could not help themselves from copying it.

The public is also concerned that young children mimic the violent behavior they see in the media. Research has found this concern to be valid (Bandura, 1978, 1979, 1982, 1985; Centerwall, 1993; Comstock et al., 1978; Liebert & Schwartzberg, 1977; Tan, 1981; Walters & Willows, 1968). For example, Centerwall says that children as young as 14 months "demonstrably observe and incorporate behavior seen on television" (p. 56). Children are aware of their copying violent acts. In a survey of young children, 60% said they frequently copied behaviors they had seen on television (Liebert et al., 1973).

Apparently the copying effect does not last more than a few months. Kniveton (1973) repeatedly observed children who were exposed to a model behaving aggressively in a film. There was an imitative effect immediately after the exposure, but it was gone within 4 months.

11. *Activation, Triggering, or Instigation.* Activation is different from imitation. With imitation, the viewer mimics behavior just seen. With activation, the media portrayal triggers a previously learned behavior. For example, after seeing cartoon characters beating each other over the head with rubber hammers, children might imitate this behavior if they have rubber hammers available at the time. But let's say that several days later they are in a toy store and they see some rubber hammers. If their memory reminds them that they learned this action, the presence of the hammers now makes it possible for them to perform the behavior. Thus, their later violent behavior was triggered by the cued memory of a violent action learned from the media. This effect sometimes goes by the term *instigation* (Caprara, D'Imperio, et al., 1984).

12. *Disinhibition.* Exposure to media violence can reduce viewers' normal inhibitions that prevent them from behaving in a violent manner. This effect has been found with children (Liebert & Baron, 1972, 1973; Lovaas, 1961), espe-

cially with boys (Liebert & Schwartzberg, 1977), and with adults (see Hearold, 1986).

Although the disinhibition effect can occur immediately after viewing, it can also last a while, especially when viewers are continually exposed to violent messages (Liebert & Schwartzberg, 1977; Tan, 1981).

13. *Attraction.* A behavioral effect that is often overlooked is attraction. Viewers keep searching out violent television shows, movies, novels, lyrics on CDs, and so on. Perhaps the reason there is not more research on this effect is that the few studies that have been reported have inexplicably concluded that violence in a show is not related to audience enjoyment or popularity of the programs. For example, Himmelweit, Swift, and Jaeger (1980) explained that the audience is the continual critic of television programming and that programmers cancel shows that people do not like and try to find shows that people will watch in large numbers. They said that "the enjoyment of a program depends on the kind of arousal it evokes" and that "the arousal is associated with enjoyment when it is moving, absorbing, and exciting, but unpleasant when it is disturbing, brutal, and unpredictable" (p. 94). In a study they conducted, Himmelweit et al. found that ratings of violence were not related to ratings of enjoyment. In addition, violence was not correlated with the attributes exciting, absorbing, or moving, but it was correlated with the attribute brutal.

Among Finnish television viewers, Mustonen and Pulkkinen (1993) found no correlation between the audience size for a program and the rate or brutality of aggression. They said that the "most popular programs such as quiz shows, news, and family serials did not contain aggression at all or were only mildly aggressive" (p. 181).

14. *Generalizing to Novel Behaviors.* The media can influence behaviors not just in specific actions, but in a general long-term manner (Comstock et al., 1978; McHan, 1985). The resulting effect can show up as behavior that is very different from any of the particular portrayals viewed by that person, because viewers can generalize from particular violent behaviors to a broader class of behaviors. For example, a woman might watch a media portrayal of a man who is unfairly denied a raise at work and then at night sneaks into his boss's office and breaks everything. Several days after seeing this portrayal, the woman's boss insults her just for being female, so that night she paints his car pink. She is not copying the media-portrayed behavior; instead, she has generalized a pattern of righteous retaliation, which she altered to fit her particular circumstances.

This effect is not a simple one; it works through several stages of influence. For example, Van der Voort (1986) found that heavier viewers of television tend to be exposed to more violence; through this exposure, they develop a liking for violent portrayals; this liking leads them to be less likely to rate the violence as terrible; their higher tolerance for violence then leads them to be more likely to act aggressively when they are given the opportunity in their lives. In contrast, children who are easily frightened and emotionally touched by the violent behavior they see in the media are more shocked by it; their shocked reactions lead them to a more critical stand when exposed to violence both in the media and in real life; their critical viewing decreases their tolerance for violence; their low toleration prevents them from choosing aggressive actions when given the chance to behave aggressively in their own lives.

COMBINATION EFFECTS

The effects presented in the preceding discussion were shown to fit relatively well into one of the 10 blocks in the grid in Table 9.1. However, other effects that are often mentioned by researchers do not fit well, primarily because they span several types. These effects are discussed here as combination effects.

Note that each of these terms refers to several discrete effects that are usually linked together in a single process; hence, the single name. But these discrete primary effects need not necessarily work in unison; some of the primary effects may be missing or may operate in an opposite manner. These differences may explain why, for some of these effect terms, the literature contains conflicting results.

15. *Catharsis.* The idea of catharsis as an effect of exposure to entertaining messages goes back to the writings of Aristotle. This idea resurfaced with Freud and most recently with Feshbach in the media effects literature. Catharsis has been conceptualized as an effect that gives viewers release from their own aggressive drives as they vicariously participate in the violence they see in drama (Feshbach, 1955), especially among viewers with weak imaginations to fantasize (Feshbach, 1972). But Gunter (1980) argued that people with well-developed imaginations are more able to become absorbed in violent portrayals and thereby discharge their anger.

Catharsis is regarded as a combination effect because it involves physiologically manifested drives that are experienced as emotions of anger or frustration. For catharsis to take place, a viewer must be aware of a heightened drive state along with strong emotions and then feel these drop throughout the exposure or at least during the climactic scenes.

Feshbach has published findings in support of catharsis (1955, 1961, 1972). For example, Feshbach and Singer (1971) found that aggressive boys were able to use exposure to media violence as a way to discharge their aggressive impulses through viewing and later not behave as aggressively.

These studies of Feshbach have been challenged because they are considered not a good test of catharsis (Comstock et al., 1978; Liebert, Sobol, & Davidson, 1972; Wells, 1973) and because no one has been able to replicate the findings, although some have tried (e.g., see Wells, 1973). Berkowitz (1962) argued that the reduction of aggression that Feshbach found was not catharsis, but inhibition induced by the experiment.

Despite the controversy, speculation continues about catharsis as an effect of watching media violence. Reviews of the effects literature continue to acknowledge this effect (Comstock et al., 1978; Gunter, 1994; Signorielli, 1991).

16. *Narcotizing.* Narcotizing is a combination effect in the way it dulls our physiological and emotional reactions while controlling our behavior in the form of continued exposure. Himmelweit et al. (1980) argued that people can become habituated to beatings and car chases as they can to barbiturates. They speculated that producers of empty excitement action series "might be tempted to increase the dosage and opt for even more violent happenings . . . but this could be self-defeating since habituation to the new level might soon set in" (p. 95).

[margin handwriting: increase dosage]

This belief that media violence could act as a narcotic has been around for many decades. Blumer (1933) warned of "media possession" in which viewers lose control over their feelings and perceptions. Preston (1941) argued that people could become addicted to media horrors. Critics—such as Edith Winn in her book *The Plug-In Drug* (1977)—caution that television hooks children into entertainment, keeps their brains functioning at a low level, and makes them passive acceptors of the media messages as presented. In addition, Marcuse (1966) argued that the mass media in the United States hammer the population into having a one-dimensional mind; that is, people's minds become paralyzed so that they are incapable of independent thought; they cannot criticize or oppose the messages in which they become immersed.

There may be something to these speculations. The *United States Statistical Abstract* (1995) says that the average person spends 3,297 hours with the media a year; that's about 9 hours each day. About half of this time is spent watching television. Even after it has been acknowledged that much of this time with the media overlaps with other activities, it is clear that most people are spending most of their waking hours exposing themselves to some form of media. Because violence is such a pervasive and continuous message throughout the media, it can be argued that people are addicted to media violence. This point, of course, is arguable. But if this point had no value, we would have to see a much more powerful and widespread criticism of media violence. Instead, it appears as if our society has gotten used to the high level of violence and no longer notices much of it.

[margin handwriting: media exposure in U.S.]

17. *Excitation Transfer.* This effect is a combination effect because it requires physiological arousal and emotional or attitudinal labeling. In addition, it is observed with behavioral measures. Zillmann (1982) makes an important distinction between two types of physiological arousal. One type is cortical arousal, which involves the processes that govern attention and perception. The

[margin handwriting: physiological or emotional or attitudinal labeling]

other type is autonomic arousal, which involves emotional reactions. Autonomic arousal is of more concern here, because it is what sets up the fight-or-flight emotion when people are exposed to violence.

Zillmann (1971) theorized that not only is arousal a key element in explaining aggressive effects from the media, but the arousal that is generated with one particular activity or message can be transferred to another activity. In an experiment, Zillmann showed participants an erotic film, an aggressive film, and a neutral film. It was not the aggressive film, but rather the erotic film, that led to the most subsequent aggression among the participants. Zillmann explained that the erotic film was more arousing than the aggressive one and that the strongest arousal leads to the strongest effects. He found that the arousal generated by the erotic film could be transferred into aggressive activity.

Zillmann (1991b) also explains that arousal is viewed as an energizer of thoughts and behaviors. It needs direction, however, because arousal by itself is not guided. So the arousal from a viewing experience can lead to either prosocial or antisocial reactions, depending on the prevailing social circumstances and the dispositions of the individual. In addition, arousal can be generated by many different kinds of media fare, especially strong violence, "titillating sexual fare and hilarious comedy" (p. 118). But the arousal from exposure to the media is short-lived, usually dissipating within several minutes after exposure.

18. *Long-Term Triggering.* Some researchers have hypothesized that television teaches people to commit criminal behavior—such as larceny—indirectly. For example, Hennigan et al. (1982) argued that exposure to affluent lifestyles on television, along with high levels of advertising for consumer goods, teaches viewers over time that to be happy in the United States (or even to be part of the mainstream) requires participation in the high level of materialism. Poor people who cannot buy goods are being tempted to commit crimes to acquire those goods.

Triggering is a combination effect because it is primarily behavioral, but the factors required in the long-term lead-up to the triggering are cognitive and attitudinal.

19. *Cultivation.* A good deal of research supports the hypothesis that heavy exposure to the world of television, which is saturated with violent portrayals, leads people to construct unrealistically high estimates of risk of victimization and a corresponding belief that the world is a mean and violent place (Bryant, Carveth, & Brown, 1981; Carveth & Alexander, 1985; Gerbner et al., 1977; Hawkins & Pingree, 1980, 1981a, 1981b; Morgan, 1983, 1986; Ogles & Hoffner, 1987; Potter, 1991a, 1991b; Rouner, 1984; Signorielli, 1990; Weaver & Wakshlag, 1986; Wober, 1978; Zillmann & Wakshlag, 1985).

This type of fear is generalized from individual instances in news and entertainment. Over time, this generalization is reinforced through continued exposure to violence in all forms across all types of messages. This type of fear shows up as a cognitive effect (overestimation of the risks from violence), as attitudinal (belief that the world is mean and violent), and behavioral (purchase of locks for doors, avoidance of strangers, etc.). The cultivation effect is measured with generalized cognitions (estimates of risk), as well as beliefs about the world's being mean and violent.

The argument has been made convincingly that the media have created a moral panic with all their coverage of crime and violence. For example, Chiricos (1996) points out that in the early 1990s, there was a particular fixation on high-profile crimes in the national news media and that during that time the percentage of Americans ranking crime or violence as the nation's foremost problem jumped from 9% to 49%.

UMBRELLA TERMS — *fear, desensitization + learning*

Finally, some frequently used terms refer to several of the effects on the preceding list. I call these umbrella terms. Umbrella terms are not the same as the terms for combination effects. Combination effects are unified processes of influence that cut across two or more of the blocks in the grid. They join two or more types, or they move from an immediate effect to a long-term effect that is more than just the continuation of an immediate effect. In contrast, an umbrella term is a popularly used phrase that appears to refer to a media effect *definition* but really indicates a variety of effects of very different types. The different effects covered by the umbrella are not usually linked together in a unified process of influence. On the contrary, they refer to several different processes requiring very different operationalizations. The use of umbrella terms is a *why umbrella* problem because we cannot be sure to which of the component effects the user *terms are a* of the term is referring. These umbrella terms are *fear, desensitization,* and *problem* especially *learning.*

Fear

There is no doubt that exposure to media violence can cause fear in viewers (for a review, see Cantor, 1994). However, the fear effect is far from monolithic, and when scholars use the term *fear,* it is difficult to understand what they mean unless they are clear in delineating which component of the fear effect they *emotional* mean. One component—the one usually addressed—is a combination of emo- *+ psychological* tion tied strongly to physiological arousal, both as an immediate effect (Cantor & Reilly, 1982; Himmelweit et al., 1958; Sapolsky & Zillmann, 1978; von Feilitzen, 1975) and as a long-term effect (Cantor, 1994). A second component considers *fear effect* to be a synonym for *cultivation,* which itself is a combina- *cognitive* tion of cognitive and attitudinal influences and measures. These two compo- *+ attitudinal* nents are very different in their conceptualizations, processes of effect, and sets of operationalizations.

Desensitization

The various uses of the term *desensitization* are very broad, spanning across all five types of effects both as an immediate effect and as a long-term effect. As an immediate effect, desensitization has been examined as a cognitive, an attitudinal, and a behavioral effect.

In looking at desensitization as an immediate cognitive effect, Feshbach and Roe (1968) examined children's perceptions of pictures of other children involved in violence. They reported that children try to distance themselves from victims of violence so that they regard themselves as less similar to the portrayals. Feshbach and Roe tried to link cognitions with affective states but found that although children could comprehend and recognize the emotional states of the children in the pictures, the participants did not automatically translate this recognition into empathy.

As an immediate attitudinal effect, exposure to media violence has been found to change the attitudes of both children and adults about violence and its victims (Thomas et al., 1977). The type of attitude most often measured in this type of experiment is toleration of violence. Tolerance for violence has been found to increase in adults who have been exposed to strong violence against women (Linz, Donnerstein, & Penrod, 1984, 1988a) or even relatively mild forms of violence (Thomas, 1982). Adult males who watched erotic aggressive films were found to be less sympathetic to rape victims. After viewing five such films in one experiment, males came to perceive the films as less violent and consider them less degrading to women (Linz et al., 1984).

As an immediate behavioral effect, children have been found to be less helpful to victims after they are exposed to violence. For example, Drabman and Thomas (1974) showed their participants (third- and fourth-grade boys and girls) a film and then had them watch other children play as the play escalated into fighting. Participants who had seen the aggressive film took longer to seek help and therefore had been desensitized to real-life violence. Similar findings are reported by Thomas and Drabman (1975), who ran their experiment on slightly younger children (first and third graders).

Over the long term, people, even children, have been shown to exhibit physiological habituation to media violence, especially among the heaviest viewers of TV violence (Cline et al., 1973). This habituation may begin even during exposure to a single program. For example, people who watch graphic violence in a film usually exhibit strong physiological responses, but these responses steadily decline during the exposure (Lazarus & Alfert, 1964; Lazarus, Speisman, Mordkoff, & Davison, 1962; Speisman, Lazarus, Mordkoff, & Davidson, 1964). Also in the long term, exposure to media violence can increase tolerance for violence (Linz, Donnerstein, & Penrod, 1988a, 1988b).

On the positive side, people can also become desensitized to the things they fear through repeated exposure to these violent characters and actions in the media. For example, experimenters have found that gradual, repeated showing of frightening material in a nonthreatening environment can gradually reduce children's fear of particular characters, such as the Incredible Hulk (Cantor & Sparks, 1984; Sparks & Cantor, 1986) or the Wizard of Oz (Cantor & Wilson, 1984; Wilson, Hoffner, & Cantor, 1987).

Learning

The most troublesome of these umbrella terms is *learning* because it has been used to refer to so many different types of effects, as well as processes of influence. Learning has been regarded as a cognitive effect, as the ability to recall how a crime was committed, or as the practice of generalizing from individual exposures to broad patterns about how the world works. The term *learning* has also been used to refer to the acquisition of a particular attitude about a victim. *Learning* has been used to refer to the exhibiting of behaviors in the short-term triggering process or the learning of social norms regarding violence throughout one's lifetime. Learning sometimes is regarded as formal learning, such as perceiving and encoding facts (or cues) about violence from a depiction, but more often it is regarded as incidental learning—coming to understand how social situations work by observing role models. In addition, these conceptions of learning have been operationalized in many different ways, such as expressing an attitude, recalling a fact, making an estimate, paying attention, copying behavior, generalizing behavior, and so on. Given all this variety, it is not possible to look at the literature and answer the seemingly simple question, Is there a learning effect from exposure to media violence?

RECOMMENDATIONS

We need to develop a broader view of effects of exposure to media violence. Exposure to media violence has many effects, both immediately and over the long term. In this chapter, I have enumerated 19 of them, but there are likely many more.

We need to use effects terms more consistently. If scholars are able to develop a consensus of the meaning of the terms used to indicate the various effects, research results can be communicated much more efficiently. At present, in some cases terms are stretched to cover several different effects, and in other cases multiple terms are used to refer to essentially the same effect.

10

Risk to viewers

How can we determine the degree of risk to viewers of media violence? This general question has three facets. First, we need to determine what the risk is for—that is, what the different effects are. Second, we need to analyze different violent portrayals to determine which elements influence the risk. Third, we need to determine what different characteristics of people place different viewers at risk.

A strong line of effects research has laid the foundation for risk assessment. We know there are many negative effects (see Chapter 9), but most of the research has been limited to the effects of disinhibition, immediate fear, and cultivation of fear. We know a good deal about which contextual factors are associated with negative effects, but we do not have a good idea of the relative strength of each of these factors, nor do we have a good idea about how these factors interact with one another. We know something about which characteristics of people put viewers at greater risk, but there is much to learn about how these characteristics interact with contextual factors.

In short, we have made a very good start in addressing the task of assessing risk, but much work remains to be done. The purpose of this chapter is to review what has been done, so as to develop a strong rationale for what effects research needs to address next.

WHAT WE KNOW

Effects research has made good progress in delineating a list of contextual factors that are associated with negative effects—at least disinhibition, fear, and desensitization—of exposure to media portrayals of violence (see Chapter 3). Key among these factors are the following: rewards and punishments, consequences, identification with perpetrators, attractiveness of perpetrators, motives, justification, appropriateness, realism, humor, production techniques, presence of weapons, and sexual portrayals linked with violence.

This list of key contextual factors gives us the terms for a risk formula, but as of now, we have very little idea how to assemble those terms into a summary index of risk. We need much more research that examines how contextual factors interact with characteristics of viewers.

Context-Context Interactions

Contextual factors in portrayals of violence in the media interact with each other. Thus far, the research has identified six interactions between pairs of contextual factors. There are likely many more. In addition, three-way and multiway interactions are likely. With all this contextual information available, it is highly likely that viewers do not regard each of these cues as equally valuable in constructing their overall judgments of the meaning of a violent episode. Instead, some interactions probably cancel out the influence of certain factors while increasing the influence of others. In this area, more research is clearly needed.

Punishment and Justification

Bryant, Carveth, and Brown (1981) ran an experiment with two treatment groups. One group was exposed to programs offering a clear triumph of justice: The transgressive acts were punished by personal vengeance, by retribution provided by an affiliated agent, or through legal restitution. The other group saw an equal number of violent acts in which there was a preponderance of injustice—the majority of transgressive acts going unpunished. The viewers in the unpunished condition developed significantly increased levels of anxiety. Thus, there appears to be an interaction between justification and punishment.

Strategy and Success

Lando and Donnerstein (1978) found an interaction between the problem-solving strategy of a filmed model and the success or failure of the strategy. Neither characteristic was significant by itself. Participants who saw a success-ful aggressive model *and* those who saw an unsuccessful nonaggressive model both showed the most aggressiveness subsequent to the viewing.

Pain and Humor

Deckers and Carr (1986) found ratings of pain to be related to the degree of humor of newspaper cartoons. Pain ratings were superior to aggression ratings in predicting cartoon humor.

Realism and Consequences

Gunter (1983) found that when consequences of violence are shown, viewers think the violence is much more serious than when no consequences are shown.

However, this finding holds only for relatively realistic content and not for fantasy.

Motive and Role

A viewer's interpretation of motive is shaped by the role of a character, and this interpretation relates to judgments of violence. To illustrate, Lincoln and Levinger (1972) showed their experimental subjects a picture of a white police officer grabbing an African American man by the shirt. Subjects who were told that the action took place at a peace rally rated the action as violent, but subjects who were told nothing assumed the police officer was subduing a criminal and did not rate the action as violent.

Fantasy and Humor

Sprafkin, Gadow, and Grayson (1988) ran an experiment on 26 emotionally disturbed children (6 to 9 years old), exposing the participants to either six aggressive cartoons or six control cartoons. The control cartoons resulted in more nonphysical aggression from participants. The investigators explained that there may have been a confounding factor in the treatment conditions. The aggressive cartoons showed fantasy characters in repeated humorous acts of aggression. The nonaggressive cartoons featured a realistic animated drama that was suspenseful throughout a narrative adventure. Therefore, the "control" materials were likely to be perceived as more realistic and arousing.

flaw

Context-Viewer Interactions

Research has documented some interactions of a contextual variable with a demographic variable, such as age, gender, race, or culture. In addition, there are reactions with psychological traits, such as locus of control. Likely many more (and untested) characteristics of individuals (e.g., intoxication) can help explain interpretations of violence across individuals.

Age

Age interacts with perceptions of reality. Hapkiewicz (1979) conducted a review of the literature on children's reactions to cartoon violence. After analyzing 10 studies, he concluded that young children (under 6) do not make good distinctions among puppets, cartoons, and humans in terms of reality. Taylor and Howell (1973) found that children's ability to distinguish reality from fantasy increases with age from 3 to 5. Wright, Huston, Reitz, and Piemyat (1994) found that by age 5, children can distinguish the factuality of programming—that is, they can tell the difference between fictional programs and news or documentary—and that they improve at this ability with age. The learning comes not in believing that TV is fiction; 5-year-olds know this. The learning comes in figuring out what is nonfiction.

Gender

Gender interacts with the influence of reality-based programming, presentational style, and humor. Hapkiewicz and Stone (1974) ran an experiment on 180 elementary school children and found no significant differences on film (real-life aggression, aggressive cartoons, or nonaggressive films), but they did find an interaction with sex. Boys who viewed a realistic aggressive film were significantly more aggressive in play than boys who viewed other films.

Alvarez, Huston, Wright, and Kerkman (1988) found that children (ages 5-11) exhibit sex differences in their attention to violence. Boys' visual attention was generally higher. Girls preferred programs with low action rather than high action. There were no differences in comprehension, which led these researchers to speculate that girls pay greater attention to verbal auditory content, while boys pay more attention to visual content.

As for humor, Mueller and Donnerstein (1977) found that males were not affected by listening to a humorous audiotape. But in females the level of arousal was reduced after listening to the low-arousal tape. The investigators found that high-arousal humor did nothing to reduce a person's level of aggression, but with females, low-arousal humor did reduce their aggression.

Race

Baron (1979) found that pain cues from a same-race victim had a stronger effect on participants' subsequent aggressive behavior than did pain cues from a victim of another race. For example, with white participants, pain cues from nonwhites were less effective than pain cues from whites in inhibiting subsequent aggression from nonangry whites and in facilitating aggression from angry whites.

Culture

There appear to be cultural differences in the interaction between heroes and seriousness. Gunter (1985) found that American viewers rated violence by villains as more serious than violence by heroes, whereas British viewers rated violence by heroes as more serious than violence by villains.

Locus of Control

Prerost (1989) ran an experiment on 144 female undergraduates in a $2 \times 2 \times 3$ design of locus of control (internal and external), arousal of anger (arousal and nonarousal), and jokes (neutral humor, aggressive humor, and nonhumorous jokes). Locus of control was significant, with internals using humor to reduce anger. Internals who were angered enjoyed the aggressive humor the most.

Intoxication

Schmutte and Taylor (1980) found that high pain feedback reduced the aggression of only nonintoxicated participants; highly intoxicated participants still behaved aggressively.

Effect Sizes

What are the comparative effect sizes among these contextual factors? Two meta reviews of the literature help us answer this question. Hearold (1986) conducted a meta-analysis of 1,043 effects studies of television on social behavior and reported that justified and realistic violence in particular had comparatively large effects. Unjustified aggression, negative consequences for violence, and a decidedly unsympathetic perpetrator were aspects that minimized the influence of the portrayal. However, cartoon violence has a larger effect than nonanimated violence. Hearold also found support for arousal theory (Zillmann, 1979): The effect was stronger when the treatment was interesting. The physiological arousal is greater for young children than for older persons. In addition, frustration and provocation have contributed to the size of effects. However, the effects are still positive and strong even when viewers are not frustrated, so frustration is not a necessary condition.

Paik and Comstock (1994) conducted a meta-analysis of 217 studies of the effects of television violence on antisocial behavior and reported the finding that portrayals in which the viewer identified with the perpetrator had a slightly higher effect. In addition, episodes with justified violence had a greater effect. Surprisingly, episodes in which violence was rewarded showed almost no difference from those that showed violence being punished.

THE NEED FOR THEORETICAL CALCULUS

Given the evidence on interactions thus far, it is likely that many other untested interactions are influencing the way viewers construct their meaning of violent portrayals. Bandura (1994) is one theoretician who acknowledges that many factors (such as the reality of the portrayals and whether the models are rewarded) are simultaneously interacting in this complex process of influence. He speculates that "reciprocality does not mean that the different sources of influences are of equal strength. Some may be stronger than others" (p. 61), but he does not elaborate on this point by specifying what those influences might be.

Thus, it is important to design effects experiments with more attention to interactions. Understandably, experiments limit their examination to a small set of key variables. The isolation of a key factor while controlling the influence of others is an important strength of the experimental methodology. This strength is responsible for our high degree of confidence that certain individual variables influence the disinhibition process. However, when violence appears on the television screen, many contextual factors appear simultaneously, and all are available to influence viewers' interpretations of the meaning of the message. Therefore, we need to focus more attention on interactions. We need to know which factors interact, if the presence of some factors amplifies the effect of particular others, or if the influence of some factors cancels out the influence of others.

Until we have more guidance from the results of multivariate experiments that focus on interactions, we are left with arbitrarily constructing scales of risk. Gerbner and his colleagues were forced to do this several decades ago when they first developed a violence index, containing three elements: "the percent of programs with any violence at all, the frequency and rate of violent episodes, and the number of roles calling for characterizations as violents, victims, or both" (Gerbner & Gross, 1976, p. 185). To compute their index, Gerbner and his colleagues took the rate figure, doubled it, and then added it to the prevalence percentage and the number of roles involved in violence. They said that the "index itself is not a statistical finding but serves as a convenient illustrator of trends and facilitates gross comparisons" (p. 185). Although the elements used to construct the scale are relevant indicators of the amount of violent portrayals on television, the problem is that no discernible logic guides the way in which these measures with different metrics are assembled into a single scale. Therefore, it is very difficult to understand what the resulting score from such an index means.

The problem Gerbner and his colleagues had two decades ago is still with us today. Although the experimental literature has elaborated the list of contextual variables that viewers use to interpret the meaning of violence, we still do not have a sense of the relative importance of these factors in contributing to risk. In sum, the theories and the experimental research have been very useful in identifying contextual characteristics that lead to risks, but they are weak in modeling processes of influence to explain how those risk factors work together.

A Test

To test the implications of arbitrarily constructing scales of risk, I constructed several alternative scales for a disinhibition effect (Potter, 1996). If several different arbitrary constructions of scales all result in the same types of programs, genres, and TV channels being ranked high on risk, then risk is robust and scale construction is not a major problem. But if the results differ significantly across scale constructions, then we have evidence that results are not robust but are sensitive to the way the scales are constructed.

For this test, I selected the seven contextual variables (rewards and punishments, consequences, motive and justification, realism, humor, identification with perpetrators, and arousal) that are most closely linked to a disinhibition effect (see Chapter 3). I assembled these seven factors into four different scales of risk. The scales differed only in terms of how the seven contextual variables were assembled; that is, each scale presented a different version of where the risk is.

To provide an empirical test of the thesis, four alternative test scales were constructed. These were not presented in a competition to identify the best among the four, because we have no criterion of judging "best" at this point. Instead, they were offered to provide a test of comparison across different kinds of operationalizations. Each of these scales differs substantially from the others in the way it assembles data from the contextual variables into a single score of risk.

One model for construction of a scale was the simple sum of the presence of the contextual measures. A second model used humor and fantasy as "toggle switches"; that is, when either of these factors was present, the value of the scale was reduced to zero. The third model highlighted interactions among pairs of variables. Thus, the presence of X or Y by itself does not increase the risk, but when both are present together, the risk is increased. The fourth model used the formula from the interaction model and then weighted the resulting values according to how imitable the particular acts of violence were.

The four risk models showed differences in patterns when compared across genres, networks, and lengths of programs. For example, the risk scores on Model 1 across networks revealed that Fox's programming shows a significantly lower risk compared to the programming of other networks. With Model 2, Fox is grouped with ABC and NBC. And with Models 3 and 4, Fox is significantly higher in risk than the other networks. NBC shows the lowest risk of all networks on Models 3 and 4, but it exhibits the highest risk in Model 2.

Clearly, the way the scales are constructed makes a difference. Using the same contextual variables, one scale construction shows that NBC presents the most risky programming. But if another construction is used, Fox presents the riskiest programming.

Which formula for scale construction of risks is the best one? This is an extremely important question. Unfortunately, we do not know the answer at this time. I do not argue for a particular scale construction above all others, because too much speculation would be required to do so. Instead, in the remainder of this chapter I present some guidelines to expand our thinking about scale construction. My intention is to stimulate creative thinking about how scales could be constructed, followed by empirical testing of those speculated constructions. Only by undertaking such a process can we develop confidence in our estimates of risk of exposure to media violence.

RECOMMENDATIONS

We need more multivariate experimental research. Most of the experimental research uses two or three independent variables. We need to expand this number to four or five independent variables tested at the same time. In this way, we can assess where the interactions are. The tests for interactions should focus both on sets of contextual variables themselves and on interactions between contextual variables and viewer characteristics.

We need a stronger focus on reporting the strength of effects. Almost all the experimental research is limited to reporting whether findings were statistically significant. Although testing for significance is important, it is only the first step. Researchers also need to provide readers with a sense of how much variance is accounted for by each variable. It is no longer sufficient merely to report that a variable showed an influence on the dependent measure; we need to see a rank ordering of the individual influences of each of the independent variables, as well as the interactions among them. The rank orderings would provide valuable information to guide the weighting of factors in scales of risk. The resulting scale scores then would give us a better sense of the probability of the effect.

We need to think more broadly in our conceptualizations of relationships among variables. The complexity of the effects process is not reflected solely in the requirement for many contributory variables. The real complexity—and the biggest challenge in theorizing—is in conceptualizing how these variables interlock as pieces in a puzzle. Once we figure out the fit of these individual pieces, we will be able to see the big picture.

We need to avoid the default thinking built into the most popular of our statistical tests of association and differences. That is, we must think beyond the idea that relationships are positive, linear, symmetrical, sufficient, general, and direct. Instead, we need to think in terms of the following eight factors: shape of relationships, symmetry, thresholds, necessary versus sufficient conditions, contingent effects, countervailing forces, direct versus indirect influences, and structural modeling. We must move beyond the limited emphasis on summary indicators of the strength of relationships and examine more deeply the *nature* of relationships.

1. *Shape of Relationships.* The usual statistics for association are tests of linear relationships. In a linear process, one unit of input is associated with one unit of output. A linear effect is illustrated when viewers who are exposed to one violent message move one step closer to an effect, and viewers who are exposed to two violent messages move two steps closer to an effect, and so on. That is, the number of exposures is an exact predictor of the number of steps toward an effect.

But the media effect process is rarely linear. For example, the learning effect is a hyperbola in which viewers keep increasing exposures with very little change in effect until a break point at which the steps toward an effect increase much faster than the number of exposures.

Media research shows many other nonlinear relationships. The S-curve expresses the rate of diffusion of innovations in a society. The J-curve expresses the relationship between the use of the mass media and the importance of an event. Other examples are the bell curve, the advertising-exposure plateau curve (3-10 exposures optimal), and the sine curve. Nonlinear relationships need not even be expressed as curves. For example, an effect could be represented as jagged peaks that indicate the sudden influence of catastrophic events.

2. *Symmetry.* The Pearson product-moment correlation test is a symmetric one. Let's say we find that $r = .15$ in a test of association between exposure to media violence and a cultivation measure. This single summary statistic ($r = .15$) is an indicator of mutual association—that is, the influence of exposure on cultivation, as well as the influence of cultivation on exposure. But if we are skeptical that both directions are equally strong, we assume there is an asymmetric relationship in which exposure influences cultivation much more strongly than cultivation influences exposure. To test this hypothesis, we need a different quantitative analysis.

To illustrate, suppose we have data from 100 respondents. We find that 40 have very high exposure to media violence and that 25 of these also have very high scores on a scale of long-term fear of the real world (the cultivation measure). If we run a symmetric test of association, we are likely to get a fairly weak coefficient—that is, a small percentage of respondents (25%) at the high end of both distributions (violence exposure and fear scale), but the remaining respondents showing little consistency in their positions in the two distributions. If we stop the analysis at this point, we are forced to conclude that the relationship is very weak or nonexistent. If we test for an asymmetric relationship, however, we find that all 25 high scorers on the fear scale also are very high on the exposure scale. We must conclude that to have a high fear score, a respondent must have very high exposure to media violence. In short, high exposure to media violence is a necessary condition for a high fear score. However, it is not a sufficient condition, because 15 respondents have high exposure without also having high fear scores. This type of relationship has been found with cultivation (Potter, 1991a).

Most tests of relationships assume a symmetric association. Thus, a finding of a weak or nonexistent relationship does not necessarily mean that there is no type of relationship, only that there is no symmetric relationship.

3. *Thresholds.* Some effects do not show up until media exposure exceeds a certain point. For example, viewing television generally does not have a negative influence on a child's academic performance until it reaches a point

of about 30 hr/week, when it really begins cutting into study time (Potter, 1987). So a student who increases her television viewing time from 10 to 20 hr/week is not likely to show a decrease in academic performance. But a student who increases his viewing from 30 to 35 hr/week is very likely to show a drop in grades.

With media violence, it is likely that exposure does not begin to have an observable influence until a person has reached a certain threshold, but this type of research has not yet been conducted. For example, in the testing of immediate effects, researchers could vary the amount, duration, and/or intensity of violence across their experimental treatments to document the point at which disinhibition effects begin to become prevalent. Until this type of research is conducted, we cannot know if the existing experimental literature has relied on treatments with violence below the threshold—in which case this set of research underestimates the disinhibition influence of media violence.

4. *Necessary and Sufficient Conditions.* With media violence, there are no sufficient conditions; that is, no single factor is sufficient to guarantee an effect. An effect is the result of many factors acting in concert. Some of these factors may be necessary; that is, the effect could not occur if such a factor was missing. However, many of the factors are not even necessary; factors can be substitutable. For example, to make a fire we need heat, oxygen, and wood. Each of these elements is a necessary condition, but none is sufficient. In addition, many things could be substituted for wood. In research on the effects of media violence, the clear framing of analyses as examinations of necessary, sufficient, and substitutable factors would orient us more efficiently toward constructing models of the influence process.

5. *Contingent Effects.* By categorizing viewers into groups, researchers can test for differential effects across those groups. If we observe that media violence affects people in each group differently, we have documented a contingent effect; that is, the effect is contingent on the group in which the person is categorized. To illustrate, suppose that Greg watches a violent fight on television and sees that the perpetrator is attractive and rewarded. Greg then begins behaving aggressively. Here, the violent message leads to aggressiveness. If Cindy has poor attention skills as she watches the same violence, she might not understand the meaning of the violence and might become confused rather than aggressive. The violence in this case leads to confusion. And Marcia watches the same violent message but laughs at it, because she thinks it is farcical and unrealistic. In this case the violence leads to laughter. From these three examples, can we say that violent messages lead to aggressive behavior? In general, there is no consistent pattern; the effect depends on the type of person. When we use an approach that takes into consideration the different types of people (as well as many other key grouping variables), we discover

that *under certain conditions* violent messages can cause aggressive behavior. In short, the effect is contingent on certain conditions.

Valkenburg and Van der Voort (1995), in a study of Dutch elementary school children, studied the effect of television viewing on daydreaming and found that there was an important interaction between type of daydreaming and type of TV program. There is more than one type of daydreaming: positive-intense (characterized by vivid, pleasant, and childlike daydreams), aggressive-heroic (action characters acting violently), and dysphoric (escapist). TV viewing in Year 1 of the study influenced daydreaming in Year 2, but not the other way around. A positive-intense daydreaming style was found to be stimulated by watching of nonviolent children's programs and to be inhibited by watching of violent dramatic programs. An aggressive-heroic daydreaming style was stimulated by watching of violent dramatic programs and inhibited by watching of nonviolent programs. This study shows a contingent effect in which certain kinds of exposure stimulate daydreaming while others inhibit it. The contingent analysis made it possible to find the countervailing factors.

Testing for contingent effects is important. Some of the major contingent variables are level of cognitive development, gender, frustration, arousal, and aggressiveness as an inherent trait.

6. *Countervailing Forces.* Sometimes two different media effects are simultaneous, each canceling out the other. One example is with the issue of children's creativity and daydreaming. Some people argue that TV stimulates daydreaming, because TV is so stimulating that viewers will want to relive those episodes. Other people argue that TV reduces daydreaming and imagination because it has such rapid pacing that it leaves children no time to stop and reflect or daydream. The ready-made images of television do not engage the imagination as a book would. In addition, TV presents so many fantasies that viewers can access with very little effort that they have little motivation for expending the creative effort needed to daydream.

With media violence, some theorists say that exposure to high amounts of explicit violence is bad, because it can trigger imitation. But other theorists say that exposure to high amounts of explicit violence might be good, because it can sensitize people to the brutal nature of violence and therefore make them more sympathetic to the victims of violence and less likely to perpetrate violence themselves. The two effects of disinhibition and sensitization may be happening simultaneously, thus canceling each other out so that on the surface there appears to be no effect.

7. *Direct and Indirect Influences.* The media effects process *can* be direct. For example, we might read about a violent crime and encode the details, thus experiencing a cognitive effect. Or we might be watching television and see an attractive character commit a justified act of violence, thus triggering an

immediate behavior to respond aggressively when our viewing is interrupted by a telephone call to the wrong number.

The effect can also be indirect, such as through institutions, which try to socialize us by instilling values about violence, among other things. Reimer and Rosengren (1990) remind us that the important agents of socialization in modern societies are family, peer group, work group, church, law, school, and large organizations representing popular movements and interest groups. The mass media can influence these institutions that in turn influence us. For example, it has been argued that the media have changed the way families are structured, so we are raised differently from how we would have been without the media. In certain families, media violence resonates with existing family values about aggressiveness and reinforces those values (see McLeod & Chaffee, 1973). In other families, media violence goes against the grain of values, so a child's intense exposure to both family and media places the child in a state of confusion.

8. *Structural Modeling.* With a multivariate-probabilistic approach, it is useful to orient toward building structural models that organize the many influences and display the paths of influence. This approach is illustrated well in the work of Malamuth and his colleagues (e.g., see Malamuth, Linz, Heavey, Barnes, & Acker, 1995), who use a confluence model to explain sexual aggression. As yet, there are no similarly elaborate structural models of the influence of media violence. However, Huesmann, Eron, and their colleagues have undertaken a strong beginning of this task.

There are three obvious advantages to building structural models. First, the process requires a truly multivariate approach. With media violence, we have identified a long list of variables that should be part of such a model, but our tests of influence largely have been confined to two or three variables. Second, a structural model reveals a pattern of influence among the variables. This pattern not only shows the interrelationships among variables but also estimates the influences of factors that are exogenous (outside the list of variables in the database) to the analysis. Third, a structural model tests the simultaneous influence of all variables such that the unique influence of each variable is revealed as the overlapping influences are removed.

The computation of structural models usually takes into consideration the issues of directionality, countervailing influences, and direct versus indirect relationships. But there are additional issues that we must consider when testing for structural influence. These issues include thresholds, necessary versus sufficient conditions, and nonlinear relationships. The first two of these issues should be considered as antecedents to particular models; that is, researchers need to do a bit of theorizing before setting up their research designs. Analysts need to move beyond the traditional correlation tests of linear relationships and test for a variety of nonlinear relationships to connect the terms in the structural model.

When we consider all these issues, the resulting model is likely to be very complex. But then the influence process itself is very complex.

The theory outlined in Chapter 15 attempts to move the research more in this direction by highlighting the variables of influence for each family of effects and by speculating on the variables that might be the most influential. But those speculations need to be tested and extended by rigorous empirical work oriented by a multivariate-probabilistic approach toward developing elaborate structural models.

We need to conceptualize more about risk at a macro level, such as harm to society. I recommend that more of this society-level research be conducted and that we expand our operationalizations of what could serve as indicators of harm in society. Perhaps there are cognitive effects, such as higher estimates of how much money is spent (or should be spent) on law enforcement, rates of crime, and so on. Perhaps there are attitudinal effects, such as beliefs about capital punishment, latitude for police to apprehend criminals and subdue them, or level of support for government spending on weapons systems. Perhaps there are aggregate emotional effects, such as a rise in the general level of frustration and anger in society, higher levels of fear when walking in one's own neighborhood, or lack of emotion when hearing about someone being killed.

Finally, we need to expand our operationalizations of evidence of behavioral effects. Perhaps the constant media portrayals of violence show up in other behavioral effects, such as higher rates of highway aggression, lower rates of volunteerism, or higher levels of voting for authoritarian law-and-order political candidates. Perhaps the level of civility in society has changed, thus allowing (or even encouraging) higher rates of aggression that can be seen in competitiveness (in career and sports participation) and in lack of politeness (being treated unjustly by sales clerks).

11

The Industry's Perspective

Criticism of violent messages has been around as long as the mass media has. In 1885, Mark Twain's book *Huckleberry Finn* was criticized for portraying Huck as faking his own death by killing a pig and smearing the pig's blood along with some of his own hair on an ax. The critic complained that boys who read this story would repeat this behavior (Bianculli, 1992). At the turn of the 20th century, the fear was that newspapers that printed gruesome and sensational stories would debase the morals of their readers. Film has also been criticized. A 1991 Associated Press poll found that 82% of Americans feel that movies are too violent (O'Donnell, 1992). With the increasing popularity of television, criticism about media violence has shifted to this pervasive medium. More than 70% of Americans feel that entertainment TV has too much violence, and 57% think that TV news gives too much attention to stories about violent crime (Galloway, 1993).

The public thinks the problem is worsening. A nationwide poll by the *Los Angeles Times* in 1997 found that two thirds of people think that television programming has become worse in the past decade, and 90% believe that television now has more violence and sex than it did 10 years ago (Lowry, 1997). Of the 21,600 respondents in a write-in poll for *USA Weekend* in 1997, 92% said they find television content more offensive than ever, especially the level of violence, sexual content, and vulgarity (Salvoza, 1997).

Members of the public feel that the TV entertainment industry does not share their values. However, polls of people working in the entertainment industry tend to indicate that entertainment workers are also critical of television violence and think it has negative effects. A *U.S. News & World Report* poll in 1994 found that 78% of Hollywood officials think TV contributes to violence in this country ("Culture & Ideas," 1994). Two years later, another *U.S. News & World Report* poll (April 1996) found that 80% of Hollywood executives questioned in a mail survey agreed that there was a link between TV violence and violence in real life.

THE INDUSTRY'S RESPONSE
TO CRITICISM

The industry has endured this criticism for a long time. When people in the media entertainment industry are criticized for presenting violence, they typically seek to avoid the criticism rather than to respond to it by changing the programming. In defending themselves against this criticism, industry people usually employ one of five types of arguments. One argument is to claim that violence is a part of life. Several decades ago, Baldwin and Lewis (1972) interviewed the producers of the top 18 series on prime-time network television at the time and found producers who held the opinion that it would be fantasy to act as if violence did not exist.

A second defense against the criticism of media violence is that all drama is based on conflict, and violence is a tool of conflict. Baldwin and Lewis (1972) quoted one producer as saying, "Violence and drama are almost synonymous" (p. 303). Another producer said, "Good drama is based on conflict which erupts in violent emotion" (p. 303).

Conflict, of course, is a necessary part of storytelling. But the more important issue is whether violence is the only tool available for portraying conflict. Are the people in the creative community really being creative, or are they relying on violence merely because it is easy? This question is reflected in the concern for quality. Are writers using violence appropriately in the telling of high-quality stories, such as *Romeo and Juliet* or *Schindler's List,* or is violence primarily linked with low-quality programming? In an effort to answer this type of question, Hamilton (1998) analyzed movies shown on 32 television channels during a 12-month period to see how critics rated those movies on a four-star rating system for quality. Among the 5,030 movies that had program indicators for violent content, only 2.8% received a four-star rating.

Third, some people in the industry say that they use violence responsibly by showing its negative side. Some in the industry point to movies and television programs in which violence is portrayed very negatively, such as dramas about child abuse and racism. It is true that there are examples of the use of violence to demonstrate its harmful and antisocial nature, but these examples are rare. In its analysis of 9,000 television programs during 3 years, the *National Television Violence Study* (1998) reported that less than 4% of all programs that contained some violence provided an antiviolence context—that is, a context in which characters showed reluctance or remorse for using violence, in which alternatives were discussed when violence was shown, or in which a good deal of pain and suffering was depicted among the victims.

A fourth defense by people working in the media industries is to claim that they are solid citizens with strong family values, just like the people who criticize them. Producers of entertainment violence "dispute the underlying notion that they are out of step with the public, insisting that the image of disengaged media moguls contradicts reality for those in the trenches" (Lowry,

Hall, & Braxton, 1997, pp. 8-9). Dick Wolf, producer of *Law & Order,* said, "The majority of people in Hollywood are involved with nuclear families with kids in school and I think are very plugged in to the concerns of most Americans" (p. 9). In addition, Sandy Grushow, president of 20th Century Fox Television, which produces shows like *The X-Files* and *The Simpsons,* said that if people throughout the country had contact with Hollywood producers and programmers, they would "realize that the values that are held by the executives in this town are consistent with America at large" (p. 9).

Fifth, some people in the industry do not believe that their fictional violence harms viewers, even children. They typically argue (Baldwin & Lewis, 1972, pp. 342-343),

> My kids know the violence they see on *Gunsmoke* is make-believe and what they see on a newscast is real.

> The medium is artificial. It deals with action that is artificial. My theory is that people know what they see on the tube is different from what happens on the street.

> Violence is a catharsis for kids. It's no accident that there's violence in fairy tales. Kids love the creepy feeling they get from grisly fairly tales and horror movies. It's a way they learn to deal with a portion of their environment.

> I don't think that violence in televised drama can inure a child to see people as objects. He knows that his brother screams and his mother bruises.

Internal Criticism

Not all producers and writers feel the need to defend the industry; some express critical opinions themselves. For example, one producer complained that violence is often sanitized to make it more acceptable to large numbers of viewers, but this sanitation has a harmful effect because children do not see violence for the harm and tawdriness it is, so viewers get the wrong idea. A chief censor for one of the networks said, "I would like to see more of the painful consequences of violence (hurt and after effects on people) but find it difficult to explain. If I were to put that into a memorandum to producers, I would be in trouble" (Baldwin & Lewis, 1972, p. 346). Some producers do get this point. One said that the aftereffects of violence have "more dramatic impact than showing the violence" (p. 345). However, most producers disagree with the claim that it is better to show more harm. One producer said, "We caution writers and directors against unnecessary exhibition of repulsive material. To make a heavy seem ruthless, you don't have to have him eviscerate someone and eat his vitals. To sicken the audience is not drama" (p. 346). And another producer says, "As escape, television can carry realism only so far" (p. 346).

Perhaps the saddest observation from an industry insider came from Richard Powell, past president of the Writers Guild of America, who said, "The so-called action shows have at their core a vacuum which can only be filled by violence. They are not about real questions; they are not about real people; they are not about real situations. The only possible controversy is through violence and therefore the supply of violence on TV will remain constant as long as there is a constant number of so-called action shows. They have nowhere else to go with these shows" (p. 357).

Internal Regulation

As their way of dealing with the problem of media violence, the commercial television networks each have their own departments of broadcasting standards. For example, ABC "employs a staff of over two dozen editors who are directly responsible for reviewing and evaluating the writing and production of all entertainment programming" (Wurtzel & Lometti, 1984, p. 90). They use what is called the Incident Classification and Analysis System, which takes into consideration four elements: type of violence, severity of the violence, the victim and consequences of the violence, and the overall context within which the violence is portrayed. All acts of violence are recorded, weighted for seriousness, and then summed for each show to arrive at a final score. The scores for new programs are compared to the typical scores for existing programs of the same type. In addition, the score for an episode of a particular program is compared to the average violence score for that series. Thus, the purpose of the system is to identify new programs and episodes that differ from the norm. Each program has its own baseline, which is determined by consideration of the unique qualities of the series, as well as the time period in which it is programmed. The score for a new episode is compared to the series' baseline and then rated as either below average, average, above average, or high in violence. In short, the goal of this procedure is to identify "elements which may be problematic or unacceptable" (p. 90)—that is, "excessive and gratuitous" (p. 91).

In addition, some of the networks have research departments that deal with the issue further. For example, NBC has a research department with seven subdepartments, most of which are concerned with generating applied research on specific problems of business (audience, programming, news, affiliate relations, marketing, and sales). One of these seven subdepartments, Social and Developmental Research, was created in 1969 to conduct studies and monitor the existing academically generated research on social problems, such as violence on television and children as consumers (Stipp, 1990). This subdepartment also addresses the task of trying to make the programming aimed at children on Saturday mornings more socially responsible by reducing the presence of elements in that programming that would likely put children at risk for a negative effect (Stipp, Hill-Scott, & Dorr, 1987). The focus of the Social and Developmental Research subdepartment has been to shift violence into the fantasy realm, in which the participants of violent acts are more likely to engage in superhuman feats and use fantasy weapons.

The television industry—both broadcast and cable—began implementing a new system for rating all programs except news and sports in October 1997. This system was designed to work with the V-chip, which became available in television sets manufactured after 1998. Using this system, each channel rates its programs according to one of six age-based levels; the rating RV-14, for example, tells parents that the program is suitable for people 14 years of age and older. In addition, in response to pressure from parents' and children's organizations, the industry agreed to augment the age-based descriptors with content-based descriptors. These content-based descriptors alert parents about the nature of the content. In this system, a *V* stands for violence, an *S* for sexual situations, and an *L* for adult language.

This labeling of programs was regarded as a major contribution of the television industry in helping parents decide the suitability of programs for their children's viewing. However, the industry has been slow in delivering on this promise of providing more information. In an analysis of the content of more than 2,000 programs shown through 1998, Kunkel et al. (1998) found that 79% of all shows containing violence did not receive a *V* content descriptor. These unlabeled shows portrayed an average of five acts of violence per hour. Kunkel et al. also found that within children's programming, 81% of the programs with violence did not receive an *FV*, for fantasy violence.

THE ECONOMIC PERSPECTIVE

The media industries are in the business of constructing audiences that can be rented to advertisers. Therefore, programmers are under pressure to select material that will appeal to the greatest number of people within a desired audience segment. The most desired audience segment is people 18 to 34 years old, because advertisers heavily target this group. Advertisers want to get their messages in front of these people, because these are the consumers with the highest needs as they set up their own households and establish brand loyalties.

People in the industry believe that violence is an essential tool in building audiences, especially younger audiences. They point out that violence excites young people and thus provides them with a release from their everyday tensions. This is why violence is used in fantasy settings and is exaggerated, such as in action-adventure programs. In addition, programmers believe that the audience wants to see a particular kind of violence—that is, the type in which a good guy is pushed to the breaking point and then fights back. Producers believe that this kind of justification for violence is very popular because it provides a buildup of tension followed by an acceptable release, which leaves the viewer sated and happy. Thus, producers recognize that following a formula for entertainment is the safest thing to do. Formulas help programmers reduce their risk that audiences will not understand or like their programs.

When programmers can rely on proven formulas to produce their shows inexpensively, they can keep the appeal of those programs high and their costs low. The results are large profits.

Economic Criticism

Although the current practice of using violent material to attract audiences produces a good economic situation for the media industries, it is a very poor one for society, according to Hamilton (1998), who argues that television violence is an example of market failure. He traces this problem to what he calls negative externalities. Negative externalities are the costs that are borne by individuals other than those involved in the production activity.

To illustrate the nature of this problem, Hamilton uses the analogy of environmental pollution. If a factory generates waste products that are hazardous to the environment, the factory can calculate the costs of cleaning up the environment and include those costs in the price of its products—thereby acting responsibly. But the factory could instead choose to ignore the cleanup costs by regarding them as outside of—external to—its decision process. By ignoring these costs, the company can sell its products at an artificially low price, thus enabling it to compete very successfully and amass a large profit. However, the environment is damaged and left to bear the costs of cleanup itself.

Moving from the manufacturing analogy to the issue of television violence, Hamilton shows that although all parties are acting rationally to advance their self-interests, society suffers in that viewers, especially children, are exposed to the constant pollution of violence. Programmers desire most the audiences of men and women of the ages 18 to 34, because advertisers are willing to pay a premium to show their messages to these high-spending audience members. These two demographics represent the largest audiences for violent programming. Therefore, it is in the best interest of individual programmers to offer violent programs to attract these desired audience segments. Other segments of the audience are less desirable, even though the total number of people in these other segments constitutes a majority of all viewers.

To make this example more concrete, suppose that Programmer X schedules Program Y at 9 p.m. because this time is when the number of viewers from 18 to 34 is largest. Program Y is violent to attract the desired advertisers: A, B, and C. Program Y does attract large numbers of the desired audience segments, but the audience also contains many children and teens who are exposed to the program. However, Programmer X does not care about these children and teens, because Advertisers A, B, and C do not care about these younger audiences. The consideration about whether Program Y will attract children and teens does not enter into the decision to schedule Program Y; thus, this consideration is external to the decision.

Hamilton says that the problem of dealing with the pollution of violence falls to individuals. But at the individual level, the costs are very high and the return very low. A parent can boycott products advertised on violent programs, but such action puts a heavy burden on an individual to monitor advertisements and shop around for substitutes. This cost seems especially high when balanced against the effect of a single person's boycott. The costs are also high to parents who want to monitor shows for their children, tape them, and play back only the acceptable ones. "The pursuit of individual self-interest by consumers, producers, and distributors of violent programming leads to undesirable social outcomes, such as the current rates of children's exposure to violent programming" (Hamilton, 1998, p. xvii).

Hamilton conducted a series of analyses that reveal that programmers are very aware of the effect of violence on creating the audiences they desire and that they adopt strategies to use violence as a tool to further their own ends. In one analysis, for example, Hamilton found that channels schedule particular types of violent programming on given days and at given times so as to build viewer expectations about program content and thus attract more viewers. They also counter program violence against popular shows (such as *Seinfeld* and *Monday Night Football*) to attract the audience away from those shows. Hamilton (1998) observes, "The scheduling of movies during the evening and daytime hours demonstrates how violent content is an externality, for the patterns follow the flow of adults in the viewing audience without a strong regard for the potential exposures of children" (p. 158). He says that the level of violence, as well as sexual content, is as high at 8 p.m. as at 10 p.m.—at both of which times the desired audience segments are viewing in large numbers. But a high concentration of children are also viewing then, especially in the earlier time period.

Hamilton also found that the movies scheduled in early afternoons on Saturday contain more violence and nudity than do movies scheduled at that time during weekdays. This difference clearly shows that programmers realize that more desired target people (males and females 18-34) are watching television on Saturday afternoons than on weekday afternoons. However, many more children are also viewing at that time, but this information again is treated as external to the decision making of programmers.

As for advertising, Hamilton says that program warnings change the mix of advertisers that support prime-time movies. Movies with warnings are less likely to attract family-oriented advertisers (food and kitchen products) and more likely to attract advertisers of alcoholic beverages and of sports and leisure products. Also on programs with violent warnings, the number of nonprogram minutes is the same as for programs without warnings, but the amount of time spent on commercial advertising is a bit less, with the difference being filled by program promotions. This loss in advertising revenue is a disincentive, so programmers frequently fail to label violent programming as such. With public criticism of the networks, incentives have shifted to cable channels, where the percentage of shows that contain violence is even higher than on the commercial television broadcast networks. In addition, because violent programming can be exported to foreign countries, producers are able to expect more revenue from these types of programs and therefore will be more likely to have higher production budgets, leading to higher production values and greater audience attraction.

From an economic point of view, programmers and producers are acting rationally but irresponsibly. It is rational to want to maximize revenue, but the narrow pursuit of revenue that does not take into consideration the polluting effects of violence on society is not responsible.

VIOLENCE AND AUDIENCE ATTRACTION

Does violence attract large audiences? It is obvious that people in the media industries believe the answer is yes. But what do the results of the research say?

Attraction and Ratings

When we examine broad patterns of programming to see if the amount of violence in a particular program is related to its rating, the research results are equivocal. For example, Clark and Blankenburg (1972) analyzed prime-time programs on three commercial networks from 1956 to 1969 and found no correlation between ratings of programs and the number of highly violent programs offered in the same year. However, when they used a 1-year lag in their analysis, they did find a strong correlation ($r = .49$) between the ratings for violent programs in one year and the number of highly violent programs in the following year. Thus, the industry appears to respond to the public's taste by increasing the number of highly violent programs for the next year when the highly violent programs receive high ratings in the current year.

The opposite findings were found in other research studies. Gerbner (1994) compared average Nielsen ratings for violent and nonviolent shows from 1988 to 1993 and found that nonviolent shows in general had a higher mean rating (11.1-13.8). Diener and De Four (1978) examined 71 prime-time episodes for elements such as suspense, emotion, sex, humor, action, and violence during a period of more than 3 months. The occurrence of none of these elements was related to program popularity as determined by industry ratings of the shows. Similar findings were reported by Himmelweit, Swift, and Jaeger (1980).

Why the Attraction?

Why are people attracted to violence, and why do they seek out violent portrayals in the media? Zillmann (1998) provided a penetrating examination of theoretical explanations for why people are attracted to violence. He dismissed explanations based on aesthetic appeal, catharsis, technological development, and conditioning by reinforcement as too superficial. He was also critical of psychoanalytical explanations, such as Jung's archetypes and Freud's idea of identification, as well as anthropological explanations based on evolution or humans' need for mastery over the environment and fate. Zillmann reasoned that humans simply want to experience the pleasure of arousal. He argued, "There can be little doubt, then, that righteous violence, however brutal but justified by the ends, will prompt gloriously intense euphoric reactions the more it is preceded by patently unjust and similarly brutal violence. In other words, *displays of monstrous gratuitous slaughter and the distress they evoke are a necessary prelude to the portrayal of righteous maiming and killing that is to spark euphoric reactions.* Without such prelude, violence cannot be righteous and hence is rendered unenjoyable—at least for nonsadists, who should constitute the vast majority of the drama-consuming public" (Zillmann, 1998, p. 208).

This arousal explanation makes a good deal of sense. But the arousal must be pleasurable (Zillmann, 1978). Himmelweit, Oppenheim, and Vince (1958) said that children like being frightened, but only to a point. When their fear is increased to a moderate point through suspense and then relieved, children find the experience very pleasurable. In repeated surveys, children have consistently said they like to be frightened by media programs. Early research found that among third graders, 86% recalled instances in which they had been very frightened by media presentations, but 82% of these children also said that they liked being frightened by movies (Blumer, 1933). In a later study, 80% of adolescents and more than 50% of elementary school children said they liked scary movies and television shows. And the same results were found in several samples by Wilson, Hoffner, and Cantor (1987). Adults also exhibit an attraction for horror (Zillmann, Weaver, Mundorf, & Aust, 1986) and crime (Oliver & Armstrong, 1995).

Most likely arousal itself and the enjoyment of that arousal are shaped by other factors, such as mood, self-concept, motivation, long-term exposure to violence, and political attitudes. As for mood, anger (Freedman & Newtson, 1975) and stress from unhappy or irritating experiences (Munakata & Kashiwagi, 1991) have been found to be related to attraction to violence. In addition, a poor self-concept was found to be related to attraction to violent video games (Dominick, 1984; Donnerstein, Slaby, & Eron, 1994).

What are the motivations for viewing graphic horror films? Johnston (1995) studied adolescents and concluded that there are four motivations: gore watching, thrill watching, independent watching, and problem watching. These motivations are related to dispositional characteristics (fearfulness, empathy, and sensation seeking), as well as cognitive and affective responses. For example, some viewers seek out graphic horror for excitement and for the opportunity to demonstrate mastery over fear. These viewers report a positive affect both before and after viewing. But viewers who watch because of anger, loneliness, or personal problems report negative feelings after viewing and attribute these feelings to the exposure; however, these people usually have negative feelings before the exposure. The type of person most at risk for subsequent violent behavior is the gore watcher, who is an adventure seeker and shows both little empathy and little fear.

Amount of television viewing has been found to be related to attraction to violence. Heavier viewers "watch violent television programs with more absorption but—ironically enough—with more detachment as well" (Van der Voort, 1986, p. 336). Van der Voort explained that viewers' enjoyment of violence keeps them absorbed in the program, so they continue to watch without interruption, but that the same viewers can also be detached; that is, they are not drawn into strong identifications with particular characters and do not feel strong emotional reactions, because they have become jaded by so much exposure to media violence. These heavier television viewers also enjoy violence more, have a clear preference for it, and are more likely to regard violence as justified. For example, Diener and De Four (1978) showed their participants an episode of *Police Woman*. One group saw the full episode, and the other group saw the episode edited to remove all violent scenes. The original version was perceived as more violent and generally was liked more than the cut version. To complicate matters further, within the group who saw the uncut version, there was a negative relationship between perceptions of how violent the episode was and how much it was liked. In another study, Diener and Woody (1981) found that only light viewers liked violent shows significantly less than nonviolent shows.

Oliver and Armstrong (1995) conducted a random telephone survey of adults to determine why people like to watch crime shows. They found higher enjoyment of reality-based crime programs among younger viewers, among viewers who watched more television in general, and among viewers with lower levels of education. In addition, enjoyment was related to punitive attitudes about crime, higher levels of racial prejudice, and higher levels of authoritarianism. In contrast, Oliver and Armstrong were unable to find any profiling differences in enjoyment among viewers of fictional crime shows.

What is it about violence that viewers like? It appears that action more than violence per se is what attracts attention. For example, Potts, Huston, and Wright (1986) showed 64 preschool boys animated and live television programs that varied in terms of violent content (high and low) and action level (high and low). Rapid character action facilitated visual attention to programs; violence per se did not facilitate attention. In addition, there appears to be a gender difference in the modality of the action. Alvarez, Huston, Wright, and Kerkman (1988) found that girls focused more on verbal auditory content of television, while boys focused more on the visual content.

Once a person's attention is attracted, how does violence hold that attention? The attentional-inertia explanation says that the viewer's attention will continue as long as distractions are low and as long as comprehensibility is high. It is assumed that viewers have a limited capacity to process information, so viewers must employ strategies to find content that fulfills their expectations. Viewers then use these strategies to determine what captures and holds their attention. But Hawkins, Tapper, Bruce, and Pingree (1995) question whether television viewers really use strategies or whether they instead use nonstrategic, automatic processes of inertial engagement. The inertia explanation also raises some questions about how viewers stay in the flow when television programs are frequently interrupted with advertisements, public service announcements, program promotions, news breaks, and so on. A possible explanation is offered by Geiger and Reeves (1993), who argue that not all interruptions and distractions are the same; that is, some require more effort from viewers to recover their attention.

This important area of concern is only sparsely addressed by the research. However, we do have a few clues about what generally attracts viewers' attention. We also have a perspective—attentional inertia—that guides our thinking about holding attention. Preliminary results indicate that some factors usually found associated with violence, rather than violence itself, are what attract and hold attention. If this finding is upheld by further research, producers might be able to use the tools of attraction without having to attach violence to them and thereby build large audiences without risking public criticism by also showing violence. But this type of resolution seems too easy. More likely certain attraction factors require violence. Whatever the case, more careful research is needed before we can understand the role of violence in attracting audiences.

RECOMMENDATIONS

We need to understand more about how programmers make their decisions. Programmers, of course, are driven by economic motives. But this issue is much more complex than this simple economy-based explanation. We need to identify all values at play in decision making.

We need to understand more about the dynamics of the attitudes exhibited by both the public and the people in the media industries. Both sets of people are motivated by two conflicting sets of beliefs. One set of beliefs says that it is important to be responsible, and therefore the amount of violence should be greatly reduced so as not to hurt children and poison society in general. The other set of beliefs says that violence is harmless entertainment and that it is okay to pursue selfish ends. The public wants the pleasure of being excited and aroused. People in the industry want to use the violence formula to build audiences and thus maximize their profits. There is dissonance in both the public and the industry. How has this condition continued to exist for well more than four decades?

PART III

Rethinking Methodology

12

Effects Methodologies and Methods

This chapter addresses the methodologies and methods that have been used to examine effects of exposure to media violence. The chapter is organized to present first the major social science methodologies that have been responsible for generating what we know about the effects of media violence. Then four methods (sampling, treatments, measurement, and data-gathering methods) are examined.

METHODOLOGIES

The primary methodologies for studying effects have been experiments, surveys, and epidemiological studies.

① Experiments

lab = immediate results
field = long term

There are two types of experiments: laboratory and field. The laboratory experiment, which is the most used methodology in research on the effects of violence in the media, is used to study immediate effects. The field experiment has also been used for immediate-effects studies, but it is more typically used to study long-term effects of exposure.

Laboratory Experiments

The prototypical laboratory experiment for studying the immediate effects of media violence uses about 50 to 200 research participants in a design that usually has several demographics as independent variables, along with a treatment variable that varies the exposure to violence in a medium, usually television or film. The dependent measure is typically a behavioral measure taken within minutes after the participants are exposed to the violence. A classic example is the 1972 experiment by Liebert and Baron, who used as participants 68 boys and 68 girls of two age levels (5-6 years and 8-9 years) and exposed half of the participants to a 3.5-minute clip from a popular television series, *The Untouchables*. The remaining children, the control group, were shown a video of a track competition. Thus, the experimental design was 2 sexes × 2 ages × 2 treatments. Participants were run individually. Immediately following the video exposure, the participants were taken from the video room into another room, where they were shown a device that they could use to help or hurt a child in another room. Participants' uses of the device were recorded as hurting or helping behavior. Finally, the child was taken to a third room that contained a variety of toys where his or her play was monitored by observers to record how much of that play was aggressive.

[handwritten margin note: typical — show clips then put in observable settings]

Almost every experiment in this literature is a variation on this basic design. The variations can be traced to the sample size and composition, the nature and timing of stimulus materials, the selection of independent variables, and the operationalization of the dependent measures. These variations are illuminated in the sections on sampling, treatments, measurement, and data gathering later in this chapter.

Field Experiments

Field experiments are not numerous in the research on media violence, but a few are worth noting. Stein and Friedrich (1972) conducted an experiment at a summer nursery school program and observed a total of 97 boys and girls (ages 3-5) during a 9-week period. The design began with a 3-week baseline period, followed by a 4-week treatment period, and finally a 2-week postviewing period. The primary treatment was the showing of 12 videos that were aggressive, prosocial, or neutral. Stein and Friedrich measured the attributes IQ, mental age, chronological age, socioeconomic status, and parents' educational and occupational status. During free-play sessions, children were observed for type of behavioral aggression (physical or verbal) and target of aggression (object, interpersonal, or fantasy).

Other scholars have conducted field experiments by interspersing treatments throughout the participants' real lives for several weeks. Although participants are exposed to the stimulus videos usually in a laboratory-type setting, the relatively long periods of time between exposures allow participants to interweave their own media patterns, conversations, and other real-life activities among the treatments (e.g., see Bryant, Carveth, & Brown, 1981).

A form of field experiment is the study of the introduction of a medium with its violent messages into a society. With this type of study, the researcher does not control the stimulus but can only respond to it by measuring its effects on individuals. Studies have examined the introduction of television into various countries, such as Australia (Campbell & Keogh, 1962), Canada (Centerwall, 1989; Williams, 1986a), Great Britain (Halloran, Brown, & Chaney, 1970),

Japan (Furu, 1962, 1971), South Africa (Centerwall, 1989), and the United States (Schramm, Lyle, & Parker, 1961). For example, Williams studied the influence of television on children when it was introduced into a rural Canadian community (Notel) in 1973. She followed 45 first and second graders for 2 years, observing the rates of inappropriate physical aggression and comparing these rates to rates of aggression exhibited by children in other rural towns, which had long-term experience with television. Although the rates of aggression (physical and verbal) did not change in the control communities, the rates of aggression among Notel children increased substantially (160%) after television was introduced.

Surveys

Researchers studying the effects of media use two kinds of surveys: cross-sectional and longitudinal. Cross-sectional surveys are more prevalent.

Cross-Sectional Surveys

Cross-sectional surveys collect data on a variety of exposure measures and a variety of effects measures at one point in time. The measures are constructed to assess typical exposure patterns that are stable for a long period of time. For example, when researchers ask, "How much television did you watch yesterday?" they are not specifically interested in yesterday's viewing time; instead, they assume that yesterday was a typical viewing day and that the measure is a good indicator of everyday viewing in general. As for effects, researchers are not particularly interested in how respondents are feeling at the time they participate in the survey; instead, they are interested in general patterns of feelings, psychological traits (not states), general knowledge structures, and typical behavioral patterns. It is assumed that the concepts being measured in this way have been built up over time as a result of many influencing factors—among them repeated exposure to media violence.

These survey studies examine the relationship between exposure to media violence and an effect variable, such as aggressive behavior, learning certain values, attitudes about violence, or certain psychological traits. Because these researchers realize that such relationships are subject to the influence of a large number of "third variables" that might intervene in the tests of the relationships, they also measure these obvious third variables and use them as controls in the computation of the primary relationship of interest to them.

Longitudinal Surveys

Longitudinal surveys are less common than cross-sectional surveys because they require a great deal more work in sampling, and they require more sophisticated designs to avoid additional threats to validity (such as participant mortality, history, and maturation). The extra work is usually worthwhile because longitudinal surveys can develop stronger claims of influence, even making a case for causality.

Longitudinal surveys vary primarily in terms of the length of time researchers follow their respondents. Some are relatively short, such as two measurement periods spaced 1 year apart (Atkin, Greenberg, Korzenny, & McDermott, 1979; Van der Voort, 1986). Some have followed respondents for 3 years (Milavsky, Kessler, Stipp, & Rubens, 1982; Sheehan, 1983) or 5 years (McCarthy, Langner, Gersten, Eisenberg, & Orzeck, 1975; Singer, Singer, & Rapaczynski, 1984).

The most extensive longitudinal studies were conducted by Huesmann, Eron, and their colleagues (Eron, Huesmann, Lefkowitz, & Walder, 1972; Huesmann & Eron, 1986; Huesmann, Eron, Lefkowitz, & Walder, 1984). They tested samples of 758 children in the United States and 220 children in Finland in each of 3 years in an overlapping longitudinal design covering Grades 1 through 5 (Huesmann, Lagerspetz, & Eron, 1984) and followed those respondents for 22 years. This longitudinal design enabled the researchers to identify a link between exposure to television violence at age 8 and antisocial behavior at age 30. Eron (1982) argued that there is a sensitive period around age 8 during which a youngster is especially susceptible to the effect of viewing violence. "One of the best predictors of how aggressive a young man would be at age 19 was the violence of the television programs he preferred when he was 8 years old. Now, because we had longitudinal data, we could say with more certainty, on the basis of regression analysis, partial correlation, path analysis, and so forth, that there indeed was a cause-and-effect relation" but that "the causal effect is probably bidirectional" (Eron, 1987, p. 438).

Epidemiological Studies

At first look, epidemiological studies might appear to be the same as intervention field studies, but there are two important differences. First, epidemiological studies do not gather measures directly from people. Instead, they use secondary data, such as aggregate crime figures gathered by law enforcement agencies. Second, epidemiological studies do not control treatments and cannot construct control groups. Because this methodology does not subject participants to experimental treatments, nor does it sensitize respondents by asking them all sorts of questions, it is more naturalistic than either experiments or surveys. Epidemiological researchers simply let things happen on their own and then look at reactive patterns on a societal level. However, making the results of these studies appear credible is a challenge. Researchers must convince the reader that the patterns they find in society are triggered by media occurrences and are not artifactual.

The literature contains two types of these studies. The first type follows changes in individuals and cultures when a new medium, such as television, is introduced and disseminated. The second type of study looks for changes in society or individual behavior following media coverage of a high-profile violent event to see if the coverage had any effect.

Dissemination of Violence —

Centerwall (1989) looked at changes in rates of violence in the United States, Canada, and South Africa (in the last case, television broadcasting was prohibited before 1975). In all three countries, the homicide rates were flat until about 10 to 15 years *after* the introduction of television, at which point they doubled. Centerwall said that television viewing is linked to about half of all homicides, rapes, assaults, and other violent crimes committed each year. He also divided the United States into nine regions and found that homicide rates increased later in areas where television was introduced later. Furthermore, this pattern was found across whites, who had received TV sets earlier than minorities. Centerwall concluded that violence affects children the most by teaching them to behave violently—a lesson they carry into adulthood, when these behaviors show up as higher rates of criminal violence.

Hennigan et al. (1982) focused on the introduction of television into the United States and looked for an impact on crime rates. Using time series analysis, they found no consistent association with rates of violent crime, burglary, or auto theft. Moreover, the introduction of television was consistently associated with increases in larceny, irrespective of whether state- or city-level data were used. Hennigan et al. speculated that television teaches people about an affluent world of easily obtainable material goods, and this lesson is what leads many people to feel deprived and frustrated enough to steal.

Messner (1986) did a macro analysis, looking for correlations between the amount of popularity of media violence in particular cities and subsequent criminal activity. Popularity of television violence within cities was estimated across demographic groups according to Nielsen ratings of all television programs. Crime data were obtained from the Federal Bureau of Investigation and broken down by city. After applying several control variables (poverty, education, and ethnicity), Messner found negative correlations between the viewing of television violence on television and crime. Apparently people living in high-crime neighborhoods are likely to avoid watching shows with high levels of violence, preferring instead more peaceful, calming shows.

High-Profile Event —

Phillips and Hensley (1984) pointed out that after highly publicized suicide stories (such as Marilyn Monroe's death), suicides in this country increased significantly. In addition, car accidents (single-car crashes) increased—also indicating an increase in suicides. Highly publicized murder-suicides are associated with an increase in multiple-car passenger deaths, but not single-car driver deaths. Murder-suicide stories were also found to be related to increases in the number of crashes of private planes. In all cases, the more publicity given to the story, the greater the rise in the number of violent deaths. After heavy-weight championship prizefights, the number of U.S. homicides increased, with the person beaten in the fight matching the pattern (in age and race) of the victims of homicides. Phillips and Hensley concluded, "Taken together, the evidence of these studies strongly suggests that some mass media stories trigger imitative increases in fatal violence" (p. 104).

The work of Phillips has its critics. For example, Baron and Reiss (1985) argued that Phillips's conclusion that high-profile violent events in the media lead to real-life violence is spurious because Phillips does not specify (a) the properties of the media portrayals that are the active agents, (b) the set of behaviors that qualify as legitimate effects, (c) the process that evokes imitative responses, and (d) the time period within which the effects should occur. In replicating the work of Phillips, Baron and Reiss concluded that the findings that the televising of prizefights leads to increases in the homicide rate in society is an artifact of Phillips's analysis and therefore is not a valid finding. Kessler and Stipp (1984) also criticized this study, arguing that Phillips got the date of the soap opera suicides wrong in 8 of 13 cases and therefore their time series analyses were off. When corrections were made in these analyses, there was no evidence of a soap opera effect on real-life suicides.

SAMPLING

Samples used in effects studies show wide variety in terms of age of partici-pants, country, and size. This variety is a strength of the research.

Range of Participants

Age

Three general age groupings show up in this literature: children, adolescents (13-18 years of age), and adults. The group studied most often is children, followed by adults, then adolescents (Hearold, 1986). Researchers have studied children as young as 3 years old (Bandura & Menlove, 1968; Friedrich & Stein, 1973; Gadow, Sprafkin, & Ficarrotto, 1987; Hoffner & Cantor, 1985; Rosekrans & Hartup, 1967), but more typically child participants are of elementary school age (e.g., see Atkin et al., 1979; Cairns, 1990; Hawkins & Pingree, 1981a, 1981b) or adolescents (Carlson, 1983; Lynn, Hampson, & Agahi, 1989; McIntyre & Teevan, 1972). As for adults, the body of literature focuses almost exclusively on college undergraduate males (Hearold, 1986), although some studies have tested noncollege adults (Gunter & Furnham, 1984), military recruits (Leyens, Cisneros, & Hossay, 1976), midlevel airline executives (Speisman, Lazarus, Mordkoff, & Davison, 1964), and married couples (Loye, Gorney, & Steele, 1977).

Country

Most of the experiments have been conducted in the United States, but studies have also been conducted on children in other countries, such as Australia (Campbell & Keogh, 1962; Perry & Perry, 1976; Sanson & Di Muccio, 1993; Sheehan, 1983), Belgium (Leyens & Dunand, 1991; Parke, Berkowitz, Leyens, West, & Sebastian, 1977), Canada (Russell, Di Lullo, & Di Lullo, 1988-1989; Williams, 1986a), Finland (Lagerspetz & Engblom, 1979), Great Britain (Gunter & Furnham, 1984; Halloran, Brown, & Chaney, 1970; Kniveton, 1973; Russell et al., 1988-1989), Italy (Caprara, D'Imperio, et al., 1984; Caprara, Renzi, Amolini, D'Imperio, & Travaglia, 1984), Japan (Furu, 1962, 1971), Lebanon (McHan, 1985), the Netherlands (Vooijs & Van der Voort, 1993), and Sweden (Frodi, 1975; Linne, 1976; Van der Voort, 1986). Some are cross-cultural: Centerwall (1989) studied South Africa and Canada; Parke et al. (1977) studied Belgium and the United States; Huesmann and Eron (1986) studied elementary school children in the United States, Australia, Finland, Poland, and the Netherlands.

Sample Size

Most of the studies use a sample of about 100 to 800 respondents. A few studies have much larger samples. The largest samples used are typically from existing national databases gathered for other purposes. For example, Gerbner and colleagues use large national databases, such as the annual National Opinion Research Corporation (NORC) General Social Survey data or the American General Election Study, which typically includes 1,500 to 2,200 respondents.

Other researchers have also used large samples. For example, Robinson and Bachman (1972) used a national probability sample of 1,500 young adult males; Lynn et al. (1989) surveyed 2,000 secondary school students; McIntyre and Teevan (1972) surveyed 2,299 adolescents; and Thornton and Voigt (1984) analyzed 3,500 questionnaires from the Louisiana Youth Survey. Some samples, however, are very small. For example, Friedman and Johnson (1972) studied only 39 aggressive male adolescents.

STIMULUS TREATMENTS

Stimulus materials vary widely. They differ by medium, type of content, time of exposure, and constructed versus natural treatments.

Medium

Most studies use a visual-motion medium (film or video), but other media are also used, such as still visuals of slides (Caprara, Renzi, et al., 1984; da Gloria,

Duda, Pahlavan, & Bonnet, 1989; Feshbach & Roe, 1968; Leyens & Parke, 1975), newspaper cartoons of *Herman* and *The Far Side* (Deckers & Carr, 1986), or photographs shown on a VCR (Zillmann, Bryant, Comisky, & Medoff, 1981). Audio stimuli have been used in the form of radio news reports (Schuck, Schuck, Hallam, Mancini, & Wells, 1971; Wilkins, Scharff, & Schlottmann, 1974) or radio plays (Siegel, 1958). And interactive media have been used, such as video games (Cooper & Mackie, 1986) and computer games (Silvern & Williamson, 1987). Some studies have compared effects from different media (e.g., Furnham & Gunter, 1987).

Type of Content

Content genres varied from cartoons (Gadow et al., 1987; Hapkiewicz & Stone, 1974; Mussen & Rutherford, 1961; Sprafkin, Gadow, & Grayson, 1988) to hockey games (Russell et al., 1988-1989), prizefights (Geen & Berkowitz, 1966, 1967), fight sequences on *Mannix* (Thomas, 1982), aggressive commercials (Caprara, D'Imperio, et al., 1984), films interrupted by commercials (Worchel, Hardy, & Hurley, 1976), gunfighters assisting residents of a Mexican village (Geen & Stonner, 1974), aggressive erotic rock videos (Peterson & and Pfost, 1989), aggressive erotic films (Donnerstein, 1980a, 1980b; Linz, Donnerstein, & Penrod, 1984, 1988b; Smeaton & Byrne, 1987), and films with happy endings (Zillmann, Johnson, & Hanrahan, 1973).

Leyens and Dunand (1991) had an unusual twist on their stimulus; rather than show their subjects a depiction of violence from the media, they merely told their male participants they were about to watch either a violent or a neutral film. "The mere anticipation of viewing an aggressive movie was already effective in producing the usual instigation effect of filmed violence" (p. 507).

Time of Exposure

Most experiments expose participants to their treatment once, and the exposure is usually completed within 15 minutes, but sometimes it is as short as 2 minutes. Other studies try to achieve a more naturalistic treatment of exposing participants repeatedly. For example, Bryant et al. (1981) had their participants in the heavy viewing condition watch a minimum of 4 hours of television per day (28 hours/week) for 6 weeks; this viewing included 5 hours/week (30 hours total) of an experimental condition in a lab. Ogles and Hoffner (1987) showed participants a total of five R-rated erotic aggressive films about every other day for about 10 days. Leyens, Camino, Parke, and Berkowitz (1975) showed their participants commercial movies every evening for a week. Steuer, Applefield, and Smith (1971) showed preschool children television programs for a total of 110 minutes during 11 days. Friedrich and Stein (1973) showed their participants 4 weeks of cartoons (*Batman* and *Superman*), prosocial programs (*Mister Rogers' Neighborhood*), or neutral films.

Constructed or Natural Treatments

Treatments range from specially constructed presentations to presentations that viewers are likely to see in their everyday lives. Some studies use unedited films that anyone could see in the movies or on television (Bryant et al., 1981; Leyens et al., 1975; Zillmann & Weaver, 1997).

In other studies, the researchers edit existing films or create new ones to fit the needs of their treatment design. For example, Lovaas (1961) edited an existing film to remove all nonaggressive parts. Donnerstein and Berkowitz (1981) edited a 5-minute film to alter outcomes in the last 30 seconds. In one version, two men were sexually aggressive with a woman who resisted and was shown suffering from their advances. In the second version, the woman succumbed and became a willing participant.

Some researchers construct their own stimulus materials from scratch. Savitsky, Rogers, Izard, and Liebert (1971) constructed their own film to show a boy interacting with a human clown—hitting it with a plastic mallet, shooting it with a toy machine gun, shaking his fist at it, or walking by it. The specific toys used in the film were then available to the participants afterward so that the experimenters could measure imitative behavior.

Additional Experimental Treatments

Although all studies in this literature have a treatment variable consisting of exposure to violence in the media, many studies add another experimental treatment variable. One prevalent treatment is the angering of participants by giving them a frustrating task to complete (Geen & Berkowitz, 1967; Mussen & Rutherford, 1961), by having the experimenter or a confederate insult them (Geen & Berkowitz, 1966, 1967; Schuck et al., 1971), by giving them electric shocks (Donnerstein, 1980a; Donnerstein & Barrett, 1978; Donnerstein, Donnerstein, & Barrett, 1976; Geen & Stonner, 1974; Hoyt, 1970; Meyer, 1972), or with children, by teasing by withholding a promised toy (Savitsky et al., 1971). Another treatment variable is to make the participants intoxicated with alcohol (Schmutte & Taylor, 1980).

In several studies, the researchers showed participants a film and told them something about that film as an additional treatment. In several experiments, for example, participants were shown a film of a prizefight in which Kirk Douglas was the protagonist, but the treatment variable was to tell participants that the name of the experimenter was either Kirk or Bob (Berkowitz & Alioto, 1973; Berkowitz & Geen, 1966; Berkowitz & Rawlings, 1963).

MEASUREMENT

We make a distinction between explanatory variables and effects variables. Explanatory variables include attributes about the participants in experiments and respondents in surveys. They also include media exposure. Effects variables can be categorized as immediate or long-term.

Explanatory Variables

Experimental designs have tested a wide range of explanatory variables in their designs. These explanatory variables are typically attributes of the experimental participants. These variables are also frequently measured in surveys. They can be grouped as demographics of the participants and psychological attributes of the participants.

Demographics

The most prevalent demographic built into the design of experiments, especially with children, is sex, but it is also frequently used with adult samples (Donnerstein & Barrett, 1978; Donnerstein & Berkowitz, 1981; Mueller & Donnerstein, 1977; Schuck et al., 1971). Other popularly used demographics are age (Liebert & Baron, 1972), socioeconomic status (Hapkiewicz & Stone, 1974), and social class (Kniveton & Stephenson, 1975).

Psychological Attributes

Experimenters have built into their designs certain traits, such as trait aggressiveness (Dubanoski & Kong, 1977; Friedrich & Stein, 1973; Josephson, 1987; Parke et al., 1977; Wilkins et al., 1974), trait anxiety (Berkowitz & Geen, 1967), trait irritability (Caprara, Renzi, et al., 1984), personal hostility (Gunter & Furnham, 1984), psychoticism (Zillmann & Weaver, 1997), and masculinity (Smeaton & Byrne, 1987). Most of these studies classify their participants into two categories (usually high and low), but some are more elaborate. For example, Lagerspetz and Engblom (1979) classified their participants into one of four personality types: aggressive, constructive, submissive, and anxious.

Media Exposure

In surveys, respondents report on their own exposure to television. Media exposure is rarely observed directly, and then only with very small samples. However, self-report measures still vary considerably. Four other types of measures of exposure are used much more often. They are global assessment, exposure to genres, exposure to particular shows, and exposure through attention.

Global Assessment

Gerbner and his colleagues typically operationalized exposure by asking people to assess total viewing of television regardless of program type or source. In most of their reports of cultivation analysis, these researchers have used databases gathered by NORC, which asked the following question about TV exposure: How many hours of television do you watch on an average day? This question has been used often by Gerbner's colleagues and former students (Gross & Jeffries-Fox, 1978; Morgan, 1983, 1984, 1986; Signorielli, 1990), as well as by others (Carveth & Alexander, 1985; O'Keefe, 1984; Tan, 1982; Volgy & Schwarz, 1980). In addition, there are slight variations on this question, such as, How many evenings per week do you watch TV for at least 1 hour? (Fox & Philliber, 1978).

Exposure to Genres

An alternative method of measuring television exposure is to present respondents with a list of television genres—action-adventure, situation comedy, afternoon soap opera, prime-time soap, news or documentary, movie, sports, cartoon, music, game show, and talk show—and ask the respondents to estimate the number of hours they view on a weekly basis within each program type (e.g., Potter, 1986, 1988b).

Exposure to Particular Shows

Some studies present their respondents with a long list of specific programs and ask them to check the programs they regularly view (Elliott & Slater, 1980; Rubin, Perse, & Taylor, 1988); some ask respondents to check the shows they have viewed in the past 7-day period (Doob & Macdonald, 1979; Weaver & Wakshlag, 1986; Wober, 1978); some ask respondents to check whether they watch the show every time, a lot, or once in a while (Carlson, 1983; Eron, Huesmann, Brice, Fisher, & Mermelstein, 1983; Friedman & Johnson, 1972; Huesmann, Lagerspetz, & Eron, 1984; McLeod, Atkin, & Chaffee, 1972; Volgy & Schwarz, 1980); and some ask respondents to specify whether they watch the show every week, most weeks, some weeks, or never (Reeves, 1978). Weaver and Wakshlag (1986) designed a prime-time television viewing diary for the prior week that listed 65 programs, and respondents checked all the programs they had viewed in the previous 7-day period.

One of the most complete forms of measuring exposure was conducted by Hawkins and Pingree (1980, 1981a), who asked their respondents to fill out a viewing diary. All programs were listed, and respondents wrote the number of minutes they had viewed each program during the measurement period.

A few studies have focused on exposure to particular shows only *within* a genre. For example, Carlson (1983) presented a list of 16 selected crime shows and had respondents use a four-point scale (ranging from never to almost always) to respond.

Several researchers have used the data from a genre exposure measure and combined it with content analysis data to compute an estimate of exposure to violence (Atkin et al., 1979; Eron, 1982; Friedman & Johnson, 1972; McLeod et al., 1972; Sheehan, 1983). In addition, Bassett, Cowden, and Cohen (1968) computed a fantasy-aggressive behavior scale, which was a self-report of the amount of time spent viewing audiovisual presentations of crime and violence.

Exposure Through Attention

Rouner (1984) used a unique assessment of exposure. She measured not hours, but self-reported attention. Specifically, she asked respondents how much attention (ranging from close attention to no attention) they paid to the "personal qualities of the characters, the characters' appearance, values and morals displayed by the characters, and the story line" (p. 171). In addition, several researchers observed how much attention children were paying to the screen during the showing of their stimulus videos (Stein & Friedrich, 1972; Van der Voort, 1986).

Measures of Immediate Effects

Timing of Measures

All studies in this literature took measures immediately after exposure (within minutes) to the media violence. Some also continued the measurement well after the exposure to determine how long the immediate effect would last. For example, Kniveton (1973) measured 7 days after treatment and then again 4 to 5 months later. He found that after watching a model hit a Bobo doll with a hammer on a 3.5-minute tape, boys imitated this aggressive behavior both immediately after the viewing and during all postviewing measurements (1 day, 1 week, and 4-5 months later).

Sometimes experimenters begin measuring their dependent variable before the treatment so that they have a baseline measure (Collins, 1973; Gadow et al., 1987). For example, Collins took baseline measures 18 days before exposure to the treatment and then again immediately after exposure.

Type of Measure

As with the timing of the dependent measure, the type of dependent measure varies. Variations include behavioral observation, behavioral self-report, attention, physiological readings, cognition and learning, emotion or mood, and psychological self-report.

Behavioral Observation. Behavioral observation is the most prevalent measure gathered by observation of participants and recording of their aggressive behavior. After the participants are exposed to the treatment(s), they are placed in a situation in which they have an opportunity to behave aggressively (or not) and their behavior is observed and recorded. For example, participants are given a chance to administer electric shocks to someone else while the number, intensity, and/or duration of those shocks are recorded as the dependent measures (Berkowitz & Alioto, 1973; Berkowitz & Geen, 1966, 1967; Donnerstein, 1980a; Donnerstein & Barrett, 1978). Variations include watching participants (a) use a noise machine in which they can give painful feedback to learners (Feshbach, 1972; Lando & Donnerstein, 1978), (b) press a lever that activates one doll hitting another (Lovaas, 1961), (c) hit a punching device (Dubanoski & Kong, 1977), or (d) hit a Bobo doll with a hammer (Bandura, Ross, & Ross, 1963a, 1963b; Kniveton, 1973). In an Australian experiment, children were given a chance to play with toys that were based on the cartoon characters they observed in the treatment conditions (Sanson & Di Muccio, 1993).

Sometimes experiments do not use a device but instead observe direct interpersonal aggression (Friedrich & Stein, 1973; Steuer, Applefield, & Smith, 1971); cooperative or competitive play (Kniveton & Stephenson, 1975); physical, nonphysical (verbal), noncompliant, and imitative behavior (Gadow et al., 1987); or speed of fist clenching (da Gloria et al., 1989).

In studies in which experimenters insult the participants, the participants are given a chance to retaliate against the experimenters by evaluating the experimenters' performance (Worchel et al., 1976; Zillmann et al., 1981; Zillmann & Sapolsky, 1977).

Some experimenters have also looked for evidence of prosocial behavior as well as antisocial behavior. For example, Friedrich and Stein (1973) measured levels of task persistence, rule obedience, and tolerance for delay. Mueller, Nelson, and Donnerstein (1977) also measured helping behaviors.

Some experimenters have attempted to observe subsequent aggressive behavior in a naturalistic setting. For example, Turner, Layton, and Simons (1975) recorded the aggressive behavior of drivers by counting instances of horn honking on public streets.

Behavioral Self-Report. Less typically, behavior is measured by participants' self-reports of what they would do in certain situations. For example, Atkin (1983) asked participants to speculate on what they would do if someone cut in ahead of them in a long line at a movie. Cahoon and Edmonds (1984, 1985) used a behavioral control index, which was a self-report of hostility in 12 hypothetical situations. Wotring and Greenberg (1973) tested the effects of viewing televised violence by using self-report measures of verbal as well as physical aggression. Collins (1973) presented his participants with six real-life situations and asked what they would do by giving them four options: physical aggression, verbal aggression, leaving the situation, or positive coping. Zillmann and Weaver (1997) measured the acceptance of violence as a means of conflict resolution by having their participants read about six hypothetical conflict situations and choose a reaction from three to six listed choices.

Sometimes experimenters use several kinds of behavioral measures (Cooper & Mackie, 1986; Liebert & Baron, 1972). For example, Cooper and Mackie (1986) read a story about a fictional child to their participants and then asked them to reward or punish the child in the story by pushing a green or a red button, respectively. In addition, the experimenters observed the children during an 8-minute period of free play immediately after the treatment and recorded the time spent playing with different types of toys that varied in aggressive potential.

Attitudes. Dominick and Greenberg (1972) used measures of attitudes in a study of elementary school children. They found that the greater the level of exposure to TV violence, the more respondents were willing to use violence, to suggest it as a solution to conflict, and to perceive it as effective.

Physiological Readings. Typically, physiological measures are taken to determine the degree of arousal. These measures include heart rate (Geen & Rakosky, 1973; Thomas, 1982), blood pressure (Donnerstein, 1980a, 1980b; Donnerstein & Barrett, 1978; Geen, 1975; McHan, 1985), skin temperature (Wilson & Cantor, 1985; Zillmann, Hay, & Bryant, 1975), skin resistance as a measure of emotionality (Geen & Rakosky, 1973; Thomas, Horton, Lippincott, & Drabman, 1977), and palmar sweat (Geen, 1975; Koriat, Melkman, Averill, & Lazarus, 1972).

Cognition or Learning. The effects measures of learning can be grouped into three categories: understanding of the narrative in the exposure, recall of information learned in the exposure, and the acquisition of norms as a result of exposure to violence.

As for understanding, some researchers have been concerned about children's ability to comprehend the motives for aggressive actions (Collins, 1973; Collins, Berndt, & Hess, 1974; Hoffner & Cantor, 1985). For example, Hoffner and Cantor showed children a narrative to a certain point and then asked the children to project what they would see next if the story continued.

As for recall, violent material in newscasts has been found to be recalled better than nonviolent material (Furnham & Gunter, 1987; Gunter, Furnham, & Gietson, 1984), especially among males (Furnham & Gunter, 1985).

Some researchers have asked their participants about their perceptions of social norms (Collins, 1973; Hoffner & Cantor, 1985; Leifer & Roberts, 1972; Linne, 1976; Siegel, 1958; Thomas & Drabman, 1978). For example, Siegel found that children use media portrayals to make attributions about real people. Children listening to a radio play about a taxi driver who used aggression to solve his problems were more likely to believe taxi drivers were aggressive than were children who had not heard this portrayal of taxi drivers.

Emotion or Mood. Some researchers have used a measure of general moods or emotions immediately following the treatment (Berkowitz & Geen, 1967; Lazarus, Speisman, Mordkoff, & Davidson, 1962; Russell et al., 1988-1989; Speisman et al., 1964). Other researchers have focused on one mood or emotion, such as fear (Hoffner, 1997; Weiss, Imrich, & Wilson, 1993), stress (Tannenbaum

& Gaer, 1965), disturbance (Gunter & Furnham, 1984), happiness (Ekman et al., 1972), or empathy with characters as indicated by participants' facial expressions (Wilson & Cantor, 1987; Zillmann & Cantor, 1977).

Psychological Self-Report. Sometimes effects researchers use an established psychological scale to measure participants' level of a particular trait or state. For example, Bryant et al. (1981) monitored the change in anxiety of their participants by asking them to fill out Taylor's Manifest Anxiety Inventory both before the 6-week period of viewing and again after.

Measures of Long-Term Effects

Long-term effects that are measured include behaviors, perceptions and cognitions, attitudes and beliefs, emotions, and psychological states.

Behaviors

The typical kind of behavior examined is aggression. Often this aggression is assessed through self-report (Belson, 1978; Lynn et al., 1989; McLeod et al., 1972; Robinson & Bachman, 1972) and delinquency (Bassett et al., 1968; Cowden, Bassett, & Cohen, 1969; Robinson & Bachman, 1972; Thornton & Voigt, 1984). Another way of measuring this variable is to have a person's peers rate his or her aggressive behavior (Eron, 1982; Eron et al. 1972; McLeod et al., 1972; Sheehan, 1983; Van der Voort, 1986).

Perceptions and Cognitions

With cultivation research, a popular measure is an assessment of respondents' perceptions about the prevalence of crime and violence (Carveth & Alexander, 1985; Doob & Macdonald, 1979; Gerbner et al., 1977; Hawkins & Pingree, 1981a; Potter, 1991a, 1991b); personal victimization through crime (Hawkins & Pingree, 1980; Morgan, 1983; Weaver & Wakshlag, 1986); and risks in life, such as being hit by lightning, flooding, and terrorist bomb attacks (Gunter & Wober, 1983; Wober & Gunter, 1985).

Attitudes and Beliefs

Cultivation researchers often assess respondents' beliefs about the mean and violent nature of the world (Bryant et al., 1981; Hawkins & Pingree, 1980; Morgan, 1986; Potter, 1988b; Rouner, 1984; Signorielli, 1990; Wober, 1978; Zillmann & Wakshlag, 1985).

Very little cultivation research has examined values. Reimer and Rosengren (1990) looked at materialism and postmaterialism. Potter (1990) focused on the themes of television programs and the values that adolescents were learning from general exposure to television, including violence.

Emotions

Aisbett and Wright (1989) found that respondents had a stronger emotional reaction to violence in news than in other types of programs. This reaction was attributed to respondents' knowledge that news is real and involves real people. In addition, older viewers and female viewers showed stronger reactions to violence and less tolerance for the depiction of violence than did younger viewers and male viewers.

As for long-term emotional states, researchers have assessed fear of victimization (Bryant et al., 1981; Morgan, 1986; Wober, 1978; Zillmann & Wakshlag, 1985), anxiety (Zillmann & Wakshlag, 1985), alienation and anomia (Gerbner, Gross, Jackson-Beeck, Jeffries-Fox, & Signorielli, 1978; Gerbner, Gross, Signorielli, Morgan, & Jackson-Beeck, 1979a, 1979b; Morgan, 1986; Signorielli, 1990), and feelings about one's life (great, calm, intense, lousy; Morgan, 1984).

Psychological Traits

Some researchers have measured stable psychological characteristics that they thought might be altered by long-term exposure to media violence. Eron (1982) used a combination of Minnesota Multiphasic Personality Inventory (MMPI) and the Psychopathic Deviate and Hypomania scales. In addition, examined characteristics were responsibility, self-concept, and emotional stability (Cowden et al., 1969); regressive anxiety, self-destructive tendencies, conflict with parents, mentation programs, fighting, delinquency, and isolation (McCarthy et al., 1975); and locus of control and anomia (Potter, 1991a, 1991b).

DATA-GATHERING METHODS

There are three primary types of survey data-gathering methods: self-administered questionnaires, phone surveys, and field interviews or observations. The most prevalent is the self-administered questionnaire (e.g., Atkin et al., 1979; Bassett et al., 1968; Carlson, 1983; Friedman & Johnson, 1972; McIntyre & Teevan, 1972; Robinson & Bachman, 1972; Weaver & Wakshlag, 1986).

Also popular is the telephone interview. Some researchers gather their own data over the phone (e.g., Einsiedel, Salomone, & Schneider, 1984). Others use data from large-scale phone surveys conducted for general purposes on nationwide probability samples (e.g., Gerbner et al., 1978).

Some researchers conduct field interviews themselves (Huesmann, Lagerspetz, & Eron, 1984). Other researchers use the databases gathered by survey research firms. For example, O'Keefe (1984) used data from a nationwide multistage probability sample collected in the homes of the 1,188 respondents by the Roper Organization.

LIMITATIONS OF EFFECTS RESEARCH   *plateau*

Social science has reached a plateau in its dealing with media violence. The good thing about this condition is that we now have much more knowledge about the phenomenon. The problem is that the increase in our knowledge seems to be leveling off because of limitations in practices. I argue that there are three such limitations.   *①*

The first limitation is the continued reliance on laboratory studies to generate *reliance* new findings. Laboratory experiments have contributed a great deal to our *on* understanding of potential effects and the factors that may be contributing to *lab results* those effects. Cook, Kendzierski, and Thomas (1983) observed, "Experiments are designed (a) to minimize internal inhibitions against aggression, (b) to minimize external cues sanctioning aggression, and (c) to maximize the clarity and intensity of short-term experimental treatments that have been deliberately chosen because they are likely to foster aggression. Although appropriate for discriminating between treatments, this strategy is not obviously relevant to regular television programming in the home, where internal cues against aggression may operate more powerfully, situational cues sanction aggression, and television aggressors are punished, usually by characters with prosocial qualities that are themselves presumably worthy of emulation. Also, the violent scenes on television are interspersed with many different types of activity, and viewers are free to watch intermittently or with low levels of involvement" (p. 180). We need to test our laboratory findings in the field; that is, we need more naturalistic research.

A second limitation is the underuse of the receiver's view of media violence. *underuse* Qualitative scholars remind us that meaning making is an individual enterprise *of* and that although we all learn how to make meaning of symbols through *viewer's* interactions with others, ultimately the meaning is ours to make. Although each *view of* television program presents a vast array of particular symbols carefully crafted *violence* to achieve a certain effect on the desired audience, each viewer interacts with those symbols in a way specific to his or her experience of meaning. Therefore, television viewing is a very active process of meaning making (Fiske & Hartley, 1978). Different individuals have learned different connotations for each symbol. Because viewers weigh the symbols differently, their individual interpretations differ widely.

There are many examples of experimenters telling their participants how to interpret certain key elements in the context of violent portrayals. In some studies, for example, participants were told that the action was either real or fictional (Berkowitz & Alioto, 1973; Geen, 1975; Thomas & Tell, 1974). Berkowitz and Alioto, for instance, showed a World War II documentary depicting U.S. Marines capturing a Japanese-held island. By taped introduction, about half of the 51 male undergraduate participants were told that the movie was a documentary, and the other half were told that the film was a Hollywood enactment. The researchers found that participants who had been told that the film was realistic exhibited more of a disinhibition effect; the interpretation of reality made a difference, but that interpretation was given to the participants.

In some studies, participants are told certain things about the perpetrators or victims of the violence. Berkowitz and Geen (1967) had an experimenter named either Kirk or Bob anger the participants and then show them a film of a prizefight in which Kirk Douglas was beaten. Participants were told that the protagonist in the fight was either a bad person or a good person, hence deserving the beating or not. In other experiments, participants were told by researchers how to interpret motivation for a particular violent act (Berkowitz & Powers, 1979; Berkowitz & Rawlings, 1963; Geen, 1981; Geen & Stonner, 1973, 1974; Hoyt, 1970) or specifically whether the violence was justified (Geen, 1981; Meyer, 1972).

There is nothing wrong with experimenters telling their participants how to interpret elements in violent portrayals, as long as the study focuses on the connection between a particular interpretation and an effect. In fact, this feature is a strength, because it ensures that all participants in a particular treatment are experiencing the same interpretation. However, when the focus is the larger task of determining how exposure leads to effects, we must recognize that interpreting symbols in the narratives, which is an essential early step in the effects *process,* is most likely to reveal a wide range of interpretations across individuals.

RECOMMENDATIONS

The recommendations in this chapter are grouped into two categories: internal and external recommendations. The internal recommendations make suggestions about the design of particular studies. The external recommendations are very broad and ask researchers to think about how their research designs can contribute more effectively to the overall development of knowledge about the effects of media violence.

Internal Recommendations

We need to use nonprobability samples more sparingly. Almost all studies in the literature use nonprobability samples. These studies have generated findings showing (a) *that* there are certain effects and (b) *that* certain characteristics in the messages contribute to those effects. The examination of these kinds of "that" issues has provided a solid beginning point. But the line of research about the effects of media violence needs to extend beyond a concern *that* an effect occurs and address the concerns of *strength* or *prevalence* of the effects. To address these concerns, probability samples are essential.

This is not to say, however, that nonprobability samples will not continue to be useful for certain purposes. Researchers who want to break new ground by examining whether an additional effect *can* occur will continue to generate appropriate results with nonprobability samples.

We need to increase our understanding of the role of frequency of violence on effects. We should focus more attention on how frequency of exposure influences the effect. With the disinhibition effect, for example, priming-effects theory predicts that the effect will happen immediately after a single exposure (Jo & Berkowitz, 1994). Other theories, however—such as social cognitive theory—posit that viewers can "acquire lasting attitudes, emotional reactions, and behavioral proclivities towards persons, places, or things that have been associated with modeled emotional experiences" (Bandura, 1994, p. 75). Although this acquisition can occur after a single exposure, what is learned can be altered and shaped over time through a process of acculturation. But the theory does not attempt to explain how additional exposures to violence shape that process.

Research has made clear that a single exposure to violence in the media can have an immediate effect. But these findings raise a series of important questions about the role of time and frequency in that effect. First, is there a threshold effect for how long a single exposure should be? The experimental literature shows a wide range of treatments in terms of length. At the short end is a 90-second film (Geen, 1975; Thomas & Tell, 1974). More typically, a film of about 5 to 7 minutes is used (Atkin, 1983; Berkowitz & Rawlings, 1963; Ellis & Sekyra, 1972; Goranson, 1969; Leyens & Picus, 1973; Turner & Berkowitz, 1972). Some researchers use longer treatments, such as a 30-minute TV show (Collins, 1973) or even a feature-length movie (Bushman & Geen, 1990). Although all these studies report a disinhibition effect, we cannot tell if the degree of disinhibition is related to the length of the exposure.

A second concern about frequency is, How much violence must a given exposure contain? And again, is there a threshold? Sometimes the length of the treatment can tell us something about how much violence was presented. For example, the 1.5-minute film of an argument escalating into a fist fight used by Geen (1975) likely contained far fewer punches (or acts of physical violence) than the 7-minute film of a prizefight used by Berkowitz and Rawlings (1963). But the 5-minute animated cartoon used by Ellis and Sekyra (1972) probably had more acts of violence than the 30-minute television drama used by Collins (1973). We cannot automatically conclude that longer treatments contain more violent acts, because the density of violence can vary significantly across treatments. Unfortunately, researchers rarely report about the frequency and kind of acts in their media treatment condition. One exception is Thomas and Drabman (1975), who said that their 15-minute edited film "contained six killings. Surrounding these killings were four arguments, seven fights and 17 shots fired" (p. 229). However, the violent-stimulus treatment is rarely described at this level of detail. And even when it is reported in detail, we still are not provided with conclusions about how strongly that degree of violence is related to an effect.

effect of multiple exposures (handwritten margin note)

A third concern about frequency is, What is the effect of multiple exposures? For example, 1 week of television viewing was controlled by Loye et al. (1977), who measured their subjects for aggression after the week was over. A 4-week period was used by Friedrich and Stein (1973). A 6-week exposure period was used by Bryant et al. (1981). But in these studies, the measurement was taken only after the treatments were completed, and it is not possible to plot the accumulation of the effect.

Multiple measurement times were used in several studies. Milavsky et al. (1982) measured 3,200 elementary school children and teenagers five times during a 3-year period. Huesmann and Eron (1986) tracked eight hundred 8-year-old children for 10 years. These long-term studies provide very useful documentation about the overall arc of the effect. But from a risk assessment point of view, these long-term studies would have been even more helpful if they had focused on identifying possible cycles within the long-term process. Perhaps disinhibition is not monotonic over the long term but instead increases and decreases given certain short-term changes in exposure patterns. Perhaps viewers recover a few hours after a session of viewing TV violence. Or perhaps a very short exposure is sufficient to disinhibit someone, and subsequent viewing throughout an evening has no additional effect. Or perhaps additional viewing of violence reinforces the disinhibition, thus requiring a longer period of time to recover afterward. We need to see researchers plot the shape of the relationship between exposure to violence and an effect—such as disinhibition—so that we can identify the points at which risk increases dramatically from the places at which risk plateaus or maybe even decreases.

We need to pay more careful attention to types of violence in designing effects studies. We should not expect all *types* of violent acts to contribute equally to risk. Hart (1986) pointed out that the frequency of violence is not the same as salience. For example, Gunter (1985) has shown that the degree of brutality in the violence influences the effect on viewers.

When we think of media content that would most likely have a negative effect on viewers, we usually begin with the core idea of criminal violence—that is, murders, rapes, serious physical assaults, and the like. These are the portrayals that would make us most uncomfortable when we think that young, impressionable minds are watching and getting ideas about how to act. When we expand our frame to more than criminal activity, we include less major assaults (such as hitting or slapping) or threats and coercion, which are ambiguous from a criminal point of view. Then there are the least serious acts of violence, which are usually verbal, such as lying, insults, put-downs, rejection, harsh criticism, and the like.

Intuition tells us that exposure to the serious, criminal acts is the most harmful. But we must be careful to define what we mean by harm. If we are watching television with a child and the narrative builds to a graphic portrayal of a nasty crime, we are likely to feel uncomfortable or even embarrassed. We want to protect the child's innocence and prevent him or her from believing that such things occur. That emotional discomfort is a negative effect. If instead the narrative portrayed less graphic crime or less serious acts of violence, we would not feel the discomfort and would avoid this effect. So we conclude that serious violence graphically portrayed should not be shown, because it obviously triggers a negative effect; but portrayals of less serious violence are acceptable. However, if we switch our focus from emotional discomfort as a negative effect to disinhibition, the risk situation changes quite a bit. The riskiest portrayals in terms of leading to disinhibition may be the least serious violence (such as lying and insults) because they are the most imitable. Would an impressionable child be more likely to tell a lie or bomb a building? Would a child be more likely to insult someone or kill her? Of course, bombing and killing are much more serious than lying and insulting. And although the concern over the seriousness of the act is important, it is secondary to the more fundamental issue of the degree to which the portrayal of an act puts a viewer at risk of disinhibition.

We need to rely less on self-report measures and more on observation. A good deal of the survey data relies on self-report of behavior or reports of others' behaviors. These data can be dangerously misleading, especially when we consider the demand effects, social desirability, and the third-person effect— each of which could contaminate self-report data.

Exposing oneself to media is a mundane behavior, and the self-reporting of mundane behaviors is very inaccurate. To illustrate, Ferguson (1994) had people watch an hour of television while he monitored how often they changed the channel with a remote control. Immediately after the viewing session, he asked people to recall how many times they changed the channel. Most people had already erased those memories and had no idea how often they had performed the mundane behavior of channel changing a few minutes earlier. More than 20% underreported their channel changing by a factor of more than 8 (e.g., a person who changed the channel 80 times but estimated the number of changes at 10 would be underreporting by a factor of 8). One person changed the channel 122 times but estimated 3; another changed channels 396 times and estimated 20; and another made 181 changes and estimated 300. People could not remember back a few minutes and make a good estimate of a mundane behavior during media exposure. Furthermore, the estimations were not all overestimates or underestimates, in which cases researchers would be able to develop a correction factor and adjust people's self-reports. Instead, the estimate patterns were random, so it is not possible to salvage the self-reported data for any meaningful analyses of channel-changing rates.

We need primary data, such as direct observations, in place of self-reports. Of course, direct observation requires a much greater time commitment from researchers. It also requires a great deal more in-depth analyses of the meanings of everyday situations. However, the current cutting edge of research has moved us beyond the point at which another study with self-reports of aggressive behaviors would add anything significant to our understanding of the effects of exposure to media violence.

We need to be more creative in operationalizing effects measures. Using a broad conceptualization of effects places a greater burden on measuring them than does a narrow conceptualization. Researchers need to continue to look for behaviors, but they also need to be more expansive in their view. It is not sufficient to look only for high-profile aggressive behaviors. Our operationalizations should also include low-profile aggressive behaviors such as impatience, rudeness, and the like. In addition, there may be some prebehavioral indicators in the areas of attitudes, emotions, and cognitions. For some effects, a chain of influence might result in a behavior. If the particular behavior (such as aggression) is not exhibited, the absence does not necessarily mean that the exposure to media violence had no effect. There might be other effects along this chain, but researchers must build in this wider view of effects so as to document patterns of how far different people are pushed along the chain leading to a high-profile behavioral effect. Limiting measurement to only an end point behavior misses the opportunity to understand the process of influence.

Some effects (such as reinforcement) show up not in change but in lack of change. This result calls for a higher level of creativity in research design in order to be able to distinguish between no change as lack of influence and no change as an indication of a reinforcement effect.

Thus, the challenge of measuring the effects of media violence is twofold. First, researchers need to hypothesize a chain of influence that includes multiple steps in which some of these steps lead to the effect while a sequence of other steps might branch off and lead to a different (perhaps opposite) effect. Second, researchers need to determine what could serve as evidence of those various steps and effects. The easiest observable measures are changes in physiology and behavior; the research to this point has been strong in documenting such measures. But the more subtle changes (or reinforcements) that build the foundation for behavioral eruptions also need to be translated into observable indicators.

We need to triangulate the measurement of concepts. Every method of measurement has its limitations. The key to developing stronger research studies is to use more than one method of measurement to triangulate each view of the phenomenon and thereby avoid the influence of any single method's limitations.

We need to be more precise in constructing grouping variables. With culture-level studies, researchers need to be more careful in selecting grouping variables. Demographic variables are relatively weak, because they are usually surrogates for the active influences on the effects. For example, almost all the time that researchers use the variable of age with children, they are really concerned with level of cognitive development. Because development varies somewhat across children of the same age, the assumption that age adequately captures cognitive development is faulty. Furthermore, not all males are alike in their interpretations, nor are all heavy viewers of television.

Grouping individuals not because they agree on interpretations but because they share an easily observable characteristic introduces error variance. Such categorization results in within-group variation that is then regarded as error. The strategy of running multivariate analyses on a large number of these grouping variables with the intention of increasing predictive power expands the total error as within-group error is increased with each additional variable entered. A better strategy would be to focus on using a person's individual interpretations of contextual information to predict that individual's summary judgment of violence in a portrayal.

We need to think more broadly about the influence of control variables. This recommendation has two facets: (a) speculation about what factors should be regarded as controls and (b) testing the nature of the controls. The typically tested "third variables" are the demographic characteristics that reflect a person's stage in life or predominant environment. For example, Gerbner and his colleagues typically use as control variables a person's age, gender, socioeconomic status, educational level, and type of neighborhood. These variables also have been measured by other researchers (McLeod et al., 1972; Robinson & Bachman, 1972). Other variables measured have been respondents' family life, such as rejection punishment (Eron, 1982); family size (Lynn et al., 1989); the influence of family, school, and peers (McLeod et al., 1972; Thornton & Voigt, 1984); reactions to TV in general, such as judged realism, fantasy, identification with TV characters (Sheehan, 1983); and psychological factors such as IQ, extroversion, neuroticism, and psychoticism (Lynn et al., 1989; Stein & Friedrich, 1972). In addition, it is important to measure participants' trait levels of aggressiveness (McLeod et al., 1972; Stein & Friedrich, 1972). As is evident, past research has paid a fair amount of attention to control variables. This focus on control variables needs to continue as we add new variables to the list.

Control variables can be used in many different ways. In cultivation analysis, for example, the control variables are tested as contaminants so that their influence is removed. Because the resulting coefficients are almost always smaller than the coefficients computed without controls, the controls act as extraneous variables. But perhaps other third variables act as suppressor variables; that is, when the influence of the suppressor variables is removed, the resulting coefficients are stronger. Perhaps some variables act as antecedents, and so on (see Rosenberg, 1968).

We need to use more multivariate analysis techniques. By *multivariate,* I do not mean the simple expansion of the Latin square experimental design into 6-way, 10-way, or 20-way analyses of variance. The demand to test all key contextual variables simultaneously would require at least a 20-way design. But even if we started small—say, a 6-way analysis with each condition having only 2 values—64 cells would be required. Editing stimulus material into suitable treatments, let alone running enough experimental participants, would be a near impossible task. Thus, moving forward using the traditional experimental design is not feasible.

I propose a hybrid design that attempts to blend the strength of the experimental method with the survey method, while being sensitive to the need for a more naturalistic perspective on both stimulus materials and viewer interpretations. The method I propose emphasizes viewer perceptions of contextual characteristics rather than experimenter-designed characteristics. Individuals construct their own interpretations of the meaning of violent portrayals. These interpretations provide researchers with a wealth of information about why different viewers experience different effects even when their exposure is the same. Ignoring this information greatly limits our ability to explain the effects processes.

Furthermore, I propose a three-part analysis strategy:

1. Use multiple regression to focus on strengths of contributions of factors in a simultaneous model in which influences of other factors are removed rather than the use of analysis of variance (ANOVA), with its focus on whether differences exist between constructed situations.

2. Treat the distributions of interpretations as continuous rather than dividing respondents into groups.

3. Conceptualize the nature of relationships and interactions more broadly.

The processes by which exposure to media violence affects viewers are complex. For us to have a good chance of increasing our understanding of that complexity, we must take a truly multivariate approach. A useful guide to this task is the work of Malamuth and his colleagues (Malamuth, Linz, Heavey, Barnes, & Acker, 1995; Malamuth, Sockloskie, Koss, & Tanaka, 1991), who have been developing a confluence model of sexual aggression. Although the model does not deal specifically with media violence, it is a useful guide because it illustrates how researchers can theorize about and then test how different variables work together in a complex interlocking process of influence. Their confluence model illustrates the structure of variables and the degree of influence each has on others in the structure.

To take advantage of the power of multiple regression analyses of many variables, it is important to treat the distributions of those variables as continuous. The practice of arbitrarily segmenting a continuous distribution places the analysis at greater risk for generating spurious results. (For a more complete development of this point, see Potter, 1994.)

Plotting the shape of those distributions would provide a graphic picture of the aggregate pattern of interpretations. By examining the range, the skew, and the densities, we can gain a better appreciation for the phenomenon.

External Recommendations

We need to conduct more naturalistic studies. The laboratory experiments have been very useful in identifying the factors that *could* have an effect on viewers. Now we need more field experiments to see if these factors *do* have an effect in naturalistic viewing situations. Researchers need to focus more on how everyday viewing distractions compete with violence for viewers' attention, how viewers talk about violence with their friends in everyday conversations, and how subtle changes in mood and behavior are associated with viewers' attraction to different kinds of portrayals.

Naturalism would be increased by the use of stimulus materials as they appear on the home screens of viewers—that is, longer narratives with frequent interruptions for commercials. Form makes a difference. For example, Liefer and Roberts (1972) ran two experiments, one with shows taped off the air as is, the other with edited tapes that removed the commercials and made the narratives shorter. Compared to children who had not seen the edited tapes, children who were shown the edited tapes were subsequently more aggressive when they viewed violence that was motivated by socially acceptable reasons and that was portrayed with no harmful consequences to the victims. However, children who saw the unedited tapes showed no such effect.

Without a significantly higher degree of naturalism in the experiments, we cannot make good assessments of the degree to which these laboratory documented effects occur when viewers' attention fades in and out and when viewers are not so sensitized to the demand characteristics of the experiments. Critics are bothered—for good reasons—about the ecological validity of generalizing laboratory-generated findings into everyday real-world situations.

We need to be more aware of the received view when designing experiments. Often experimenters tell their participants what to think about the portrayals of violence rather than letting participants construct their own judgments. To illustrate, let's take the classic experiment in which two groups see the same violent video clip. Before viewing the clip, Group A is told that the aggressor is a bully, and Group B is told that the aggressor is a good person who is retaliating for a previous attack on his defenseless child. After the viewing, participants are given a chance to exhibit aggression against someone who previously angered them. In typical experiments, the researchers assume that all participants in the A condition will perceive the violence as unjustified and that all participants in the B condition will regard the violence as justified. If researchers conduct a manipulation check, they will likely see that the interpretations of justification vary. At this point, the researchers can do one of two things. One path—the one almost always chosen—is to run a test of differences across the two groups to see if ratings of justification differ significantly. If a significant difference is found, this measure is left behind as the analysis continues. With this analysis path, the within-group variation on the manipulation check variable is regarded as error. A second path is to regard the variance on the "manipulation check" variable as valuable data and test that variable as a possible predictor of the dependent measure. With this analysis path, the variation is used, not discarded; there is a concern for individual differences in interpretation.

We need to be clear about the level of phenomenon we are examining. It is best not to assume that a study is tapping into only one level. Instead, empiricists should conduct their analyses to determine how the variance is apportioned across levels. In this way the level at which the phenomenon is strongest will become clearer.

We need to get away from the assumption that all viewers are subjected to the same effect of violence when they see the same message. This simply is not the case. Viewers make a wide range of interpretations, and if we, as researchers, are to understand more fully how media violence affects viewers, we need to focus on both interpretation and influences, as illustrated in the individual-interpretations model.

With humor, for example, it appears that this would be an individual-differences phenomenon. But it is possible that after years of conditioning by laugh tracks, we all have come to share the same reactions to situations as far as humor is concerned. This conclusion is speculation. The purpose of research is to test speculations such as this one.

We need to conduct more meta reviews. Some important findings can be generated only by reanalysis of the data across many comparable studies. This is especially the case when the analyst challenges some of the assumptions in previous analyses. For example, Hogben (1998) analyzed 56 different studies in a meta review of survey literature on the influence of viewing violence on behavioral aggression. His quantitative meta-analysis did not assume a linear relationship, but instead tested for an asymptotic relationship on age and geographic location. For example, he found that although children may watch more television than adults on any given day, their total exposure is much smaller, because they have not yet experienced decades of viewing. Therefore, adults are more likely than children to have reached an asymptotic level; that is, adults have reached a ceiling for the effect of viewing, so additional exposure will not translate into as much aggression as would additional viewing by children. As for geography, Hogben found indicators that viewers in the United States have reached an asymptote compared to viewers in other countries.

We need to conduct more analytical and critical reviews of the literature. Typically, when social scientists think of analysis, they think quantitative analysis—that is, using statistical tests to move from numerical data to results. However, there is a qualitative task that all quantitative researchers conduct within each study. That qualitative analysis always begins the manuscripts and sets up the quantitative part of the studies; this is the rationale and review of the literature. This qualitative analysis entails two tasks: (a) to argue persuasively that this study undertakes a worthwhile task and that the design is a good means to accomplish the task and (b) to position the study in the field. Of course, these two tasks overlap. Within the media violence literature, we could do a better job on both tasks.

The first task—making a case for the value of a particular study—has been harder to achieve as more research has been published. It is no longer sufficient to acknowledge a few peripheral studies on a particular topic and then conclude that X has yet to be done, so therefore it is important to do X in this study. That rationale is very weak. Not all gaps in the literature are equally important, and some could remain gaps without damaging the overall thrust of the literature.

With more research over time, the gaps between studies grow smaller, and the task of acknowledging previous research relevant to the topic becomes more involved. In addition, as this line of research grows, it is not sufficient merely to acknowledge previous studies by simply describing them one by one in paragraph after paragraph. Instead, it becomes more important to review those studies in meaningful sets and to do so critically. Grouping studies into meaningful sets is not a single task, but a multifaceted task, because the scholar should arrange the studies into sets according to their theoretical approaches, operational decisions (especially in the areas of measurement, treatment specifics, and procedures), analyses, and findings. So the review of the literature is really an integrated set of reviews of the literature in which each paragraph deals analytically with a different issue rather than dealing descriptively with another study. Furthermore, the reviews should be critical. When dealing with a particular issue (such as measurement), not all studies in the literature have employed equally good measurement tools. Some are better than others, and the writer of the manuscript needs to tell the reader which measurement tools are better and why.

Scholars who follow the suggestions in the previous paragraph will be able to build the review of the literature to a persuasive set of conclusions about the conceptual approach, operational decisions, analysis, and expected findings. Such conclusions position the new study within the growing line of research. By clearly presenting this qualitatively derived context for the current study, a scholar provides the reader with the means to appreciate the results more fully. In addition, the writer is provided with a means to check whether his or her study is going to make a substantial contribution to the line of research or whether it is making the same mistakes that have limited the findings of previous studies.

Thus, the qualitative part of any quantitative study is essential. If the quantitative scholar cannot get over the qualitative hurdle of critically analyzing the literature, developing a persuasive voice to argue for the usefulness of his or her decisions and providing adequate context for the reader to appreciate the results, then the study (no matter how sophisticated the quantitative analysis and powerful the tests) will not contribute much to readers' understanding of the phenomenon. Thus, the line of research is neither strengthened nor moved forward. (For more information on the qualitative approach for quantitative scholars, see Potter, 1996.)

13

Content Analysis of Media Violence

The decisions made by the designers of content analyses of violence literature are remarkably diverse. This chapter deals with decisions about five methods: coding violence, sampling, defining units of analysis, assessing reliability, and analyzing context.

5 methods

CODING VIOLENCE

How much violence is there on television? At first glance, this question appears to be simple and straightforward. But there are several very different answers to this question—all legitimate—depending on how one goes about answering it. For example, a content analysis might require coders simply to record the number of times a violent act occurs. If an act meets the requirements of the definition of violence, it is coded as present; all other acts are ignored (e.g., see Baxter, Riemer, Landini, Leslie, & Singletary, 1985; Poulos, Harvey, & Liebert, 1976; Sherman & Dominick, 1986; Smythe, 1954).

The simple counting of violent instances can be misleading. For example, if one show presents 12 individual slaps and another show presents 4 brutal murders, a simple counting of acts makes the first show seem much more violent than the second. To avoid such a problem, some coding designs direct coders to make a series of additional decisions when they see the presence of violence and code the type and/or duration of the violence. For example, the *National Television Violence Study* (NTVS) asked coders to record violence as a credible threat, as having harmful consequences only, or as a behavioral act. Greenberg, Edison, Korzenny, Fernandez-Collado, and Atkin (1980) used four codes: physical aggression, verbal aggression, theft, and deceit. Oliver (1994) also categorized aggressive behaviors into four types: verbal aggression, threat of physical aggression, unarmed physical aggression, and armed physical aggression. Brown and Campbell (1986) had their coders choose from among 22 antisocial acts.

Some studies used a nested set of types. For example, Potter and Ware (1987) subdivided their construct of aggression into two types (physical and symbolic), each of which had several levels. The physical category included destruction of property, larceny, burglary, robbery, armed robbery, assault without a weapon, assault with a weapon, rape, and killing. The symbolic category included minor deceit, insult delivered in a kidding manner, genuine insult intended to hurt the feelings or pride of another, threat of loss of reputation or peace of mind, major deceit, threat of loss of money or property, nonverbal threat of physical force, and verbal threat of physical force. Potter et al. (1995) revised this scheme to include 43 levels nested within the two types of violence: verbal and physical.

When the coding categories for type of violence have an ordinality, researchers can address the issue of relative seriousness of differences in portrayals across shows. For example, the Center for Media and Public Affairs (1994) had coders choose from a list of acts ranging from pushing, menacing threats, and slaps to serious assaults, assaults with weapons, and suicides. In their analyses, coders converted these individual codes into a scale of seriousness. In addition, Mustonen and Pulkkinen (1993) constructed a scale for brutality in their analysis based on coders' ratings of three variables: realism, justification, and injury. The most brutal acts were those that "contained realistic, and unjustified violence with severe injuries emphasized with TV effects" (p. 178). Mustonen and Pulkkinen argue that a "weakness of TV-content analysis is the counting of aggressive acts without considering the interpretations and responses of the audience" (p. 176). Thus, they make a clear distinction between frequency and salience.

Duration also provides a piece of the picture about the presence of violence. One program might contain only one act of violence, but that act might last 10 minutes, while a second program might show 12 acts of violence, each lasting 2 seconds. Unfortunately, few researchers measure duration. But the studies that do, typically find the amount of time violence is on the screen to be very small. For example, Gerbner, Gross, Signorielli, Morgan, and Jackson-Beeck (1979b) computed the length of violent incidents and found an average of 2.4 min/hr, which is about 4% of total programming. The *National Television Violence Study* (1997, 1998) also measured duration of violence, as did studies conducted in Finland (Mustonen & Pulkkinen, 1993) and Japan (Iwao, de Sola Pool, & Hagiwara, 1981a).

SAMPLING

Four aspects of the variety of sampling decisions can be examined: sample size, the nature of the sampling units, how the units are selected, and whether the sample is cross-sectional or longitudinal.

Sample Size

Within this body of literature, the samples range from 12 hours of programming to more than 2,700 hours, but most of the studies have samples of between 70 and 110 hours of programming. Typically, the samples are of a composite week of prime-time programs from the commercial networks (Center for Media and Public Affairs, 1994; Harvey, Sprafkin, & Rubinstein, 1979; Potter & Ware, 1987; Potter et al., 1995) or of prime-time and Saturday morning programs (Gerbner, Gross, Morgan, & Signorielli, 1980; Greenberg et al., 1980). The reasoning behind this selection of shows is that each sample would capture the programming watched by the greatest number of viewers. Williams, Zabrack, and Joy (1982) used this criterion of popular viewership most clearly when they selected the top-rated 100 programs for adults, the top 100 for teenagers, and the top 100 for children; of course, there was a great deal of overlap in popularity of shows among the three demographic groups, as indicated by the fact that the total size of the sample was 109 programs. The Center for Media and Public Affairs (1994) selected only the premiere episodes of prime-time fictional series, assuming that these would be the most watched.

There are many variations on this norm. The variations are a function of number of days sampled, hours per day, number of channels, and limitations on types of programming. For example, Lichter and Amundson (1992) selected a single day of programming (April 2, 1992). Some researchers have constructed 2 composite weeks (Broadcasting Standards Council, 1993; Potter & Ware, 1987) or 4 weeks (Gunter & Harrison, 1995). Oliver (1994) looked at all episodes of five series for 3 months.

Although most analyses are limited to prime time, some look at shorter time periods. For example, Poulos et al. (1976) looked at two Saturday mornings only. Some studies look at a longer time span, such as all parts of the day (Gunter & Harrison, 1995; Mustonen & Pulkkinen, 1993; *National Television Violence Study*, 1997, 1998).

The number of channels also varies around the norm of 3 or 4 channels (Center for Media and Public Affairs, 1994; Gerbner, Gross, Morgan, & Signorielli, 1980; Greenberg et al., 1980; Kapoor, Kang, Kim, & Kim, 1994; Mustonen & Pulkkinen, 1993; Potter et al., 1995; Potter & Ware, 1987; Poulos et al., 1976; Sherman & Dominick, 1986). But some studies look at more channels—for example, 5 (Schramm, Lyle, & Parker, 1961), 7 (Smythe, 1954), 8 (Gunter & Harrison, 1995), 10 (Lichter & Amundson, 1992), or 23 (*National Television Violence Study*, 1997, 1998, 1999).

Some studies have limited their analyses to one genre, such as music videos (Baxter et al., 1985; Brown & Campbell, 1986; Sherman & Dominick, 1986; Sommers-Flanagan, Sommers-Flanagan, & Davis, 1993), Saturday morning programs only (Poulos et al., 1976), crime drama (Dominick, 1973; Estep & Macdonald, 1983), or reality-based programming (Oliver, 1994).

But the "general" content analyses also impose programming limits on themselves. For example, many have limited themselves to fiction, thus screening out news, sports, documentaries, and other forms of nonfiction (Center for Media and Public Affairs, 1994; Greenberg et al., 1980; Potter & Ware, 1987; Potter et al., 1995). Some are even more limited, to comedy and dramatic series, thus screening out variety programs and movies (Dominick, 1973). But other analyses are all-inclusive, even encompassing news (Gunter & Harrison, 1995; Mustonen & Pulkkinen, 1993). Some even include the analysis of nonprogram elements. For example, Lichter and Amundson (1992) examined a total of 5,997 units, which included product commercials, promotions for TV shows and movies, news stories, music videos, and entertainment programs.

The broadest-based sample has been the *National Television Violence Study* (1997, 1998, 1999), which each year sampled about 3,000 programs (a composite week of programming from 6 a.m. to 11 p.m. across 23 broadcast and cable channels).

Sampling Units

Almost all content analyses look at the programs themselves. There is one exception: Clark and Blankenburg (1972) collected their data by analyzing the program synopses printed in *TV Guide.*

How Units Are Sampled

Some studies do not use sampling; that is, they construct their sampling frame so that it is possible to select all sampling units and therefore conduct an examination of the entire population of interest. For example, the Center for Media and Public Affairs (1994) constructed a sampling frame of the premiere episodes of prime-time fictional series for the 1992-1993 television season, and they were able to code all 73 episodes. Williams et al. (1982) selected all the top-rated 100 shows in each of three demographic viewing groups.

Because the designers of most content analyses of violence want to generalize to all television, they must sample. Most of the studies say they select television shows randomly, but often the shows are not the sampling unit. For example, Dominick (1973) sampled 1 week and took the intact week of programming. Gunter and Harrison (1995) selected 4 weeks and then took all programming intact. Potter et al. (1995) sampled days, then took a day's programming (6 p.m. until midnight) intact, and Brown and Campbell (1986) selected an evening and then took that entire evening's set of music videos intact. Lichter and Amundson (1992) selected 1 day and then took the programming from the entire day as the sample.

The most sophisticated sampling scheme was used by the NTVS project, which used a sampling frame of all programs within 23 channels from 6 a.m. to 11 p.m. during a 26-week schedule. Individual programs were selected from this sampling frame such that each was given an equal chance of being chosen. To construct a full composite week for each of the 23 channels, the sampling was stratified within channels.

Longitudinal Studies   *examining trends across years*

Most content analyses of violence are cross-sectional; that is, they examine the violent content at one point in time, even if that point is a week long. But several studies take a longitudinal perspective so that they can examine trends across years. For example, Greenberg and colleagues (mid-1970s) and the NTVS projects (mid-1990s) each constructed a 3-year composite of television programming. The study by Clark and Blankenburg (1972) spanned 15 years, from 1953 to 1969. The longest longitudinal study was begun in 1967 by Gerbner and his colleagues and continued yearly for more than two decades.

DEFINING UNITS OF ANALYSIS

Television shows are complex narratives. In analyzing them, researchers need to recognize that the meaning of the violence can be conveyed in different narrative strata. For example, within television shows are brief incidents of violence, each typically lasting several seconds and each telling its own ministory about a character interaction. There are also scenes, each lasting perhaps a minute or two. And at the most macro level, a narrative spans the entire length of the program and provides a more complete context for interpreting violent scenes and violent interactions.

Content analyses of television violence typically use one of these three levels. At the macro level, the entire show is the unit. If violence occurs anywhere in the show, the entire program is categorized as violent. The problem with this approach is that a 2-hour movie that contains one act of violence would be put in the same category as a half-hour cartoon with 20 acts of violence.

The micro level focuses on the individual act of violence. Each time a violent act (such as a slap) is committed, it is recorded as a unit of violence. The problem with this unit is that in some instances, such as fights, the counting of each individual act might be regarded as inflating the frequency of violence. For example, if Characters X and Y each throw 20 punches at each other during a 1-minute fight, use of a micro unit would require the coder to code each of the 40 punches as individual acts of violence. But if the fight were used as the unit, one act of violence would be coded.

Most studies focus on one unit—usually the interaction or the scene. Some studies, however, used multiple units of analysis. For example, Williams et al. (1982) coded at two levels. The global level was the program; coders rated the tone of the program and general characteristics of the characters. The second level was the segment, which was defined by a change in setting or time or both. Several studies coded at the program and act levels (Gerbner, Gross, Morgan,

& Signorielli, 1980; McCann & Sheehan, 1985). Gunter and Harrison (1995) coded at both the act and the sequence levels.

The NTVS used three units: program, sequence, and what they call PAT, which is a violent interaction of act (A) between a perpetrator (P) and target (T). Each time one of these elements changed, a new PAT was coded throughout the continuing violent sequence. But as long as all PAT elements remained the same, even though there were multiple instances of the same act, such as repeated punches, only one unit was coded.

Another issue of unitizing is whether units are constructed before the coding or whether the units evolve from the coding itself. For example, researchers could break programs down into narrative scenes and then have coders record which of the scenes contained violence and which did not. However, it is sometimes difficult to divide a narrative into clean scene units. A way around this problem is to divide the program into time blocks. For example, Sommers-Flanagan et al. (1993) analyzed the content of 40 MTV videos by breaking them down into 30-second segments and then coding each segment as either containing violence or not.

In most content analyses, the units evolve from the coding itself. Using this approach, coders monitor a program but do not record anything until they see something that qualifies as violence, and they begin coding the sequence of events until the elements that qualify the sequence as violence cease. Thus, the parts of the program that do not have violence are not coded. It is clear that Mustonen and Pulkkinen (1993) use this approach to unitizing when they say their unit of analysis is "a coherent uninterrupted sequence of aggressive actions (one or several) involving the same agents in the same roles" (p. 178). In addition, the Center for Media and Public Affairs (1994) grouped acts into sequences, which they defined as "a group of interconnected actions and dialogue that take place in the same location, in the same time frame, between a similar group of characters" (p. 4).

Another alternative is unitizing by characters instead of actions. For example, Oliver (1994) organized her analysis not on scenes but on characters. She found 696 characters (351 criminal suspects and 345 police officers). These characters became the units, which were recorded as exhibiting violence or not.

ASSESSING RELIABILITY

Content analysis is a social scientific methodology that requires researchers who use it to make a strong case for the reliability of their data. Content analysts must design a procedure in which at least two coders assess the same content so that their judgments can be compared for consistency. If coders exhibit a high degree of agreement, the case is made for good consistency, hence reliability. Reliability raises four issues: manifest versus latent content, coder overlap, size of the reliability sample, and computing coefficients of reliability.

155 lues

1. Manifest Versus Latent Content

With some kinds of content, the judgments are easy to make, and the consistency among coders is usually very high. Such is the case with manifest content. Manifest content is content that is on the surface and easily observable, such as the appearance of a particular object or word. For example, we could count how many times a weapon appears or how many times a character uses the word *kill.*

The coding of violence is a much more complex task, because violence is almost always regarded as latent content. We can write a long list of specific coding rules, but those rules will never fully capture the essence of violence. Coders should be guided by those rules, but they will always be required to exercise some judgment. Coders will always have to infer if certain patterns underlie portrayals, and if so, whether those particular patterns qualify as violence. With latent content, the testing of reliability is difficult, but it is a more important task because coders must use their own judgments in addition to the coding rules. If the judgment making is consistent across coders, reliability will be high. For a more detailed treatment of this issue, see Potter and Levine-Donnerstein (in press).

2. Number and Overlap of Coders

To test the degree of consistency in decision making across coders, the coding must overlap somewhat; that is, at least two coders must make judgments on the same material. The typical test of intercoder reliability in content analysis methodology is to have a pair of coders analyze the same subset of the sample. Within this dually coded portion of the sample, the judgments of the two coders can be compared directly (e.g., see Kaplan & Baxter, 1982; Mustonen & Pulkkinen, 1993; Potter & Ware, 1987). In some studies, researchers have more than two coders available, such as five (Oliver, 1994), six (Williams et al., 1982), or seven coders coding tests run by pairs (Dominick, 1973; Potter et al., 1995), 12 to 18 coders working in pairs coding the entire sample (Gerbner & Gross, 1976), 27 (Kunkel et al., 1998) or as many as 40 coders (*National Television Violence Study,* 1997). Even studies with many coders pair coders on segments of the sample so that the reliability test compares the judgments of at most two coders. There are two exceptions to this setup (Kunkel et al., 1998; *National Television Violence Study,* 1997), in which many coders were trained and at least half the coders participated in the same recording for the reliability test.

3. Size of the Reliability Sample

When samples are relatively small, researchers tend to test the entire sample for reliability. For example, Kaplan and Baxter (1982) analyzed 22 episodes of prime-time series and were able to double-code the entire sample. However, in some cases relatively large samples are double-coded, as with the cultural indicators project, which collected a sample of about 100 hours of programming each year (Gerbner & Gross, 1976). It is more common to use a small percentage of the sample for reliability, such as 10% (Potter et al., 1995; Potter & Ware, 1987), 15% (Williams et al., 1982), or 23% (Dominick, 1973).

When choosing the material to be coded in the test of reliability, researchers should, of course, use random selection. If the researcher can make a case that the difficulty of the coding decisions is uniform throughout the material to be coded, then a relatively small overlap is required to set up a fair test of reliability. But if the material to be coded contains segments that present different degrees of coding difficulty, each of those segments should be represented in the overlap to provide a fair test of reliability. To illustrate, the challenge of coding television programs for violence includes many different genres of television programming. There is good reason to believe that some of these genres may be much easier to code for violence than others. Action-adventure shows with a great deal of crime, gunplay, fights, car chases, property destruction, and so on, are relatively easy to code. The violence is formulaic and overtly portrayed. However, other genres treat "violent" acts differently, making it very difficult for coders to apply a single definition consistently. For example, coders may have different challenges in analyzing (a) cartoons with their humorous contexts, (b) situation comedies with their verbal aggression, (c) news programs with their recounting of violent acts (but not showing them) after their actual occurrence, and (d) music videos with their ambiguous images stylized into montages. Thus, in this situation, a fair test of reliability would require the overlap to include at least one program from each of these genres.

Computing Coefficients of Reliability

When coders use continuous scales (i.e., scales of ordinal, interval, or ratio-level measurement), well-established methods exist to test for consistency (see Traub, 1994). These methods typically involve the computing of appropriate correlation coefficients. For example, one could compute the Pearson product-moment correlation coefficient with a Spearman-Brown correction (Anastasi, 1976). Correlation coefficients typically have an accompanying probability value (p value) to help researchers interpret the level of significance (and confidence) that corresponds to the statistical results. Furthermore, in these situations, the "reliability coefficient is also a coefficient of determination" (Kerlinger, 1996, p. 412). Hence, r^2 indicates "how much of the total variance of a measure is true variance" (p. 412).

Most of the measures in content analyses of media violence are nominal. With nominal-level judgments, we could simply compute a phi coefficient and use that as the reliability coefficient. While phi is the chi-square corrected for number of observations, it offers no correction for chance agreement. A much more common procedure for computing a reliability coefficient is to find the percentage of agreement among coders and then correct for chance agreement by employing one of three popularly used methods: Scott's pi, Cohen's kappa, and Krippendorff's alpha. Each method makes its correction in a different manner.

Methods range from no reporting (Iwao et al., 1981a; Lichter & Amundson, 1994) to reporting simple percentages of agreement (Mustonen & Pulkkinen, 1993), Scott's pi (Dominick, 1973; Kaplan & Baxter, 1982; Potter et al., 1995; Potter & Ware, 1987), Krippendorff's alpha (Gerbner & Gross, 1976; Williams et al., 1982), and the binomial correction (Kunkel et al., 1998).

ANALYZING CONTEXT

In general, the most popular contextual variables of violence have been (a) outcome of the violent act for the perpetrator (reward vs. punishment, or whether the act was successful), consequences of the act for the victim (harm and pain), and motivation (intent or reasons) of the aggressor. Also becoming popular are the variables of realism (setting in place or time), humor (tone), use of weapons, graphicness (gratuitousness), and justification.

Results are always presented as a series of univariate or bivariate findings. In a univariate presentation, for example, a study would report the percentage of programs with violence and then present the hourly rate of violence across all programs, the number of violent acts found, the percentage of violent acts in which the perpetrator was punished, and on and on, one variable at a time. In a bivariate presentation, a study might report perpetrator gender and age together (e.g., the percentage of violent acts committed by teenage males or by elderly females) or present a character variable and context variable together (e.g., the percentage of male perpetrators that are rewarded compared to the percentage of female perpetrators that are rewarded).

What has been missing from the literature thus far is an elaboration of the picture of violence that can be constructed only through an examination of many contextual factors simultaneously to determine which characteristics cluster together. This is a troubling limitation, because the context of violent portrayals on television is always an interweaving of these factors, and viewers likely draw information from many of these contextual factors simultaneously when interpreting the meaning of violent acts. Therefore, it is important to examine how these factors group into a pattern.

We need to ask, Is there a formula underlying the presentation of violence on television? If there is a formula, we should expect to find a regular pattern in the way violence is portrayed; that is, there should be strong associations among the contextual variables. Furthermore, we should expect to see this pattern consistently across many different types of programming. If a strong association exists among contextual variables, we can conclude that writers and producers are consciously or unconsciously using a general formula. If so, when a particular contextual variable is present in a portrayal, certain other contextual variables very likely will also appear. The variables in this "formula set" are identified through their strong association with one another. Other contextual variables not strongly associated with the variables in this set cannot be regarded as part of the formula.

Several steps to overcoming this limitation were taken recently in a study that addressed the issue of a formula underlying the portrayal of TV violence (Potter & Smith, in press). Using the large data set from the NTVS project, we examined the degree to which certain factors of prevalence and contextual variables cluster together. It was reasoned that a strong association among a set of variables across the television landscape would be evidence that a formula for violence exists. That is, if a portrayal contains Factor A, then it is highly probable that Factors X, Y, and Z will also be present; a producer who puts A in her program will automatically put in X, Y, and Z. Therefore, a violence formula is in evidence in the recurring patterns of contextual factors.

Evidence suggests that certain contextual variables do indeed cluster together. When graphicness is high, pain is higher, depictions of harm are more realistic, and there are fewer sequences per hour. When harm is depicted realistically, more harm is shown and there are fewer PATs. In contrast, when the violence is sanitized (i.e., harm is unrealistic), there is likely to be no harm, pain, or graphicness, and it is likely to appear in programs with higher rates of PATs and sequences per hour. This clustering—contextual web—was found across programs of different genres.

This illustration shows why the concept of the contextual web is so important. Although the presence of individual contextual characteristics varies across genres, the structure of relationships among those contextual characteristics remains relatively stable. Thus, the contextual web tells viewers what to look for. When viewers notice the presence of a particular characteristic, they know that the other characteristics in the cluster are also likely to be present, and this knowledge makes their meaning processing more efficient.

RECOMMENDATIONS

We need to use multiple measures of prevalence. The assessment of violence on television requires multiple measures if the findings are to present a fair and accurate picture of the presence of violence. The counting of acts, the assessing of type, and the recording of length are three different measures that can result in three different—and often conflicting—findings about the presence of violence across the television landscape or within a particular show. To avoid presenting misleading results, content analysts need to incorporate all three kinds of measures into their coding designs.

We need to construct samples representing the entire television landscape. Programs should be the sampling units, and they should be selected from the universe of programs in a probabilistic manner so that the resulting sample represents the entire universe. The universe should be the entire television landscape, including all genres, channel types, and parts of the day.

When the entire television landscape is the universe, the resulting sample provides a rich context for the interpretation of any one data point. For example, reporting that the genre of music videos presents an average of three violent acts per hour would take on much more meaning in the context of reporting the hourly rates of other genres.

We need to make assessments at multiple levels. Particular contextual characteristics can vary across levels, thus leading viewers (and researchers) to interpret the meaning of the violence differently. Each of these interpretations presents a partial picture. To achieve a more complete picture, content analysts need to examine multiple levels of the narrative.

Researchers who need to make a case for the reliability and validity of coded data of latent content should follow three steps. First, decide whether the standard of agreement should be criterion-based as determined by experts or norm-based as set by coding patterns. When coding manifest content, experts can set a good standard. But if the content is latent, then using a norm-based standard is likely to generate more convincing results. Although objectivity may be a reasonable goal for the coding of manifest content, it is not a realistic goal for the coding of latent content. Instead, the proper goal of coding latent content seems to be intersubjectivity. When a high percentage of coders who are given the task of assessing latent content arrive at the same inferences, the subjectively derived interpretations of individuals have converged. This convergence is convincing evidence of coder consistency, even though the coders did not use a purely objective, systematic method to arrive at their judgments. In fact, because all coders inferred the same pattern using their different subjective perceptual and reasoning processes, this evidence seems to be *more* convincing that the patterns of latent content exist as coded. Intersubjective convergence gives readers the sense that the patterns in the latent content are fairly robust and that if the readers were to code the same content, they too would make the same judgments.

As a second step, it is strongly recommended that researchers who choose a norm-based standard use multiple coders assigned to the same overlap of units. This approach provides for a much more powerful test of consistency of decision making across coders. When researchers have many coders available, they must make an important decision. They can either (a) divide coders into pairs (or small subgroups) and assign each pair to code a separate set of material or (b) have all coders independently code the same material. Given a fixed set of coder resources, this decision forces a trade-off between the number of sampling units in the overlap and the number of coders assigned to the same overlap. Splitting the pool of coders into many pairs gives the researcher the advantage of stretching the coding resources across a larger proportion of the sample. In contrast, keeping all coders on the same overlap reduces the size of the sample in the reliability test, but it gives the researcher a stronger platform for assessing consistency across coders.

In practice, most researchers choose the first option (pairing coders), because it then allows for maximizing the proportion of the sample in the reliability test. This approach, however, has a problem. If researchers arrange coders into pairs, it is impossible to observe whether there are patterns of widespread agreement. When a pair of coders agree, there is no way of knowing if this agreement is an anomaly or if many other people also would have agreed with them. If the pair of coders disagree, it is impossible to tell which of the two would be in the majority of coders if many coders had completed the same task. Thus, the question arises of whose decisions are more normative—that is, whose decisions are consistent with those of other coders. Unfortunately, one is unable to address this question when comparing coding decisions within a pair of coders. So with an overlap of only two coders, the reliability analysis focuses on how consistently the two coders agree with one another *across decisions.* This matter is different from the issue of how widespread agreement is *across different coders,* which is more at the heart of the reliability issue of reproducibility. Although both concepts of consistency are relevant to the issue of reliability, readers of content analyses are more concerned about whether they personally would have made the same decisions as the coders. Therefore, it is a relatively weak argument to show that a particular pair of coders agree as compared to an argument showing that, for example, six out of six or even six out of eight coders agree. (For a more in-depth treatment of this topic, see Potter and Levine- Donnerstein, 1996.)

When the content analyst has access to a relatively large number of coders, those coders should be used to create a powerful test of reliability. All coders should be assigned to the same task in the overlap to maximize the comparative power.

Researchers also need to address the issue of selection of the overlap conceptually by thinking about the degree of uniformity across the units in the sample. If the units are not uniform in terms of the difficulty in coding, then the overlap should be stratified to include all subsets of units.

As a third step, it is recommended that percentages of agreement be translated into reliability coefficients by use of a formula that removes chance agreement. The binomial correction method provides the most accurate estimate of consistency corrected for chance agreement. Each of the other methods of determining intercoder reliability has limitations. The percentage-of-agreement method results in inflated coefficients, because it does not correct for chance agreement. The computation of a proportional reduction of error (PRE) measure corrects for chance agreement, but a limit exists in using pairs of coders, such as with Scott's pi. Cohen's kappa allows for multiple coders, but it overcorrects for chance agreement, and this overcorrection is especially serious when larger numbers of coders are used. Krippendorff's alpha can be used in more situations than either Scott's pi or Cohen's kappa, but it is very complex and very difficult to set up and compute.

We need to determine the web of context. Determining the web of context shifts the focus away from the presence of individual contextual characteristics and places it instead on structure—that is, how those contextual characteristics cluster together. Meaning is in the pattern of context—the web—much more than in a list of individual contextual characteristics.

PART IV

Lineation Theory

14

Axioms and Dictionary

lineation (handwritten)

In this chapter, I lay the groundwork for a general theory of media violence. First, I present four axioms that underlie the theory. These are the fundamental tenets on which this theory is based. Second, I present a dictionary of key terms. Then in the next chapter, I present a set of propositions.

I have named this set of propositions lineation theory to refer to its multiple uses of the line metaphor. *Lineation* means "marking with lines; a system or series of lines; dividing into lines" (*Webster's New World,* 1964, p. 852). The metaphor of line is used in four key ways: *programming line* for thinking about the industry and how it produces as well as programs violence; *narrative line* for thinking about content; the *line of influence* for thinking about how to connect violent portrayals with effects; and *threshold lines* that divide the qualitatively different kinds of processing of media messages.

AXIOMS

Lineation theory is built on four axioms. These fundamental assumptions underlie and support the theory. They are presented here as arguments to convince you, the reader, that they are useful tenets. First, we need a broader perspective on the phenomenon itself. Second, we need a broader conceptualization of the focal constructs of *violence* and *effects*. Third, we need an even more multivariate examination with a focus on probabilistic effects. And fourth, we need to recognize the importance of individual interpretations.

These arguments reveal that lineation theory is positioned primarily within the social science paradigm. However, it would be a mistake to characterize the theory as an example of the powerful effects tradition, which has been discredited for more than half a century. Instead, this theory is much more in the tradition of social cognitions, which has been gaining prominence during the past several decades. In addition, some of the thinking within social cognition reaches into the humanistic paradigm, in which focusing on the uniqueness of

[margin note: post-modern]

individuals in meaning making has value over directing attention solely on patterns in the aggregate. Although this characteristic of unique interpretations is supported most strongly by the fourth argument, it appears in all four arguments. Each argument is elaborated in the discussion that follows.

① Broader View of the Phenomenon

A general theory of media violence should take a broad view of the phenomenon. This means looking beyond effects and content to examine also the media industries and the processes of influence. These four elements (effects, content, media industries, and processes) are very different facets of the same phenomenon. I argue that the more we know about one of these facets, the better we can understand the nature of the other facets. Therefore, it is useful to incorporate all four facets into one system of explanation. In addition, it is useful to broaden our conception of the four facets themselves.

Effects

[margin note: need more on fear + desensitization]

A great deal of research has focused on the effects of media violence, but this research has concentrated primarily on immediate effects, and there it is largely limited to the one effect of disinhibition. We need much more investigation into the more-difficult-to-determine long-term effects. The much smaller literatures on fear and desensitization are promising and need to be extended. And a wide range of other cognitive, emotional, and drive-altering effects also need to be examined.

Content

During the past several decades, analyses of content have been moving beyond the simple counting of occurrences of violence and have been incorporating the examination of the context within which it is presented. However, a nagging question remains: Are we missing something important in the context? This question becomes more significant when we consider violence presented in fantasy and/or humorous contexts. The terms *fantasy* and *humor* likely are too general. For example, there are many different kinds of humor, and not all humor has the same meaning or is interpreted in the same way. So perhaps we should analyze humor by breaking it down into meaningful subtypes and then monitoring the appearance of those subtypes in the context of violence in the media.

[margin note: context as web]

We also need to go beyond the examination of context as a list of discrete characteristics. Instead, we need to think of context as a web in which the individual elements (such as reward, consequences, weapons, graphicness, character attractiveness, and many other factors) are woven together into a pattern. The pattern is in the web, not within any single characteristic. We need to focus on how the contextual factors form a web and how the web signals meaning to viewers.

Another content limitation is that the examination of violence has been focused largely within the realm of television, and within television it is limited primarily to entertainment programming. More needs to be done to analyze news and perhaps ads within television. And we need to monitor the violent messages in other media, especially on the Internet and in video games, lyrics of popular music, and portrayals in print.

The most striking limitation of this literature has been its focus on the *what* of media violent content and its almost complete lack of examination of the *why*. We need to ask, Why is violence in the media the way it is? That is, why does it usually follow a standard formula? Furthermore, why does it appear continually across so much of the television landscape? And why is children's programming so saturated with violence?

Media Industries

This part of the media violence phenomenon is the facet most overlooked by communication researchers. Effects researchers and content analysts often suggest that if their research findings were powerful enough of an indictment of the industry, then programmers and producers would automatically change their practices. But this continues *not* to be the case. The industry is not acting out of ignorance, but social scientists often mount their criticisms out of ignorance of the industry. Therefore, researchers need to conduct better investigations of the stated and implied goals and practices of the industry. A good line of research is examining the news segment of the industry (e.g., see Altheide & Snow, 1979; Fishman, 1980; Tuchman, 1978), but unfortunately this research does not deal much with the issue of violence. Understanding more about the economic environments and organizational cultures will help us understand the content better.

We need to elaborate our findings about violent content and effects within the mind-set of decision makers operating from an economic point of view. Programmers are most interested in the acquisition and use of resources. Their goal is to maximize their primary asset, which is the audience.

Processes

We need to go beyond documenting what an effect is and address the questions of *how* and *why* more fully. What processes lead to those various effects? What factors increase the probability of these effects? With cultivation theory, for example, there is support for the prediction *that* viewers will be influenced by television. But not much work reflects *how* viewers are being influenced. Because of this lack of direction for examining how the process works, the process is limited simply to building an inventory of topics in which television exposure has a cultivation effect.

Some theories have provided guidance to answer these questions and have become even more useful as they have evolved into more cognitive approaches to media effects. For example, Bandura has extended social learning theory into social cognitive theory, and Berkowitz has extended cue theory into construct activation theory.

Broader Conceptualization of Focal Constructs

The two most important constructs concerning media violence are violence and effects. These are the two focal constructs of lineation theory. Research and theorizing to this point have presented a variety of elements for both violence and its effects. Although all these elements are useful, we need a clear, broad definition of each.

A broader definition of violence would guide future content analyses to inventory all gradations of violence. Readers of the results of such analyses would have the option of excluding certain types of enactments if they so desired. In addition, readers who wanted to assemble their own configurations could do so. But to provide these options, we must have the broadest resource so that scholars have a complete set from which to work. Similarly, with the focal construct of effects, the definition must be very broad to stimulate research across the full spectrum.

Multivariate-Probabilistic Approach

Many factors about the audiences, the messages, and the environment influence the way in which media violence affects viewers. Decades of research on this topic have shown us that the range of influences is very wide. We need to think in terms of biological variables, such as drives, instincts, and hormones. We must consider variables from the ecological theories, such as sociological factors, that dominate the real-world environment (family, networks of friends, and the institutions of religion, education, government, etc.), as well as the media environment. We must also look at the variables suggested by cognitive theories, such as traits (developmental level of cognitive abilities, cognitive style, personality, lifestyle) and states (motivations, arousal levels).

All these factors (and perhaps others) exert simultaneous influences in any exposure situation and likely work in concert to shape effects. If we are to move closer to understanding the complexity of this influence process, we must account for many (if not all) of these factors simultaneously in our analyses. Thus, it is essential that the analysis be truly multivariate.

My use of the term *multivariate* is not concerned with the number of variables as much as with the simultaneity of influences. Some studies in the effects literature build four or five variables into a design but then look at the influence of each only one at a time. This approach is not multivariate in the sense I mean. My argument for multivariate analyses pushes the focus onto the interactions among variables, as well as their unique combinations after controlling for the influences of other variables in the analyses.

probable causes

When examining the relationships among all these factors, we should be careful to use probabilistic instead of deterministic language. Doing so forces us to think about the nature of causation, a condition that requires three characteristics (e.g., see Babbie, 1992, p. 72). First, there must be a relationship between the hypothesized cause and the observed effect. Second, the cause must always precede the effect in time. And third, we must rule out all alternative causes for the effect. The more we know about the influence of the media, the more challenge we have in meeting the latter two conditions. These conditions present formidable barriers to making deterministic claims. As long as we hold deterministic causation as a goal, we will fail. And as long as we allow the public, policymakers, and programmers to continue perceiving our goal as discovering causal factors, we will forever be seen as falling short in our efforts. Instead, we need to acknowledge more visibly the goal of achieving probabilistic causation.

Media effects are almost always probabilistic, and they are influenced by many different factors simultaneously. As social scientists, we know this; this is nothing new. But knowing it and giving that knowledge stronger weight so that it forms a perspective from which we design research are two different things. As Chapter 12 demonstrated, the experimental literature is very good at identifying variables that have an effect, but much weaker at telling us the relative strengths of the effects of the multiple variables within different effects processes. The reason is that the analysis of data in experiments is largely limited to simply examining whether differences exist across treatment groups. Missing are multivariate studies that look at the simultaneous interaction of influences among many variables. The literature reviews also reflect this univariate limitation as they present their lists of variables that have been found to lead to negative effects. In some cases, reviewers highlight interactions between two variables, but no review builds toward a full model of effect and illuminates the unique probabilistic contributions of each variable. Knowledge of the effects process stops here. This is the frontier.

Highlighting Individual Interpretations

As social scientists, sometimes we focus so much on looking for aggregate patterns that we ignore the differences across individuals. This is a problem with media texts. For example, Hall (1980) reminds us that television programs do not have a single meaning, but instead they are what he calls "open texts," which are subject to different readings by different people. Newcomb (1978) reinforces this position by saying that messages do not speak for themselves and that we cannot predict a viewer's response by looking solely at the message or text. Instead, it must be understood that viewers constantly interact with the messages in a kind of dialogue. As Newcomb pointed out, opinion about any given show usually varies widely, and even people who share a common reaction to a particular program often have very different reasons for doing so.

These researchers explained that viewers bring values and attitudes, a universe of personal experiences and concerns to the texts, and by so doing, a viewer examines, acknowledges, and makes texts of his or her own. These multiple readings of television shows are made possible because viewers are individuals who bring different values and social histories to the task (Allen, 1987).

Of course, social scientists have known that there is always a range of reaction to any media message for a much longer time than critics have been writing about it. Anyone who has conducted an experiment has observed that a given stimulus affects different people differently. It is not that social science is insensitive to individual differences; rather, social science is more interested in aggregates than in differences among individuals. So, differences among participants in a treatment group are regarded as a low level of noise that must be tolerated, and this noise is relegated to the bin of error variance. This error variance (the differences among participants) is neatly partitioned and used as a comparison for the signal (which is the variance between groups) to construct ratios of variance. The higher the ratio, the more significant the results. And to get a high ratio, the differences between groups must be much larger than the variance within groups. Because effect sizes (differences across treatment groups) are usually small in social science, we try to construct research designs to minimize within-group variance; that is, we try to construct treatments in such a way that all participants in a treatment group behave in the same way or construct the same interpretations.

Therefore, although social scientists recognize the importance of individual differences at the conceptual level, they lose sight of the importance of this variation when they get down into the empirical trenches and hope that their manipulation checks result in a pattern of uniform reaction among all participants within each different treatment condition. At best, they acknowledge individual differences by trying to tie them to several variables (usually demographics of sex, age, etc.) and then covary out their effect in the analysis. This approach keeps the focus sharply on the treatment variables, but it loses all the information about how characteristics of individuals are keyed into making the treatment work and contrasting them with the characteristics that work against the effect—as participants constantly do outside the laboratory, where they are ordinary television viewers.

I am not arguing that we abandon the quest to find general patterns in the aggregate. Instead, I am arguing for an expanded goal for research: to try to explain individual differences in interpretation. Rather than treating within-group variation as error and setting it aside, let's also analyze that variance. We begin to focus on individual interpretations by asking people to articulate their own meanings rather than imposing meanings on them in experimental situations (such as telling them whether a portrayal is real or justified) or constraining meaning choices by a questionnaire.

definitions

TABLE 14.1 Focal Constructs

Violence

Any action that harms a person or something a person values, such as physical property, reputation, or cherished idea. The action can be physical or verbal; the resulting harm can be physical, emotional, or psychological.

Intentionality is an important element in this definition. When the perpetrator can conceive of intentions, there must be an intention to harm. However, when the perpetrator cannot be motivated by intentions, as in acts of nature, the act need only exhibit harm to be considered violent. Acts that are intended to do harm but fail are also included.

The act can be presented in any kind of context. It can be serious or humorous. It can be literal reality (as in news), fiction, or pure fantasy. And it can happen on-screen or off-screen if clearly implied.

Violence is distinguished from aggression in the sense that aggression is defined as having a goal-directed drive that lacks an intention to harm.

Effect

A change in a person as a result of exposure to one or more violent messages in the media. The change can be negative or positive; can be immediate or take a long time to occur; can dissipate very quickly or persist a long time; and can be physiological, cognitive, attitudinal, emotional, behavioral, or any combination of these. It can be very large, clearly observable, and direct, such as copycat criminal behavior immediately following an exposure to specific actions in a television show. But it can also be subtle, very difficult to observe, and indirect, such as people's expressing opinions that the rate of crime has been going up dramatically in their neighborhoods when the crime rate actually has remained at a steady, very low level.

The idea of change is not limited to behavior. Change can happen cognitively (adding or subtracting from a person's set of information), attitudinally (creating or reversing opinions), physiologically (increasing heart rate and blood pressure), or emotionally (shifting from calm to fear).

In a subtle but profound sense, change is also conceptualized as the reinforcing of existing knowledge, attitudes, or behaviors. From an observational point of view, nothing seems to have changed. But the reinforcement effect gives greater weight to what already exists, and that is what is meant by change in this sense.

There are five families of effects: learning or imitation, fear, desensitization, drive altering, and societal effects (see Table 14.2). Note that this table reconfigures and extends the effects outlined in Chapter 9.

DICTIONARY

In this dictionary, I distinguish among four different types of terms. First are the focal constructs—violence and effects—which are the most important ideas in the theory (see Tables 14.1 and 14.2). I define these two terms differently

TABLE 14.2 The Effects Typology

Learning or Imitation Effects
1. Cognitive encoding
2. Generalizing to novel behaviors
3. Disinhibition
4. Triggering
5. Learning social norms about violence

Fear Effects
1. Immediate emotional reaction
2. Cultivation of fear

Desensitization
1. Immediate change of attitudes
2. Reinforcement of attitudes
3. Habituation

Drive-Altering Effects
1. Temporary physiological arousal
2. Catharsis
3. Narcotizing

Societal Effects
1. Attraction to the fringe
2. Reshaping institutions

---

from how any other scholars define them. Because these definitions are different and because the differences are so important to lineation theory, they are regarded as focal terms, and their definitions are carefully laid out in detail in this section. (For a discussion of the importance of explicating focal constructs, see Chaffee, 1991.)

Second are many key constructs in addition to the two focal constructs (see Table 14.3). These are also important terms that have special meaning in lineation theory. However, they are less central to the theory than are the two focal constructs. They are organized in four groups: media industries, content, effects, and processes. Most of these definitions appear at the appropriate places in the theory itself, which is presented in Chapter 15. For each group, the most important term is defined first, and the other terms, listed alphabetically, are defined under that term.

Third are the primitive terms that I am leaving undefined in the belief that scholars reading this book would share the same meanings for these terms. For these terms, the everyday meaning, which is shared by most people, is the

TABLE 14.3 Key Constructs

Media Industry Terms

Programming Line A norm of programming that is imagined by programmers, such that appeal is increased as high as possible without going so far as to offend audience members. Programmers push the line (relineation) by getting away from old, tired portrayals and presenting little surprises intended to shock the audience pleasantly and hold their attention.

Audience The set of people exposed to a message. Typically, the audience is a target in the minds of programmers. Generally programmers think in terms of two kinds of audiences: mass and niche.

Mass Audience For the dominant media, programmers regard everyone as a potential audience member, so they try to appeal to as many people as possible. Broadcast television is one dominant medium; it tries to develop programming to appeal to everyone in the country over 2 years of age and living in a television household. Other dominant media are certain cable channels (such as TBS and USA), Hollywood films, some magazines (such as *Time* and *TV Guide*), newspapers, and mass market books.

Niche Audience With most media and vehicles, programmers think in terms of smaller sets of people, such as niches, to whom they can appeal. These sets are usually defined with demographics (Nickelodeon aiming at children; Lifetime aiming at women) or personal interests (Fox Sports Network, History Channel, *Soldier of Fortune* magazine, books on how to build a bomb).

Audience Appeal The primary tool used by programmers to attract the attention of as many people in an audience as possible. Programmers believe that appeal is created by arousing the viewers and triggering strong emotions in a pleasant way.

Creative Bandwidth The range of different variations on characters and narratives that programmers try. If programmers limit message elements to very minor deviations from the formula, the creative bandwidth is very small.

Least Objectionable Programming (LOP) The selecting of content units that have the lowest probability of offending (or challenging) viewers.

Lowest Common Denominator (LCD) Programming for the lowest requirements of viewers. Such programming is based on the belief that programs that are more efficient (that are easier to watch and deliver more emotional appeal without offending) will attract the lower tiers of viewers (people of lower socioeconomic status and of lower IQ or education) without losing the upper tiers (people who want more challenging programming).

Media The major channels of information and entertainment dissemination in this culture. Television (broadcast and cable) is regarded as the dominant medium, because people spend more time with TV than with any other medium and therefore are likely to be affected more by it; thus, most of the research and theorizing has focused on television. This theory builds from that television research but generalizes it, where possible, to all media, including print (newspapers, magazines, books), radio, film, audio recordings, and computers (games, the Internet, etc.).

Programmers and Producers The people who create and make decisions about content units. Producers (novelists, screenwriters, songwriters, reporters, etc.) create those units. Programmers are the gatekeepers of the media; they decide which content units are produced or disseminated in the media.

Relineation of Programming Line Redrawing the programming line to keep up with what appeals most to society while avoiding criticism.

Responsibility To media programmers, avoiding offending audiences—that is, not crossing the programming line of good taste.

Vehicle That which delivers the media messages. For example, television is a medium, and programs (evening news, *ER,* etc.) are the vehicles; newspaper is a medium, and the *New York Times* is a vehicle.

Viewer An audience member who is exposed to a content unit of media violence. Strictly speaking, the term refers to someone exposed to television or film; in lineation theory, it is used in a more general sense.

(continued)

TABLE 14.3 Continued

Content Terms

Narrative Line A formula for the way violence is portrayed in the media. Although deviations from this formula exist across media and across vehicles within a medium, a fairly consistent set of characteristics is usually found with violence. The formula for media violence is as follows: "Bad" characters commit transgressive violence—that is, aggressively harmful acts that are first strikes against other characters or objects. These transgressive acts are motivated out of a selfish desire on the part of bad characters. "Good" characters, the ones wronged by the transgressive acts or who serve in roles to protect good characters (such as family and friends) or society (such as police), are thereby given a motivation to retaliate strongly against the bad characters. The good characters are positioned in the violent narrative so that the audience will identify with them; that is, they are attractive in some way, and the story is told from their point of view. The bad characters typically commit multiple violent acts so as to build the conflict throughout the narrative progression. These acts usually attain their goals and almost never are punished. This pattern arouses the emotions of viewers, who feel that the bad characters are "getting away with something" by being allowed to continue their behavior and being successful. The audience is directed to want revenge. Throughout the narrative, the good characters become stronger and more successful in their own acts of violence until the conflict builds to its highest point, at which the violence of the good characters is stronger and more successful than the violence of the bad characters. As a result of this climactic scene, order is restored, in the form of the transgressors finally being stopped and sometimes punished.

Content Unit A meaningful segment of media programming. With newspapers or magazines, it is the story (fiction or news). With radio and audio recordings, it is usually the song. With computers on the Internet, it is a visit to a site. With television, the unit is the program; however, the program can be subdivided into smaller units: sequence, scene, or interaction.

Contextual Characteristics Individual features about the way violence is portrayed that provide viewers with information about how to interpret the meaning of the portrayal. Contextual characteristics include features about the perpetrator (such as demographics, appearance, role, consequences), the victim, environment (such as realism), the narrative (such as justification and appropriateness of the act), and the violent act itself (such as use of weapons and graphicness).

Contextual Web The pattern of contextual variables in a media violence portrayal.

Duration An indicator of saturation of violence in a narrative; for television or film, it is usually expressed either in seconds or as a percentage of total narrative time; for example, "2% of narrative time was violent."

Prevalence An indicator of how widespread violence is throughout a medium's total programming; with the medium of television, programs are used as units of comparison; for example, "80% of all programs were found to contain some violence."

Rate An indicator of the frequency of occurrence of discrete violent actions; usually normed by the hour of programming; for example, "there were six acts of violence per hour."

TABLE 14.3 Continued

Effects Terms

Line of Influence The connection between exposure to media violence and a particular effect. The goal of researchers studying the effects of media violence is to construct this path.

Arousal Jag The excited feeling associated with the physiological effect of heightened heart rate and blood pressure. It can be triggered by different kinds of real-life experiences and media portrayals, especially violence.

Attraction to the Fringe A society-level effect. As the amount of violent portrayals that are dumped into the culture from the media increases, so does the number of people who are attracted away from the mainstream and toward the fringe.

Catharsis Viewers' use of violent messages in the media to release their aggressive drives vicariously.

Cognitive Encoding Coding that takes place immediately during exposure as the viewer inserts new information from an exposure into an existing script, either by altering it or by reinforcing existing patterns. This coding engages three elements: facts of the violent portrayal, meaning of the act as determined by context, and emotional reaction.

Cultivation of Fear A long-term effect that has both emotional and cognitive aspects that portray the world as threatening. After years of exposure to violent messages in the media, a person has developed scripts with emotional feelings linked to cognitive information.

Delineation The construction of a line of influence that links together exposure to media violence and an effect.

Desensitization The erosion of one's natural feelings of sympathy for victims of violence or of existing beliefs that violence is bad, harmful, or punishable.

Disinhibition An immediate effect that reduces barriers to performing aggressively during exposure to media violence or shortly thereafter. This effect puts viewers in a ready state in which they think and feel that behaving aggressively is good, or at least not bad.

Generalizing Constructing a pattern out of individual portrayals of media violence and projecting this pattern onto the real world, into the future, or onto another class of behaviors, people, or settings.

Habituation A long-term physiological effect that is linked to emotional tolerance.

Learning Acquisition of an element related to media violence. Learning can be a cognitive (a fact in the content unit), emotional, or physiological reaction to a content unit. The element is coded into a script from which it can be retrieved.

Narcotization A long-term effect that builds up a dependence on exposure to portrayals of media violence. Development of this effect begins with an arousal jag with each exposure; that is, viewers experience a heightened heart rate and blood pressure that they find pleasant. Over time, however, it takes stronger depictions of violence and more of them in rapid succession for viewers to experience the arousal jag. So viewers have a stronger and stronger drive to seek out media violence.

Reshaping Institutions A society-level effect. The media portrayals of violence gradually change societal institutions (such as family, government, court system, education, and religion).

Social Norms Patterns of thinking and behavior as prescribed by society. Such prescriptions are the commonly shared rules and perspectives held by most members of the society.

Triggering An immediate effect that takes viewers from the ready state into behavioral performance.

(continued)

TABLE 14.3 Continued

Processing Terms

Script Relineation Altering an existing script by making it more general (leveling) so that a portrayal discrepant with the script can be made to fit, or elaborating an existing script (sharpening) by adding more detail so that it becomes a more useful guide in making finer discriminations among portrayals.

Associational Network The pattern of connections among ideas and images in a person's mind.

Construct Accessibility The retrieval of information from one's psychological schemas when cues in the media are perceived. During exposure to media violence, people will seek out cues in the media portrayal and use this cuing information to look for appropriate schemas to use as a guide in interpreting those portrayals of character, plot point, setting, and so on. The schemas that are most likely to be accessed are those that have been used most recently or those that are the most often used.

Liminal Thresholds The boundaries marking the four channels of perception.

Perceptual Channels Levels of perception by viewers exposed to media violence. There are four perceptual channels: subliminal, automatic, attentional, and self-reflexive. These four channels of processing are rather like steps in a hierarchy of awareness. Each step is marked by a liminal threshold that requires a different kind of perceptual processing.

Perceptual Flow The uninterrupted continuation in a perceptual channel during an exposure session. There is an inertia to the flow; the longer people stay in a perceptual flow, the harder it is to interrupt that flow.

Scripts Templates that people use to (a) guide their perceptions during exposures and (b) interpret the meaning of messages in their exposures. Media scripts are accessed when a person is exposed to a content unit, searches the content for a few salient characteristics, and then matches those content characteristics to various scripts in order to pick the most appropriate one to make meaning of the current content unit. Scripts are constructions by individuals and are the product of their experiences filtered through their mental processes of sorting and meaning making. Although schemas are static frames, such as classification rules that draw boundaries for us, scripts are sequences of frames that tell us how action should progress.

---

meaning that is used in this theory. Thus, these terms have no special—or technical—meaning when used in this theory. Examples of these terms include *characters, perpetrators, targets, victims, weapons, television, newspapers, magazines, books, radio, news, fiction, viewing, reading, listening, children, adolescents,* and *adults.*

Fourth and last is a group of terms I call viewer-defined terms. These terms are best not defined by researchers or theoreticians; these terms are often used in everyday language by all people. People have a clear, intuitively derived meaning for these terms, although sometimes it is difficult for them to articulate that meaning. But they know it when they see it.

Interestingly, each of these terms is likely to have a range of meanings in the general population. That is, not everyone defines the term in precisely the same way. For example, think of the term *attractiveness*. Most people, whether social

TABLE 14.4 Some Viewer-Defined Terms

Attractive

Bad versus good

Consequences
   Pain or harm
   Successful versus unsuccessful
   Reward versus punishment

Graphic or explicit

Hero versus villain

Humorous

Justified

Negative versus positive

Offensive

Real versus fantasy

---

scientists or couch potatoes, know what this term means to them. However, the meanings of *attractiveness* differ substantially across individuals. What a 14-year-old boy thinks of as attractive is most likely something very different from what a 35-year-old woman thinks of as attractive. Furthermore, a Beverly Hills plastic surgeon, a 5-year-old girl hugging a teddy bear, a gay Olympic gymnast, and a poor migrant worker from a Third World country are all familiar with the term *attractiveness* but are likely to have very different definitions for it.

What is important for lineation theory is the recognition that this type of term exists and that many examples of such terms are essential for the explanatory propositions in the theory (see Table 14.4). Although these terms are very important in lineation theory, I prefer they that they be treated descriptively, not prescriptively; that is, I am arguing that we as researchers need to inventory the variety of meanings so that we can understand how they are used in common, everyday language in the general population. Once those receiver definitions are described, the meanings should be related to the influence process outlined in the theory. But rather than have these definitions imposed by the theory, it would be much more useful for researchers to inventory the various meanings of each term and then try to test that variety of meanings in the propositions in which the term appears. This is one of the ways the theory respects the interpretive nature of an individual's meaning making.

15

Propositions

In this final chapter, I present a large set of propositions that attempt to provide a systematic explanation for media violence in its widest sense. These propositions (summarized in Table 15.1) seek to explain violence across all media by focusing attention on the media violence narrative line. Furthermore, they seek to explain more than one facet of media violence by examining not only effects but also media industries, content, process patterns, and general influence.

Some media scholars, particularly those most focused on psychological experimentation, might have a tighter view of what a theory is and object to my characterizing what follows as a theory. Empirical researchers who are used to encountering theories that have a single proposition (or small set of propositions) will find this theory very unwieldy, because there is no way to operationalize a study to test this theory fully in a single research design.

However, what follows is a theory. It presents an integrated set of propositions, each of which can be transduced into a hypothesis that can be tested (some might require a bit more creative thinking than others). Those tests can result in findings that do not support part of the theory, so the propositions can be falsified.

This theory of media violence attempts to build on the key ideas from both theoretical thinking and empirical testing. It draws heavily on the ideas in the theories reviewed in Chapter 2. It also builds from the many empirical findings (reviewed in Chapters 3 and 4) that have attained the status of laws.

At first glance, what follows might look somewhat like *Human Behavior: An Inventory of Scientific Findings,* published by Berelson and Steiner in 1964, because of the way in which the major propositions are highlighted and the paragraphs are numbered to show the nested structure. However, this theory is different in two major ways. First, its focus on media violence is much more narrow than that of Berelson and Steiner, who looked at all communication. Second, lineation theory is more than an inventory; it is a synthesis—not a list—of empirical findings. In addition, it includes my speculations. Some of

225

TABLE 15.1 Outline of Propositions

Content

11. Presence of violence
    11.1. Prevalence
    11.2. Rate
    11.3. Duration
12. Typified narrative line
    12.1. Contextual web
    12.2. Character portrayals

Media Industry

21. Goal of programmers
    21.1. Appeal
    21.2. Responsibility
22. Setting the line of programming
    22.1. Least objectionable programming
    22.2. Fear of labeling
    22.3. Appeal belief
    22.4. Appeal of news
23. Changing the violence narrative line
    23.1. Audience support of the narrative line
    23.2. Creative bandwidth

Process

31. Perceptual channels
    31.1. Subliminal channel
    31.2. Automatic channel
    31.3. Attentional channel
    31.4. Self-reflexive channel
32. Perceptual flow
    32.1. General viewing style
    32.2. Special motives
33. Perceptual inertia
    33.1. Typical channel
    33.2. Changes in channels
34. Scripts
    34.1. General script
    34.2. Subscripts
35. Selection of scripts
    35.1. Perceptual channels
        35.1.1. Efficiency
        35.1.2. Accuracy

TABLE 15.1 Continued

35.2. Encountering minor deviations
    35.2.1. Ignore discrepant elements
    35.2.2. Seek alternative messages
    35.2.3. Alter the script
35.3. Encountering major deviations
    35.3.1. Seek more appropriate script
    35.3.2. Terminate exposure
    35.3.3. Significantly alter the script
35.4. Encountering no deviations
    35.4.1. Seek out another exposure
    35.4.2. Continue the exposure
36. Script alterations
  36.1. Controlled alterations
  36.2. Unconscious alterations

4 General Influence

41. Sets of general influence factors
  41.1. Perceptual channels
    41.1.1. Type of perceptual channel
    41.1.2. Interaction with contextual factors
  41.2. Content factors
    41.2.1. Type of violence
    41.2.2. Context of the portrayal
    41.2.3. Frequency of exposure
  41.3. Viewer factors
  41.4. Long-term environment
  41.5. Situational cues
42. Synergistic interaction of general influence factors
  42.1. Factors work in interaction
  42.2. Factors work in a cumulative probabilistic manner

5 Families of Effects

51. Learning and imitation
  51.1. Cognitive encoding
  51.2. Generalizing to novel behaviors
  51.3. Disinhibition
  51.4. Triggering
  51.5. Learning social norms
  51.6. Influences on learning or imitation
    51.6.1. Characteristics of the exposure situation
    51.6.2. Content characteristics

(continued)

TABLE 15.1 Continued

51.6.3. Viewer traits
51.6.4. Viewer states
51.6.5. General environment
51.6.6. Situational cues
52. Fear
52.1. Immediate emotional reaction
52.2. Cultivation of fear
53. Desensitization
53.1. Immediate change of attitudes
53.2. Reinforcement of attitudes
53.3. Habituation
53.4. Influences on desensitization effects
53.4.1. Characteristics of the exposure situation
53.4.2. Content characteristics
53.4.3. Viewer traits
54. Drive-altering effects
54.1. Temporary physiological arousal
54.2. Catharsis
54.3. Narcotization
54.4. Influences on drive-altering effects
54.4.1. Content characteristics
54.4.2. Viewer traits
54.4.3. Viewer states
55. Societal effects
55.1. Moving the mean more toward a fight-or-flight mentality
55.2. Changing institutions
55.3. Factors that contribute to a societal effect
55.3.1. Saturation with violence
55.3.2. Constancy of the contextual web

these speculations have been suggested by a study or two, but some are logical extensions between two other points in the theory so as to bridge a gap between them. These speculations draw primarily on the arguments presented in Chapters 5 through 13.

This chapter is organized to highlight five facets of media violence: content, media industry, process, general influence, and families of effects. Because this chapter contains many propositions, they have been numbered in five series to allow quick identification of a proposition with the facet it is addressing. The propositions that address the content facet are numbered in the 10 series (which begins with 11), propositions addressing the media industry facet in the 20 series (which begins with 21), process propositions in the 30 series, general-influence propositions in the 40 series, and family-of-effects propositions in the 50 series (see Table 15.1).

CONTENT

2 propositions

Lineation theory presents two sets of content propositions: (a) the presence of violence in the television world and (b) the media violence narrative line. These are lawlike propositions because they are supported by numerous content analysis studies, all of which confirm the findings. In addition, they are descrip- *descriptive* tive: They simply describe elements in the narrative line, rather than attempting an explanation for why the narrative line exists the way it does.

11. *Presence of Violence.* Violence is widespread throughout the media. Violence appears in books, magazines, newspapers, films, and musical lyrics in recordings and on radio broadcasts. Violence is especially prevalent on television, which is the dominant medium because it reaches larger audiences and those audiences spend more time with it than with any other medium. Within the television world, violence appears frequently in all genres, during all parts of the day, and on all channels.

TV

11.1. *Prevalence.* Violence is found in 60% of all programs across the television landscape. It is especially high (about 80%) among programs watched by most people—that is, on prime-time commercial broadcast stations.

11.2. *Rate.* Rates of violence are high. When a content unit (film, TV program, song lyric, etc.) contains a violent portrayal, usually several or many violent portrayals are contained in that content unit; that is, seldom is there a single act of violence.
11.2.1. Rates are higher for verbal violence than for physical violence. In fictional narratives on television, characters are more likely to insult, lie to, yell at, or commit some other form of verbal aggression intended to harm another person than they are to commit a physical act of aggression.
11.2.2. Rates are shifting from major to minor types of violence. Although the overall rate of violence in the television world has not changed much since its earliest days of broadcasting, recently there has been a shift away from the more serious portrayals of violence. Within the category of physical violence, there are now fewer murders and rapes, but more assaults. In addition, the rate of physical violence seems to be declining gradually while the rate of verbal violence has increased.

11.3. *Duration.* Violence appears only a small percentage of time in television programming. Violent incidents in fictional narratives are usually very brief. In television fiction, violence appears on the screen only 2% to 5% of the time, depending on the type of program.

12. *Narrative Line.* Violence is portrayed in the media according to a typified narrative line. Of course, deviations from this narrative line exist across media and across vehicles within a medium. However, a fairly consistent set of characteristics usually is found in line with violence.

The narrative line is reflected in the propositions about the contextual web and character portrayals. These propositions have been derived largely from content analyses of television content. However, given the stability of these findings across all genres of television (drama series, situation comedies, news, movies, talk shows, children's shows, etc.) and given the pervasiveness of television throughout the culture, it is reasonable to speculate that this narrative line applies to all violence presented in the media.

12.1. *The contextual web supporting portrayals of violence is similar across the television landscape.* The heart of interpreting media violence is in the *way it is portrayed.* Viewers use contextual factors to guide their interpretations of the meaning of violence.

12.1.1. Much of the violence is portrayed as good. Perpetrators are often "good" characters who are created to be attractive to viewers. They are usually successful in their use of violence and are rarely punished for their actions. In addition, violent acts are frequently portrayed as justified, even though most violent acts are intentional and have motives that are not prosocial.

12.1.2. Most of the violence is trivialized. Violence is often shown in fantasy contexts and linked with humor, as in situation comedies; sometimes it is shown in both contexts (fantasy and humor), such as in cartoons. The harmful consequences to the victims are rarely shown, either immediately following the act or later in the program. Not only is the physical recovery rarely depicted, but sensitive portrayals of the emotional and psychological trauma are almost nonexistent.

12.1.3. Almost all the violence is sanitized. The presentation style is rarely graphic and explicit. Violence is rarely shown close-up or in much detail. Blood and gore are rarely shown. Often the violence happens off-screen, but the body is shown or the audience is told of the violent incident in a verbal recounting of the violent action. Such portrayal prevents shocking the viewers, but it still gets the message across that the media world contains a good deal of violence.

12.1.4. Violence is portrayed unrealistically. This part of the media violence narrative line is deceptive. In fictional narratives, the settings almost always appear realistic or may even be actual locations that viewers have visited. The characters are almost always humans who are acting very similar to how viewers act. But the unrealism comes in the form of exaggerated rates and depictions that give viewers false information about patterns of perpetrators and victims.

In addition, violence is unrealistic in "informational" programs, such as news and documentaries. With both fiction and news, the rates of violence portrayed are much higher than the rates in real life, and the pain and suffering of victims are either abstracted or ignored.

12.2. *Character patterns in the portrayals of violence are similar across the television landscape.* The research on characters involved in media violence has concentrated on television. Within the world of television is a strong profile of perpetrators and victims, as follows:

12.2.1. Most perpetrators are males.

12.2.2. Most perpetrators are white.

12.2.3. Most perpetrators are middle-aged.

12.2.4. Victims and perpetrators are demographically similar.

12.2.5. A high proportion of the violence is committed by "good" characters.

To put these profile propositions into context, I must point out that males make up about 75% of all characters on television, whites about 80%, and middle-aged people (30-50 years old) more than 50%. So, the character profile of violence follows the same line as the general profile for television characters. No type of character is significantly overrepresented as a perpetrator or victim of violence compared to their base levels of appearance in the television world. However, young children are almost never shown as either perpetrators or victims.

In summary, the typified narrative line focuses on a central character who is attractive and will stimulate a high level of identification with many viewers. Villain characters commit unjustified violence against "throw-away" targets, who are rarely shown in pain and who disappear after they are victimized. Often the central character is also victimized, but in such cases rarely is there any lasting harm—at least, no harm that would prevent that character from retaliating. Up to this point in the narrative line, the villains are portrayed as successful and often rewarded with physical possessions or praise from other characters. Rarely is any of this violence shown close-up or highly graphically. Eventually the central character retaliates with justified violence against the villains, subduing them (but not necessarily punishing them), and through this climax the world is put back in order and accounts are balanced. This narrative line extends through almost all episodes of crime and action-adventure series; it also extends through all genres of television programs, so its continual presence is a low-level hum throughout the media environment.

MEDIA INDUSTRY

The important questions with the media industries are, Why program violence? and Why is the narrative line the way it is? The three propositions in this section are speculative explanations. They are based on some research, but they need a good deal more empirical support before they can be regarded as laws.

Although the media industries themselves constitute a very important part of the media violence phenomenon, very little research has been conducted on this area compared to areas of content, process, and effects. Therefore, these propositions are much more speculative. They are also more explanatory than descriptive.

21. *Goal of Programmers.* Media programmers regard their goal as entertaining the greatest number of people within a potential audience. To serve this purpose well, they base their programming decisions about violent narratives on the dual criteria of appeal and responsibility. Therefore, they construct a programming line that maximizes positive appeal without going too far in triggering negative reactions.

21.1. *Appeal is used to increase audience size.* Producers believe that appeal is created by arousing the audience and triggering strong emotions in a pleasant way.

21.1.1. Violence is used to increase appeal, because violence is believed to be efficient. In other words, a strong emotional reaction can be elicited with a small amount of effort (writing creativity, production costs, and acting ability). It is easy to have a character pull a gun or shout a harsh invective. Violent acts appeal to the stronger and baser emotions in a primal way.

From the audience member's point of view, it is relatively easy to process violent messages because of so much conditioning from the media through years of exposure. With very little processing effort, viewers experience a strong emotional reaction in return.

21.1.2. The violence narrative line is believed to be the best way to present violence. Producers believe that the violence narrative line is a very good (if not the best) way to achieve high program appeal because the media violence narrative line arouses viewers, gives power to the most attractive characters, and appears justified. The violence is used to "right things" by putting the world back in order, and it does so in a sanitized manner so as not to offend viewers. Using the violence narrative line, producers can make viewers identify with the perpetrators by making those characters attractive and successful. The violence puts the viewers in vicarious fight-or-flight situations in which they always survive and triumph in a pleasant way.

21.2. *To media programmers, responsibility means avoiding offending the audience.* In the minds of programmers a line seems to divide acceptable portrayals from unacceptable portrayals. Part of being a successful programmer is to learn where the programming line is. It is different with different types of audiences, and it moves as the public's expectations and tolerance levels change.

21.2.1. Feedback from offended viewers signals programmers when they have crossed the line into poor responsibility. When programmers perceive themselves as crossing the line, they back off.

21.2.2. Programmers fear the damage to audience size, which is indicated by angry feedback. By the time programmers receive angry feedback (phone calls and letters expressing outrage about program elements), the damage has been done. Thus, programmers fear the threat of angry feedback, and they take steps to avoid triggering such feedback.

21.2.3. Given their purpose of increasing audience size, programmers do not define responsibility in terms of a public health issue, as public policy-makers would like them to do. In addition, programmers do not define responsibility in terms of risk to individuals, as social scientists would like them to do. Thus, the debate about what to do about media violence (or even if anything needs to be done) masks the more fundamental difference about conceptions of responsibility.

22. *The Programming Line.* Programmers push the line of violent programming as far as they can to increase the size of their audiences.

22.1. *For a dominant medium, such as broadcast television, programmers believe that the best strategy to reach the largest audience is through programming to the lowest common denominator (LCD) with the least objectionable programming (LOP).* Programmers believe that shows that are more efficient (i.e., that are easier to watch and deliver more emotional appeal without offending) attract the lower tiers of viewers (people of lower socioeconomic status and lower IQ or education) without losing the upper tiers (people who want more challenging programming). Thus, programming in the dominant media conforms more closely to the media violence narrative line.

22.1.1. The LOP strategy is less important when programming to niche audiences. Niche audiences are more homogeneous and thus have a narrower range of interests. The program is aimed directly at the niche audience rather than being stretched to appeal to many different kinds of people. Therefore, programmers aiming at a niche audience develop a different narrative line for violence if those differences increase appeal to the members of that particular niche.

22.1.2. As more viewers leave the mass audience, programmers lose their ability to condition viewers to the violence narrative line. However, viewers who have already been conditioned by the violence narrative line will expect to see that formula when they shift their exposures to niche programming. For example, some viewers might shift their viewing away from the commercial networks and to the science fiction channel. Such a shift is not stimulated by a desire to avoid violence. Instead, the shift is likely stimulated by a desire to experience different settings and different types of characters, but the expectation to have plots follow the violence narrative line remains.

22.2. *Programmers fear the labeling of programs for violent content because such labels have the potential to reduce audience size and anger viewers about programming.* Programmers believe that labels will scare potential viewers away from exposure to their programs. In addition, if they do not label programs according to the expectations of all individual viewers, some viewers will be angered by what they perceive as false labeling.

22.3. *The more widespread the appeal belief is among programmers, the more violence will be commissioned and the fewer alternatives there will be.* Content units that follow the narrative line of media violence are more likely to pass through the programming gate. Programmers commission content units that follow the narrative line, because they believe those units will appeal to a wider audience. This idea is a belief, and the belief of programmers is what counts. As long as that belief exists, programmers will commission violent programs. Over time in an environment of violence saturation, the choice is not really between violence and nonviolence, but among different configurations of violence, all of which are variations on the media violence narrative line.

22.4. *With informational content units (such as news), programmers are oriented primarily toward appeal.* Because news workers are almost never at the scene when a violent act occurs, news coverage is never an eidetic report. Instead, it is always a reconstruction that is shaped by the values of the news workers. News programmers value most a story focused on elements that will capture and hold viewers' attention. Therefore, like entertainment programming, news stories are constructed to appeal to the emotions.

The criterion of responsibility does not operate in the same way with news programmers. If a news program crosses the line of public tolerance, programmers can say that they are only reporting what happened and that they would be irresponsible if they did not report it. For example, suppose a bank robbery goes awry and the fleeing thieves shoot a young child in the arm. News stories typically focus on the dramatic aspects of the occurrence. Rather than providing viewers with a broader context of bank robberies in the area, along with rates of arrests, convictions, and punishments, the news story would focus on the child—and likely show close-ups of the bleeding arm and crying face. The dramatic approach is more emotional. But if some audience members complained that the news story crossed the line by showing the child's bleeding arm, news programmers would likely say that it was the criminals who crossed the line by shooting the child and that the news story was merely reporting that fact.

23. *Changing the Violence Narrative Line.* When pushing the line of programming, programmers must change the violence narrative line. Producers and programmers continually test variations of this main narrative line through a process of programming relineation. In doing so, they exhibit a sort of Darwinian perspective on the survival of the fittest permutations. In this metaphor, the violence narrative line is the focal species, and the variational characteristics are the types of characters, types of acts, pacing, plot twists, use of weapons, special effects, language patterns, and so on. Characteristics that are not successful in creating and holding audiences die off; those that are successful become stronger and are gradually incorporated more centrally into the

violence narrative line. Thus, the violence narrative line continually changes in characterization while remaining the same species. The change (and the stasis) of the narrative line is governed by two forces: audience support and creative bandwidth.

23.1. *Programmers believe that the audience likes certain variations in the violent narrative line.* Programmers notice support when a particular change is tried and the resulting audience is larger than expected. Programmers then try this characteristic again in the form of sequels, spin-offs, and replications. If the characteristic develops a track record of large audiences, then programmers keep requesting this characteristic in new programs. Over time, this characteristic gradually is incorporated into the violence narrative line.

[margin handwriting: variations audience like]

23.2. *Typically, the creative bandwidth is fairly small, because programmers are conservative and do not want to deviate much from a successful narrative line.* Programmers limit message elements to very minor deviations from the narrative line. However, the implication of this strategy is that audiences are given little variety and therefore are not given an opportunity to show that very different characteristics can achieve audience support. The long-term implications of this strategy are that the narrow creative bandwidth reinforces the existing violence narrative line and thereby fixes in the minds of the audience the following equation: Narratives must be violent.

[margin handwriting: don't mess w/ success]

Furthermore, audiences are conditioned not to expect more than minor deviations from the narrative line, so when audience members are exposed to a major deviation, they become cognitively confused or emotionally upset. Programmers interpret this confusion or upset as signaling lack of audience support. However, this confusion could be interpreted in other ways. One alternative interpretation is that audiences need more conditioning with major deviations from the narrative line, so that when they are confronted with some forms of major deviations, audiences will strongly support some of those major differences. Thus, the widening of the creative bandwidth is likely to accelerate the evolution of the violence narrative line by requiring the accommodation of major (rather than only very minor) variations in narrative characteristics.

PROCESS

How do people process violent messages in the media? The key ideas here are perceptual channels, liminal thresholds, perceptual flow, and perceptual scripts. These process propositions address the issues of the nature of perceptual channels, how viewers use them, how viewers create and maintain perceptual flow, and how people deal with perceptual scripts during exposure to media violence.

Perception

31. _Perceptual Channels._ People's levels of awareness or concentration vary along a continuum as they are exposed to media messages. This continuum ranges from subliminal to automatic and upward to attentional and finally self-reflexive processing. These four perceptual channels of processing are rather like steps along the overall continuum. Each step is marked by a liminal threshold (line of perception) that requires a different kind of perceptual processing.

31.1. _In the subliminal channel, no perceptions are processed._ The subliminal elements of a message are below the perceptual sensitivities of humans, so these elements do not enter into perception as elements; they are transformed into something else. For example, when people watch a movie, they are exposed to individual static images projected at about 24 images per second. During the brief time between each image projection, the screen is blank. But these blanks appear and disappear so fast that this activity is below the threshold of perception; that is, we do not perceive the blanks. In addition, the human eye-brain connection is not quick enough to process the individual frames of still image, blank, still image, blank, and so on. Instead, it processes the flow of images as smooth, uninterrupted motion.

With television, the picture is composed of more than 250,000 glowing dots of color (called pixels). Each dot glows and fades 30 times each second as it is guided by an interlaced scan of every other line across a 525-line grid. Unless we put our nose on the screen, we cannot see the individual dots. Nor do we see the 525 individual lines of glowing dots. Nor do we see a full screen pattern of dots and lines. Instead, we perceive images and motion. With audio stimuli, humans have a range of hearing of 1,000 to 10,000 megahertz. Humans cannot hear sounds of lower or higher pitch.

Thus, if violent sounds are outside of humans' auditory range (i.e., the frequency is too high or too low), we cannot perceive those sounds and are therefore not exposed to the violence. If a single violent image is projected on a film or television screen for less than $\frac{1}{24}$ of a second, that individual element cannot be perceived. And if several dozen of these images are projected in sequence, we still do not perceive the individual elements, but we perceive something else—a flow of motion.

31.2. _In the automatic perceptual channel, message elements are perceived but processed automatically in an unconscious manner._ This channel resides above the threshold of human sensory perception but below the threshold of conscious awareness. In this channel, perceptual flow continues until an interruption stops the exposure or "bumps" the person's perceptual processing into the next higher channel of attention.

31.3. *In the attentional perceptual channel, message elements are processed consciously.* This channel is above the threshold of human conscious processing. In this channel, humans actively interact with the elements in the messages. In this perceptual channel, people can exercise some control over the processing, which can range from partial to quite extensive, depending on the number of elements handled and the depth of analysis used.

31.4. *In the self-reflexive perceptual channel, people are consciously aware not only of the elements in the message, but also of their processing of those elements.* This perceptual channel is the highest in awareness and concentration. Viewers are aware not only of the messages, but also of their processing of those messages; that is, they experience their own processing. In this perceptual channel, the viewer exercises the greatest control over perceptions by reflecting on questions such as, Why am I watching this? and Why am I making these interpretations of meaning? There is not only analysis, but meta-analysis.

32. *Perceptual Flow.* Often we select a channel unconsciously and effortlessly as we flow through exposures. The content cues guide us into an efficient channel, and we stay there as long as the flow of cues does not interrupt our comfort level, which is an intuitive feeling that we are at home in this channel. That is, we feel we are not expending too much or too little effort in the exposure, given our general viewing style and special motives.

32.1. *Perceptual flow is influenced by a person's general viewing style for media violence, which can be predominantly ritualistic or instrumental.* People with a ritualistic motive for exposure to media violence usually select the automatic processing channel and continue in that flow as long as the typical media violence narrative line continues. Such people enjoy the types of characterizations and flow of the narrative line. They focus little on particular characters or differences across violent programs; instead, they enjoy experiencing the characteristics of the narrative line. Thus, they habitually seek out examples of the violent narrative line. For example, a person who likes reading crime, detective, or mystery novels ritualistically will read continually in this genre regardless of the author.

People with an instrumental motive for exposure to media violence consciously seek out certain kinds of portrayals to serve a particular purpose. For example, some people want to learn what happened with a particular crime, so they seek out news programs that report on this action. Or some people might enjoy a particular kind of violence, such as fantasies with state-of-the-art special effects, so they check movie listings and go to video stores to find examples. They consciously seek out particular kinds of characters (or actors), particular settings (such as outer space, wartime Germany, or urban police stations), or particular types of plot points (such as heroes rescuing damsels in distress, or tough cops eliciting a confession from punk criminals). People who have instrumental motives typically use an attentional or self-reflexive channel for the exposure.

32.2. *Special motives for exposure to violence also influence the perceptual flow.* Even people who have a predominantly ritualistic style of exposure occasionally exhibit a special need for a favorite type of violent program or character.

33. *Perceptual Inertia.* When the violent content elements flow along with expectations, the perceptual channel remains unchanged. When message elements do not surprise or challenge a person's perceptual flow, the flow continues in the same channel of perception. The longer a person stays with a particular channel of perception, the more surprising or challenging a content element will need to be to trigger a change in perceptual channel. This is a more general concept than attentional inertia, because it predicts perceptual inertia several perceptual channels beyond attention.

33.1. *Perception is typically in the automatic processing channel.* The default channel is automatic processing, and processing continues in that channel as long as a person's emotional or cognitive states do not dramatically change and thus alter his or her comfort level. Violence that follows the typical narrative line tends to keep people in the automatic perceptual channel. This use continues as long as the cues (visual, auditory, pacing, etc.) flow in the ritualistic mode.

There are several reasons for instrumental exposure. If the reason is entertainment, then automatic processing is used. If the reason is information, then higher channels are more likely to be used.

33.2. *During perceptual flow, people can gradually or suddenly change perceptual channels.*

33.2.1. Gradual Change. When emotions or cognitive demands continue to increase during an exposure session, the person is likely to flow gradually into another perceptual channel. People who are in the automatic channel could experience a heightening of their emotions or a need for information and find themselves shifting into attentional perception. They gradually become uncomfortable that they are not getting enough out of their exposure, so they become more involved so that they are prepared to encode more emotional and cognitive information and be able to recall it more quickly.

In contrast, people in the attentional perceptual channel who are watching a challenging narrative (one with different kinds of characters, settings, plot pacing, etc.) become accustomed to the narrative conventions and feel that they can reduce their effort of perception and can gradually slip into the automatic perceptual channel.

33.2.2. Sudden Change. When emotions or cognitive elements change dramatically, viewers quickly shift perceptual channels. People in the attentional channel could experience sudden heightening of their emotions (such as through content cues of explicit or graphic violence) and quickly shift into the self-reflexive channel, in which they are aware of their shock and outrage and see themselves arguing against the producers of the program who felt it necessary to show such a depiction.

In contrast, people who are enjoying their favorite program and viewing it in the attentional channel, might suddenly have that enjoyment interrupted by a break for commercials, and they shift down suddenly into the automatic perceptual channel throughout the string of ads.

Processing Meaning

34. *Scripts.* Viewers use a preexisting script as a guide in their exposures to each media message. Scripts are templates. They help us during media exposures by guiding us to place certain elements in the foreground (pay more attention to them) and to place others in the background, thus making exposure sessions more efficient and more meaningful. When the flow of message elements conforms to our script-based expectations, our processing is automatic and reinforces the script being used. The scripts are delineations (sketches of the outline) of our experiences.

viewer templates

34.1 *All viewers have learned a general script for media violence: the media violence narrative line.* Because the media violence narrative line has been used so consistently, because its use is so widespread, and because viewers have had so much exposure to it, it is a dominant script. Its dominance makes it highly accessible, so it is quickly brought into use when viewers begin exposure to media violence.

general script

34.2 *Viewers construct subscripts to elaborate the general script for media violence.* Viewers who spend more of their media exposure time in the higher perceptual channels and who are more analytical develop subscripts nested under this general media violence script. For example, the general media violence script might be divided into subscripts for cartoon violence, farcical violence, criminal violence, interpersonal violence, and so on. Furthermore, cartoon violence may be divided into subscripts for humorous violence and for action-adventure violence. In addition, viewers who have a higher need for conceptual differentiation construct more subscripts, and these numerous subscripts branch a good deal into different types and nesting in a hierarchy. The subscripts in this set are likely to be sharpened—that is, highly elaborated, thus making them more specialized—and their use becomes limited for particular shows or particular types of violence.

subscripts

35. _Selection of Scripts._ In selecting a script, we use the dual criteria of efficiency and accuracy.

35.1 _The relative importance of these two criteria varies by channel of perception._

35.1.1. In the automatic perceptual channel, viewers are guided primarily by efficiency. When people are confronted with an event, they use the most accessible construct to help them make sense of that event. Constructs are more accessible when they have been used more recently, when they are linked with many other constructs, and when they are clearly cued by emotions or motivations in the portrayals.

35.1.2. In higher channels of perception, viewers are guided more by accuracy. People operating in higher channels of perception are willing to expend more mental energy. Such viewers pay more attention to the flow of message elements because they have conscious goals for information or entertainment. Therefore, they are more motivated to be accurate in their perceptions, and those perceptions are governed by salience.

35.1.2.1. The most salient elements in the beginning of the perceptual flow are the most important. Once perceived, these salient elements are matched with scripts. This matching method results in selection of the most accurate script to guide a viewer's perceptual flow.

35.1.2.2. What people look for varies across acts, because the salience of certain meaning factors changes across acts. We latch on to the most salient factor for each situation. We all recognize the same salient meaning element in a given portrayal; however, this does not mean that we all interpret it in the same way. The salient element sets the agenda by telling us what to pay attention to; then we apply our judgment. And these judgments vary across individuals, although we are all dealing with the same salient meaning element(s). (For example, see Chapter 9 for interpretations about violence and justification.)

35.2. _Minor Deviations._ When viewers encounter minor discrepancies between our selected script and the flow of program elements, they do one of three things: ignore the message elements, seek out alternative messages, or alter the script.

35.2.1. Viewers ignore discrepant message elements, thus giving prominence to the script.

35.2.1.1. Viewers can deal with this dissonance by regarding the deviations as temporary surprises.

35.2.1.2. People stay with an existing script when the script is so important that changing it would create dissonance. Such is the case with strongly held opinions and beliefs, such as religious and political ones.

35.2.1.3. People often stay with a script when they are in low perceptual states and do not want to process message elements more carefully.

35.2.2. Viewers will not change the script but will seek out an alternative media message in which there are no deviations or the deviations are minor and pleasant.

35.2.3. Viewers will alter the script.

35.2.3.1. Sharpening. Viewers elaborate their scripts by adding new information, which makes the scripts more detailed and thus less general.

35.2.3.2. Leveling. Viewers erode the key points (soften the criteria) of an existing script so that the script can be of continued use in processing the flow of message elements that deviate from the existing script.

35.3. *Major Deviations*. If something happens in the portrayal to indicate a major deviation from the script (very large discrepancies that cannot be tolerated by the viewer), viewers do one of three things: seek a more appropriate script, terminate the exposure, or significantly alter the script.

35.3.1. Viewers may look for a more appropriate script by moving out on the associative network for the next available option. In the automatic processing channel, people select a script very intuitively and quickly—usually by locating the most salient set of cues in the portrayal and matching it to the most appropriate accessible script. Continued exposure tends to rely on the existing script and reinforce its elements.

35.3.2. Viewers may terminate the exposure, because more mental effort is required than they are willing to give.

35.3.3. Viewers may significantly alter the existing script to bring it into line with the portrayal. In this alteration, the person must determine if the discrepancies signal a general problem with the script. If so, the entire script is relineated to fit the portrayal. If the person determines that the portrayal differs in specifics and not in general pattern, he or she can construct a subscript to fit this portrayal.

35.4. *No Deviations*. When people encounter no discrepancies between their selected script and the flow of program elements, they do one of two things: become bored and seek out another exposure, or continue the exposure.

35.4.1. In higher channels of perception, viewers become bored when there are no deviations from the script and seek out an exposure in which the deviations are minor and pleasant.

35.4.2. In the automatic perceptual channel, people continue their exposure, even when they are being exposed multiple times to the same message (such as watching reruns). As long as the present exposure delivers a pleasant feeling of familiarity and as long as memory lapses lead to minor discrepancies, the exposure continues.

36. *Script Alterations (Relineations)*. As viewers use their perceptual scripts, they continually alter them. Scripts are constructed and changed in two primary ways: controlled or unconscious.

36.1. *In controlled script alteration, the viewer consciously perceives a relatively large discrepancy between an existing script and a flow of message elements.* At this point, the viewer significantly alters the existing script. This process of alteration may result in a new script while preserving the old script as is. This is a copying-alteration procedure, in which the old script is maintained while a copy of the old script is altered into a new script.

36.2. *Unconscious script alteration takes place in the automatic perceptual channel.* In this situation, scripts are changed outside of the person's control or awareness by a process of accretion. That is, when the media continually present a certain message pattern that is outside of a viewer's perception, the script is shaped by the media, not by the viewer. When viewers watch television, for example, they can recognize acts of violence, but over the long term of viewing they cannot "recognize" an accurate percentage of violent perpetrators who are male. No one keeps a running count of all perpetrators categorized by demographics, so the processing of this type of information is outside of the perception of viewers. For example, because television has been constant for the past 50 years in showing about 70% of all perpetrators of violence to be male, over time viewers have become accustomed to expect males to be the perpetrators.

GENERAL INFLUENCE   *expose → effect — not a clear line*

The challenge of research on the effects of media violence is to trace a line from some sort of exposure to violence to some sort of effect. Rarely are these lines straight; instead, they are embraided with all kinds of influencing factors that twist and bend the shape of the line. These connecting lines go in and out of focus as the length of time extends between an observed effect and the hypothesized exposure pattern. Because of these challenges inherent in tracing the line of influence, it is best to use a multivariate, probabilistic approach in which tests of association focus on curvilinear patterns.

This set of propositions deals with the question of what factors increase the probability of an effect from exposure to media violence. Of course, such exposure has many different possible effects; that issue will be addressed later in the chapter. Here I focus on the factors that are so central to the process by which media violence affects viewers that they should be considered with any effect.

41. *General Influence Factors.* Five sets of factors influence the probability that viewers will experience an effect from exposure to media violence: perceptual channels during exposure, content factors, viewer factors, long-term environment, and situational cues.

41.1. *The perceptual channels used during exposures influence the probability and strength of an effect.*

41.1.1. Viewers gain more control over the effects process if they spend less time in the automatic perceptual channel.

41.1.1.1. In the subliminal perceptual channel, there is no effect. The reason is that the message cannot penetrate a person's sense organs. No effect is possible at this channel.

41.1.1.2. In the automatic perceptual channel, message elements are perceived but are processed automatically in an unconscious manner. This channel is where the greatest negative effects occur. The most prevalent effect at this channel is reinforcement of existing aggressive attitudes and behaviors. In addition, particular facts and images creep into viewers' scripts without their conscious control, so scripts can be altered over time through a process of accretion.

[margin handwriting: greatest negative effects]

41.1.1.3. Because the attentional perceptual channel is above the threshold of human conscious processing, message elements are processed under the viewer's control. In this channel, humans are aware that elements in the messages are actively interacting with them. This control can range from partial to quite extensive, depending on the number of elements handled and the depth of analysis used.

41.1.1.4. In the self-reflexive channel, the viewer exercises the greatest control, and positive effects are maximized while negative effects are minimized. Because people are aware not only of the messages, but also of their processing of them, they are examining the implications of the exposure and actively seeking particular satisfactions and effects.

41.1.1.5. Awareness of processing is not enough by itself for controlling the processing in a useful direction. The person must also be aware of the risks of effects to control them.

41.1.2. Perceptual channels interact with contextual factors in violent messages. This interaction is especially true of the contextual factors humor and fantasy. Judging the reality of media portrayals of violence is a complex task based on individual interpretation. The same is true of humor. Humor and fantasy are judgments constructed by viewers, and these judgments are highly sensitive to a person's level of cognitive development.

Early in an exposure session to media violence, viewers decide whether humor and fantasy exist in the message. If either of these characteristics is found, viewers are likely to enter and stay in the automatic channel of perception. This is an implicit decision to discount risk of a harmful effect; that is, viewers think that the message is not real or serious, so it cannot influence them. It is just fun or fluff—a mild diversion. As long as the media violence follows the standard script (such as cartoon violence or the farcical violence of the Three Stooges), viewers will stay with that script and remain comfortably in the automatic perceptual channel. If the message breaks with the typical narrative line (e.g., shifting back and forth between seriousness and humor or shifting from fantasy to reality—highly unique or unexpected humor or fantasy, such as in a Shakespearean play), viewers with a ritualistic motivation or with little need for entertainment likely will switch to another message flow. In contrast, viewers with an instrumental motive for more challenging messages will switch to another perceptual channel, such as the attentional or the self-reflexive channel.

41.1.2.1. Interpretations of reality are likely to be cued to the setting, the genre, and the matching of characteristics in the portrayals to real life. A person's judgment about the reality of a media message is also multidimensional. The dimensions typically include three dimensions: magic window, social expectations, and identity (see Potter, 1988a). A person might judge the reality of a particular television show high on one dimension but low on other dimensions. These differences in judgment are related to other factors about a person. For example, young children mature on one of these dimensions (magic window) during the preschool years so that they develop an "adult discount" that leads them to be skeptical of the factuality of portrayals. But it is likely that children mature in their judgment-making ability on the other dimensions of perceived reality and that this maturation is influenced by a person's emotional maturity, social skills, and personality, as well as many other factors. In short, we know that judging reality is a complex interpretive process. And we know that people who judge a portrayal of media violence to be realistic are more likely to experience a disinhibition effect.

41.1.2.2. Humor also plays a complex role in the perceptions of viewers, for several major reasons. One reason is that there are many different types of humor. Another reason is that humor can be used in many ways, either to heighten dramatic effect, as a catharsis from serious scenes, or to trivialize otherwise serious situations. But perhaps the most important reason is that humor appears to be very personal; that is, each person is likely to read the cues differently and react differently to the humor in a violent act.

41.1.2.3. The complexity of understanding the factors of fantasy and humor is magnified in the genre of cartoons. In cartoons, these two highly interpretive factors interact and lead to the public opinions that cartoons do not contain violence. The presence of these factors shifts the attention to the violence down into the automatic perceptual channel.

41.2. _Content factors include type of violence, context of the portrayal, and frequency of exposure._

41.2.1. The different types of violence range from serious assaults resulting in great pain and death to minor acts of verbal aggression. Viewers distinguish among acts in terms of seriousness.

41.2.2. Context matters. People use the contextual web to interpret the meaning of violent portrayals. People's judgments about the meaning of violence are related to the effects the exposure will have on them. The interpretive process is complex. It is noteworthy that television viewers do not base their ratings of the degree of violence on harm to the victim. Thus, our intuitive guesses do not always bear out; that is, sometimes we are not aware of how we make the thousands of daily decisions we take for granted.

41.2.3. Frequency of exposure is related to effects. Some effects can occur after only one exposure: cognitive encoding, generalizing to novel behaviors, disinhibition, triggering, immediate emotional reaction, immediate change of attitudes, temporary physiological arousal, and catharsis. Other effects require a gradual accumulation of exposures through a long period of time: learning of social norms about violence, cultivation of fear, reinforcement of attitudes, habituation, narcotization, attraction to the fringe, and changing institutions. In addition, some of the immediately occurring effects can be reinforced or altered over time with additional exposure to media violence.

41.3. *Viewer factors shape the effects process.* The effect of exposure to media violence is influenced by the susceptibility of the viewer. Traits (such as general aggressiveness) and states (arousal, frustration, anger) influence the probability of an effect. Especially important are a person's cognitive, emotional, and moral development. As children age, their minds mature to allow them to operate in higher cognitive channels. Because young children differ in their ability to attend to, process, and make meaning of media messages compared to older children and adults, they experience different effects from the exposure to violence in the media. People see images on TV and in other media before they see the real thing in life. With violence, often they never see a truly violent occurrence, so they are left with the media images as their reality. When they do see a murder or a serious accident in real life, it becomes just another image.

41.4. *A person's long-term environment is important.* The effects process of media violence is shaped by socialization, the process by which everyone in a society gradually learns the rules and norms of that society through exposure to agents, such as parents, siblings, institutions, and the media.

Especially important are two environmental influences: family and peers. These influences act together in shaping a person's behavior such that children raised in coercive families are likely to adapt their behavior to be aversive and aggressive, and when this behavior is negatively reinforced at home (being left alone) and positively reinforced by peers (acceptance), the aggressive behavior is strengthened.

41.5. *Situational cues influence the probability that an effect will occur.* The effect of media violence is influenced by situational cues, such as the presence of an aversive stimulus (annoying sound, threat to safety, etc.), triggering cues from media exposure (particular weapons, speech patterns, etc.), or an opportunity to aggress (sanctioned situation, threat of retaliation lacking, etc.).

42. *Synergistic Interaction of General Influence Factors.* These five sets of factors work together synergistically to influence the effects process.

42.1. *These influence factors interact with each other, because they are all linked together.* Exposure to media violence is likely linked with heightened blood pressure, hostile thoughts, angry feelings, and aggressive motor responses. According to cognitive-neoassociation theory, any aversive event stimulates a chain reaction through associative networks that link physiological reactions, emotions, thoughts or memories, and motor responses.

42.1.1. These factors interact within groups. For example, gender, age, and aggressive traits interact; younger aggressive boys are most likely to exhibit disinhibition from exposure to media violence.

42.1.2. These factors interact across groups. For example, a person's stage of moral development interacts with his or her understanding of the contextual factor of motivation.

42.2. *These factors work in a cumulative probabilistic manner.* The presence of each factor (or set of factors) alters the probability of a particular effect. No single factor is sufficient to cause any effect, and no set of factors can determine an effect.

FAMILIES OF EFFECTS

The effects of exposure to media violence are arranged into five families: learning and imitation, fear, desensitization, drive-altering effects, and societal effects. As you will notice, the effects within a family are related to each other; that is, there is a progression from simpler, more immediate effects to longer-term effects.

51. *Learning and Imitation.* The learning or imitation sequence begins with the progression of cognitive encoding and moves on to generalizing to novel behaviors. At this point it branches into either (a) a behavioral progression of disinhibition and triggering or (b) a cognitive progression into learning of social norms.

The primary progression of learning or imitation includes two effects: cognitive encoding and generalizing to novel behaviors. The behavioral progression builds on the primary progression and moves on to the effects of disinhibition and then triggering. The cognitive progression builds on the primary learning or imitation progression and moves on to the effect of learning social norms.

51.1. *Cognitive encoding of observed behaviors is an effect in the primary sequence.* This effect of exposure to media violence is the most common as viewers select elements in a violent portrayal and encode them into memory.

This encoding takes place immediately during exposure. Images of violence can evaporate quickly if they are not encoded meaningfully into a script; that is, if a violent image is left unencoded or "dumped" into an unscripted bin, the image will not be retrieved after several hours. When it is encoded into a script, it either elaborates the script by adding new information (cognitive or emotional) or reinforces the existing script, thus making the script more resistant to change.

Encoding engages three elements. First, and at minimum, the facts of the violent act (such as whether a weapon was used or not, how the weapon was used, how the characters accomplished the violence, etc.) are encoded. Second, the meaning of the violent act is usually part of the encoding. This meaning is derived from matching the contextual web surrounding the violent act (whether it was successful, the harm to victims, the appearance of perpetrators, etc.) to the contextual web in the viewer's script. Third, viewers can encode their emotional reactions to the act. Typically the facts, meaning, and emotions are intertwined in a gestalt-like manner; that is, the combination carries the information. This combination varies across viewers to the extent that viewers perceive different contextual characteristics in the portrayed violence and hence fixate on different facts, interpret meanings differently, and experience different emotions. This combination is uniform across viewers to the extent that viewers share the same scripts for violence.

51.2. *Generalizing to novel behaviors is a cognitive effect in the primary sequence.* Viewers generalize from one (or several) acts of violence in the media to patterns of behavior. Viewers also generalize from media violence to real-world violence.

This process of generalizing can happen immediately. During the exposure or immediately after, viewers can revisit the script they used and fill in the gaps—that is, imagine similar and related behaviors, contextual characteristics, meanings, and emotions that fit the sketchy pattern outlined in the existing script. In this process, viewers may substitute themselves for the portrayed perpetrator. Then, by mentally "rehearsing" the act, they can make changes to fit themselves more comfortably into the narrative in the script.

Generalizing to novel behaviors can be a long-term effect when people sort through the images in their scripts and reorganize them. This reorganization requires the mind to arrange images into sets by comparing and contrasting the image elements to look for patterns among groups of images. In looking for patterns, the mind can fill in gaps between examples, thus inferring new examples of violent portrayals.

51.3. *Disinhibition is an immediate effect that reduces barriers to performing aggressively during exposure to media violence or shortly thereafter.* This effect puts viewers in a ready state in which they think and feel that behaving aggressively is a good idea. The important influences of disinhibition are in the media content and the person's existing scripts about violence. When a person's script about performing violent acts contains only weak inhibitions, media portrayals of violence need only present minor contextual prompts—such as attractiveness and success of the perpetrator or lack of harm to the victim. When people's scripts contain strong inhibitions preventing them from performing violent acts, then media portrayals of violence need strong, multiple contextual prompts.

51.4. *Triggering is an immediate effect that takes viewers from the ready state into behavioral performance.* Triggering depends on an environment that makes aggression possible (suitable victim and means are present) and that is perceived to hold a threat of sanctions that is weaker than the person's motivation to aggress.

For triggering to work, people must first be primed; then something in the environment cues the aggressive behavior. Therefore, personal factors, as well as a match between factors in the media and factors in the environment, are key. For example, Berkowitz's priming-effects theory explains that anger and media violence prime people. Then, when these angry people see certain elements in their environment that remind them (because they associate them with scripts) of the violent portrayals they just witnessed, they are cued to behave aggressively.

51.5. *Learning of social norms is a long-term effect that requires viewers to be exposed to many portrayals of violence, interspersed with imaginative rehearsals and feedback from behaviors in the real world.* This combination of experiences builds a cognitive belief system (in the form of a script) that tells viewers about the role of violence in the real world. Some of the information structures in the script have been put there from cognitive encoding during direct observations. But many of the information structures are generalizations—that is, patterns constructed by viewers to infer information in the gaps that would otherwise exist between encoded observations. This inferred pattern tells the viewer about how much violence exists in the real world, who perpetrates it, what happens to the perpetrators as well as to the victims, and so on.

After people are exposed to a great many violent portrayals over a long time, they look for broad-scale patterns across scripts. Their goal in this pattern searching is to understand how the real world works. With exposure to a good deal of media violence over time, people see a pattern of high rates of violence. They construct a belief that more people are involved in criminal activity and law enforcement than is really the case. They tend to think that most criminals are violent and wreak a great deal of havoc but are almost always caught and removed from society.

51.6. *Learning and imitation effects are generally increased with particular characteristics in six groups: characteristics of the exposure situation, content characteristics, viewer traits, viewer states, long-term environment, and situation.*

51.6.1. Characteristics of the Exposure Situation. If the viewer processes the violence at a higher level, especially in the self-reflexive perceptual channel, the viewer will be able to exercise some control over the process of influence. If instead the exposure environment presents many distractions, such as extraneous noise, people talking, and other demands on one's attention, the exposure is likely to be experienced in the automatic perceptual channel and the viewer will lose control over the effects process.

However, greater control does not lead directly to avoidance of negative effects. For the self-reflexive processing to be more powerful, viewers need to be at higher levels of cognitive, moral, and emotional development and to have more elaborate scripts from which to work.

51.6.2. Content Characteristics. A learning effect increases when a modeled behavior is rewarded (or at least not punished), when neither the victim nor the perpetrator suffers any serious negative consequences, when the violence is portrayed as justified, when the violence is portrayed as realistic, and when the violence is linked with eroticism. Arousing portrayals (even if not violent) are more likely to lead to aggressive behavior.

51.6.3. Viewer Traits. Both demographics and psychological traits are influential.

51.6.3.1. The demographics of age, gender, socioeconomic status, and ethnicity are especially influential. Younger children, boys, people of lower socioeconomic status, and minorities are more affected. These characteristics are not usually regarded as active influences; rather they are surrogates for more active variables, as described in the next paragraph.

51.6.3.2. The psychological traits of developmental level, IQ, amount of exposure to television in general (and violence in particular), and aggressive traits are especially influential. People at lower levels of cognitive and moral development are more affected. People with higher levels of exposure (which is related to low socioeconomic status, lower IQ, ethnic minorities, and immigrant groups) show more vulnerability to this effect. Children who have lower IQs, who have learning disabilities, who are emotionally disturbed, or who are generally more aggressive are more likely to be affected.

51.6.4. Viewer States. Degrees of physiological arousal, anger, and frustration have all been found to increase the probability of a negative effect, especially disinhibition and imitation. Viewers who are upset by the media exposure (stimuli with negative hedonic value) are more likely to aggress, especially when they are left in a state of unresolved excitement. Frustration has been found to be an important antecedent to aggression, as was first suggested by the frustration-aggression hypothesis. In addition, it has been well established that the more a person, especially a child, identifies with a character, the more likely that person will pay attention to, encode information about, and be influenced by the character's behavior.

What leads a viewer to identify with a character? One answer is that viewers have been found to identify more with characters who are similar to them. If the perpetrator is perceived as similar to the viewer, the likelihood of learning to behave aggressively increases. Another answer is that viewers identify with characters they regard as attractive. When an attractive character performs violence, the probability of aggression by the viewer increases. A third characteristic that increases identification is the portrayal of the character who commits violence as a hero.

51.6.5. General Environment. Family life is an important contributing factor. Children who are abused by parents watch more violence and identify with violent heroes more. Furthermore, children receive less support and are more vulnerable in families with high-stress environments.

Socialization against aggression is also important. Children in households with strong norms against violence are not as strongly affected behaviorally. But children in households in which parents exhibit sociopathic belief systems are more affected by exposure to violent content.

51.6.6. Situational Cues. Viewers who perceive cues in a real-world situation that remind them of a media portrayal are likely to feel negative arousal. This negative arousal is likely to be associated with certain scripts that lay out the details of a violent act, thus priming viewers for aggressive action. Once the viewer is primed, the presence of weapons or cue value of perpetrators (such as their names) can lead to negative behavior.

52. _Fear._ Fear effects include the short-term effect of emotional reaction and the long-term effect of cultivation of fear.

52.1. _Immediate emotional reaction is a physiological and emotional reaction of fight or flight._ It is triggered immediately during certain types of violent portrayals. If the physiological reaction is weak or moderate, it can be pleasant for viewers. When it is strong, however, most viewers find it very upsetting. Immediate fear effects generally increase with particular characteristics in five groups: characteristics of the exposure situation, content characteristics, viewer traits, viewer states, and situational cues.

52.1.1. Characteristics of the Exposure Situation. Typically, fear-inducing portrayals of violence shift viewers up from the automatic perceptual channel into the attentional channel. The physiological arousal heightens their concentration and awareness. If viewers are able to move themselves up again, to the self-reflexive perceptual channel, they can put some cognitive distance between themselves and the portrayals. Thus, by consciously analyzing the unfolding portrayals, self-reflexive people are able to pull themselves out of the emotional flow and thereby reduce its fear effect.

52.1.2. Content Characteristics. Certain content characteristics influence the effect, especially production and narrative elements. The use of sudden loud special effects, close framing, shadowy lighting, suspenseful narrative, and evil characters can all increase the immediate fear effect. In addition, a person in an attentional channel, feeling a high state of physiological arousal, viewing alone in a strange, unfamiliar environment with a reputation for violence, and experiencing symbols in real life like the symbols in the media portrayal is highly likely to experience an immediate fear effect.

Fear effects increase when "bad" characters are shown committing a great deal of unjustified violence and when they are shown as successful and never stopped. Furthermore, fear increases when the violence is shown graphically and the victims are shown suffering. Finally, realistic portrayals also increase fear effects.

52.1.3. Viewer Traits. Psychological traits of developmental level, imagination, and locus of control are important predictors. Children at lower levels of development are more likely to experience fear triggered by production elements, such as loud noises and gruesome images. Children at higher levels of development are more likely to experience fear triggered by narrative elements of building suspense and character motivations. Children with more highly developed imaginations likely increase the fear of the media portrayal by extending it through their ability to project themselves into even more fearful situations. Finally, people who have a strong external locus of control are likely to have a stronger fear reaction, because they feel powerless in the face of forces outside themselves. In contrast, people who have an internal locus of control can be more successful at discounting fear effects by believing they can exercise more control and get themselves out of threatening situations.

52.1.4. Viewer States. Degree of physiological arousal and identification with characters can increase the probability of an immediate fear effect. Physiological arousal (increased heart rate and blood pressure) is essential for a strong fear effect. When people are in this state, they tend to feel a strong emotion and seek to label it. Some people who feel this strong arousal while watching media violence label it as fear, but others could label it as anger, frustration, or the like.

Furthermore, the more a person, especially a child, identifies with a character in danger, the more likely the person will experience an immediate fear effect. Identification sets up a vicarious experience such that when the character is in danger, the viewer who identifies with that character also feels the danger.

52.1.5. Situational Cues. The fear effect is increased if the person is in a generally fearful environment and if that environment presents many cues to trigger associations with the fearful script.

52.2. *Cultivation of fear is a long-term effect that has both emotional and cognitive aspects.* After years of exposure to violent messages in the media, a person has developed scripts with emotional feelings linked to cognitive information. Over time, people sort out their scripts by looking for patterns. They use the information they have to fill in the blanks, thus creating a more complete pattern. If the information they have is skewed (e.g., all images of criminals are violent), then they likely will generalize an inaccurate pattern—that is, a distortion of the real world. In addition, inaccuracies can be inferred from attempts to generalize from too few cases or by making errors in the generalization process (ignoring the majority of cases and instead using a single high-profile case as a base for generalization).

The cultivation effect is stronger with people in an anomic state. Such people have not been socialized and have few interpersonal contacts, so media violence has more of an unhindered effect on them.

53. *Desensitization.* Desensitization effects include the immediate change in attitudes and the long-term effects of reinforcement of attitudes and habituation.

53.1. *Immediate Change of Attitudes.* Exposure to even a single violent message can result in a drop in sensitivity. Most people feel a natural sympathy for others who suffer, but this attitude can be changed when violence is portrayed as not leading to suffering. This effect usually appears in people who have the weakest inherent feelings of empathy. This effect is also enhanced when the violence is shown as justified and the victims are shown as relatively unharmed. With such a portrayal, viewers learn that violence is often deserved and that it therefore does not warrant sympathy.

53.2. *Reinforcement of Attitudes.* People who are exposed to a great many violent portrayals over a long time come to be more accepting of violence and less likely to feel sympathy for victims. Although this attitude is learned from media exposure and then reinforced through repeated viewing, the attitude can be generalized beyond the media world to apply also to real-world instances.

53.3. *Habituation.* This long-term physiological effect is linked to emotional tolerance. Over time, people do not react as strongly to a particular portrayal of violence. When programmers present the same elements over and over, the repeated portrayal loses its ability to put viewers in a fight-or-flight mode and increase their heart rates and blood pressures. To achieve the same physiological effect each time, the portrayal has to be stronger each time. If portrayals do not get stronger, heavily exposed people lose the "arousal jag," the pleasant feeling of being excited. In normal everyday viewing of violence in the media, habituation usually takes a very long time, such as years.

53.4. *Desensitization effects generally increase with particular characteristics in three groups: characteristics of the exposure situation, content characteristics, and viewer traits.*
53.4.1. Characteristics of the Exposure Situation. If the viewer processes the violence at a higher perceptual level and if the viewer is more media literate, the effect is reduced. But in the automatic channel of processing, the continual flow of unexamined messages is likely to erode dispositions of empathy.

53.4.2. Content Characteristics. A desensitization effect increases when violence is shown graphically and humorously. For example, cartoons are highly desensitizing when they continuously show victims being blown to bits, followed by the bits reassembling themselves and thus restoring the character. Such portrayals lead us to laugh away the horror until gradually we lose sympathy for victims of violence.

Justification and attractiveness are also important content factors in this process. When attractive characters are repeatedly shown as justified in committing violence against unattractive victims, viewers come to believe that violence is deserved by victims.

53.4.3. Viewer Traits. Some viewers are socialized to have empathetic value systems. These people start from a stronger position, and it takes more counterconditioning to reduce this disposition for empathy. When viewing media violence, empathic people are more likely to identify with the victims or at least to feel their pain.

54. *Drive-Altering Effects.* Exposure to media violence triggers physiological effects that shape drives. This shaping can work immediately by increasing drives (temporary physiological arousal) or decreasing drives (catharsis). It can also have a long-term shaping effect: narcotization.

54.1. *Temporary Physiological Arousal.* Violent portrayals have been found to arouse viewers during an exposure and to last up to about an hour afterward. Sometimes viewers are unaware of this arousal, but most often they are aware of it and attempt to label it. Excitation transfer theory explains that viewing media violence energizes viewers, and this energy needs direction. The direction process is influenced by the prevailing social circumstances and the dispositions of the individual. When individuals label the arousal as unpleasant (anger, frustration), they will want the drive to be reduced and will try to find a way to dissipate the energy through aggressive behavior.

54.2. *Catharsis.* In catharsis, violent messages in the media are used to release aggressive drives vicariously. Viewers seek out violent messages in which they can identify closely with characters so that when the narrative climaxes, the viewers' drives will be released safely through the character and not require the viewers to behave violently in the real world, where they would put themselves at risk of harm or punishment.

54.3. *Narcotization.* This long-term effect builds up a dependence on exposure to portrayals of media violence. Development of this effect begins with an arousal jag with each exposure; that is, viewers experience a heightened heart rate and blood pressure that they find pleasant. Over time, however, it takes stronger depictions of violence and more of them in rapid succession for viewers to experience the arousal jag. So viewers have a stronger and stronger drive to seek out media violence.

54.4. *Drive-altering effects generally increase with particular charac-teristics in three groups: content characteristics, viewer traits, and viewer states.*

54.4.1. Content Characteristics. A drive-increasing effect is likely when viewers identify with attractive characters who get deeper and deeper into danger; when those characters are unjustly victimized by violence perpetrated by "bad" and unattractive characters; and when the narrative is realistic, nonhumorous, and erotic. A drive-decreasing effect happens suddenly when those attractive characters turn the tables and commit appropriately strong, justified violence on their previous tormentors.

54.4.2. Viewer Traits. When viewers have chosen to live most of their experiences through the media, the effect is strong because it is not counterbal-anced by real-life experiences. Viewers who are younger, less educated, of lower income, and of lower socioeconomic status usually find a much greater variety of experiences in the media than they find in their real lives compared with people who are older, more educated, and in control of more resources— financially and cognitively.

In addition, people with generally higher aggressive traits, aggressive in-stincts, or particular hormones are more motivated to seek out media violence to shape their drives. Some humans have a stronger instinct toward aggression, and when their energy in this area builds to a high point, they must act aggressively to relieve the hostility. Furthermore, exposure to violence can increase levels of the hormone testosterone; a person with higher levels of testosterone is more likely to seek out violence in the media and enjoy those exposures. In short, levels of hormones in the bloodstream are reciprocally related to the aggressive behavior of humans.

54.4.3. Viewer States. Degrees of physiological arousal, anger, and frustra-tion all shape drives. Portrayals (even if they are not violent) that leave viewers in an aroused state of unresolved excitement are more likely to lead to aggres-sive behavior. Viewers who are upset by the media exposure (stimuli with negative hedonic value) are more likely to aggress.

55. *Societal Effects.* Media violence can exert effects at the macro level of society and its institutions.

55.1. *Moving the Mean of Society Toward More of a Fight-or-Flight Men-tality.* We can envision the aggregate of society arrayed as a normal distribution, with most people clustered in the center in terms of their socialized beliefs and behaviors regarding violence. On one side of the distribution (the prosocial tail) are the people who have a very high degree of inhibition preventing them from behaving aggressively; these people also have a high degree of sensitivity to violence and sympathy for all its victims. On the opposite side of the distribu-tion (the antisocial tail) are the people who have very low inhibitions toward behaving aggressively; these people also have very low levels of sympathy for victims of violence.

When violence permeates the media year after year in all kinds of programming and when the message of that violence is antisocial (violence is usually justified, successful, and harmless to victims), the mean of society is likely to move gradually in the antisocial direction. That is, the norms of society (as evidenced by the beliefs and behaviors clustered close to the mean) will show a gradual movement in the direction of a fight-or-flight mentality. The fight component is exhibited by an erosion of inhibitions to violent behavior. The flight component is exhibited by a gradual increase in generalized fear along with an erosion of sympathy for victims of violence.

Societies have drawn a line on the antisocial tail that divides socially tolerated antisocial behavior (such as rudeness, selfish aggression, etc.) from antisocial behavior that the society cannot tolerate (usually labeled as criminal behavior for which society has prescribed clear penalties). All societies have a few people with extreme deviant behavior—that is, people who cross the line that is set by society.

As the entire distribution shifts more toward a fight-or-flight mentality (in the antisocial direction), differences are observable not only in the mean, but also at the tails of the distribution. As the antisocial tail also moves to more of a fight-or-flight mentality, more people on that tail have crossed the line. In addition, it takes even more outrageous behavior to label someone truly deviant.

55.2. *Changing Institutions.* When violence permeates the media year after year in all kinds of programming and when the message of that violence is antisocial, institutions feel the influence and gradually change. For example, the criminal justice system experiences stronger conflicting forces. On the one side is greater fear in society that asks this institution to be more aggressive at removing deviants from society and thus reduce the fear. On the other side is a greater tolerance for many forms of deviant behavior that have become relatively less threatening to society (thefts and assaults) compared to other more deviant acts (such as bombing federal buildings, sending letter bombs to individuals' homes, teenage snipers killing classmates during false-alarm fire drills).

In a larger sense, perhaps the institution of government is changing as a result of these conflicting forces. On the one hand, the public is asking government for more personal freedom, perhaps as a way of getting back some of their lives that they perceive as being taken away by their increasing fear of others. On the other hand, the public asks for a more authoritarian response (more laws, more law enforcement personnel, stronger punishments) to the shifts in society.

The educational system has also changed to deal with the stronger fight-or-flight mentality among students. Instead of being able to operate at higher levels of a goals hierarchy (such as self-actualization) in which students can concentrate on more abstract ideas, teachers must respond to more basic concerns of students that are moving toward the lower end of a goals hierarchy (survival).

Religion may be changing as people turn to that institution because of a generalized fear or a rejection of the changing norms of society. In addition, religions may be more aggressive at drawing the line of acceptable behaviors in order to stop the shift of society in an antisocial direction. Thus, religion is becoming more concerned with moral issues than spiritual ones. The focus may be shifting more toward prescribing everyday behaviors and away from the awe and mystery of creation and humans' place in the universe and eternity.

The institution of family may also be changing as a result of the forces brought about by media violence. Perhaps the generalized fear has made parents less trusting of their children. Perhaps couples are less willing to deal with their arguments by looking for peaceful solutions and compromising. Instead, couples may be looking for more fights to act on their aggressive impulses, feel more justified in those confrontations, and thus want to dominate the other in their resolutions. Such adversarial behaviors are likely to lead to more breakups and more people choosing to live alone.

55.3. *The primary factors that contribute to societal effects are the degree of saturation of the culture with violence and the constancy of the contextual web.*

55.3.1. When the society is saturated with violent messages to a point at which the violence is a part of the culture, violence is taken for granted—like a low-level hum in the background—and therefore not challenged. It is merely accepted as a part of life and becomes a tenet of socialization.

55.3.2. When the contextual web is constant, the meaning it portrays exerts a cumulative effect. With a cumulative effect, the frequency of the messages is a good predictor of how far the effect will go. But if the web varies in its meaning, then conflicting messages about violence are projected into the society and the frequency is not as good a predictor.

CONCLUSIONS

The set of propositions presented in this chapter constitutes what I call the lineation theory of media violence. To get to this point, I have stood on the shoulders of the many giants with considerable talents of theoretical speculation and empirical testing. But despite all their guidance, this theory should not be regarded as a definitive statement about media violence. Instead, I hope this effort will be treated as a useful place of reflection on the rugged path toward greater understanding of this complex phenomenon. I hope this theory will be viewed as a working document to stimulate greater debate and testing that will take us to the next plateau of understanding. My expectation is that parts of this theory will be falsified, other parts altered, some elaborated, and even some accepted as trustworthy explanations. Which parts are which? Let's find out.

References

Adler, R. P., Lesser, G. S., Meringoff, L. K., Robertson, T. S., Rossiter, J. R., & Ward, S. (1980). *The effects of television advertising on children: Review and recommendations.* Lexington, MA: Lexington Books.

Aisbett, K., & Wright, A. (1989, November). Views on the news. *Media Information Australia, 54,* 13-16.

Allen, M., D'Alessio, D., & Brezgel, D. (1995). A meta-analysis summarizing the effects of pornography II: Aggression after exposure. *Human Communication Research, 22,* 258-283.

Allen, R. C. (1987). Reader oriented criticism and television. In R. C. Allen (Ed.), *Channels of discourse: Television and contemporary criticism* (pp. 74-112). Chapel Hill: University of North Carolina Press.

Altheide, D. L., & Snow, R. P. (1979). *Media logic.* Beverly Hills, CA: Sage.

Alvarez, M. M., Huston, A. C., Wright, J. C., & Kerkman, D. D. (1988). Gender differences in visual attention to television form and content. *Journal of Applied Developmental Psychology, 9,* 459-475.

Anastasi, A. (1976). *Psychological testing* (4th ed.). New York: Macmillan.

Anderson, C. A. (1983). Imagination and expectation: The effect of imagining behavioral scripts on personal intentions. *Journal of Personality and Social Psychology, 45,* 293-305.

Andison, F. S. (1977). TV violence and viewer aggression: A cumulation of study results. *Public Opinion Quarterly, 41,* 314-331.

Applebome, P. (1995, January 12). Fear of violence affecting daily lives of U.S. teens. *Santa Barbara News Press,* pp. A1, A2.

Atkin, C. (1983). Effects of realistic TV violence vs. fictional violence on aggression. *Journalism Quarterly, 60,* 615-621.

Atkin, C., Greenberg, B. S., Korzenny, F., & McDermott, S. (1979). Selective exposure to televised violence. *Journal of Broadcasting, 23,* 5-13.

Atkin, C. K. (1982). Television advertising and socialization to consumer roles. In D. Pearl, L. Bouthilet, & J. Lazar (Eds.), *Television and behavior: Ten years of scientific progress and implications for the eighties: Vol. 2. Technical reviews* (pp. 191-200). Rockville, MD: U.S. Department of Health and Human Services.

Averill, J. R., Malmstrom, E. J., Koriat, A., & Lazarus, R. S. (1972). Habituation to complex emotional stimuli. *Journal of Abnormal Psychology, 1,* 20-28.

Babbie, E. (1992). *The practice of social research* (6th ed.). Belmont, CA: Wadsworth.

Baker, R. K., & Ball, S. J. (1969). *Violence and the media.* Washington, DC: Government Printing Office.

Baldwin, T. F., & Lewis, C. (1972). Violence in television: The industry looks at itself. In G. A. Comstock & E. A. Rubinstein (Eds.), *Television and social behavior: Reports and papers: Vol. 1: Media content and control* (pp. 290-373). Washington, DC: Government Printing Office.

Ball-Rokeach, S. J. (1972). The legitimation of violence. In J. F. Short, Jr., & M. E. Wolfgang (Eds.), *Collective violence* (pp. 100-111). Chicago: Aldine-Atherton.

Ball-Rokeach, S. J. (1980). Normative and deviant violence from a conflict perspective. *Social Problems, 28,* 45-62.

Bandura, A. (1965). Influence of models' reinforcement contingencies on the acquisition of imitative responses. *Journal of Personality and Social Pychology, 1,* 589-595.

Bandura, A. (1973). *Aggression: A social learning analysis.* Englewood Cliffs, NJ: Prentice Hall.

Bandura, A. (1977). Self-efficacy: Toward a unifying theory of behavioral change. *Psychological Review, 84,* 191-215.

Bandura, A. (1978). A social learning theory of aggression. *Journal of Communication, 28*(3), 12-29.

Bandura, A. (1979). Psychological mechanisms of aggression. In M. von Cranach, K. Foppa, W. Lepenies, & D. Ploog (Eds.), *Human etholody: Claims and limits of a new discipline* (pp. 316-356). Cambridge, UK: Cambridge University Press.

Bandura, A. (1982). Self efficacy mechanism in human agency. *American Psychologist, 27*(2), 122-147.

Bandura, A. (1985). *Social foundations of thought and action.* Englewood Cliffs, NJ: Prentice Hall.

Bandura, A. (1986). *Social foundations of thought and action: A social cognitive theory.* Englewood Cliffs, NJ: Prentice Hall.

Bandura, A. (1994). Social cognitive theory of mass communication. In J. Bryant & D. Zillmann (Eds.), *Media effects* (pp. 61-90). Hillsdale, NJ: Erlbaum.

Bandura, A., & Menlove, F. L. (1968). Factors determining vicarious extinction of avoidance behavior through symbolic modeling. *Journal of Personality and Social Psychology, 3,* 99-108.

Bandura, A., Ross, D., & Ross, S. A. (1961). Transmission of aggression through imitation of aggressive models. *Journal of Abnormal and Social Psychology, 63,* 575-582.

Bandura, A., Ross, D., & Ross, S. A. (1963a). Imitation of film-mediated aggressive models. *Journal of Abnormal and Social Psychology, 66,* 3-11.

Bandura, A., Ross, D., & Ross, S. A. (1963b). Vicarious reinforcement and imitative learning. *Journal of Abnormal and Social Psychology, 67,* 601-607.

Baron, J. N., & Reiss, P. C. (1985). Same time, next year: Aggregate analysis of the mass media and violent behavior. *American Sociological Review, 50,* 347-363.

Baron, R. A. (1971a). Aggression as a function of magnitude of victim's pain cues, level of prior anger arousal, and aggressor-victim similarity. *Journal of Personality and Social Psychology, 18,* 48-54.

Baron, R. A. (1971b). Magnitude of victim's pain cues and level of prior anger arousal as determinants of adult aggressive behavior. *Journal of Personality and Social Psychology, 17,* 236-243.

Baron, R. A. (1977). *Human aggression.* New York: Plenum.

Baron, R. A. (1978). Aggression-inhibiting influence of sexual humor. *Journal of Personality and Social Psychology, 36,* 189-197.

Baron, R. A. (1979). Effects of victim's pain cues, victim's race, and level of prior instigation upon physical aggression. *Journal of Applied Social Psychology, 9*(2), 103-114.

Bassett, H. T., Cowden, J. E., & Cohen, M. F. (1968). The audio-visual viewing habits of selected subgroups of delinquents. *Journal of Genetic Psychology, 112,* 37-41.

Baxter, R. L., Riemer, C. D., Landini, A., Leslie, L., & Singletary M. W. (1985). A content analysis of music videos. *Journal of Broadcasting & Electronic Media, 29,* 333-340.

Belson, W. (1978). *Television violence and the adolescent boy.* Farnborough, UK: Saxon House, Teakfield.

Berelson, B. R., & Steiner, G. (1964). *Human behavior: An inventory of scientific findings.* New York: Harcourt, Brace and World.

Berger, A. A. (1988). Humor and behavior: Therapeutic aspects of the comedic techniques and other considerations. In B. D. Ruben (Ed.), *Information and behavior* (pp. 226-247). New Brunswick, NJ: Rutgers University Press.

Berger, P. L., & Luckmann, T. (1966). *The social construction of reality.* Garden City, NY: Doubleday.

Berkowitz, L. (1962). *Aggression: A social-psychological analysis.* New York: McGraw-Hill.

Berkowitz, L. (1965). Some aspects of observed aggression. *Journal of Personality and Social Psychology, 2,* 359-369.

Berkowitz, L. (1970). Aggressive humors as a stimulus to aggressive responses. *Journal of Personality and Social Psychology, 16,* 710-717.

Berkowitz, L. (1974). Some determinants of impulsive aggression: The role of mediated associations with reinforcements for aggression. *Psychological Review, 81,* 165-176.

Berkowitz, L. (1984). Some effects of thoughts on anti- and prosocial influences of media events: A cognitive-neoassociation analysis. *Psychological Bulletin, 95,* 410-427.

Berkowitz, L. (1993). *Aggression: Its causes, consequences, and control.* Philadelphia: Temple University Press.

Berkowitz, L. (1994). Is something missing? Some observations prompted by the cognitive-associationist view of anger and emotional aggression. In L. R. Huesmann (Ed.), *Aggressive behavior: Current perspectives* (pp. 35-57). New York: Plenum.

Berkowitz, L., & Alioto, J. T. (1973). The meaning of an observed event as a determinant of its aggressive consequences. *Journal of Personality and Social Psychology, 28,* 206-217.

Berkowitz, L., & Geen, R. G. (1966). Film violence and the cue properties of available targets. *Journal of Personality and Social Psychology, 3,* 525-530.

Berkowitz, L., & Geen, R. G. (1967). Stimulus qualities of the target of aggression: A further study. *Abnormal and Social Psychology, 65,* 197-202.

Berkowitz, L., & LePage, A. (1967). Weapons as aggression-eliciting stimuli. *Journal of Personality and Social Psychology, 7,* 202-207.

Berkowitz, L., & Powers, P. C. (1979). Effects of timing and justification of witnessed aggression on the observers' punitiveness. *Journal of Research in Personality, 13,* 71-80.

Berkowitz, L., & Rawlings, E. (1963). Effects of film violence on inhibitions against subsequent aggression. *Journal of Abnormal and Social Psychology, 66,* 405-412.

Berry, G. L., & Mitchell-Kernan, C. (Eds.). (1982). *Television and the socialization of the minority child.* New York: Academic Press.

Bianculli, D. (1992). *Teleliteracy: Taking television seriously.* New York: Continuum.

Biocca, F. (1991). *Television and political advertising.* Hillsdale, NJ: Erlbaum.

Bjorkqvist, K., & Lagerspetz, K. (1985). Children's experience of three types of cartoons at two age levels. *International Journal of Psychology, 20,* 77-93.

Blumer, H. (1933). *Movies and conduct.* New York: Macmillan.

Borduin, C. M., Mann, B. J., Cone, L. T., & Henggeler, S. W. (1995). Multi systematic treatment of serious juvenile offenders: Long term prevention of criminality and violence. *Journal of Consulting and Clinical Psychology, 63,* 569-578.

Bridis, T. (1997, December 5). Teen describes similar shooting scene from movie. *Santa Barbara News Press,* p. A8.

British Broadcasting Corporation. (1972). *Violence on television: Programme content and viewer perceptions.* London: Author.

Broadcasting Standards Council. (1993). *Monitoring report II.* London: Author.

Broadcasting Standards Council. (1995). *Children and violence. The report of the commission on children and violence.* London: Gulbenkian Foundation.

Bronfenbrenner, U. (1979). Contexts of child rearing: Problems and prospects. *American Psychologist, 34*(10), 844-850.

Brown, J. D., & Campbell, K. (1986). Race and gender in music videos: The same beat but a different drummer. *Journal of Communication, 36*(1), 94-106.

Brown, R. C., Jr., & Tedeschi, J. T. (1976). Determinants of perceived aggression. *Journal of Social Psychology, 100,* 77-87.

Browning, G. (1994). Push-button violence. *National Journal, 26,* 458-463.

Bruner, J. S. (1957). On perceptual readiness. *Psychological Review, 64,* 123-152.

Bruner, J. S., Goodnow, J., & Austin, G. A. (1956). *A study of thinking.* New York: John Wiley.

Bryan, J. H., & Schwartz, T. (1971). Effects of film material upon children's behavior. *Psychological Bulletin, 75,* 50-59.

Bryant, J., Carveth, R. A., & Brown, D. (1981). Television viewing and anxiety: An experimental examination. *Journal of Communication, 31*(1), 106-119.

Buckingham, D. (1993). *Children talking television: The making of television literacy.* London: Falmer.

Bushman, B., & Geen, R. (1990). Role of cognitive-emotional mediators and individual differences in the effects of media violence on aggression. *Journal of Personality and Social Psychology, 58,* 156-163.

Buss, A., Booker, A., & Buss, E. (1972). Firing a weapon and aggression. *Journal of Personality and Social Pscyhology, 22,* 296-302.

Butterfield, F. (1996, April 22). Crime may not pay, but it costs America plenty. *Santa Barbara News Press,* p. A1.

Bybee, C., Robinson, D., & Turow, J. (1982, May). *Mass media scholars' perceptions of television's effects on children.* Paper presented at the annual convention of the American Association for Public Opinion Research, Hunt Valley, MD.

Cahoon, D. D., & Edmonds, E. M. (1984). Guns/no guns and the expression of social hostility. *Bulletin of the Psychonomic Society, 22,* 305-308.

Cahoon, D. D., & Edmonds, E. M. (1985). The weapons effect: Fact or artifact? *Bulletin of the Psychonomic Society, 23,* 57-60.

Cairns, E. (1990). Impact of television news exposure on children's perceptions of violence in Northern Ireland. *Journal of Social Psychology, 130,* 447-452.

Campbell, W. J., & Keogh, R. (1962). *Television and the Australian adolescent.* Sydney, Australia: Angus Robertson.

Cantor, J. (1994). Fright reactions to mass media. In J. Bryant & D. Zillmann (Eds.), *Media effects: Advances in theory and research* (pp. 213-245). Hillsdale, NJ: Erlbaum.

Cantor, J., & Hoffner, C. (1990). Children's fear reactions to a televised film as a function of perceived immediacy of depicted threat. *Journal of Broadcasting & Electronic Media, 34,* 421-442.

Cantor, J., & Reilly, S. (1982). Adolescents' fright reactions to television and films. *Journal of Communication, 32*(1), 87-99.

Cantor, J., & Sparks, G. C. (1984). Children's fear responses to mass media: Testing some Piagetian predictions. *Journal of Communication, 34*(2), 90-103.

Cantor, J., & Wilson, B. J. (1984). Modifying fear responses to mass media in preschool and elementary school children. *Journal of Broadcasting, 28,* 431-443.

Cantor, J., Wilson, B. J., & Hoffner, C. (1986). Emotional responses to a televised nuclear holocaust film. *Communication Research, 13,* 257-277.

Cantor, J., Ziemke, D., & Sparks, G. G. (1984). Effect of forewarning on emotional responses to a horror film. *Journal of Broadcasting, 28,* 21-31.

Cantor, J., Zillmann, D., & Bryant, J. (1975). Enhancement of experienced sexual arousal in response to erotic stimuli through misattribution of unrelated residual excitation. *Journal of Personality and Social Psychology, 32,* 69-75.

Cantril, H. (1940). *The invasion from Mars: A study in the psychology of panic.* Princeton, NJ: Princeton University Press.

Caprara, G. V., D'Imperio, G. D., Gentilomo, A., Mammucari, A., Renzi, P. G., & Travaglia, G. (1984). The intrusive commercial: Influence of aggressive TV commercials on aggression. *European Journal of Social Psychology, 14,* 23-31.

Caprara, G. V., Renzi, P., Amolini, P., D'Imperio, G., & Travaglia, G. (1984). The eliciting cue value of aggressive slides reconsidered in a personological perspective: The weapons effect and irritability. *European Journal of Social Psychology, 14,* 313-322.

Carlson, J. M. (1983). Crime show viewing by preadults: The impact on attitudes toward civil liberties. *Communication Research, 10,* 529-552.

Carlson, M., Marcus-Newhall, A., & Miller, N. (1990). Effects of situational aggression cues: A quantitative review. *Journal of Personality and Social Psychology, 58,* 622-633.

Carver, C., Ganellen, R., Fromming, W., & Chambers, W. (1983). Modeling: An analysis in terms of category assessibility. *Journal of Experimental Social Psychology, 19,* 403-421.

Carveth, R., & Alexander, A. (1985). Soap opera viewing motivations and the cultivation hypothesis. *Journal of Broadcasting & Electronic Media, 29,* 259-273.

Center for Media and Public Affairs. (1994). *Violence in prime time television.* Washington, DC: Author.

Centerwall, B. S. (1989). Exposure to television as a risk factor for violence. *Journal of Epidemiology, 129,* 643-652.

Centerwall, B. S. (1993). Television and violent crime. *Public Interest, 111,* 56-71.

Chaffee, S. H. (1972). Television and adolescent aggressiveness (overview). In G. A. Comstock & E. A. Rubinstein (Eds.), *Television and social behavior: Reports and papers: Vol. 3. Television and adolescent aggressiveness* (pp. 1-34). Washington, DC: Government Printing Office.

Chaffee, S. H. (1991). *Explication.* Newbury Park, CA: Sage.

Chaffee, S. H., & McLeod, J. M. (1972). Adolescent television use in the family context. In G. A. Comstock & E. A. Rubinstein (Eds.), *Television and social behavior: Vol. 3. Television and adolescent aggressiveness* (pp. 149-172). Washington, DC: Government Printing Office.

Chiricos, T. (1996). Moral panic as ideology: Drugs, violence, race and punishment in America. In M. J. Lynch & E. B. Patterson (Eds.), *Justice with prejudice: Race and criminal justice in America* (pp. 19-48). New York: Harrow & Heston.

Chiricos, T., Eschholz, S., & Gertz, M. (1997). Crime, news and fear of crime: Toward an identification of audience effects. *Social Problems, 44,* 342-357.

Chiricos, T., Hogan, M., & Gertz, M. (1997). Racial composition of neighborhood and fear of crime. *Criminology, 35,* 107-131.

Clark, D. G., & Blankenburg, W. B. (1972). Trends in violent content in selected mass media. In G. Comstock & E. Rubinstein (Eds.), *Television and social behavior: Reports and papers: Vol. 1. Media content and control* (pp. 188-243). Washington, DC: Government Printing Office.

Cline, V. B., Croft, R. G., & Courrier, S. (1973). Desensitization of children to television violence. *Journal of Personality and Social Psychology, 27,* 260-265.

Cole, J. (1995). *The UCLA television violence monitoring report.* Los Angeles: UCLA Center for Communication Policy.

Cole, J. (1996). *The UCLA television violence monitoring report.* Los Angeles: UCLA Center for Communication Policy.

Collins, W. A. (1973). Effect of temporal separation between motivation, aggression, and consequences: A developmental study. *Developmental Psychology, 8*(2), 215-221.

Collins, W. A. (1983). Interpretation and inference in children's television viewing. In J. Bryant & D. R. Anderson (Eds.), *Children's understanding of television: Research on attention and comprehension* (pp. 125-150). New York: Academic Press.

Collins, W. A., Berndt, T. J., & Hess, V. L. (1974). Observational learning of motives and consequences for television aggression: A developmental study. *Child Development, 45,* 799-802.

Columbia Broadcasting System. (1980). *Network prime time violence tabulations for 1978-1979 season.* New York: Author.

Comisky, P., & Bryant, J. (1982). Factors involved in generating suspense. *Human Communication Research, 9,* 49-58.

Comstock, G. A. (1985). Television and film violence. In S. Apter & A. Goldstein (Eds.), *Youth violence: Programs and prospects* (pp. 178-218). New York: Pergamon.

Comstock, G., Chaffee, S., Katzman, N., McCombs, M., & Roberts, D. (1978). *Television and human behavior.* New York: Columbia University Press.

Comstock, G., & Strasburger, C. C. (1990). Deceptive appearances: Television violence and aggressive behavior. *Journal of Adolescent Health Care, 11*(1), 31-44.

Condry, J. (1989). *The psychology of television.* Hillsdale, NJ: Erlbaum.

Cook, T. D., Kendzierski, D. A., & Thomas, S. A. (1983). The implicit assumptions of television research: An analysis of the 1982 report on "Television and behavior." *Public Opinion Quarterly, 47,* 161-201.

Cooper, J., & Mackie, D. (1986). Video games and aggression in children. *Journal of Applied Social Psychology, 16,* 726-744.

Cowden, J. E., Bassett, H. T., & Cohen, M. F. (1969). An analysis of some relationships between fantasy-aggressive and aggressive behavior among institutionalized delinquents. *Journal of Genetic Psychology, 114,* 179-183.

Culture & ideas: Special report [On-line]. (1994). *U.S. News & World Report Online.* Available E-mail: webmaster@usnews.com.

Cumberbatch, G., Jones, I., & Lee, M. (1988). Measuring violence on television. *Current Psychology: Research & Reviews, 7,* 10-25.

Cumberbatch, G., Lee, M., Hardy, G., & Jones, I. (1987). *The portrayal of violence on British television.* London: British Broadcasting Corporation.

da Gloria, J., Duda, D., Pahlavan, F., & Bonnet, P. (1989). "Weapons effect" revisited: Motor effects of the reception of aversive stimulation and exposure to pictures of firearms. *Aggressive Behavior, 15,* 265-271.

Davidson, P. O., & Hiebert, S. F. (1971). Relaxation training, relaxation instruction, and repeated exposure to a stressor film. *Journal of Abnormal Psychology, 78,* 154-159.

Deckers, L., & Carr, D. E. (1986). Cartoons varying in low-level pain ratings, not aggression ratings, correlate positively with funniness ratings. *Motivation and Emotion, 10,* 207-216.

Diener, E., & De Four, D. (1978). Does television violence enhance programme popularity? *Journal of Personality and Social Psychology, 36,* 333-341.

Diener, E., & Woody, L. W. (1981). TV violence and viewer liking. *Communication Research, 8,* 281-306.

Dishion, T. J., Patterson, G. R., & Griesler, P. C. (1994). Peer adaptations in the development of antisocial behavior: A confluence model. In L. R. Huesmann (Ed.), *Aggressive behavior: Current perspectives* (pp. 61-95). New York: Plenum.

Dollard, J., Doob, L. W., Miller, N. E., Mowrer, O. H., & Sears, R. R. (1939). *Frustration and aggression.* New Haven, CT: Yale University Press.

Dominick, J. (1973). Crime and law enforcement on prime-time television. *Public Opinion Quarterly, 37,* 241-250.

Dominick, J. R. (1984). Videogames, television violence, and aggression in teenagers. *Journal of Communication, 34*(2), 136-147.

Dominick, J. R., & Greenberg, B. S. (1972). Attitudes towards violence: The interaction of television exposure, family attitudes, and social class. In G. A. Comstock & E. A. Rubinstein (Eds.), *Television and social behavior: Reports and papers: Vol. 3. Television and adolescent aggressiveness* (pp. 314-335). Washington, DC: Government Printing Office.

Donnerstein, E. (1980a). Aggressive erotica and violence against women. *Journal of Personality and Social Psychology, 39,* 269-277.

Donnerstein, E. (1980b). Pornography and violence against women: Experimental studies. *Annals of the New York Academy of Sciences, 347,* 277-288.

Donnerstein, E., & Barrett, G. (1978). Effects of erotic stimuli on male aggression toward females. *Journal of Personality and Social Psychology, 36,* 180-188.

Donnerstein, E., & Berkowitz, L. (1981). Victim reactions in aggressive erotic films as a factor in violence against women. *Journal of Personality and Social Psychology, 41,* 710-724.

Donnerstein, E., Donnerstein, M., & Barrett, G. (1976). Where is the facilitation of media violence: The effects of nonexposure and placement of anger arousal. *Journal of Research in Personality, 10,* 386-398.

Donnerstein, E., Donnerstein, M., & Evans, R. (1975). Erotic stimuli and aggression: Facilitation or inhibition. *Journal of Personality and Social Psychology, 32,* 237-244.

Donnerstein, E., & Hallam, J. (1978). Facilitating effects of erotica on aggression against women. *Journal of Personality and Social Psychology, 36,* 1270-1277.

Donnerstein, E., Slaby, R. G., & Eron, L. D. (1994). The mass media and youth aggression. In L. D. Eron, J. H. Gentry, & P. Schlegel (Eds.), *Reason to hope: A psychological perspective on violence and youth* (pp. 219-250). Washington, DC: American Psychological Association.

Doob, A. N., & Climie, R. J. (1972). Delay of measurement and the effects of film violence. *Journal of Experimental Social Psychology, 8*(2), 136-142.

Doob, A. N., & Macdonald, G. E. (1979). Television viewing and fear of victimization: Is the relationship causal? *Journal of Personality and Social Psychology, 37,* 170-179.

Dorr, A. (1980). When I was a child I thought as a child. In S. B. Withey & R. P. Abeles (Eds.), *Television and social behavior: Beyond violence and children* (pp. 191-230). Hillsdale, NJ: Erlbaum.

Dorr, A. (1981). Television and affective development and functioning: Maybe this decade. *Journal of Broadcasting, 25,* 335-345.

Downs, A. C. (1990). Children's judgments of televised events: The real versus pretend distinction. *Perceptual and Motor Skills, 70,* 779-782.

Drabman, R. S., & Thomas, M. H. (1974). Does media violence increase children's toleration of real-life aggression? *Developmental Psychology, 10,* 418-421.

Dubanoski, R. A., & Kong, C. (1977). The effects of pain cues on the behavior of high and low aggressive boys. *Social Behavior and Personality, 5,* 273-279.

Dysinger, W. S., & Ruckmick, C. A. (1933). *The emotional responses of children to the motion picture situation.* New York: Macmillan.

Einsiedel, E. F., Salomone, K. L., & Schneider, F. P. (1984). Crime: Effects of media exposure and personal experience on issue salience. *Journalism Quarterly, 61,* 131-136.

Ekman, P., Liebert, R. M., Friesen, W. V., Harrison, R., Zlatchin, C., Malmstrom, E. J., & Baron, R. A. (1972). Facial expressions of emotion while watching televised violence as predictors of subsequent aggression. In G. A. Comstock, E. A. Rubinstein, & J. P. Murray (Eds.), *Television and social behavior: Reports and papers: Vol. 5. Television's effects: Further explorations* (pp. 22-58). Washington, DC: Government Printing Office.

Elliott, W. R., & Slater, D. (1980). Exposure, experience and perceived TV reality for adolescents. *Journalism Quarterly, 57,* 409-414, 431.

Ellis, D. P., Wienir, P., & Miller, L. (1971). Does the trigger pull the finger? *Sociometry, 34,* 453-465.

Ellis, G. T., & Sekyra, F., III. (1972). The effect of aggressive cartoons on the behavior of first grade children. *Journal of Psychology, 81,* 37-43.

Eron, L. D. (1982). Parent-child interaction, television violence, and aggression of children. *American Psychologist, 37,* 197-211.

Eron, L. D. (1987). The development of aggressive behavior from the perspective of a developing behaviorism. *American Psychologist, 42,* 435-442.

Eron, L. (1994). Theories of aggression: From drives to cognitions. In L. R. Huesmann (Ed.), *Aggressive behavior: Current perspectives* (pp. 1-11). New York: Plenum.

Eron, L. D., Huesmann, L. R., Brice, P., Fisher, P., & Mermelstein, R. (1983). Age trends in the development of aggression, sex typing, and related habits. *Developmental Psychology, 19,* 71-77.

Eron, L. D., Huesmann, L. R., Lefkowitz, M. M., & Walder, L. O. (1972). Does television violence cause aggression? *American Psychologist, 27,* 253-263.

Estep, R., & Macdonald, P. T. (1983). How prime time crime evolved on TV, 1976-1981. *Journalism Quarterly, 60,* 293-300.

Ferguson, D. A. (1994). Measurement of mundane TV behaviors: Remote control device flipping frequency. *Journal of Broadcasting & Electronic Media, 38,* 35-47.

Feshbach, N. D., & Roe, K. (1968). Empathy in six- and seven-year-olds. *Child Development, 39,* 133-145.

Feshbach, S. (1955). The drive-reducing function of fantasy behavior. *Journal of Abnormal and Social Psychology, 50,* 3-11.

Feshbach, S. (1961). The stimulating versus cathartic effects of a vicarious aggressive activity. *Journal of Abnormal and Social Psychology, 63,* 381-385.

Feshbach, S. (1972). Reality and fantasy in filmed violence. In J. P. Murray, E. A. Rubinstein, & G. A. Comstock (Eds.), *Television and social behavior: Reports and papers: Vol. 2. Television and social learning* (pp. 318-345). Washington, DC: Government Printing Office.

Feshbach, S. (1976). The role of fantasy in the response to television. *Journal of Social Issues, 32*(4), 71-89.

Feshbach, S., & Singer, R. D. (1971). *Television and aggression.* San Francisco: Jossey-Bass.

Fishman, M. (1980). *Manufacturing the news.* Austin: University of Texas Press.

Fiske, J., & Hartley, J. (1978). *Reading television.* London: Methuen.

Fiske, S. T., & Taylor, S. E. (1991). *Social cognition* (2nd ed.). New York: McGraw-Hill.

Flavell, J. H. (1977). *Cognitive development.* Englewood Cliffs, NJ: Prentice Hall.

Forgas, J. P., Brown, L. B., & Menyhart, J. (1980). Dimensions of aggression: The perception of aggressive episodes. *British Journal of Social and Clinical Psychology, 19,* 215-227.

Forum for Children's Television. (1982). *TV and children's health.* Tokyo: Author.

Forum for Children's Television. (1988). *How TV has been commercialized.* Tokyo: Author.

Fox, W. S., & Philliber, W. W. (1978). Television viewing and the perception of affluence. *Sociological Quarterly, 19,* 103-112.

Franzblau, S., Sprafkin, J. N., & Rubinstein, E. (1977). Sex on TV: A content analysis. *Journal of Communication, 27*(2), 164-170.

Freedman, J., & Newtson, R. (1975, September). *The effect of anger on preference for filmed violence.* Paper presented at the annual conference of the American Psychological Association, Chicago.

Freedman, J. L. (1984). Effect of television violence on aggressiveness. *Psychological Bulletin, 96*(2), 227-246.

Freud, S. (1933). *New introductory lectures on psycho-analysis.* New York: Norton.

Freud, S. (1960). *Jokes and their relation to the unconscious* (Std. ed., Vol. 8). London: Hograth.

Friedman, H. L., & Johnson, R. L. (1972). Mass media use and aggression: A pilot study. In G. A. Comstock & E. A. Rubinstein (Eds.), *Television and social behavior: Reports and papers: Vol. 3. Television and adolescent aggressiveness* (pp. 336-360). Washington, DC: Government Printing Office.

Friedrich, L. K., & Stein, A. H. (1973). Aggressive and prosocial programs and the natural behavior of preschool children. *Monographs of the Society for Research in Child Development, 38* (4, Serial No. 151).

Friedrich-Cofer, L., & Huston, A. C. (1986). Television violence and aggression: The debate continues. *Psychological Bulletin, 100,* 364-371.

Frodi, A. (1975). The effect of exposure to weapons on aggressive behavior from a cross-cultural perspective. *International Journal of Psychology, 10,* 283-292.

Furnham, A., & Gunter, B. (1985). Sex, presentation mode, and memory for violent and non-violent news. *Journal of Educational Television, 11,* 99-105.

Furnham, A., & Gunter, B. (1987). Effects of time of day and medium of presentation on immediate recall of violent and non-violent news. *Applied Cognitive Psychology, 1,* 255-262.

Furu, T. (1962). *Television and children's life: A before-after study.* Tokyo: NHK Radio and Television Culture Research Institute.

Furu, T. (1971). *The function of television for children and adolescents.* Tokyo: Sophia University Press.

Gadow, K. D., Sprafkin, J., & Ficarrotto, T. J. (1987). Effects of viewing aggression-laden cartoons on preschool-aged emotionally disturbed children. *Child Psychiatry and Human Development, 17,* 257-273.

Galloway, S. (1993, July 27). U.S. rating system: Sex before violence. *Hollywood Reporter,* p. 31.

Gardner, H. (1983). *Frames of mind: The theory of multiple intelligences.* New York: Basic Books.

Gardner, R. W. (1968). *Personality development at preadolescence.* Seattle: University of Washington Press.

Geen, R. G. (1975). The meaning of observed violence: Real vs. fictional violence and consequent effects on aggression and emotional arousal. *Journal of Research in Personality, 9,* 270-281.

Geen, R. G. (1981). Behavioral and physiological reactions to observed violence: Effects of prior exposure to aggressive stimuli. *Journal of Personality and Social Psychology, 40,* 868-875.

Geen, R. G. (1994). Television and aggression: Recent developments in research and theory. In D. Zillmann, J. Bryant, & A. C. Huston (Eds.), *Media, children, and the family* (pp. 151-162). Hillsdale, NJ: Erlbaum.

Geen, R. G., & Berkowitz, L. (1966). Name mediated aggressive cue properties. *Journal of Personality, 34,* 456-465.

Geen, R. G., & Berkowitz, L. (1967). Some conditions facilitating the occurrence of aggression after the observation of violence. *Journal of Personality, 35,* 666-676.

Geen, R. G., & Rakosky, J. J. (1973). Interpretations of observed aggression and their effect on GSR. *Journal of Experimental Research in Personality, 6,* 289-292.

Geen, R. G., & Stonner, D. (1973). Context effects in observed violence. *Journal of Personality and Social Psychology, 25,* 145-150.

Geen, R. G., & Stonner, D. (1974). The meaning of observed violence: Effects on arousal and aggressive behavior. *Journal of Research in Personality, 8,* 55-63.

Geiger, S., & Reeves, B. (1993). We interrupt this program . . . Attention for television sequences. *Human Communication Research, 19,* 368-387.

Gerbner, G. (1969). Towards "cultural indicators": The analysis of mass mediated message systems. *AV Communication Review, 17,* 137-148.

Gerbner, G. (1972). Violence in television drama: Trends and symbolic functions. In G. Comstock & E. Rubinstein (Eds.), *Television and social behavior: Reports and papers: Vol. 1. Media content and control* (pp. 28-187). Washington, DC: Government Printing Office.

Gerbner, G. A. (1994, January 27). *Highlights of the television violence profile no. 16.* Remarks prepared for the National Association of Television Executives annual conference, Miami Beach, FL.

Gerbner, G., & Gross, L. (1976). Living with television: The violence profile. *Journal of Communication, 26*(2), 172-199.

Gerbner, G., Gross, L., Eleey, M. F., Jackson-Beeck, M., Jeffries-Fox, S., & Signorielli, N. (1977). Television violence profile no. 8: The highlights. *Journal of Communication, 27*(2), 171-180.

Gerbner, G., Gross, L., Jackson-Beeck, M., Jeffries-Fox, S., & Signorielli, N. (1978). Cultural indicators: Violence profile no. 9. *Journal of Communication, 28*(3), 176-207.

Gerbner, G., Gross, L., Morgan, M., & Signorielli, N. (1980). The "mainstreaming" of America: Violence profile no. 11. *Journal of Communication, 30*(3), 10-29.

Gerbner, G., Gross, L., Morgan, M., & Signorielli, N. (1981). A curious journey into the scary world of Paul Hirsch. *Communication Research, 8,* 39-72.

Gerbner, G., Gross, L., Morgan, M., & Signorielli, N. (1982). Charting the mainstreaming: Television's contributions to political orientations. *Journal of Communication, 32*(2), 100-127.

Gerbner, G., Gross, L., Morgan, M., & Signorielli, N. (1986). Living with television: The dynamics of the cultivation process. In J. Bryant & D. Zillmann (Eds.), *Perspectives on media effects* (pp. 17-40). Hillsdale, NJ: Erlbaum.

Gerbner, G., Gross, L., Morgan, M., & Signorielli, N. (1994). Growing up with television: The cultivation perspective. In J. Bryant & D. Zillmann (Eds.), *Media effects* (pp. 17-41). Hillsdale, NJ: Erlbaum.

Gerbner, G., Gross, L., Signorielli, N., & Morgan, M. (1980). Aging with television: Images on television drama and conceptions of social reality. *Journal of Communication, 30*(1), 37-47.

Gerbner, G., Gross, L., Signorielli, N., Morgan, M., & Jackson-Beeck, M. (1979a). The demonstration of power: Violence profile no. 10. *Journal of Communication, 29*(3), 177-196.

Gerbner, G., Gross, L., Signorielli, N., Morgan, M., & Jackson-Beeck, M. (1979b). *Violence profile no. 10: Trends in network television drama and viewer conceptions of social reality, 1967-78.* Unpublished manuscript, Annenberg School of Communications, University of Pennsylvania.

Gerbner, G. A., & Signorielli, N. (1990). *Violence profile 1967 to 1988-89: Enduring patterns.* Unpublished manuscript, Annenberg School of Communications, University of Pennsylvania, Philadelphia.

Gilligan, C. (1993). *In a different voice.* Cambridge, MA: Harvard University Press.

Goldenstein, A. P. (1994). *The ecology of aggression.* New York: Plenum.

Goleman, D. (1995). *Emotional intelligence.* New York: Bantam.

Goonasekera, A., & Lock, Y. K. (1990). Violence on television in Asia. *Asian Journal of Communication, 1*(1), 136-146.

Goranson, R. (1969). *Observed violence and aggressive behavior: The effects of negative outcomes to the observed violence.* Unpublished doctoral dissertation, University of Wisconsin-Madison.

Goranson, R. E. (1970). Media violence and aggressive behavior: A review of the experimental research. In L. Berkowitz (Ed.), *Advances in experimental social psychology* (Vol. 5, pp. 1-31). New York: Academic Press.

Greenberg, B. S. (1975). British children and television violence. *Public Opinion Quaterly, 39,* 521-547.

Greenberg, B. S. (1980). *Life on television.* Norwood, NJ: Ablex.

Greenberg, B. S. (1988). Some uncommon television images and the drench hypothesis. In S. Oskamp (Ed.), *Applied social psychology annual: Vol. 8. Television as a social issue* (pp. 88-102). Beverly Hills, CA: Sage.

Greenberg, B. S., Edison, N., Korzenny, F., Fernandez-Collado, C., & Atkin, C. K. (1980). In B. S. Greenberg (Ed.), *Life on television: Content analysis of U.S. TV drama* (pp. 99-128). Norwood, NJ: Ablex.

Greenberg, B. S., & Gordon, T. F. (1972). Social class and racial differences in children's perceptions of television violence. In G. A. Comstock, E. A. Rubinstein, & J. P. Murray (Eds.), *Television and social behavior: Reports and papers: Vol. 5. Television's effects: Further explorations* (pp. 211-230). Washington, DC: Government Printing Office.

Groebel, J., & Krebs, D. (1983). A study of the effects of television on anxiety. In C. D. Spielberger & R. Diaz-Guerrero (Eds.), *Cross-cultural anxiety* (Vol. 2, pp. 89-98). New York: Hemisphere.

Gross, L., & Jeffries-Fox, S. (1978). What do you want to be when you grow up little girl? In G. Tuchman, A. K. Daniles, & J. Benet (Eds.), *Hearth and home: Images of women in the mass media* (pp. 240-265). New York: Oxford University Press.

Guerre, N. G., Nucci, L., & Huesmann, L. R. (1994). In L. R. Huesmann (Ed.), *Aggressive behavior: Current perspectives* (pp. 13-33). New York: Plenum.

Gunter, B. (1980). The cathartic potential of television drama. *Bulletin of the British Psychological Society, 36,* 166-168.

Gunter, B. (1983). Personality and perceptions of harmful and harmless TV violence. *Personality and Individual Differences, 4,* 665-670.

Gunter, B. (1985). *Dimensions of television violence.* Aldershot, UK: Gower.

Gunter, B. (1987). *Television and the fear of crime.* London: John Libbey.

Gunter, B. (1994). The question of media violence. In J. Bryant & D. Zillmann (Eds.), *Media effects: Advances in theory and research* (pp. 163-211). Hillsdale, NJ: Erlbaum.

Gunter, B., & Furnham, A. (1983). Personality and the perception of TV violence. *Personality and Individual Differences, 4,* 315-321.

Gunter, B., & Furnham, A. (1984). Perceptions of television violence: Effects of programme genre and type of violence on viewers' judgements of violent portrayals. *British Journal of Social Psychology, 23,* 155-164.

Gunter, B., Furnham, A., & Gietson, G. (1984). Memory for the news as a function of the channel of communication. *Human Learning, 3,* 265-271.

Gunter, B., & Harrison, J. (1995). *Violence on television in the United Kingdom: A content analysis.* Sheffield, UK: Department of Journalism Studies, University of Sheffield.

Gunter, B., & Wober, M. (1983). Television viewing and the public trust. *British Journal of Social Psychology, 22,* 174-176.

Hagiwara, S. (1990). Violence on television in Asia: Japaneses study. *KEIO Communication Review, 11,* 3-23.

Halderman, B. L., & Jackson, T. T. (1979). Naturalistic study of aggression: Aggressive stimuli and horn honking. *Psychological Reports, 45,* 880-882.

Hall, S. (1980). Encoding and decoding (Rev. extract). In S. Hall (Ed.), *Culture, media, language,* (pp. 128-138). London: Hutchinson.

Halloran, J. D., Brown, R. L., & Chaney, D. C. (1970). *Television and delinquency.* Leicester, England: Leicester University Press.

Halloran, J. D., & Croll, P. (1972). Television programmes in Great Britian. In G. A. Comstock & E. A. Rubinstein (Eds.), *Television and social behavior: Reports and papers: Vol. 1. Media content and control* (pp. 415-492). Washington, DC: Government Printing Office.

Hamilton, J. T. (1998). *Channeling violence: The economic market for violent television programming.* Princeton, NJ: Princeton University Press.

Hapkiewicz, W. G. (1979). Children's reactions to cartoon violence. *Journal of Clinical Child Psychology, 8*(1), 30-34.

Hapkiewicz, W. G., & Stone, R. D. (1974). The effect of realistic versus imaginary aggressive models on children's interpersonal play. *Child Study Journal, 4*(2), 47-58.

Hare, R. D., & Blevings, G. (1975). Defense responses to phobic stimuli. *Biological Psychology, 3,* 1-13.

Hart, A. (1986). Children and television: Audience and influence. *Media in Education and Development, 19*(2), 80-85.

Harvey, S. E., Sprafkin, J. N., & Rubinstein, E. (1979). Prime time television: A profile of aggressive and prosocial behaviors. *Journal of Broadcasting, 23,* 179-189.

Hashway, R. M., & Duke, L. I. (1992). *Cognitive styles: A primer to the literature.* Lewiston, NY: Edwin Mellen.

Hawkins, R. P. (1977). The dimensional structure of children's perceptions of television reality. *Communication Research, 4,* 299-320.

Hawkins, R. P., & Pingree, S. (1980). Some processes in the cultivation effect. *Communication Research, 7,* 193-226.

Hawkins, R. P., & Pingree, S. (1981a). Uniform messages and habitual viewing: Unnecessary assumptions in social reality effects. *Human Communication Research, 7,* 291-301.

Hawkins, R. P., & Pingree, S. (1981b). Using television to construct social reality. *Journal of Broadcasting, 25,* 347-364.

Hawkins, R. P., & Pingree, S. (1982). Television's influence on social reality. In D. Pearl, L. Bouthilet, & J. Lazar (Eds.), *Television and behavior: Ten years of scientific progress and implications for the eighties* (Vol. 2, pp. 224-247). Rockville, MD: U.S. Department of Health and Human Services.

Hawkins, R. P., Tapper, J., Bruce, L., & Pingree, S. (1995). Strategic and nonstrategic explanations for attentional inertia. *Communication Research, 22,* 188-206.

Head, S. W. (1954). Content analysis of television drama programs. *Quarterly of Film, Radio and Television, 9,* 175-194.

Hearold, S. (1986). A synthesis of 1043 effects of television on social behavior. In G. Comstock (Ed.), *Public communication and behavior* (Vol. 1, pp. 65-133). San Diego, CA: Academic Press.

Heath, L., Bresolin, L. B., & Rinaldi, R. C. (1989). Effects of media violence on children. *Archives of General Psychiatry, 46,* 376-379.

Hennigan, K. M., Del Rosario, M. L., Heath, L., Cook, T. D., Wharton, J. D., & Calder, B. J. (1982). Impact of the introduction of television on crime in the United States: Empirical findings and theoretical implications. *Journal of Personality and Social Psychology, 42,* 461-477.

Hicks, D. J. (1965). Imitation and retention of film-mediated aggressive peer and adult models. *Journal of Personality and Social Psychology, 2,* 97-100.

Himmelweit, H., Oppenheim, A., & Vince, P. (1958). *Television and the child.* London: Oxford University Press.

Himmelweit, H. T., Swift, B., & Jaeger, M. E. (1980). The audience as critic: A conceptual analysis of television entertainment. In P. H. Tannenbaum (Ed.), *The entertainment functions of television* (pp. 67-106). Hillsdale, NJ: Erlbaum.

Hodge, R., & Tripp, D. (1986). *Children and television: A semiotic approach.* Stanford, CA: Stanford University Press.

Hoffner, C. (1997). Children's emotional reactions to a scary film: The role of prior outcome information and coping style. *Human Communication Research, 23,* 323-341.

Hoffner, C., & Cantor, J. (1985). Developmental differences in responses to a television character's appearance and behavior. *Developmental Psychology, 21,* 1065-1074.

Hoffner, C., & Cantor, J. (1991). Perceiving and responding to mass media characters. In J. Bryant & D. Zillmann (Eds.), *Responding to the screen* (pp. 63-101). Hillsdale, NJ: Erlbaum.

Hogben, M. (1998). Factors moderating the effect of television aggression on viewer behavior. *Communication Research, 25,* 220-247.

Hollenbeck, A. R., & Slaby, R. G. (1979). Infant visual and vocal responses to television. *Child Development, 50,* 41-45.

Horney, K. (1939). *New ways in psychoanalysis.* New York: Norton.

Howitt, D., & Cumberbatch, G. (1974). Audience perceptions of violent television content. *Communication Research, 1,* 204-223.

Howitt, D., & Cumberbatch, G. (1975). *Mass media violence and society.* New York: John Wiley.

Hoyt, J. L. (1970). The effect of media "justification" on aggression. *Journal of Broadcasting, 6,* 455-464.

Huesmann, L. R. (1986). Psychological processes promoting the relation between exposure to media violence and aggressive behavior by the viewer. *Journal of Social Issues, 42*(3), 125-139.

Huesmann, L. R. (1988). An information processing model for the development of aggression. *Aggressive Behavior, 14,* 13-24.

Huesmann, L. R., & Eron, L. D. (1986). *Television and the aggressive child: A cross-national comparison.* Hillsdale, NJ: Erlbaum.

Huesmann, L. R., Eron, L. D., Guerra, N. G., & Crawshaw, V. B. (1994). Measuring children's aggression with teachers' predictions of peer nominations. *Psychological Assessment, 6,* 329-336.

Huesmann, L. R., Eron, L. D., Lefkowitz, M. M., & Walder, L. O. (1984). Stability of aggression overtime and generations. *Developmental Psychology, 20,* 1120-1134.

Huesmann, L. R., Lagerspetz, K., & Eron, L. D. (1984). Intervening variables in the TV-violence-aggression relation: Evidence from two countries. *Developmental Psychology, 20,* 746-775.

Huesmann, L. R., & Miller, L. S. (1994). Long term effects of repeated exposure to media violence in childhood. In L. R. Huesmann (Ed.), *Aggressive behavior: Current perspectives* (pp. 153-186). New York: Plenum.

Huston, A., Wright, J. C., Rice, M. L., Kerkman, D., Seigle, J., & Bremer, M. (1983). *Family environment and television use by preschool children.* Paper presented at the biennial meeting of the Society for Research on Child Development, Detroit, MI. (ERIC Document No. ED 230 293)

Huston-Stein, A., Fox, S., Greer, D., Watkins, B. A., & Whitaker, J. (1981). The effects of TV action and violence on children's social behavior. *Journal of Genetic Psychology, 138,* 183-191.

Iwao, S., de Sola Pool, I., & Hagiwara, S. (1981a). Content analysis of TV dramatic programs. *Hoso Bunka Foundation Research Report, 14,* 291-294.

Iwao, S., de Sola Pool, I., & Hagiwara, S. (1981b). Japanese and U.S. media: Some cross-cultural insights into TV violence. *Journal of Communication, 31*(2), 28-36.

Jo, E., & Berkowitz, L. (1994). A priming effect analysis of media influences: An update. In J. Bryant & D. Zillmann (Eds.), *Media effects: Advances in theory and research* (pp. 43-60). Hillsdale, NJ: Erlbaum.

Johnston, D. D. (1995). Adolescents' motivations for viewing graphic horror. *Human Communication Research, 21,* 522-552.

Jones, G. W., Jr. (1971). *The relationship of screen-mediated violence to antisocial behavior.* Unpublished doctoral dissertation, Syracuse University, Syracuse, NY (University Microfilms No. 72-60,592).

Josephson, W. (1987). Television violence and children's aggression: Testing the priming, social script, and disinhibition predictors. *Journal of Personality and Social Psychology, 53,* 882-890.

Kagan, J., Rosman, D., Day, D., Albert, J., & Phillips, W. (1964). Information processing in the child: Significance of analytic and reflective attitudes. *Psychological Monographs, 78,* 1.

Kane, T., Joseph, J. M., & Tedeschi, J. T. (1976). Personal perception and the Berkowitz paradigm for the study of aggression. *Journal of Personality and Social Psychology, 33,* 663-673.

Kaplan, R. M., & Singer, R. D. (1976). Psychological effects of television violence: A review and methodological critique. *Journal of Social Issues, 34*(1), 176-188.

Kaplan, S. J., & Baxter, L. A. (1982). Antisocial and prosocial behavior on prime-time TV. *Journalism Quarterly, 59,* 478-482.

Kapoor, S., Kang, J. G., Kim, W. Y., & Kim, S. K. (1994). Televised violence and viewers' perceptions of social reality: The Korean case. *Communication Research Reports, 11,* 189-200.

Kashiwagi, A., & Munakata, K. (1985). Research on the relationship between influence by children's exposure to TV films with high violence ratings and family background. *Hoso Bunka Foundation Research Report, 8,* 58-66.

Kerlinger, F. N. (1996). *Foundations of behavioral research.* New York: Holt, Rinehart and Winston.

Kessler, R. C., & Stipp, H. (1984). The impact of fictional television suicide stories on U.S. fatalities: A replication. *American Journal of Sociology, 90,* 151-167.

Kintsch, W., & van Dijk, T. A. (1978). Toward a model of text comprehension and production. *Psychological Review, 85,* 363-394.

Klapper, J. (1960). *The effects of mass communication.* New York: Free Press.

Kniveton, B. H. (1973). The effect of rehearsal delay on long-term imitation of filmed aggression. *British Journal of Psychology, 64,* 259-265.

Kniveton, B. H. (1976). Social learning and imitation in relation to TV. In R. Brown (Ed.), *Children and television* (pp. 237-266). Beverly Hills, CA: Sage.

Kniveton, B. H., & Stephenson, G. M. (1975). The effects of an aggressive film model on social interaction in groups of middle-class and working-class boys. *Journal of Psychological Psychiatry, 16,* 301-313.

Kohlberg, L. (1966). Moral education in the schools: A developmental view. *School Review, 74,* 1-30.

Kohlberg, L. (1981). *The philosophy of moral development: Moral stages and the idea of justice.* New York: Harper & Row.

Koriat, A., Melkman, R., Averill, J. R., & Lazarus, R. S. (1972). The self-control of emotional reactions to a stressful film. *Journal of Personality, 40,* 601-619.

Kunkel, D., Farinola, W. J. M., Cope, K. M., Donnerstein, E., Biely, E., & Zwarun, L. (1998). *Rating the TV ratings: One year out.* Menlo Park, CA: Henry J. Kaiser Family Foundation.

Lagerspetz, K. M. J., & Bjorkqvist, K. (1994). Indirect aggression in boys and girls. In L. R. Huesmann (Ed.), *Aggressive behavior: Current perspectives* (pp. 131-150). New York: Plenum.

Lagerspetz, K. M. J., & Engblom, P. (1979). Immediate reactions to TV-violence by Finnish pre-school children of different personality types. *Scandinavian Journal of Psychology, 20,* 43-53.

Lando, H. A., & Donnerstein, E. I. (1978). The effects of a model's success or failure on subsequent aggressive behavior. *Journal of Research in Personality, 12,* 225-234.

Larsen, O. N., Gray, L. N., & Fortis, J. G. (1968). Achieving goals through violence on television. In O. N. Larsen (Ed.), *Violence and the mass media* (pp. 97-111). New York: Harper & Row.

Lazarus, R. S., & Alfert, E. (1964). Short-circuiting of threat by experimentally altering cognitive appraisal. *Journal of Abnormal and Social Psychology, 69,* 195-205.

Lazarus, R. S., Opton, E. M., Nomikos, M. S., & Rankin, N. O. (1965). The principle of short-circuiting of threat: Further evidence. *Journal of Personality, 33,* 622-635.

Lazarus, R. S., Speisman, J. C., Mordkoff, A. M., & Davidson, L. A. (1962). A laboratory study of psychological stress produced by a motion picture film. *Psychological Monographs: General and Applied, 76*(34, Whole No. 553).

Leifer, A. D., & Roberts, D. F. (1972). Children's responses to television violence. In J. P. Murray, E. A. Rubinstein, & G. A. Comstock (Eds.), *Television and social behavior: Vol. 2. Television and social learning* (pp. 43-180). Washington, DC: Government Printing Office.

Lesser, H. (1977). *Television and the preschool child.* New York: Academic Press.

Leyens, J.-P., Camino, L., Parke, R. D., & Berkowitz, L. (1975). Effects of violence on aggression in a field setting as a function of group dominance and cohesion. *Journal of Personality and Social Psychology, 32,* 346-360.

Leyens, J.-P., Cisneros, T., & Hossay, J.-F. (1976). Decentration as a means for reducing aggression after exposure to violent stimuli. *European Journal of Social Psychology, 6,* 459-473.

Leyens, J.-P., & Dunand, M. (1991). Priming aggressive thoughts: The effect of the anticipation of a violent movie upon the aggressive behaviour of the spectators. *European Journal of Social Psychology, 21,* 507-516.

Leyens, J.-P., & Parke, R. D. (1975). Aggressive slides can induce a weapons effect. *European Journal of Social Psychology, 5,* 229-236.

Leyens, J.-P., & Picus, S. (1973). Identification with the winner of a fight and name mediation: Their differential effects upon subsequent aggressive behaviour. *British Journal of Social and Clinical Psychology, 12,* 374-377.

Lichter, L. S., & Lichter, S. R. (1983). *Prime time crime.* Washington, DC: Media Institute.

Lichter, S. R., & Amundson, D. (1992). *A day of television violence.* Washington, DC: Center for Media and Public Affairs.

Lichter, S. R., & Amundson, D. (1994). *A day of TV violence: 1992 vs 1994.* Washington, DC: Center for Media and Public Affairs.

Lieberman Research. (1975). *Children's reactions to violent material on television: 5th year report.* Unpublished manuscript.

Liebert, R. M. (1972). Television and social learning: Some relationships between viewing violence and behaving aggressively (overview). In J. P. Murray, E. A. Rubinstein, & G. A. Comstock (Eds.), *Television and social behavior: Reports and papers: Vol. 2. Television and social learning* (pp. 1-42). Washington, DC: Government Printing Office.

Liebert, R. M., & Baron, R. A. (1972). Short-term effects of television aggression on children's aggressive behavior. In J. P. Murray, E. A. Rubinstein, & G. A. Comstock (Eds.), *Television and social behavior: Reports and papers: Vol. 2. Television and social learning* (pp. 181-252). Washington, DC: Government Printing Office.

Liebert, R. M., & Baron, R. A. (1973). Some immediate effects of televised violence on children's behavior. *Developmental Psychology, 6,* 469-475.

Liebert, R. M., Neale, J. M., & Davidson, E. A. (1973). *The early window: Effects of television on children and youth.* New York: Pergamon.

Liebert, R. M., & Poulos, R. W. (1975). Television and personality development: The socializing effects of an entertainment medium. In A. Davids (Ed.), *Child personality and psychopathology: Current topics* (Vol. 2, pp. 61-97). New York: John Wiley.

Liebert, R. M., & Schwartzberg, N. S. (1977). Effects of mass media. *Annual Review of Psychology, 28,* 141-173.

Liebert, R. M., Sobol, M. P., & Davidson, E. S. (1972). Catharsis of aggression among institutionalized boys: Fact or artifact? In G. A. Comstock, E. A. Rubinstein, & J. P. Murray (Eds.), *Television and social behavior: Vol. 5. Television's effects: Further explorations* (pp. 351-359). Washington, DC: Government Printing Office.

Lincoln, A., & Levinger, G. (1972). Observers' evaluations of the victim and the attacker in an aggressive incident. *Journal of Personality and Social Psychology, 22,* 202-210.

Linne, O. (1976). The viewers aggression as a function of variously edited TV-films. *Communications, 2*(1), 101-111.

Linz, D. G., Donnerstein, E., & Penrod, S. (1984). The effects of multiple exposures to filmed violence against women. *Journal of Communication, 34*(3), 130-147.

Linz, D. G., Donnerstein, E., & Penrod, S. (1988a). Effects of long-term exposure to violent and sexually degrading depictions of women. *Journal of Personality and Social Psychology, 55,* 758-768.

Linz, D. G., Donnerstein, E., & Penrod, S. (1988b). Sexual violence in the mass media: Social psychological implications. In P. Shaver & C. Hendrick (Eds.), *Review of personality and social psychology* (Vol. 7, pp. 95-123). Beverly Hills, CA: Sage.

Lippmann, W. (1922). *Public opinion.* New York: Harcourt Brace.

Liss, M. B., Reinhardt, L. C., & Fredriksen, S. (1983). TV heroes: The impact of rhetoric and deeds. *Journal of Applied Developmental Psychology, 4,* 175-187.

Lorenz, K. Z. (1963). *On aggression.* New York: Harcourt, Brace & World.

Lovaas, O. I. (1961). Effect of exposure to symbolic aggression on aggressive behavior. *Child Development, 32,* 37-44.

Lowry, B. (1997, September 21). TV on decline but few back U.S. regulation. *Los Angeles Times,* pp. A1, A40, A41.

Lowry, B., Hall, J., & Braxton, G. (1997, September 21). There's a moral to this. *Los Angeles Times Calendar,* pp. 8-9, 72-73.

Loye, D., Gorney, R., & Steele, G. (1977). An experimental field study. *Journal of Communication, 27,* 206-216.

Lyle, J., & Wilcox, W. (1963). Television news—An interim report. *Journal of Broadcasting, 7,* 157-166.

Lynn, R., Hampson, S., & Agahi, E. (1989). Television violence and aggression: A genotype-environment, correlation and interaction theory. *Social Behavior and Personality, 17,* 143-164.

Maccoby, E. E. (1964). Effects of the mass media. In M. L. Hoffman & L. W. Hoffman (Eds.), *Review of child development research* (pp. 323-348). New York: Russell Sage.

Malamuth, N. M., & Check, J. V. P. (1980). Sexual arousal to rape and consenting depictions: The importance of women's arousal. *Journal of Abnormal Psychology, 89,* 763-766.

Malamuth, N. M., Linz, D., Heavey, C. L., Barnes, G., & Acker, M. (1995). Using the confluence model of sexual aggression to predict men's conflict with women: A 10-year follow-up study. *Journal of Personality and Social Psychology, 69,* 353-369.

Malamuth, N. M., Sockloskie, R. J., Koss, M. P., & Tanaka, J. S. (1991). Characteristics of aggressors against women: Testing a model using a national sample of college students. *Journal of Consulting and Clinical Psychology, 59,* 670-681.

Marcuse, H. (1966). *One-dimensional man.* London: Routledge & Kegan Paul.

McCann, T. E., & Sheehan, P. W. (1985). Violent content in Australian television. *Australian Psychologist, 20*(1), 33-42.

McCarthy, E. D., Langner, T. S., Gersten, J. C., Eisenberg, J. G., & Orzeck, L. (1975). Violence and behavior disorders. *Journal of Communication, 25*(4), 71-85.

McGuire, W. J. (1973). Persuasion, resistance, and attitude change. In I. de Sola Pool, W. Schramm, F. W. Frey, N. Maccoby, & E. B. Parker (Eds.), *Handbook of communication* (pp. 216-252). Chicago: Rand McNally.

McGuire, W. J. (1986). The myth of massive media impact: Savagings and salvagings. In G. Comstock (Ed.), *Public communication and behavior* (Vol. 1, pp. 173-257). San Diego, CA: Academic Press.

McHan, E. J. (1985). Imitation of aggression by Lebanese children. *Journal of Social Psychology, 125,* 613-617.

McIntyre, J., & Teevan, J. J., Jr. (1972). Television violence and deviant behavior. In G. A. Comstock & E. A. Rubinstein (Eds.), *Television and social behavior: Reports and papers: Vol. 3. Television and adolescent aggressiveness* (pp. 383-435). Washington, DC: Government Printing Office.

McLeod, J. M., Atkin, C. K., & Chaffee, S. H. (1972). Adolescents, parents, and television use: Adolescent self-report measures from Maryland and Wisconsin samples. In G. A. Comstock & E. A. Rubinstein (Eds.), *Television and social behavior: Reports and papers: Vol. 3. Television and adolescent aggressiveness* (pp. 173-238). Washington, DC: Government Printing Office.

McLeod, J. M., & Chaffee, S. H. (1973). Interpersonal approaches to communication research. *American Behavioral Scientist, 16*, 469-499.

Meadowcroft, J., & Reeves, B. (1989). Influence of story schema on development of children's attention to television. *Communication Research, 16*, 352-374.

Mees, U. (1990). Constitutive elements of the concept of human aggression. *Aggressive Behavior, 16*, 285-295.

Messner, S. F. (1986). Television violence and violent crime: An aggregate analysis. *Social Problems, 33*, 218-235.

Meyer, T. P. (1972). Effects of viewing justified and unjustified real film violence on aggressive behavior. *Journal of Personality and Social Psychology, 23*, 21-29.

Mikami, S. (1993). A cross-national comparison of the U.S.-Japanese TV drama: International cultural indicators. *KEIO Communication Review, 15*, 29-44.

Milavsky, J. R., Kessler, R. C., Stipp, H. H., & Rubens, W. S. (1982). *Television and aggression: A panel study.* New York: Academic Press.

Mills, S., & Kemper, B. (1998, March 29). Profiles of young suspects emerge. *Santa Barbara News Press*, p. A3.

Molitor, F., & Hirsch, K. W. (1994). Children's toleration of real life aggression after exposure to media violence: A replication of the Drabman and Thomas studies. *Child Study Journal, 24*(3), 191-207.

Morgan, M. (1983). Symbolic victimization and real world fear. *Human Communication Research, 9*, 146-157.

Morgan, M. (1984). Heavy television viewing and perceived quality of life. *Journalism Quarterly, 61*, 499-504, 740.

Morgan, M. (1986). Television and the erosion of regional diversity. *Journal of Broadcasting & Electronic Media, 30*, 123-139.

Morley, D. (1980). *The "nationwide" audience: Structure and decoding.* London: British Film Institute.

Morrison, D. E. (1993). The idea of violence. In A. M. Hargrave (Ed.), *Violence in factual television, Annual review 1993* (pp. 124-129). London: John Libbey.

Mueller, C., & Donnerstein, E. (1977). The effects of humor-induced arousal upon aggressive behavior. *Journal of Research in Personality, 11*, 73-82.

Mueller, C., Nelson, R., & Donnerstein, E. (1977). Facilitative effects of media violence on helping. *Psychological Reports, 40*, 775-778.

Mullin, C. R., & Linz, D. (1995). Desensitization and resensitization to violence against women: Effects of exposure to sexually violent films on judgments of domestic violence victims. *Journal of Personality and Social Psychology, 69*, 449-459.

Munakata, K., & Kashiwagi, A. (1991). Effect of viewing TV programs with violence on children and their families: Five years later. *Hoso Bunka Foundation Research Report, 14*, 275-278.

Muncer, S. J., Gorman, B., & Campbell, A. (1986). Sorting out aggression: Dimensional and categorical perceptions of aggressive episodes. *Aggressive Behavior, 12,* 327-336.

Murphy, K., & McDermott, T. (1998, May 22). Shooter kills 1, injures 22 at Oregon school. *Los Angeles Times,* pp. A1, A26.

Mussen, P., & Rutherford, E. (1961). Effects of aggressive cartoons on children's aggressive play. *Journal of Abnormal and Social Psychology, 62,* 461-464.

Mustonen, A., & Pulkkinen, L. (1993). Aggression in television programs in Finland. *Aggressive Behavior, 19,* 175-183.

National Institute of Mental Health. (1982). *Television and behavior: Ten years of scientific progress and implications for the eighties.* Washington, DC: Government Printing Office.

National television violence study (Vol. 1). (1997). Thousand Oaks, CA: Sage.

National television violence study (Vol. 2). (1998). Thousand Oaks, CA: Sage.

National television violence study (Vol. 3). (1999). Thousand Oaks, CA: Sage.

NCTV says violence on TV up 16%. (1983, March 22). *Broadcasting Magazine,* p. 63.

Newcomb, H. (1978). Assessing the violence profile of Gerbner and Gross: A humanistic critique and suggestions. *Communication Research, 5,* 264-282.

Nomikos, M., Opton, E., Averill, J., & Lazarus, R. (1968). Surprise versus suspense in the production of stress reaction. *Journal of Personality and Social Psychology, 8,* 204-208.

O'Donnell, P. (1992, Summer). Killing the golden goose: Hollywood's death wish. *Beverly Hills Bar Association Journal, 34,* 103.

Ogles, R. M., & Hoffner, C. (1987). Film violence and perceptions of crime: The cultivation effect. In M. L. McLaughlin (Ed.), *Communication yearbook 10* (pp. 384-394). Newbury Park, CA: Sage.

O'Keefe, G. J. (1984). Public views on crime: Television exposure and media credibility. In R. N. Bostrom (Ed.), *Communication yearbook 8* (pp. 514-535). Beverly Hills, CA: Sage.

Oliver, M. B. (1994). Portrayals of crime, race, and aggression in "reality based" police shows: A content analysis. *Journal of Broadcasting & Electronic Media, 38,* 179-192.

Oliver, M. B., & Armstrong, B. (1995). Predictors of viewing and enjoyment of reality-based and fictional crime shows. *Journalism & Mass Communication Quarterly, 72,* 559-570.

Osborn, D. K., & Endsley, R. C. (1971). Emotional reactions of young children to TV violence. *Child Development, 42,* 321-331.

Page, D., & O'Neal, E. (1977). "Weapons effect" without demand characteristics. *Psychological Reports, 41,* 29-30.

Page, M. M., & Scheidt, R. J. (1971). The elusive weapons effect: Demand awareness, evaluation apprehension, and slightly sophisticated subjects. *Journal of Personality and Social Psychology, 20,* 304-318.

Paik, H., & Comstock, G. (1994). The effects of television violence on antisocial behavior: A meta-analysis. *Communication Research, 21,* 516-546.

Parke, R. D., Berkowitz, L., Leyens, J.-P., West, S., & Sebastian, R. J. (1977). The effects of repeated exposure to movie violence on aggressive behavior in juvenile delinquent boys: Field experimental studies. In L. Berkowitz (Ed.), *Advances in experimental social psychology* (Vol. 8). New York: Academic Press.

Parke, R. D., & Slaby, R. G. (1983). The development of aggression. In P. H. Mussen (Ed.), *Handbook of child psychology* (4th ed., pp. 547-642). New York: John Wiley.

Patterson, G. R. (1974). Interventions for boys with conduct problems: Multiple settings, treatments, and criteria. *Journal of Consulting and Clinical Psychology, 42,* 471-481.

Patterson, G. R., Reid, J. B., & Dishion, T. J. (1992). *Antisocial boys.* Eugene, OR: Castalia Press.

Perry, D. G., & Perry, L. C. (1976). Identification with film characters, covert aggressive verbalization, and reactions to film violence. *Journal of Research in Personality, 10,* 399-409.

Peterson, D. L., & Pfost, K. S. (1989). Influence of rock videos on attitudes of violence against women. *Psychological Reports, 64,* 319-322.

Phillips, D. P., & Hensley, J. E. (1984). When violence is rewarded or punished: The impact of mass media stories on homicide. *Journal of Communication, 34*(3), 101-116.

Pillard, R. C., Atkinson, K. W., & Fisher, S. (1967). The effect of different preparations on film-induced anxiety. *Psychological Record, 17,* 35-41.

Potter, W. J. (1986). Perceived reality in the cultivation hypothesis. *Journal of Broadcasting & Electronic Media, 30,* 159-174.

Potter, W. J. (1987). Does television viewing hinder academic achievement among adolescents? *Human Communication Research, 14,* 27-46.

Potter, W. J. (1988a). Perceived reality in television effects research. *Journal of Broadcasting & Electronic Media, 32,* 23-41.

Potter, W. J. (1988b). Three strategies for elaborating the cultivation hypothesis. *Journalism Quarterly, 65,* 930-939.

Potter, W. J. (1990). Adolescents' perceptions of the primary values of television programming. *Journalism Quarterly, 67,* 843-851.

Potter, W. J. (1991a). Examining cultivation from a psychological perspective: Component subprocesses. *Communication Research, 18,* 77-102.

Potter, W. J. (1991b). The relationships between first and second order measures of cultivation. *Human Communication Research, 18,* 92-113.

Potter, W. J. (1994). A methodological critique of cultivation research. *Journalism Monographs, 147.*

Potter, W. J. (1996). *An analysis of thinking and research about qualitative methods.* Hillsdale, NJ: Erlbaum.

Potter, W. J., & Berry, M. (1999). *A schema explanation for viewers' judgments of television violence.* Unpublished manuscript.

Potter, W. J., & Berry, M. (1999, May). *A schema explanation for viewers' judgments of television violence.* Paper presented at the annual meeting of the International Communication Association, San Francisco.

Potter, W. J., & Chang, I. K. (1990). Television exposure measures and the cultivation hypothesis. *Journal of Broadcasting & Electronic Media, 34,* 313-333.

Potter, W. J., & Levine-Donnerstein, D. (1996, May). *Content analysis methodology: Assessing reliability for multiple coders.* Paper presented at the annual meeting of the International Communication Association, Chicago.

Potter, W. J., & Levine-Donnerstein, D. (in press). Rethinking reliability and validity in content analysis. *Journal of Applied Communication Research.*

Potter, W. J., & Smith, S. L. (1999). *Patterns of graphicness in portrayals of television violence.* Unpublished manuscript.

Potter, W. J., & Smith, S. L. (in press). Consistency in contextual cues across multiple levels of analysis. *Journal of Communication.*

Potter, W. J., & Vaughan, M. (1997). Aggression in television entertainment: Profiles and trends. *Communication Research Reports, 14,* 116-124.

Potter, W. J., Vaughan, M., Warren, R., Howley, K., Land, A., & Hagemeyer, J. (1995). How real is the portrayal of aggression in television entertainment programming? *Journal of Broadcasting & Electronic Media, 39,* 496-516.

Potter, W. J., & Ware, W. (1987). An analysis of the contexts of antisocial acts on prime-time television. *Communication Research, 14,* 664-686.

Potter, W. J., & Warren, R. (1996). Considering policies to protect children from TV violence. *Journal of Communication, 46*(4), 116-138.

Potter, W. J., & Warren, R. (1998). Humor as camouflage of television violence. *Journal of Communication, 48*(2), 40-57.

Potter, W. J., Warren, R., Vaughan, M., Howley, K., Land, A., & Hagemeyer, J. (1997). Antisocial acts in reality programming on television. *Journal of Broadcasting & Electronic Media, 41,* 69-75.

Potts, R., Huston, A. C., & Wright, J. C. (1986). The effects of television form and violent content on boys' attention and social behavior. *Journal of Experimental Child Pschology, 41,* 1-17.

Poulos, R. W., Harvey, S. E., & Liebert, R. M. (1976). Saturday morning television: A profile of the 1974-75 children's season. *Psychological Reports, 39,* 1047-1057.

Prerost, F. J. (1989). Humor as an intervention strategy during psychological treatment: Imagery and incongruity. *Journal of Human Behavior, 26*(4), 34-40.

Preston, M. I. (1941). Children's reactions to movie horrors and radio crime. *Journal of Pediatrics, 19,* 147-168.

Pritchard, D. A. (1975). Leveling-sharpening revised. *Perceptual and Motor Skills, 40,* 111-117.

Ragan, T. (1998, February 2). Survey: Doctors consider gunshot wounds epidemic. *Santa Barbara News Press,* p. A3.

Reeves, B. (1978). Perceived TV reality as a predictor of children's social behavior. *Journalism Quarterly, 55,* 682-695.

Reimer, B., & Rosengren, K. E. (1990). Cultivated viewers and readers: A life-style perspective. In N. Signorielli & M. Morgan (Eds.), *Cultivation analysis: New directions in media effects research* (pp. 181-206). Newbury Park, CA: Sage.

Roberts, D. F., & Maccoby, N. (1985). Effects of mass communication. In G. Lindzey & E. Aronson (Eds.), *Handbook of social psychology: Vol. 2. Special fields and applications* (3rd ed., pp. 539-598). New York: Random House.

Roberts, D. F., & Schramm, W. (1971). Children's learning from the mass media. In W. Schramm & D. F. Roberts (Eds.), *The process and effects of mass communication* (Rev. ed., pp. 596-611). Urbana: University of Illinois Press.

Robinson, J. P., & Bachman, J. G. (1972). Television viewing habits and aggression. In G. A. Comstock & E. A. Rubinstein (Eds.), *Television and social behavior: Reports and papers: Vol. 3. Television and adolescent aggressiveness* (pp. 372-382). Washington, DC: Government Printing Office.

Rosekrans, M. A., & Hartup, W. W. (1967). Imitative influences of consistent and inconsistent response consequences to a model on aggressive behavior in children. *Journal of Personality and Social Psychology, 7,* 429-434.

Rosenberg, M. (1968). *The logic of survey analysis.* New York: Basic Books.

Rouner, D. (1984). Active television viewing and the cultivation hypothesis. *Journalism Quarterly, 61,* 168-174.

Rubin, A. M., Perse, E. M., & Taylor, D. S. (1988). A methodological examination of cultivation. *Communication Research, 15,* 107-133.

Rule, B. G., & Ferguson, T. J. (1986). The effects of media violence on attitudes, emotions, and cognitions. *Journal of Social Issues, 42*(3), 29-50.

Russell, G. W., Di Lullo, S. L., & Di Lullo, D. (1988-1989). Effects of observing competitive and violent versions of a sport. *Current Psychology: Research & Reviews, 7,* 312-321.

Salovey, P., & Mayer, J. D. (1990). Emotional intelligence. *Imagination, Cognition, and Personality, 9,* 185-211.

Salvoza, M. F. (1997, May 16-18). Readers rate TV worse than ever. *USA Weekend,* p. 20.

Sanbonmatsu, D. M., & Fazio, R. H. (1991). Construct accessibility: Determinants, consequences, and implications for the media. In J. Bryant & D. Zillmann (Eds.), *Responding to the screen: Reception and reaction processes* (pp. 45-62). Hillsdale, NJ: Erlbaum.

Sander, I. (1995). *How violent is TV-violence? An empirical investigation of factors influencing viewers' perceptions of TV-violence.* Paper presented at the annual conference of the International Communication Association, Albuquerque, NM.

Sanders, G. S., & Baron, R. S. (1975). Pain cues and uncertainty as determinants of aggression in a situation involving repeated instigation. *Journal of Personality and Social Psychology, 32,* 495-502.

Sanson, A., & Di Muccio, C. (1993). The influence of aggressive and neutral cartoon and toys on the behaviour of preschool children. *Australian Psychologist, 28,* 93-99.

Sapolsky, B. S., & Zillmann, D. (1978). Experience and empathy: Affective reactions to witnessing childbirth. *Journal of Social Psychology, 105,* 131-144.

Savitsky, J. C., Rogers, R. W., Izard, C. E., & Liebert, R. M. (1971). Role of frustration and anger in the imitation of filmed aggression against a human victim. *Psychological Reports, 29,* 807-810.

Schachter, S., & Singer, J. (1962). Cognitive, social, and physiological determinants of emotional state. *Psychological Review, 69,* 379-399.

Schmutte, G. T., & Taylor, S. P. (1980). Physical aggression as a function of alcohol and pain feedback. *Journal of Social Psychology, 110,* 235-244.

Schramm, W., Lyle, J., & Parker, E. P. (1961). *Television in the lives of our children.* Stanford, CA: Stanford University Press.

Schuck, S. Z., Schuck, A., Hallam, E., Mancini, F., & Wells, R. (1971). Sex differences in aggressive behavior subsequent to listening to a radio broadcast of violence. *Psychological Reports, 28,* 931-936.

Sheehan, P. W. (1983). Age trends and the correlates of children's television viewing. *Australian Journal of Psychology, 35,* 417-431.

Sherman, B. L., & Dominick, J. R. (1986). Violence and sex in music videos: TV and rock 'n' roll. *Journal of Communication, 36*(1), 79-93.

Shinar, D., Parnes, P., & Caspi, D. (1972). Structure and content of television broadcasting in Israel. In G. A. Comstock & E. A. Rubinstein (Eds.), *Television and social behavior: Reports and papers: Vol. 1. Media content and control.* (pp. 415-492). Washington, DC: Government Printing Office.

Shirley, K. W. (1973). *Television and children: A modeling analysis review essay.* Unpublished doctoral dissertation, University of Kansas, Lawrence.

Siegel, A. E. (1958). The influence of violence in the mass media upon children's role expectations. *Child Development, 29,* 35-56.

Signorielli, N. (1990). Television's mean and dangerous world: A continuation of the cultural indicators perspective. In N. Signorielli & M. Morgan (Eds.), *Cultivation analysis: New directions in media effects research* (pp. 85-106). Newbury Park, CA: Sage.

Signorielli, N. (1991). Adolescents and ambivalence toward marriage: A cultivation analysis. *Youth & Society, 23*(1), 121-149.

Signorielli, N., & Morgan, M. (Eds.). (1990). *Cultivation analysis: New directions in media effects research.* Newbury Park, CA: Sage.

Silvern, S. B., & Williamson, P. A. (1987). The effects of video game play on young children's aggression, fantasy, and prosocial behavior. *Journal of Applied Developmental Psychology, 8,* 453-462.

Singer, J. L. (1971). The influence of violence portrayed in television or motion pictures upon overt aggressive behavior. In J. L. Singer (Ed.), *The control of aggression and violence: Cognitive and physiological factors.* New York: Academic Press.

Singer, J. L., Singer, D. G., & Rapaczynski, W. (1984). Family patterns and television viewing as predictors of children's beliefs and aggression. *Journal of Communication, 34*(2), 73-89.

Sixth-graders were planning sniper attack at school, police say. (1998, May 23). *Los Angeles Times,* p. A19.

Slaby, R. G., Quarfoth, G. R., & McConnachie, G. A. (1976). Television violence and its sponsors. *Journal of Communication, 26*(1), 88-96.

Smeaton, G., & Byrne, D. (1987). The effects of R-rated violence and erotica, individual differences, and victim characteristics on acquaintance rape proclivity. *Journal of Research in Personality, 21,* 171-184.

Smith, P. K., & Cowie, H. (1988). *Understanding children's development.* Oxford, UK: Basil Blackwell.

Smith, S. L., Wilson, B. J., Kunkel, D., Linz, D., Potter, W. J., Colvin, C. M., & Donnerstein, E. (1999). Violence in television programming overall: University of California, Santa Barbara study. In *National Television Violence Study* (Vol. 3, pp. 5-220). Thousand Oaks, CA: Sage.

Smythe, D. W. (1954). Reality as presented by television. *Public Opinion Quarterly, 18,* 143-156.

Sniffen, M. J. (1998, April 13). Gangs, violent crimes up in schools. *Santa Barbara News Press,* pp. A1, A10.

Sommers-Flanagan, R., Sommers-Flanagan, J., & Davis, B. (1993). What's happening on music television? A gender role content analysis. *Sex Roles, 28,* 745-753.

Sparks, G. G. (1986). Developing a scale to assess cognitive responses to frightening films. *Journal of Broadcasting & Electronic Media, 30,* 65-73.

Sparks, G. G., & Cantor, J. (1986). Developmental differences in fright responses to a television program depicting a character transformation. *Journal of Broadcasting & Electronic Media, 30,* 309-323.

Speisman, J. C., Lazarus, R. S., Mordkoff, A., & Davidson, L. (1964). Experimental reduction of stress based on ego-defense theory. *Journal of Abnormal and Social Psychology, 68,* 367-380.

Sprafkin, J., Gadow, K. D., & Grayson, P. (1987). Effects of viewing aggressive cartoons on the behavior of learning disabled children. *Journal of Psychological Psychiatry, 28,* 387-398.

Sprafkin, J., Gadow, K. D., & Grayson, P. (1988). Effects of cartoons on emotionally disturbed children's social behavior in school settings. *Journal of Psychological Psychiatry, 29,* 91-99.

Sprafkin, J. N., Liebert, R. M., & Abelman, R. (1992). *Television and the exceptional child: A forgotten audience.* Hillsdale, NJ: Erlbaum.

Steenland, S. (1993, March 23). Violence is spilling into our lives. *Philadelphia Inquirer,* p. B2.

Stein, A. H., & Friedrich, L. K. (1972). Television content and young children's behavior. In J. P. Murray, E. A. Rubinstein, & G. A. Comstock (Eds.), *Television and social behavior: Reports and papers: Vol. 2. Television and social learning* (pp. 202-317). Washington, DC: Government Printing Office.

Sternberg, R. J., & Berg, C. A. (1987). What are theories of adult intellectual development theories of? In C. Schooler & K. W. Schaie (Eds.), *Cognitive functioning and social structure over the life course* (pp. 3-23). Norwood, NJ: Ablex.

Steuer, F. B., Applefield, J. M., & Smith, R. (1971). Television aggression and the interpersonal aggression of preschool children. *Journal of Experimental Child Psychology, 11,* 442-447.

Stipp, H. (1990). Research at a commercial television network in the United States. *Medien Psychologie, 2,* 85-99.

Stipp, H., Hill-Scott, K., & Dorr, A. (1987). Using social science to improve children's television: An NBC case study. *Journal of Broadcasting & Electronic Media, 31,* 461-473.

Stipp, H., & Milavsky, J. R. (1988). U.S. television programming's effects on aggressive behavior of children and adolescents. *Current Psychology: Research & Reviews,* 7(1), 76-92.

Surbeck, E. (1975). Young children's emotional reactions to T.V. violence: The effects of children's perceptions of reality. *Dissertation Abstracts International, 35,* 5139-A.

Swart, C., & Berkowitz, L. (1976). Effects of a stimulus associated with a victim's pain on later aggression. *Journal of Personality and Social Psychology, 33,* 623-631.

Tan, A. S. (1981). *Mass communication theories and research.* Columbus, OH: Grid.

Tan, A. S. (1982). Television use and social stereotypes. *Journalism Quarterly, 59,* 119-122.

Tangney, J. P. (1988). Aspects of the family and children's television viewing content preferences. *Child Development, 59,* 1070-1079.

Tangney, J. P., & Feshbach, S. (1988). Children's television viewing frequency: Individual differences and demographic correlates. *Aggressive Behavior, 14,* 145-158.

Tannenbaum, P. H. (1972). Studies in film- and television-mediated arousal and aggression: A progress report. In G. A. Comstock, E. A. Rubinstein, & J. P. Murray (Eds.),

Television and social behavior: Reports and papers: Vol. 5. Television's effects: Further explorations (pp. 309-350). Washington, DC: Government Printing Office.

Tannenbaum, P., & Gaer, E. P. (1965). Mood changes as a function of stress of protagonist and degree of identification in film-viewing situation. *Journal of Personality and Social Psychology, 2,* 612-616.

Tannenbaum, P. H., & Zillmann, D. (1975). Emotional arousal in the facilitation of aggression through communication. In L. Berkowitz (Ed.), *Advances in experimental social psychology* (Vol. 8, pp. 149-192). New York: Academic Press.

Taylor, S. E., & Howell, R. J. (1973). The ability of three-, four-, and five-year-old children to distinguish fantasy from reality. *Journal of Genetic Psychology, 122,* 315-318.

Thomas, M. H. (1982). Physiological arousal, exposure to a relatively lengthy aggressive film, and aggressive behavior. *Journal of Research in Personality, 16,* 72-81.

Thomas, M. H., & Drabman, R. S. (1975). Toleration of real life aggression as a function of exposure to televised violence and age of subject. *Merrill-Palmer Quarterly, 21,* 227-232.

Thomas, M. H., & Drabman, R. S. (1978). Effects of television violence on expectations of others' aggression. *Personality and Social Psychology Bulletin, 4,* 73-76.

Thomas, M. H., Horton, R. W., Lippincott, E. C., & Drabman, R. S. (1977). Desensitization to portrayals of real-life aggression as a function of exposure to television violence. *Journal of Personality and Social Psychology, 35,* 450-458.

Thomas, M. H., & Tell, P. M. (1974). Effects of viewing real versus fantasy violence upon interpersonal aggression. *Journal of Research in Personality, 8,* 153-160.

Thornton, W., & Voigt, L. (1984). Television and delinquency: A neglected dimension of social control. *Youth & Society, 15,* 445-468.

Traub, R. E. (1994). *Reliability for the social sciences: Theory and applications.* Thousand Oaks, CA: Sage.

Tuchman, G. (1978). *Making news: A study in the construction of reality.* New York: Free Press.

Turner, C. W., & Berkowitz, L. (1972). Identification with film aggressor (covert role taking) and reactions to film violence. *Journal of Personality and Social Psychology, 21,* 256-264.

Turner, C. W., Layton, J. F., & Simons, L. S. (1975). Naturalistic studies of aggressive behavior: Aggressive stimuli, victim visibility, and horn honking. *Journal of Personality and Social Psychology, 31,* 1098-1107.

United States statistical abstract. (1995). Washington, DC: U.S. Department of Commerce.

Valkenburg, P. M., & Van der Voort, T. H. A. (1995). The influence of television on children's daydreaming styles: A 1-year panel study. *Communication Research, 22,* 267-287.

Van der Voort, T. H. A. (1986). *Television violence: A child's-eye view.* Amsterdam: North-Holland.

Velicer, W. F., Govia, J. M., Cherico, N. P., & Corriveau, D. P. (1985). Item format and structure of the Buss-Durkee Hostility Inventory. *Aggressive Behavior, 11,* 65-82.

Volgy, T. J., & Schwarz, J. E. (1980). Television entertainment programming and sociopolitical attitudes. *Journalism Quarterly, 57,* 150-155.

von Feilitzen, C. (1975). Findings of Scandinavian research on child and television in the process of socialization. *Fernsehen und Bildung, 9,* 54-84.

Vooijs, M. W., & Van der Voort, T. H. A. (1993). Learning about television violence: The impact of a critical viewing curriculum on children's critical judgments of a crime series. *Journal of Research and Development in Education, 26,* 133-142.

Wald, M. L. (1997, July 18). "Violent aggressive" motorists account for 28,000 deaths. *Santa Barbara News Press,* p. B6.

Walters, R. H., & Parke, T. D. (1964). Influence of response consequences to a social model on resistance to deviation. *Journal of Experimental Child Psychology, 1,* 269-280.

Walters, R. H., & Willows, D. C. (1968). Imitative behavior of disturbed and nondisturbed children following exposure to aggressive and nonaggressive models. *Child Development, 39,* 79-89.

Wartella, E. (1981). The child as viewer. In M. E. Ploghoft & J. A. Anderson (Eds.), *Education for the television age* (pp. 17-28). Springfield, IL: Charles C Thomas.

Wartella, E., Olivarez, A., & Jennings, N. (1998). Children and television violence in the United States. In U. Carlsson & C. von Feilitzen (Eds.), *Children and media violence* (pp. 55-62). Goteborg, Sweden: UNESCO International Clearinghouse on Children and Violence on the Screen.

Wartella, E., Whitney, C., Lasorsa, D., Danielson, W., Olivarez, A., Lopez, R., Jennings, N., & Klijn, M. (1998). Television violence in "reality" programming: University of Texas at Austin study. In *National television violence study* (Vol. 2, pp. 205-266). Thousand Oaks, CA: Sage.

Weaver, J., & Wakshlag, J. (1986). Perceived vulnerability to crime, criminal victimization experience, and television viewing. *Journal of Broadcasting & Electronic Media, 30,* 141-158.

Webster's new universal unabridged dictionary. (1989). New York: Barnes & Noble.

Webster's new world dictionary. (1964). New York: World Publishing.

Webster's ninth new collegiate dictionary. (1983). Springfield, MA: Merriam-Webster.

Weiss, A. J., Imrich, D. J., & Wilson, B. J. (1993). Prior exposure to creatures from a horror film: Live versus photographic representations. *Human Communication Research, 20,* 41-66.

Wells, W. D. (1973). *Television and aggression: Replication of an experimental field study.* Unpublished manuscript, Graduate School of Business, University of Chicago.

Wertham, F. (1954). *Seduction of the innocent.* New York: Rinehart.

Whitney, C., Wartella, E., Lasorsa, D., Danielson, W., Olivarez, A., Lopez, R., & Klijn, M. (1997). Television violence in "reality" programming: University of Texas at Austin study. In *National television violence study* (Vol. 1, pp. 269-359). Thousand Oaks, CA: Sage.

Wilkins, J. L., Scharff, W. H., & Schlottmann, R. S. (1974). Personality type, reports of violence, and aggressive behavior. *Journal of Personality and Social Psychology, 30,* 243-247.

Williams, T. M. (Ed.). (1986a). *The impact of television.* Orlando, FL: Academic Press.

Williams, T. M. (1986b). The overt aggression scale for the objective rating of verbal and physical aggression. *American Journal of Psychiatry, 143*(1), 35-39.

Williams, T. M., Zabrack, M. L., & Joy, L. A. (1982). The portrayal of aggression on North American television. *Journal of Applied Social Psychology, 12,* 360-380.

Wilson, B. J. (1985). Developmental differences in empathy with a television protagonist's fear. *Journal of Experimental Child Psychology, 39,* 284-299.

Wilson, B. J., & Cantor, J. (1985). Developmental difference in empathy with a television protagonist's fear. *Journal of Experimental Child Psychology, 39,* 284-299.

Wilson, B. J., & Cantor, J. (1987). Reducing children's fear reactions to mass media: Effects of visual exposure and verbal explanation. In M. McLaughlin (Ed.), *Communication yearbook 10* (pp. 553-573). Beverly Hills, CA: Sage.

Wilson, B. J., Hoffner, C., & Cantor, J. (1987). Children's perceptions of the effectivenss of techniques to reduce fear from mass media. *Journal of Applied Developmental Psychology, 8,* 39-52.

Wilson, B. J., Kunkel, D., Linz, D., Potter, J., Donnerstein, E., Smith, S. L., Blumenthal, E., & Berry, M. (1998). Violence in television programming overall: University of California, Santa Barbara. In *National television violence study* (Vol. 2, pp. 3-204). Thousand Oaks, CA: Sage.

Wilson, B. J., Kunkel, D., Linz, D., Potter, J., Donnerstein, E., Smith, S. L., Blumenthal, E., & Gray, T. (1997). Television violence and its context: University of California, Santa Barbara study. In *National television violence study* (Vol. 1, pp. 3-268). Thousand Oaks, CA: Sage.

Winn, E. (1977). *The plug-in drug.* New York: Viking.

Witkin, H. A., & Goodenough, D. R. (1977). Field dependence and interpersonal behavior. *Psychological Bulletin, 84,* 661-689.

Wober, J. M. (1978). Televised violence and paranoid perception: The view from Great Britain. *Public Opinion Quarterly, 42,* 315-321.

Wober, M., & Gunter, B. (1985). Patterns of television viewing and of perceptions of hazards to life. *Journal of Environmental Psychology, 5,* 99-108.

Wood, W., Wong, F. Y., & Chachere, J. G. (1991). Effects of media violence on viewers' aggression in unconstrained social interaction. *Psychological Bulletin, 109,* 371-383.

Worchel, S., Hardy, T. W., & Hurley, R. (1976). The effects of commercial interruption of violent and nonviolent films on viewers' subsequent aggression. *Journal of Experimental Social Psychology, 12,* 220-232.

Wotring, C. W., & Greenberg, B. S. (1973). Experiments in televised violence and verbal aggression: Two exploratory studies. *Journal of Communication, 23*(4), 446-460.

Wright, J. C., Huston, A. C., Reitz, A. L., & Piemyat, S. (1994). Young children's perceptions of television reality: Determinants and developmental differences. *Developmental Psychology, 30,* 229-239.

Wurtzel, A., & Lometti, G. (1984). Determining the acceptability of violent program content at ABC. *Journal of Broadcasting, 28,* 89-97.

Zillmann, D. (1971). Excitation transfer in communication-mediated aggressive behavior. *Journal of Experimental Social Psychology, 7,* 419-434.

Zillmann, D. (1978). Attribution and misattribution of excitatory reactions. In J. H. Harvey, W. Ickes, & R. F. Kidd (Eds.), *New directions in attribution research* (Vol. 2, pp. 335-368). Hillsdale, NJ: Erlbaum.

Zillmann, D. (1979). *Hostility and aggression.* Hillsdale, NJ: Erlbaum.

Zillmann, D. (1982). Television viewing and arousal. In D. Pearl, L. Bouthilet, & J. Lazar (Eds.), *Television and behavior: Ten years of scientific progress and implications for the eighties: Vol. 2. Technical reviews* (pp. 53-67). Rockville, MD: U.S. Department of Health and Human Services.

Zillmann, D. (1991a). Empathy: Affect from bearing witness to the emotions of others. In J. Bryant & D. Zillmann (Eds.), *Responding to the screen* (pp. 135-167). Hillsdale, NJ: Erlbaum.

Zillmann, D. (1991b). Television viewing and physiological arousal. In J. Bryant & D. Zillmann (Eds.), *Responding to the screen* (pp. 103-133). Hillsdale, NJ: Erlbaum.

Zillmann, D. (1998). The psychology of appeal of portrayals of violence. In J. H. Goldstein (Ed.), *Why we watch: The attractiveness of violent entertainment* (pp. 179-211). New York: Oxford University Press.

Zillmann, D., Bryant, J., Comisky, P. W., & Medoff, N. J. (1981). Excitation and hedonic valence in the effect of erotica on motivated intermale aggression. *European Journal of Social Psychology, 11,* 233-252.

Zillmann, D., & Cantor, J. R. (1977). Affective responses to the emotions of a protagonist. *Journal of Experimental Social Psychology, 13,* 155-165.

Zillmann, D., Hay, T. A., & Bryant, J. (1975). The effect of suspense and its resolution on the appreciation of dramatic presentations. *Journal of Research in Personality, 9,* 307-323.

Zillmann, D., Johnson, R. C., & Hanrahan, J. (1973). Pacifying effect of happy endings of communications involving aggression. *Psychological Reports, 32,* 967-970.

Zillmann, D., & Sapolsky, B. S. (1977). What mediates the effect of mild erotica on annoyance and hostile behavior in males? *Journal of Personality and Social Psychology, 35,* 587-596.

Zillmann, D., & Wakshlag, J. (1985). Fear of victimization and the appeal of crime drama. In D. Zillmann & J. Bryant (Eds.), *Selective exposure to communication* (pp. 141-156). Hillsdale, NJ: Erlbaum.

Zillmann, D., & Weaver, J. B. (1997). Psychoticism in the effect of prolonged exposure to gratuitous media violence on the acceptance of violence as a preferred means of conflict resolution. *Personality and Individual Differences, 22,* 613-627.

Zillmann, D., Weaver, J. B., Mundorf, N., & Aust, C. F. (1986). Effects of an opposite gender companion's affect to horror on distress, delight, and attraction. *Journal of Personality and Social Psychology, 51,* 586-594.

Author Index

Abelman, R., 30
Acker, M., 150, 190
Adler, R. P., 129
Agahi, E., 172, 173, 181, 189
Aisbett, K., 92, 182
Albert, J., 115
Alexander, A., 15, 134, 177, 181
Alfert, E., 38, 39, 136
Alioto, J. T., 33, 34, 79, 104, 175, 179, 183
Allen, M., 35
Allen, R. C., 216
Altheide, D. L., 213
Alvarez, M. M., 29, 142, 162
Amolini, P., 35, 103, 173, 176
Amundson, D., 44, 48, 49, 58, 197, 198, 203
Anastasi, A., 202
Anderson, C. A., 31, 117
Andison, F. S., 28
Applebome, P., 1
Applefield, J. M., 174, 179
Armstrong, B., 161, 162
Atkin, C., 34, 129, 179, 170, 172, 177, 182, 185
Atkin, C. K., 31, 44, 47, 48, 49, 50, 51, 69, 71, 72, 74, 78, 93, 106, 117, 177, 181, 189, 195, 197, 198
Atkinson, K. W., 39
Aust, C. F., 161
Austin, G. A., 114
Averill, J., 37
Averill, J. R., 38, 39, 180

Babbie, E., 215
Bachman, J. G., 173, 181, 182, 189
Baker, R. K., 26
Baldwin, T. F., 154, 155
Ball, S. J., 26
Ball-Rokeach, S. J., 90
Bandura, A., 19, 20, 22, 32, 65, 88, 95, 130, 143, 172, 179, 185, 214
Barnes, G., 150, 190
Baron, J. N., 172
Baron, R. A., 31, 32, 79, 94, 102, 130, 142, 168, 176, 179, 181
Baron, R. S., 32
Barrett, G., 36, 102, 175, 176, 179, 180
Bassett, H. T., 177, 181, 182
Baxter, L. A., 44, 70, 201, 203
Baxter, R. L., 44, 48, 195, 197
Belson, W., 181
Berelson, B. R., 129, 225
Berg, C. A., 113
Berger, A. A., 94
Berger, P. L., 13, 14
Berkowitz, L., 20, 21, 30, 31, 32, 33, 34, 35, 36, 66, 78, 79, 91, 94, 102, 104, 105, 117, 132, 173, 174, 175, 176, 179, 180, 183, 184, 185, 214, 248
Berndt, T. J., 33, 129, 180
Berry, G. L., 29
Berry, M., 47, 49, 52, 53, 54, 55, 56, 89
Bianculli, D., 153
Biely, E., 43, 45, 157, 201, 203
Biocca, F., 85

Bjorkqvist, K., 34, 81
Blankenburg, W. B., 44, 47, 48, 160, 198, 199
Blevings, G., 37
Blumenthal, E., 47, 49, 50, 52, 53, 54, 55, 56
Blumer, H., 125, 133, 161
Bonnet, P., 174, 179
Booker, A., 35
Borduin, C. M., 29, 112
Braxton, G., 155
Bremer, M., 110
Bresolin, L. B., 27, 29, 31, 32, 112
Brezgel, D., 35
Brice, P., 177
Bridis, T., 121
British Broadcasting Corporation, 45, 74
Broadcasting Standards Council, 45, 57, 58, 59, 197
Bronfenbrenner, U., 13
Brown, D., 15, 25, 38, 134, 140, 168, 174, 175, 181, 182, 186
Brown, J. D., 44, 48, 70, 196, 197, 198
Brown, L. B., 74
Brown, R. C., Jr., 33, 34, 82, 104
Brown, R. L., 41, 168, 173
Browning, G., 1
Bruce, L., 163
Bruner, J. S., 17, 114
Bryan, J. H., 32
Bryant, J., 15, 25, 30, 31, 34, 36, 37, 38, 134, 140, 168, 174, 175, 179, 180, 181, 182, 186
Buckingham, D., 76, 97
Bushman, B., 185
Buss, A., 35
Buss, E., 35
Butterfield, F., 2
Bybee, C., 122
Byrne, D., 36, 102, 174, 176

Cahoon, D. D., 35, 179
Cairns, E., 172
Calder, B. J., 41, 134, 171
Camino, L., 174, 175
Campbell, A., 66
Campbell, K., 44, 48, 70, 196, 197, 198
Campbell, W. J., 41, 168, 173
Cantor, J., 31, 36, 37, 38, 39, 81, 91, 93, 105, 117, 126, 127, 128, 135, 137, 161, 172, 180, 181
Cantor, J. R., 37, 181
Cantril, H., 126
Caprara, G. V., 35, 102, 130, 173, 174, 176

Carlson, J. M., 172, 177, 182
Carlson, M., 28, 30, 35, 36
Carr, D. E., 140, 174
Carver, C., 78
Carveth, R., 15, 134, 177, 181
Carveth, R. A., 15, 25, 38, 134, 140, 168, 174, 175, 181, 182, 186
Caspi, D., 45, 58, 59
CBS, Office of Social Research, 44
Center for Media and Public Affairs, 43, 45, 47, 48, 52, 53, 56, 68, 70, 71, 72, 196, 197, 198, 200
Centerwall, B. S., 41, 130, 168, 169, 171, 173
Chachere, J. G., 28
Chaffee, S., 19, 26, 29, 30, 31, 32, 89, 122, 130, 131, 132, 133
Chaffee, S. H., 26, 29, 31, 40, 93, 106, 117, 150, 177, 181, 189, 218
Chambers, W., 78
Chaney, D. C., 41, 168, 173
Chang, I. K., 41
Check, J. V. P., 123
Cherico, N. P., 66
Chiricos, T., 101, 103, 135
Cisneros, T., 35, 172
Clark, D. G., 44, 47, 48, 160, 198, 199
Climie, R. J., 124
Cline, V. B., 39, 125, 130, 136
Cohen, M. F., 177, 181, 182
Cole, J., 43, 45, 70
Collins, W. A., 29, 32, 33, 110, 128, 129, 178, 179, 180, 185
Columbia Broadcasting System, 43, 44, 47
Colvin, C. M., 47, 49, 52, 53, 54, 55, 56
Comisky, P., 34, 37
Comisky, P. W., 30, 31, 36, 174, 179
Comstock, G., 19, 26, 27, 28, 29, 30, 31, 32, 35, 89, 122, 130, 131, 132, 133, 143
Comstock, G. A., 27, 31, 32, 36, 89
Condry, J., 122
Cone, L. T., 29, 112
Cook, T. D., 41, 134, 171, 183
Cooper, J., 174, 179
Cope, K. M., 43, 45, 157, 201, 203
Corriveau, D. P., 66
Courrier, S., 39, 125, 130, 136
Cowden, J. E., 177, 181, 182
Cowie, H., 110
Crawshaw, V. B., 40
Croft, R. G., 39, 125, 130, 136
Croll, P., 45, 67
Cumberbatch, G., 27, 45, 56, 57, 58, 67, 73, 82

da Gloria, J., 173, 179
D'Alessio, D., 35
Danielson, W., 48, 50, 53, 54, 55
Davidson, E. A., 27, 128, 130
Davidson, E. S., 19, 132
Davidson, L. A., 39, 136, 180
Davidson, P. O., 39
Davis, B., 44, 48, 69, 72, 197, 200
Davison, L., 38, 39, 136, 172, 180
Day, D., 115
Deckers, L., 140, 174
De Four, D., 74, 160, 162
Del Rosario, M. L., 41, 134, 171
de Sola Pool, I., 45, 57, 58, 59, 67, 196, 203
Diener, E., 74, 160, 162
Di Lullo, D., 173, 174, 180
Di Lullo, S. L., 173, 174, 180
D'Imperio, G., 35, 102, 173, 176
D'Imperio, G. D., 130, 173, 174
Di Muccio, C., 173, 179
Dishion, T. J., 13, 82
Dollard, J., 17, 65
Dominick, J., 44, 50, 51, 52, 53, 54, 56, 87,
    197, 198, 201, 202, 203
Dominick, J. R., 44, 48, 49, 51, 53, 55, 56, 67,
    87, 161, 180, 195, 197
Donnerstein, E., 2, 30, 34, 35, 36, 42, 43, 45,
    47, 49, 50, 52, 53, 54, 55, 56, 79, 91, 94,
    102, 136, 142, 157, 161, 174, 175, 176,
    179, 180, 201, 203
Donnerstein, E. I., 32, 140, 179
Donnerstein, M., 36, 175
Doob, A. N., 15, 177, 181, 124
Doob, L. W., 17, 65
Dorr, A., 31, 38, 117, 156
Downs, A. C., 91
Drabman, R. S., 39, 78, 125, 127, 128, 129,
    130, 136, 180, 185
Dubanoski, R. A., 102, 176, 179
Duda, D., 174, 179
Duke, L. I., 113
Dunand, M., 173, 174
Dysinger, W. S., 37, 126

Edison, N., 44, 47, 48, 49, 50, 51, 69, 71, 72,
    74, 78, 195, 197, 198
Edmonds, E. M., 35, 179
Einsiedel, E. F., 182
Eisenberg, J. G., 170, 182
Ekman, P., 31, 180
Eleey, M. F., 15, 44, 134, 181

Elliott, W. R., 177
Ellis, D. P., 35
Ellis, G. T., 185
Endsley, R. C., 39, 91, 126
Engblom, P., 30, 173, 176
Eron, L., 21
Eron, L. D., 2, 29, 31, 34, 40, 67, 112, 117,
    150, 161, 170, 173, 177, 181, 182, 189
Eschholz, S., 101
Estep, R., 44, 53, 54, 197
Evans, R., 36

Farinola, W. J. M., 43, 45, 157, 201, 203
Fazio, R. H., 17
Ferguson, D. A., 187
Ferguson, T. J., 27, 30, 31, 32, 90
Fernandez-Collado, C., 44, 47, 48, 49, 50, 51,
    69, 71, 72, 74, 78, 195, 197, 198
Feshbach, N. D., 37, 136, 174
Feshbach, S., 19, 29, 34, 112, 132, 179
Ficarrotto, T. J., 172, 174, 178, 179
Fisher, P., 177
Fisher, S., 39
Fishman, M., 213
Fiske, J., 97, 183
Fiske, S. T., 85
Flavell, J. H., 16
Forgas, J. P., 74
Fortis, J. G., 52, 54
Forum for Children's Television, 45, 59
Fox, S., 34
Fox, W. S., 177
Franzblau, S., 44
Fredriksen, S., 31, 93, 105, 117
Freedman, J., 161
Freedman, J. L., 28
Freud, S., 11, 12, 94, 161
Friedman, H. L., 173, 177, 182
Friedrich, L. K., 27, 29, 30, 82, 89, 168, 102,
    172, 174, 176, 178, 179, 186, 189
Friedrich-Cofer, L., 27
Friesen, W. V., 31, 181
Frodi, A., 35, 173
Fromming, W., 78
Furnham, A., 38, 74, 86, 91, 101, 103, 172,
    173, 174, 176, 180
Furu, T., 41, 169, 173

Gadow, K. D., 29, 103, 141, 172, 174, 178, 179
Gaer, E. P., 31, 37, 93, 106, 117, 180

Galloway, S., 153
Ganellen, R., 78
Gardner, R. W., 112, 114
Geen, R., 185
Geen, R. G., 27, 30, 31, 33, 34, 38, 78, 91,
    102, 104, 125, 174, 175, 176, 179, 180,
    183, 184, 185
Geiger, S., 163
Gentilomo, A., 130, 173, 174
Gerbner, G., 14, 15, 16, 42, 43, 44, 47, 50, 51,
    55, 57, 68, 69, 70, 71, 72, 73, 78, 99, 128,
    129, 134, 144, 173, 176, 177, 181, 182,
    189, 196, 197, 198, 199, 201, 202, 203
Gerbner, G. A., 47, 48, 49, 160
Gersten, J. C., 170, 182
Gertz, M., 101, 103
Gietson, G., 180
Gilligan, C., 119
Goldenstein, A. P., 12
Goleman, D., 116
Goodenough, D. R., 113
Goodnow, J., 114
Goonasekera, A., 45, 57
Goranson, R., 32, 79, 185
Goranson, R. E., 27
Gordon, T. F., 74, 89
Gorman, B., 66
Gorney, R., 172, 186
Govia, J. M., 66
Gray, L. N., 52, 54
Gray, T., 47, 49, 50, 52, 53, 54, 55, 56
Grayson, P., 29, 103, 141, 174
Greenberg, B. S., 29, 43, 44, 47, 48, 49, 50, 51,
    69, 70, 71, 72, 74, 78, 89, 130, 170, 172,
    177, 179, 180, 182, 195, 197, 198, 199
Greer, D., 34
Griesler, P. C., 13
Groebel, J., 38
Gross, L., 15, 16, 42, 44, 47, 50, 51, 68, 73,
    78, 99, 128, 129, 134, 144, 177, 181, 182,
    196, 197, 199, 201, 202, 203
Guerra, N. G., 40
Guerre, N. G., 22
Gunter, B., 19, 31, 32, 38, 39, 45, 56, 66, 68,
    72, 73, 74, 86, 89, 90, 91, 95, 99, 101,
    103, 122, 132, 133, 140, 142, 172, 173,
    174, 176, 180, 181, 186, 197, 198, 200

Hagemeyer, J., 45, 47, 48, 49, 51, 52, 53, 54,
    55, 56, 58, 69, 70, 72, 87, 196, 197, 198,
    201, 202, 203
Hagiwara, S., 45, 57, 58, 59, 67, 196, 203

Halderman, B. L., 35
Hall, J., 155
Hall, S., 215
Hallam, E., 30, 102, 174, 175, 176
Hallam, J., 36
Halloran, J. D., 41, 45, 67, 168, 173
Hamilton, J. T., 154, 158, 159
Hampson, S., 172, 173, 181, 189
Hanrahan, J., 174
Hapkiewicz, W. G., 27, 79, 102, 141, 142,
    174, 176
Hardy, G., 45, 56, 57, 58, 67
Hardy, T. W., 30, 174, 179
Hare, R. D., 37
Harrison, J., 45, 68, 72, 99, 197, 198, 200
Harrison, R., 31, 181
Hart, A., 186
Hartley, J., 97, 183
Hartup, W. W., 31, 32, 172
Harvey, S. E., 44, 49, 51, 195, 197
Hashway, R. M., 113
Hawkins, R. P., 15, 41, 92, 128, 134, 163, 172,
    177, 181
Hay, T. A., 180
Head, S. W., 44
Hearold, S., 28, 31, 32, 122, 131, 143, 172
Heath, L., 27, 29, 31, 32, 41, 112, 134, 171
Heavey, C. L., 150, 190
Henggeler, S. W., 29, 112
Hensley, J. E., 41, 171, 172
Hennigan, K., M., 41, 134, 171
Hess, V. L., 33, 129, 180
Hicks, D. J., 29, 31, 117
Hiebert, S. F., 39
Hill-Scott, K., 156
Himmelweit, H., 37, 126, 135, 161
Himmelweit, H. T., 131, 133, 160
Hirsch, K. W., 129
Hodge, R., 100, 112
Hoffner, C., 37, 38, 93, 105, 126, 128, 134,
    137, 161, 172, 174, 180
Hogan, M., 103
Hogben, M., 192, 193
Hollenbeck, A. R., 110
Horney, K., 12
Horton, R. W., 39, 125, 127, 130, 136, 180
Hossay, J.-F., 35, 172
Howell, R. J., 92, 106, 141
Howitt, D., 27, 73, 82
Howley, K., 45, 47, 48, 49, 51, 52, 53, 54, 55,
    56, 58, 69, 70, 72, 87, 196, 197, 198,
    201, 202, 203
Hoyt, J. L., 33, 104, 175, 184

Huesmann, L. R., 22, 29, 31, 34, 40, 67, 112, 117, 150, 170, 173, 177, 181, 182, 186
Hurley, R., 30, 174, 179
Huston, A., 110
Huston, A. C., 27, 29, 92, 106, 141, 142, 162
Huston-Stein, A., 34

Imrich, D. J., 180
Iwao, S., 45, 56, 57, 58, 59, 67, 196, 203
Izard, C. E., 175

Jackson, T. T., 35
Jackson-Beeck, M., 15, 44, 50, 68, 73, 128, 134, 181, 182, 196
Jaeger, M. E., 131, 133, 160
Jeffries-Fox, S., 15, 44, 68, 73, 128, 134, 177, 181, 182
Jennings, N., 2, 54, 55
Jo, E., 34, 36, 185
Johnson, R. C., 174
Johnson, R. L., 173, 177, 182
Johnston, D. D., 161
Jones, G. W., Jr., 27
Jones, I., 45, 56, 57, 58, 67
Joseph, J. M., 34, 104
Josephson, W., 102, 176
Joy, L. A., 45, 47, 48, 49, 51, 52, 53, 54, 55, 56, 57, 67, 68, 71, 72, 87, 99, 197, 198, 199, 201, 202, 203

Kagan, J., 115
Kane, T., 34, 104
Kang, J. G., 45, 57, 58, 67, 197
Kaplan, R. M., 27, 128, 130
Kaplan, S. J., 44, 70, 201, 203
Kapoor, S., 45, 57, 58, 67, 197
Kashiwagi, A., 40, 161
Katzman, N., 19, 26, 29, 30, 31, 32, 89, 122, 130, 131, 132, 133
Kemper, B., 121
Kendzierski, D. A., 183
Keogh, R., 41, 168, 173
Kerkman, D., 110
Kerkman, D. D., 29, 142, 162
Kerlinger, F. N., 202
Kessler, R. C., 170, 172, 186
Kim, S. K., 45, 57, 58, 67, 197
Kim, W. Y., 45, 57, 58, 67, 197
Kintsch, W., 85
Klapper, J., 126

Klijn, M., 48, 50, 53, 54, 55
Kniveton, B. H., 27, 102, 130, 173, 176, 178, 179
Kohlberg, L., 118, 119
Kong, C., 102, 176, 179
Koriat, A., 38, 39, 180
Korzenny, F., 170, 172, 177, 182
Korzenny, R., 44, 47, 48, 49, 50, 51, 69, 71, 72, 74, 78, 195, 197, 198
Koss, M. P., 190
Krebs, D., 38
Kunkel, D., 43, 45, 47, 49, 50, 52, 53, 54, 55, 56, 157, 201, 203

Lagerspetz, K., 29, 31, 34, 40, 117, 170, 177, 182
Lagerspetz, K. M. J., 30, 81, 173, 176
Land, A., 45, 47, 48, 49, 51, 52, 53, 54, 55, 56, 58, 69, 70, 72, 87, 196, 197, 198, 201, 202, 203
Landini, A., 44, 48, 195, 197
Lando, H. A., 32, 140, 179
Langner, T. S., 170, 182
Larsen, O. N., 52, 54
Lasorsa, D., 48, 50, 53, 54, 55
Leslie, L., 44, 48, 195, 197
Layton, J. F., 35, 179
Lazarus, R., 37
Lazarus, R. S., 38, 39, 136, 172, 180
Lee, M., 45, 56, 57, 58, 67
Lefkowitz, M. M., 40, 112, 170, 181
Leifer, A. D., 128
LePage, A., 35
Lesser, G. S., 129
Lesser, H., 27
Levine-Donnerstein, D., 201, 206
Levinger, G., 141
Lewis, C., 154, 155
Leyens, J.-P., 31, 35, 79, 105, 117, 172, 173, 174, 175, 176, 185
Lichter, L. S., 43, 44, 47
Lichter, S. R., 43, 44, 47, 48, 49, 58, 197, 198, 203
Lieberman Research, 31, 93, 94, 106
Liebert, R. M., 19, 27, 30, 31, 32, 44, 49, 51, 102, 122, 128, 130, 131, 132, 168, 175, 176, 179, 181, 195, 197
Liefer, A. D., 180, 191
Lincoln, A., 141
Linne, O., 128, 173, 180
Linz, D., 39, 47, 49, 50, 52, 53, 54, 55, 56, 150, 190

Linz, D. G., 42, 136, 174
Lippincott, E. C., 39, 125, 127, 130, 136, 180
Lippmann, W., 13
Liss, M. B., 31, 93, 105, 117
Lock, Y. K., 45, 57
Lometti, G., 68, 72, 156
Lopez, R., 48, 50, 53, 54, 55
Lorenz, K. Z., 11
Lovaas, O. I., 130, 175, 179
Lowry, B., 122, 153, 154
Loye, D., 172, 186
Luckmann, T., 13, 14
Lyle, J., 41, 44, 47, 48, 49, 126, 169, 197
Lynn, R., 172, 173, 181, 189

Maccoby, E. E., 27
Maccoby, N., 27
Macdonald, G. E., 15, 177, 181
Macdonald, P. T., 44, 53, 54, 197
Mackie, D., 174, 179
Malamuth, N. M., 123, 150, 190
Malmstrom, E. J., 31, 39, 181
Mammucari, A., 130, 173, 174
Mancini, F., 30, 102, 174, 175, 176
Mann, B. J., 29, 112
Marcuse, H., 133
Marcus-Newhall, A., 28, 30, 35, 36
Mayer, J. D., 116
McCann, T. E., 45, 57, 58, 67, 99, 200
McCarthy, E. D., 170, 182
McCombs, M., 19, 27, 29, 30, 31, 32, 89, 122,
    130, 131, 132, 133
McConnachie, G. A., 44, 67
McDermott, S., 170, 172, 177, 182
McDermott, T., 121
McGuire, W. J., 28, 129
McHan, E. J., 131, 173, 180
McIntyre, J., 172, 173, 182
McLeod, J. M., 29, 31, 40, 93, 106, 117, 150,
    177, 181, 189
Meadowcroft, J., 85
Medoff, N. J., 30, 31, 36, 174, 179
Mees, U., 65, 66, 89
Melkman, R., 38, 180
Menlove, F. L., 172
Menyhart, J., 74
Meringoff, L. K., 129
Mermelstein, R., 177
Messner, S. F., 41, 171
Meyer, T. P., 32, 33, 104, 175, 184
Mikami, S., 45, 67

Milavsky, J. R., 28, 170, 186
Miller, L., 35
Miller, L. S., 40, 67
Miller, N., 28, 30, 35, 36
Miller, N. E., 17, 65
Mills, S., 121
Mitchell-Kernan, C., 29
Molitor, F., 129
Mordkoff, A., 38, 39, 136, 172, 180
Mordkoff, A. M., 39, 136, 180
Morgan, M., 15, 16, 41, 42, 44, 47, 50, 51, 78,
    99, 129, 134, 177, 181, 182, 196, 197, 199
Morley, D., 101
Morrison, D. E., 75
Mowrer, O. H., 17, 65
Mueller, C., 94, 102, 142, 176, 179
Mullin, C. R., 39
Munakata, K., 40, 161
Muncer, S. J., 66
Mundorf, N., 161
Murphy, K., 121
Mussen, P., 79, 174, 175
Mustonen A., 4, 57, 58, 68, 70, 71, 72, 87, 89,
    131, 196, 197, 198, 200, 201, 203

National Institute of Mental Health, 27
National Television Violence Study, 43, 45, 47,
    51, 52, 53, 55, 56, 67, 68, 72, 74, 87, 89,
    98, 122, 154, 195, 196, 197, 198, 201
Neale, J. M., 27, 128, 130
Nelson, R., 179
Newcomb, H., 215
Newtson, R., 161
Nomikos, M., 37
Nomikos, M. S., 38
Nucci, L., 22

O'Donnell, P., 153
Ogles, R. M., 38, 134, 174
O'Keefe, G. J., 177, 182
Olivarez, A., 2, 48, 50, 53, 54, 55
Oliver, M. B., 45, 49, 50, 52, 54, 56, 69, 70,
    72, 161, 162, 195, 197, 200, 201
O'Neal, E., 35
Oppenheim, A., 37, 126, 135, 161
Opton, E., 37
Opton, E. M., 38
Orzeck, L., 170, 182
Osborn, D. K., 39, 91, 126

Page, D., 35
Page, M. M., 35
Pahlavan, F., 174, 179
Paik, H., 28, 31, 32, 35, 143
Parke, R. D., 12, 13, 35, 173, 174, 175, 176
Parke, T. D., 32
Parker, E. P., 41, 44, 47, 48, 49, 126, 169, 197
Parnes, P., 45, 58, 59
Patterson, G. R., 13, 82
Penrod, S., 42, 136, 174
Perry, D. G., 31, 93, 105, 106, 117, 173
Perry, L. C., 31, 93, 105, 106, 117, 173
Perse, E. M., 177
Peterson, D. L., 36, 174
Pfost, K. S., 36, 174
Philliber, W. W., 177
Phillips, D. P., 41, 171, 172
Phillips, W., 115
Picus, S., 31, 79, 105, 117, 185
Piemyat, S., 92, 106, 141
Pillard, R. C., 39
Pingree, S., 15, 41, 128, 134, 163, 172, 177, 181
Potter, J., 47, 49, 50, 52, 53, 54, 55, 56
Potter, W. J. 15, 41, 44, 45, 47, 48, 49, 50, 51, 52, 53, 54, 55, 56, 58, 54, 55, 69, 70, 71, 72, 73, 78, 87, 89, 92, 95, 98, 128, 134, 144, 147, 148, 177, 181, 182, 191, 194, 196, 197, 198, 201, 202, 203, 204, 206, 244
Potts, R., 162
Poulos, R. W., 27, 44, 49, 51, 195, 197
Powers, P. C., 33, 104, 184
Prerost, F. J., 142
Preston, M. I., 133
Pritchard, D. A., 115
Pulkkinen, L., 4, 57, 58, 68, 70, 71, 72, 87, 89, 131, 196, 197, 198, 200, 201, 203

Quarfoth, G. R., 44, 67

Ragan, T., 1
Rakosky, J. J., 38, 180
Rankin, N. O., 38
Rapaczynski, W., 170
Rawlings, E., 32, 33, 79, 104, 175, 184, 185
Reeves, B., 85, 163, 177
Reid, J. B., 82
Reilly, S., 126, 135
Reimer, B., 150, 181

Reinhardt, L. C., 31, 93, 105, 117
Reiss, P. C., 172
Reitz, A. L., 92, 106, 141
Renzi, P., 35, 102, 173, 176
Renzi, P. G., 130, 173, 174
Rice, M. L., 110
Riemer, C. D., 44, 48, 195, 197
Rinaldi, R. C., 27, 29, 31, 32, 112
Roberts, D., 19, 27, 29, 30, 31, 32, 89, 122, 130, 131, 132, 133
Roberts, D. F., 27, 128, 180, 191
Robertson, T. S., 129
Robinson, D., 122
Robinson, J. P., 173, 181, 182, 189
Roe, K., 37, 136, 174
Rogers, R. W., 175
Rosekrans, M. A., 31, 32, 172
Rosenberg, M., 189
Rosengren, K. E., 150, 181
Rosman, D., 115
Ross, D., 32, 179
Ross, S. A., 32, 179
Rossiter, J. R., 129
Rouner, D., 15, 134, 178, 181
Rubens, W. S., 170, 186
Rubin, A. M., 177
Rubinstein, E., 44, 197
Ruckmick, C. A., 37, 126
Rule, B. G., 27, 30, 31, 32, 90
Russell, G. W., 173, 174, 180
Rutherford, E., 79, 174, 175

Salomone, K. L., 182
Salovey, P., 116
Salvoza, M. F., 153
Sanbonmatsu, D. M., 17
Sander, I., 39
Sanders, G. S., 32
Sanson, A., 173, 179
Sapolsky, B. S., 30, 36, 37, 126, 135, 179
Savitsky, J. C., 175
Schachter, S., 125
Scharff, W. H., 102, 174, 176
Scheidt, R. J., 35
Schlottmann, R. S., 102, 174, 176
Schmutte, G. T., 143, 175
Schneider, F. P., 182
Schramm, W., 27, 41, 44, 47, 48, 49, 126, 169, 197
Schuck, A., 30, 102, 174, 175, 176
Schuck, S. Z., 30, 102, 174, 175, 176

Schwartz, T., 32
Schwartzberg, N. S., 27, 30, 31, 32, 122, 130, 131
Schwarz, J. E., 177
Sears, R. R., 17, 65
Sebastian, R. J., 173, 176
Seigle, J., 110
Sekyra, F., III, 185
Sheehan, P. W., 45, 57, 58, 67, 99, 170, 173, 177, 181, 189, 200
Sherman, B. L., 44, 48, 49, 51, 53, 55, 56, 67, 87, 195, 197
Shinar, D., 45, 58, 59
Shirley, K. W., 27
Siegel, A. E., 128, 129, 174, 180
Signorielli, N., 15, 16, 19, 41, 42, 44, 47, 48, 49, 50, 51, 55, 68, 71, 74, 78, 81, 99, 122, 128, 129, 133, 134, 177, 181, 182, 196, 197, 200
Silvern S. B., 174
Simons, L. S., 35, 179
Singer, D. G., 170
Singer, J., 125
Singer, J. L., 27, 170
Singer, R. D., 27, 128, 130, 132
Singletary, M. W., 44, 48, 195, 197
Slaby, R. G., 2, 12, 13, 44, 67, 110, 161
Slater, D., 177
Smeaton, G., 36, 102, 174, 176
Smith, P. K., 110
Smith, R., 174, 179
Smith, S. L., 47, 49, 50, 52, 53, 54, 55, 56, 98, 204
Smythe, D. W., 44, 47, 49, 55, 195, 197
Sniffen, M. J., 2
Snow, R. P., 213
Sobol, M. P., 19, 132
Sockloskie, R. J., 190
Sommers-Flanagan, J., 44, 48, 69, 72, 197, 200
Sommers-Flanagan, R., 44, 48, 69, 72, 197, 200
Sparks, G. C., 38, 126, 137
Sparks, G. G., 37, 38, 126, 137
Speisman, J. C., 38, 39, 136, 172, 180
Sprafkin, J., 29, 103, 141, 172, 174, 178, 179
Sprafkin, J. N., 30, 44, 197
Steele, G., 172, 186
Steenland, S., 1
Stein, A. H., 27, 29, 30, 82, 89, 102, 168, 172, 174, 176, 178, 179, 186, 189
Steiner, G., 129, 225
Stemberg, R. J., 113
Stephenson, G. M., 102, 176, 179

Steuer, F. B., 174, 179
Stipp, H., 28, 156, 172
Stipp, H. H., 170, 186
Stone, R. D., 79, 102, 142, 174, 176
Stonner, D., 31, 33, 104, 174, 175, 184
Strasburger, C. C., 27, 31, 32
Surbeck, E., 38, 91
Swart, C., 32
Swift, B., 131, 133, 160

Tan, A. S., 128, 129, 130, 131, 177
Tanaka, J. S., 190
Tangney, J. P., 29, 112
Tannenbaum, P., 31, 37, 93, 106, 117, 180
Tannenbaum, P. H., 27, 30, 124
Tapper, J., 163
Taylor, D. S., 177
Taylor, S. E., 85, 92, 106, 141
Taylor, S. P., 143, 175
Tedeschi, J. T., 33, 34, 82, 104
Teevan, J. J., Jr., 172, 173, 182
Tell, P. M. 34, 78, 104, 183, 185
Thomas, M. H., 30, 34, 39, 78, 104, 125, 127, 128, 129, 130, 136, 174, 180, 183, 185
Thomas, S. A., 183
Thornton, W., 173, 181, 189
Traub, R. E., 202
Travaglia, G., 35, 102, 130, 173, 174, 176
Tripp, D., 100, 112
Tuchman, G., 213
Turner, C. W., 31, 35, 79, 105, 117, 179, 185
Turow, J., 122

United States Statistical Abstract, 133

Valkenburg, P. M., 149
Van der Voort, T. H. A., 25, 75, 76, 77, 92, 111, 112, 119, 126, 131, 149, 162, 170, 173, 178, 181
van Dijk, T. A., 85
Vaughan, M., 45, 47, 48, 49, 50, 51, 52, 53, 54, 55, 56, 58, 69, 70, 71, 72, 78, 87, 196, 197, 198, 201, 202, 203
Velicer, W. F, 66
Vince, P., 37, 126, 135, 161
Voigt, L., 173, 181, 189
Volgy, T. J., 177
von Feilitzen, C., 38, 126, 135
Vooijs, M. W., 173

Wakshlag, J., 15, 134, 177, 181, 182
Wald, M. L., 1
Walder, L. O., 40, 112, 170, 181
Walters, R. H., 32, 130
Ward, S., 129
Ware, W., 44, 47, 48, 49, 50, 51, 52, 53, 54, 69, 70, 71, 72, 87, 196, 197, 198, 201, 202, 203
Warren, R., 45, 47, 48, 49, 51, 52, 53, 54, 55, 56, 58, 69, 70, 72, 87, 95, 196, 197, 198, 201, 202, 203
Wartella, E., 2, 48, 50, 53, 54, 55, 111
Watkins, B. A., 34
Weaver, J., 15, 134, 177, 181, 182
Weaver, J. B., 129, 161, 175, 176, 179
Webster's New Universal Unabridged Dictionary, 81
Webster's New World Dictionary, 211
Webster's Ninth New Collegiate Dictionary, 80
Weiss, A. J., 180
Wells, R., 30, 102, 174, 175, 176
Wells, W. D., 19, 132
Wertham, F., 126
West, S., 173, 176
Wharton, J. D., 41, 134, 171
Whitaker, J., 34
Whitney, C., 48, 50, 53, 54, 55
Wienir, P., 35
Wilcox, W., 44, 48
Wilkins, J. L., 102, 174, 176

Williams, T. M., 41, 45, 47, 48, 49, 51, 52, 53, 54, 55, 56, 57, 67, 68, 71, 72, 87, 99, 168, 169, 173, 197, 198, 199, 201, 202, 203
Williamson, P. A., 174
Willows, D. C., 130
Wilson, B. J., 38, 39, 47, 49, 50, 52, 53, 54, 55, 56, 126, 137, 161, 180, 181
Winn, E., 133
Witkin, H. A., 113
Wober, J. M., 15, 134, 177, 181, 182
Wober, M., 181
Wong, F. Y., 28
Wood, W., 28
Woody, L. W., 74, 162
Worchel, S., 30, 174, 179
Wotring, C. W., 179
Wright, A., 92, 182
Wright, J. C., 29, 92, 106, 110, 141, 142, 162
Wurtzel, A., 68, 72, 156

Zabrack, M. L., 45, 47, 48, 49, 51, 52, 53, 54, 55, 56, 57, 67, 68, 71, 72, 87, 99, 197, 198, 199, 201, 202, 203
Ziemke, D., 37
Zillmann, D., 15, 18, 27, 30, 31, 34, 36, 37, 94, 124, 125, 126, 129, 133, 134, 135, 143, 160, 161, 174, 175, 176, 179, 180, 181, 182
Zlatchin, C., 31, 181
Zwarun, L., 43, 45, 157, 201, 203

Subject Index

ABC, 145
  Incident Classification and Analysis System, 156
Adult discount, 92, 244
Aggression, 71-72
  and long-term media violence exposure, 26, 40-41, 42
  catharsis and, 18-19
  definitions of, 65-67, 68-70
  dimensions of, 66
  frustration and, 18
American General Election Study, 173
America's Funniest Home Videos, 75
America's Most Wanted, 52
Antisocial behavior, 71
  definitions of, 79
Aristotle, 19, 132. *See also* Catharsis
Arousal, 122
  as thought/behavior energizer, 18
  autonomic, 134
  cortical, 133
  residual, 18
  versus desensitization, 122
Arousal Jag, 221
Arousal states, media and, 18
Associational network, 222
Attraction to the fringe, 218, 221, 245
Attraction to violence, 160-163
  action, 162
  amount of television viewing, 162
  attentional-inertia explanation, 162-163
  graphic horror films, 161
  See also Arousal

Audience, 219
  appeal, 219, 232
  mass, 219, 233
  niche, 219, 233
Aversive children, 13

Batman, 93, 174
Biological theories, media violence, 11-12
  eros, 11
  hormones, 12
  instinct, 11-12
  testosterone, 12
  thanatos, 11
Black Entertainment Television, 48
Bugs Bunny, 75
Bullet approach, 100
Buss-Durkee Hostility Inventory, 66

Cartoons, 75, 244
  public's view of, 73-74
  See also specific cartoons
Catharsis, 18-19, 23, 122, 132-133, 218, 221, 228, 244, 245, 253
  and aggression, 18-19
  criticisms of, 19
Character portrayals, 226, 230
  attractive characters, 231
  good characters commit violence, 231
  male perpetrators, 231
  middle-aged perpetrators, 231

victims and perpetrators demographically similar, 231
white perpetrators, 231
Children, susceptibility of to violence, 109-110. *See also* Cognitive development; Emotional development; Moral development
Children's programming, 48, 49
Coding violence, 195
Coefficients. *See* Reliability, coefficients of
Cognitive development, 109-115
adult, 112-115
and media, 110-111
differential, 112
emotional development and, 116, 118
expansion of beyond childhood, 119
See also Cognitive styles; Intelligence
Cognitive encoding, 218, 221, 227, 245, 246-247
Cognitive-neoassociation theory, 20
anger and, 20-21
attribution, 21
spreading activation, 21
See also Cue theory
Cognitive styles:
conceptual differentiation, 113, 114-115
field dependency, 113-114
reflection versus impulsivity, 113, 115
tolerance for ambiguity, 113, 114
Cognitive theories, media violence, 11, 16-17
cognitive abilities, 16-17
construct accessibility, 17
See also Piaget, Jean
Comedy series, 48, 49
Complex society:
United States as, 14
versus primitive society, 14
Confluence theory, 13. *See also* Families, coercive; Peer influence
Construct accessibility, 222
Content analysis, 204-207, 204-207
analyzing context, 195, 203-204
assessing reliability, 195, 200-203
coding violence, 195
defining units of analysis, 195, 199-200
sampling, 195, 196-199
See also Content analysis, levels of
Content analysis, levels of, 98-99, 199-200
act, 99, 199
brief incidents, 98, 199
macro, 98, 99, 199
micro, 98, 99, 199

PAT, 99, 200, 204
program, 98, 199, 200
scenes, 98, 99, 199
segment, 99, 199
sequences, 99, 200, 204
See also Contextual web
Content unit, 220
Contextual characteristics, 220
Contextual web, 98, 220, 226, 230, 244-245
across narrative strata, 98
constancy of, 228, 256
importance of, 204
Conversation, reality maintenance and, 14
Cops, 52
Creative bandwidth, 219, 226, 235
Crime rates, television viewing and, 41
Criticism of media violence:
public's, 153
television industry's response to, 154-157
Cue theory, 20-21, 23. *See also* Cognitive-neoassociation theory
Cultivation of fear, 218, 221, 228, 245, 251-252
Cultivation theorists, 41-42
Cultivation theory, 14-16, 42, 122, 134-135
central proposition, 15-16
cultivation indicators, 15
mainstreaming, 16
refined, 16
resonance, 16
television exposure, 15

Delineation, 221
Desensitization, 25, 26, 39, 42, 122, 136-137, 139, 218, 221, 246, 252-253
immediate change of attitudes, 228, 245, 252
portrayal factors, 39
reinforcement of attitudes, 228, 252
viewer factors, 39
See also Desensitization effects, influences on; Habituation
Desensitization effects, influences on, 228
Developmental differences research, media violence and
limitations, 109
See also Cognitive development; Emotional development; Moral development
Disinhibition, 26-36, 122, 124, 130-131, 139, 218, 221, 227, 244, 245, 247-248
cognitive factors, 40
cultural factors, 40

environmental factors, 40
  familial factors, 40-41
Drama series, 47-48
Drive-altering effects, 228, 246
  influences on, 228, 253-254
  temporary physiological arousal, 228, 245,
    253
  See also Catharsis; Narcotization
Drive theories, 17-18, 218
  frustration-aggression hypothesis, 17-18
Drive theorists, 18
Duration, 220

Ecological theories, media violence, 11, 12-16
  church, 13
  education, 12
  family, 12, 13, 245
  media, 12, 13
  neighborhood, 13
  parents, 13
  peers, 13, 245
  physical, 12
  religion, 12
  school, 13
  social, 12
  See also Confluence theory; Cultivation
    theory; Socialization
Effects. See specific types of media violence
    effects; Media violence effects; Media
    violence effects, immediate; Media vio-
    lence effects, long-term; Media violence
    effects research; Media violence effects
    research methodologies; Media violence
    effects typology
Emotional development, 116-118
  cognitive development and, 116, 118
  emotional self-awareness, 116
  empathy, 116
  handling relationships, 116
  harnessing emotions productively, 116
  managing emotions, 116
  viewer-message interaction, 117-118
  See also Schemas
ER, 219
Excitation transfer theory, 18, 23, 133-134,
    253. See also Arousal

Families, coercive, 13
Fantasy:
  and perceptions of violence, 82-83, 244

"Far Side, The," (newspaper cartoon), 174
Fear effects, 25, 26, 36-39, 41-42, 122, 135,
    139, 218, 246, 250-252
  cultivation of fear, 218, 221, 228, 245,
    251-252
  immediate emotional reaction, 228, 245, 250
  portrayal factors, 38
  viewer factors, 37-38
Fight or flight, 20
  moving mean toward mentality of, 228,
    254-255
  temporary, 124, 218
Fox, 145
Fox Sports Network, 219
Freud, Sigmund, 132
Freudian theory, 18
Frustration:
  as aggression antecedent, 18
  without aggression, 18

Gangs, fear of, 1
Generalizing, 218, 221
  to novel behaviors, 227, 245, 246, 247
Graphicness, 38, 39, 55, 73, 75
Grouping variables, using, 107
Grushow, Sandy, 155
Gunsmoke, 155

Habituation, 218, 221, 228, 245, 252. See also
    Media violence effects, long-term
Harm, 75
  possible types of, 66
"Herman," (newspaper cartoon), 174
History Channel, 219
Humor, 39, 55, 93-95, 139
  and perceptions of violence, 82-83, 244
  to trivialize violence, 95
Hypodermic needle approach, 100

Incredible Hulk (character), 137
Intelligence:
  crystalline, 113
  fluid, 113
Interactionist theory, media violence, 11,
    17-22
  as person-environment event, 17
  environmental factors, 17
  intraindividual characteristics, 17

See also Catharsis theory; Cue theory;
    Drive theories; Excitation transfer theory;
    Social learning theory

Laurel and Hardy films, 93, 94
Law & Order, 155
Learning effects, 137, 218, 221, 227, 246
    influences on, 227
Least objectionable programming (LOP), 219,
    226, 233
Lifetime, 219
Liminal thresholds, 222, 235
Lineation theory, 6, 211
    axioms underlying, 211-216
    content propositions, 229-231
    content terms, 220
    effects terms, 221
    focal constructs, 217-218
    general influence factors, 242-246
    key constructs, 219-222
    line metaphor in, 211
    media industry propositions, 231-235
    media industry terms, 219
    primitive terms, 218, 222
    processing terms, 222
    processing violent messages, 235-242
    social cognition theory and, 211-212
    viewer-defined terms, 222-223
    See also Media violence theory, proposed
Line of influence, 221
Louisiana Youth Survey, 173
Lowest Common Denominator (LCD), 219,
    233

Magic window, 92, 244
Mannix, 174
Media, 219
    as socialization agent, 13
"Media possession," 133
Media violence, 5
    frequency of exposure to, 227
    type, 227
    See also Lineation theory; Media violence
        effects; Media violence theory, proposed;
        Television violence
Media violence effects, 25, 121-122, 217
    attitudinal, 124, 129-130
    behavioral, 124, 130-132
    cognitive, 124, 127-129
    combination, 312-135

emotional, 124, 125-127
imitation, 122
incitement of violent acts, 122
learning to behave aggressively, 25, 122
need for broader view of, 137
need for more consistent use of terms, 137
negative effects, 25, 122
observational learning, 122
overview, 124
physiological, 123-125
prosocial effects, 25
See also Arousal; Cartharsis; Cultivation
    theory; Desensitization; Disinhibition;
    Fear effects; Media violence effects, im-
    mediate; Media violence effects, long-
    term; Media violence effects research
    methodologies
Media violence effects, immediate, 25, 26-39,
    42, 100, 245
    activation/triggering/instigation, 124, 130
    antisocial behavior, 28
    attraction, 124, 131
    creation/change of attitudes, 124, 129, 218
    imitation/copying, 124, 130
    increased subsequent aggression, 26-28
    learning specific acts/lessons, 124, 127
    portrayal characteristics, 28, 31-36, 38
    situational cues, 28, 36, 227, 228, 245, 250,
        251
    temporary fear, 124, 125-126
    temporary fight or flight, 124, 218
    viewer demographics, 28, 29
    viewer states, 28, 30-31, 228
    viewer traits, 28, 29-30, 228
    See also Desensitization; Disinhibition;
        Fear effects
Media violence effects, long-term, 25, 26, 39-
    42, 100, 227, 245
    and aggression, 40-41
    emotional habituation, 124, 126-127, 218
    generalizing patterns, 124, 128, 131-132,
        218
    learning social norms, 124, 128-129, 218,
        245
    physiological habituation, 124-125, 218
    reinforcement of attitudes/beliefs, 124, 129-
        130, 218, 245
Media violence effects research:
    external recommendations for improving,
        191-194
    internal recommendations for improving,
        184-191

levels of analysis in, 99-101, 106
limitations, 183-184
See also Media violence effects research
    methodologies
Media violence effects research methodolo-
    gies, 167-172
  cross-sectional surveys, 169
  epidemiological studies, 170-172
  field experiments, 168-169
  field interviews/observations, 182
  laboratory experiments, 167-168
  longitudinal surveys, 169-170
  measurement, 175-182
  phone surveys, 182
  sampling, 172-173
  self-administered questionnaires, 182
  stimulus treatments, 173-175
Media violence effects typology, 218
Media violence literature, 8
Media violence theories, 11-22, 23-24. *See
    also* Biological theories, media violence;
    Cognitive theories, media violence; Eco-
    logical theories, media violence; Inter-
    actionist, media violence; Lineation the-
    ory; Media violence theory, proposed
Media violence theory, proposed, 256
  changing the violence narrative line, 226,
    234-235
  content propositions, 226, 228, 229-231
  desensitization, 228, 252-253
  drive-altering effects, 228, 253-254
  duration of violence, 226, 229
  families of effects, 227-228, 246-256
  fear effects, 228, 250-252
  general influence factors, 227, 228, 242-245
  goal of programmers, 226, 232-233
  learning and imitation, 227, 246-250, 246,
    248-249
  media industry propositions, 226, 228,
    231-235
  perceptual channels, 226, 236-237
  perceptual flow, 226, 237-238
  perceptual inertia, 226, 238-239
  presence of violence, 226, 229
  prevalence of violence, 229
  processing meaning, 239
  process propositions, 226-227, 228, 235-242
  programming line, 226, 233-234
  rate of violence, 226, 229
  script alterations (relineations), 227,
    241-242
  script selection, 226-227, 240

societal effects, 228, 254-256
synergistic interaction of general influence
    factors, 227, 246
typified narrative line, 226, 230-231
See also Lineation theory
Minnesota Multiphasic Personality Inventory
    (MMPI), 182
Mister Rogers' Neighborhood, 174
Monday Night Football, 159
Moral development, 118-119
  age and, 119
  and human development, 119-120
  conventional level, 118
  gender difference, 119
  postconventional level, 118-119
  preconventional level, 118
Movies, 47. *See also specific movies*
MTV, 48
  music videos, 48, 49, 200

Narcotization, 133, 218, 221, 228, 245,
    253-254
Narrative line, violence, 220, 230
  audience support, 226, 235
  changing, 226, 234-235
  See also Creative bandwidth
National Cable Television Association, 43, 44
National Coalition of Television Violence, 71
National Opinion Research Corporation
    (NORC), 177
  General Social Survey data, 173
National Television Violence Study, 43, 48, 50,
    52, 54-55, 70, 200
  content levels of analysis, 99, 200
  data set, 204
  See also Author Index
NBC, 145
  Social and Developmental Research sub-
    department, 156-157
Nickelodeon, 219

"Open texts," 215

Peer influence, 13, 245
Perceptions of Danger Index, 16
Perceptual channels, 222, 226, 235, 236, 242
  attentional, 226, 237, 239, 243
  automatic, 226, 236, 238, 239, 243
  interaction with contextual factors, 227

self-reflexive, 226, 237, 243
subliminal, 226, 236, 243
type, 227
Perceptual flow, 222, 226, 235, 237
general viewing style, 226, 237-238
gradual change, 238
special motives, 226, 238
sudden change, 239
Perceptual inertia, 226
changes in channels, 226
typical channel, 226
Perceptual scripts, 235
Piaget, Jean, 16, 109, 110, 112, 118, 119
stages of cognitive development, 16
Police Woman, 162
"Pollution of violence," 158-159
Powell, Richard, 156
Prevalence, 220
Priming effects theory, 20-21, 23. *See also*
Cognitive-neoassociation theory; Cue
theory
Producers, 219
Programmers, 219
appeal, 226, 232
goal, 232
responsibility, 219, 226, 232-233
Programming line, 219, 233
relineation, 219
Programming line, setting the, 226
appeal belief, 226, 232, 234
appeal of news, 226, 234
fear of labeling, 226, 233
See also Least objectionable programming
Program types, violence across, 47-48. *See
also specific types of television programs*
Public:
criticism of media violence, 153
violence definition of, 73-74, 75, 76, 77

Qualitative scholars, media violence level of
analysis by, 97, 100-101
Quantitative scholars, media violence level of
analysis by, 97, 100
identification as illustration of, 105-106

Rate, 220
Rating system, television, 157. *See also* V-chip
Realism, 31, 34, 38, 46, 56, 75, 87, 91-92, 139
cuing, 91-92
genre, 91-92

interpretation, 92
setting, 91
type of characters, 91
Reality-based programs, 48, 49, 52, 55. *See
also specific programs*
Reliability, assessing, 200-203
coder overlap, 200, 201
computing coefficients of reliability, 200,
202-203
manifest versus latent content, 200, 201
sample size, 200, 201-202
Reliability, coefficients of, 202-203
Cohen's kappa, 203, 207
Krippendorf's alpha, 203, 207
Pearson product-moment correlation, 202
phi coefficient, 202
Scott's pi, 203, 207
Spearman-Brown correction, 202
Ren and Stimpy, 75
Reshaping institutions, 218, 221
Risk, conceptualization of, 5
Risk assessment, television violence, 139-143,
146-151
context-context interactions, 140-141
context-viewer interactions, 141-143
effect sizes, 143
need for theoretical calculus, 143-145
See also ABC; Fox; NBC
Road Runner, 75
"Road Runner paradox," 82
Romeo and Juliet, 154
Roper Organization, 182

Sampling, 196-199
longitudinal studies, 199
size, 197-198
units, 198-199
Saturation, violence, 228, 256
Schemas, 85, 86, 117
Schema theory, 85-86
recommendations, 96
Schindler's List, 154
Schools:
violent crime in, 2
weapons in, 1
Script alterations (relineations), 222, 227,
241-242
controlled, 227, 241, 242
unconscious, 227, 241, 242
Scripts, 85-86, 222, 226, 239, 248
as templates, 239

general, 226, 239
  subscripts, 226, 239
Scripts, selection of, 226-227, 240-241
  encountering major deviations, 227, 241
  encountering minor deviations, 227, 240-241
  encountering no deviations, 227, 241
  perceptual channels, 226, 240
Script theory, 22
Seinfeld, 159
Simpsons, The, 155
Social cognitive theory, 19, 20, 21-22, 23, 95
  explanatory constructs, 22
  main proposition, 21
  See also Script theory
Social expectations, 92, 244
Socialization:
  definition, 13
  externalization, 13, 14
  internalization, 13, 14
  main processes, 13-14
  objectivation, 14
  See also Conversation
Social learning theory, 19-20, 23
  environmental cues, 19
  imitation subprocesses, 19
  See also Social cognitive theory
Social norms, 218, 221
  learning, 227, 248
Social science practices, limitations of,
    101-105
  lower-level measurement preference, 103
  method/level of phenomenon mismatch,
    103-104
  using poor grouping methods, 101-102
  using surrogate variables, 102-103
Societal effects, 218, 228, 246
  changing institutions, 228, 245, 255-256
  factors contributing to, 228
  moving mean toward fight-or-flight mental-
    ity, 228, 254-255
Sorting strategies, 115
Superman, (cartoon), 174

Taylor's Manifest Anxiety Inventory, 181
TBS, 219
Teenagers:
  carrying weapons to school, 1
  living in fear, 1
Television characters, violent:
  parasocial interaction with, 13
  profiles of, 46, 51-52

Television violence:
  duration of, 50
  frequency of versus real-life frequency of,
    50-51
  portrayed as good, 230
  portrayed unrealistically, 230
  presence of, 46, 47-51
  rates of, 48, 56-57
  sanitized, 230
  trivialized, 230
  types of, 50
  See also Television violence, analyses of
Television violence, analyses of, 43
  content findings, 46
  Gerbner's, 43, 44
  Greenberg's, 43, 44
  non-U.S., 45, 56-59
  U.S., 44-45
  See also National Television Violence Study
Television violence, industry perspective on,
    153, 163
  economic criticism, 158-160
  economic view, 157-160
  internal criticism, 155-156
  internal regulation, 156-157
  response to criticism, 154-157
  violence and audience attraction, 160
Three Stooges films, 75, 93, 94, 243
Tom and Jerry, 75, 76
Triggering, 134, 218, 221, 227, 245, 248
20th Century Fox Television, 155

U.S. Department of Justice, 2
U.S. Surgeon General's Advisory Committee,
    27
U.S. Surgeon General's Report (1972), 27
UCLA Television Monitoring Project, 70
Units of analysis, defining, 199-200
Untouchables, The, 168
USA (cable network), 219

V-chip:
  programming help, 6
  rating system and, 157
Vehicle, 219
Verbal violence, rates of, 49-50
Viewer, 219
Viewer demographics:
  age, 29
  ethnicity, 29

gender, 29
socioeconomic status, 29
Viewer factors, 227
Viewer states, 228, 245, 249, 251, 254
 aroused, 30
 degree of identity, 31, 244
 emotional reaction, 31
Viewer traits, 228, 245, 249, 251, 253, 254
 cognitive processing, 30
 intelligence, 29
 personality type, 30
 socialization against aggression, 29
Violence:
 as epidemic, 1
 as public health problem, 1, 7
 causes, 2
 economic implications, 2
 media amplification of, 1
 media reconfiguration of, 1
 See also Media violence; Television violence; Violence, definitions of
Violence, definitions of, 4, 63-64, 68, 71, 79-
  83, 217
 analysis of, 71-73
 by theoreticians, 65-67
 comparing, 72-73
 differences in, 75-77
 Gerbner's, 67
 implications for research, 78-79

in content analysis literature, 67-71
 key elements, 64
 need for broader, 78-79, 79-82
 public's, 73-74, 75, 76, 77
 social scientists', 75-76, 77
 understanding public definition of, 82-83
Violent portrayals, contextual variables and,
  31-36, 46, 52-56, 96, 227
 consequences, 31, 32, 46, 53, 87, 88-89, 139
 eroticism, 31, 35-36, 139
 identification, 87, 93, 105-106, 139
 importance of, 87-95
 justification, 31, 32-34, 46, 54, 87, 90, 139
 motives, 87, 89-90, 139
 presence of weapons, 31, 35, 46, 55, 139
 production techniques, 31, 34-35, 139
 rewards and punishments, 31, 32, 46, 53-54,
  87-88, 139
 See also Humor; Realism

Weapons effect, 35
Wizard of Oz (character), 137
Wolf, Dick, 155
Writers Guild of America, 156

X-Files, The, 155

About the Author

W. James Potter is currently Professor in the Department of Communication at Florida State University. He has conducted research on media violence for the past 15 years and served as one of the Principal Investigators on the National Television Violence Study. He recently published books entitled *Media Literacy* and *An Analysis of Thinking and Research About Qualitative Methods.*